Untouchable Bodies, Resistance, and Liberation

Currents of Encounter

STUDIES IN INTERRELIGIOUS AND INTERCULTURAL RELATIONS

Editor-in-Chief
Marianne Moyaert (*Vrije Universiteit Amsterdam, the Netherlands*)

Editorial Board
Catherine Cornille (*Boston College, USA*) – Marion Grau (*MF Norwegian School of Theology, Norway*) – Paul Hedges (*NTU, Singapore*) – Henry Jansen (*Vrije Universiteit Amsterdam, the Netherlands*) – Bagus Laksana (*Sanata Dharma University in Yogyakarta, Indonesia*) – Willie L. van der Merwe (*Vrije Universiteit Amsterdam, the Netherlands*) – Jonathan Tan (*Case Western Reserve University, USA*)

Founding Editors
Jerald D. Gort
Hendrik M. Vroom (†)

Advisory Board
Gavin d'Costa (*University of Bristol, Department of Religion and Theology*)
Lejla Demiri (*University of Tubingen, Center for Islamic Theology*)
Nelly van Doorn-Harder (*Wake Forest University School of Divinity*)
Jim Heisig (*Nanzan Institute for Religion & Culture*)
Mechteld Jansen (*Protestant Theological University, Amsterdam*)
Edward Kessler (*Woolf Institute and Fellow of St Edmund's College, Cambridge*)
Oddbjorn Leirvik (*University of Oslo, Faculty of Theology*)
Hugh Nicholson (*Loyola University Chicago, Department of Theology*)
Anant Rambachan (*St. Olaf College, Northfield, USA*)
John Sheveland (*Gonzaga University*)
Mona Siddiqui (*University of Edingburgh, School of Divinity*)
Pim Valkenberg (*Catholic University of America*)
Michelle Voss Roberts (*Wake Forest University School of Divinity*)
Ulrich Winkler (*University of Salzburg, Center for Intercultural Theology and the Study of Religions*)

VOLUME 61

The titles published in this series are listed at *brill.com/coe*

Untouchable Bodies, Resistance, and Liberation

A Comparative Theology of Divine Possessions

By

Joshua Samuel

BRILL
RODOPI

LEIDEN | BOSTON

Cover illustration: Image by Immanuel Vivekanandh. Used with kind permission by the artist.

The Library of Congress Cataloging-in-Publication Data is available online at http://catalog.loc.gov
LC record available at http://lccn.loc.gov/2019056284

Typeface for the Latin, Greek, and Cyrillic scripts: "Brill." See and download: brill.com/brill-typeface.

ISSN 0923-6201
ISBN 978-90-04-42003-8 (paperback)
ISBN 978-90-04-42005-2 (e-book)

Copyright 2020 by Koninklijke Brill NV, Leiden, The Netherlands.
Koninklijke Brill NV incorporates the imprints Brill, Brill Hes & De Graaf, Brill Nijhoff, Brill Rodopi,
Brill Sense, Hotei Publishing, mentis Verlag, Verlag Ferdinand Schöningh and Wilhelm Fink Verlag.
All rights reserved. No part of this publication may be reproduced, translated, stored in a retrieval system,
or transmitted in any form or by any means, electronic, mechanical, photocopying, recording or otherwise,
without prior written permission from the publisher.
Authorization to photocopy items for internal or personal use is granted by Koninklijke Brill NV provided
that the appropriate fees are paid directly to The Copyright Clearance Center, 222 Rosewood Drive,
Suite 910, Danvers, MA 01923, USA. Fees are subject to change.

This book is printed on acid-free paper and produced in a sustainable manner.

To
Prof. James Hal Cone
Whose Writings inspired me to study Liberation Theology
and
my Amma & Appa
Who show me how to embody and live it

∵

Contents

Acknowledgments   XI

PART 1
Dalit Bodies and Divine Possessions

Introduction: a Comparative Theology from a Dalit Perspective   5

1   **Toward a Comparative Theology of Liberation**   32
   1   Comparative Theology   32
      1.1   *Interrogating Comparative Theology*   34
      1.2   *Prioritization of Texts*   35
         1.2.1   Lingering Western/Christian Supremacy   35
         1.2.2   Disregarding Agency of Faith Communities   37
         1.2.3   Perpetuation of Hierarchies   39
   2   Dalit Theology   41
      2.1   *New Directions in Dalit Theology*   42
         2.1.1   Binarism   43
         2.1.2   Identitarianism   44
         2.1.3   Christian-Centrism   46
   3   A Comparative Theology of Liberation from a Dalit Perspective   49
      3.1   *People Centered Theology*   50
      3.2   *Non-Othering Theology*   51
      3.3   *Comparative Liberation Theology*   53

2   **Dalit Body—the Untouchable Sacrament**   56
   1   The Dalit Body   56
      1.1   *Bodies That 'Don't' Matter*   57
      1.2   *Disciplining the Bodies*   61
   2   Theological Significance of the Dalit Body   66
      2.1   *Body in Christianity*   66
      2.2   *Sacramentality of the Dalit Body*   70
   3   Choosing a Category for Comparison   72
      3.1   *Divine Possessions as Vague Comparative Category*   73

VIII

CONTENTS

PART 2
Divine Possessions among Hindu and Christian Dalits

3   Dalits and Hinduism   79
  1   Dalit Religion and Hinduism   79
      1.1   *The Modern Birth of Hinduism*   80
      1.2   *The Unity of Traditions within Hinduism*   85
      1.3   *Distinct Features of Dalit Religion*   88
  2   Hindu Dalit Goddesses   91
      2.1   *Goddess(es) of Hinduism*   91
      2.2   *Paraiyar Goddesses*   94
  3   Dalit Goddesses and Liberation   99
      3.1   *The Ambivalence of the Goddess(es) and Its Impact on
            Liberation Theology*   102

4   Divine Possessions among Hindu Dalits   105
  1   Divine Possessions: an Overview   105
      1.1   *Divine Possessions*   106
      1.2   *Types of Possessions*   106
            1.2.1   Enduring Possessions   107
            1.2.2   Temporary Possessions   109
  2   Divine Possessions: a Closer View   111
      2.1   *Preparing for the Possessions*   111
      2.2   *Experience of Being Possessed*   115
  3   Divine Possessions: Inferences and Interpretations   119
      3.1   *Not 'Possession' but Grace*   119
      3.2   *Interweaving of Traditions*   120
      3.3   *Background of the Possessed Devotees*   120
      3.4   *Sexual Ambiguity*   121
      3.5   *Body and Collective Memories*   122
      3.6   *Liberative Elements in Possessions*   124

5   Dalit Christianity and Theology   127
  1   Dalit Christianity   127
      1.1   *The Beginnings*   127
            1.1.1   Rajanaiken of Tanjore (1700–1771)   128
            1.1.2   Maharasan Vedamanickam of Travancore
                    (1772–1827)   129
      1.2   *Mass Movements*   131
      1.3   *Dalit Christianity Today*   137

CONTENTS   IX

2   Dalit 'God-Talk'   141
    2.1   *The 'Broken' God*   141
    2.2   *Problematizing Dalit God-Talk*   145
    2.3   *New Trends in Dalit Theology: Re-Turning to the Body*   147

6   Divine Possessions among Christian Dalits   150

1   Holy Spirit Possessions   150
    1.1   *Praise as Preparation*   152
    1.2   *Receiving the Spirit*   153
    1.3   *Interpreting Holy Spirit Possessions*   155
    1.4   *After Holy Spirit Anointing, It Is Bible Time*   157
2   Embodied Divine Mediation through *Avi Kattu*   159
3   Divine Embodiment through Sacraments   160
4   Christian Divine Possessions: Prospects and Possibilities   162
    4.1   *Centering the Body*   162
    4.2   *Dalit Religious Elements*   164
    4.3   *Divine-Human Agency*   165
    4.4   *Possibilities of Resistance and Liberation*   167
    4.5   *Reimagining Evil*   169

PART 3
Possessions as Kairos: an Embodied Constructive Theology

7   Divine Possessions as Dalit Resistance   175

1   Paraiyar Dalit Religion   175
2   Comparing Hindu and Christian Possessions   180
    2.1   *Setting*   181
    2.2   *Experiences of the Devotees*   183
    2.3   *Role of the Divine*   184
3   Possession as Liberation   188
    3.1   *Bodies That Want to Be Mattered*   188
    3.2   *Looking beyond Protests*   190
    3.3   *Hidden Transcripts and Infrapolitics*   191
    3.4   *Divine Possession as Dalit Resistance: Reimagining
          Liberation*   194
    3.5   *Possessions as Alternative Resistance*   201

8   Envisioning an Embodied Comparative Theology of Liberation   205

1   Possessions as *Kairos*   205
    1.1   Kairos   206

	1.2	*Paul Tillich's Conceptualization of* Kairos 208
	1.3	*Possessions as* Kairoi *in/of the Margins* 213
	1.4	*Re-Visioning* Kairos *Using Divine Possessions* 215
2	Toward an Embodied Theology of *Kairos* 218	
	2.1	*Christ and* Kairoi 219
	2.2	*Spirit Christology* 220
	2.3	*Spirit Christology and Religious Diversity* 221
	2.4	*The Untouchable God in Untouchable Bodies: A Constructive Theological Imagination* 224
		2.4.1 Untouchable Divine Immanence 224
		2.4.2 Transgressive Creativity 228
		2.4.3 Empowering Be(com)ing 232

Epilogue: Marginalized Bodies and Comparative Theology   238

1   Re-Visioning Comparative Theology from and at the Margins   238

   1.1   *Beyond Texts to Bodies*   238

   1.2   *Beyond Borders to Living at the Boundaries*   240

2   Some Confessions and Justifications   241

3   Looking Ahead   243

Bibliography   245

Index   259

Acknowledgments

Many good people have supported and sustained me through the journey of writing this book. I am thankful to my *doktorvater*, John Thatamanil, who guided me with compassion and wisdom in the early stages of this book as a dissertation. I cannot thank him enough for being a motivating teacher and a generous friend who believed in me more than I ever did myself. My thanks are also due to the illustrious members of my dissertation committee—Sathianathan Clarke, Paul Knitter, Rachel McDermott, and Cornel West—whose constructive criticisms helped me to revise a graduate school thesis into publishable material. I am also indebted to all my teachers, both in India and the United States, especially, Jayakiran Sebastian, John Mohan Razu, Roger Haight, Jerusha Lamptey, Ulrike Auga, Hyun Kyun Chung, and Samuel Cruz for teaching me the tools to think critically and creatively. In particular, I am ever grateful to my beloved teacher, the Late. Prof. James Cone (to whom I have dedicated this book) for constantly reminding me that my voice mattered and that I needed to write, not for my sake, but to further the cause of justice for the oppressed. I am overwhelmed by the love and faith that these people have in me as a scholar, and though I may not reach their levels of academic excellence, I sincerely hope that I would be able to emulate their spirit of kindness and humility.

As I was completing this book, I was invited to serve on the faculty of the Episcopal Divinity School at Union Theological Seminary, NY, as Visiting Lecturer for Theology, Global Christianity, and Mission. It is an honor for me to serve with Kelly Brown Douglas, Dean of EDS@Union who inspires me with her scholarship and her passion for justice. My heartfelt thanks to Miguel Escobar, the Director of the Anglican Studies program, whose friendship pushes me to widen my horizons of knowledge and be a publicly engaged theologian.

This book revolves around the ethnographic study that I conducted in Tamilnadu, India, during the summer of 2016, and my earlier researches in 2010–12. I am thankful to the Dalit communities of Kottaikarai, Pulichapallam, Annai Nagar, Vichur, Periyapalayam, Chekkanur, Thannirkulam, Aranvayil, and Pandur for opening their hearts and lives to me and sharing their religious beliefs and experiences. I also cannot forget the assistance and support rendered by my two research associates, Lazar and Arputharaj, who not only introduced and accompanied me to different research sites and helped me with the interviews, but also made perceptive observations that I may have never noticed otherwise.

When this project was still in its embryonic stage, I had the privilege of gaining from the wisdom of many scholars. In particular, I am thankful for the insights I received from the representing faculty and students at the Trans-Atlantic (now Global) Ph.D. Seminar held at the University of KwaZulu-Natal, South Africa, in 2014, and at the Union Theological Seminary, New York, in 2015. I am also grateful for the opportunity to attend the Asian Theological Summer Institute (ATSI) at the United Lutheran Seminary, Philadelphia, in 2016 where the facilitators and fellow participants helped me to fine-tune the focus and the argument of my book.

Many friends in the academy and the church have been part of this exciting journey. I thank Sunder John Boopalan, Joseph Prabhakar Dayam, Peniel Jesudasan Rufus Rajkumar, Balasubramaniam Jeyapal, John Jeyaharan, Samuel Logan Rathnaraj, Esther Parajuli, Abidhanandhar John, Jamal Calloway, and Christopher Ficci with whom I held enlightening discussions at different stages of writing. I am also grateful to Kyeongil Jung, Makito Nagasawa, Ruth Batausa, Lisa and Joel Pratt, Mary Jett, Stewart Everett, Crystal Hall, Amy Meverden, Vinod Wesley, Sweety Helen, Poonam Rai, and Janet Okang for enriching my life with their friendship.

When I began looking for publishers, I am glad that Paul Hedges suggested and recommended my proposal to Brill and put me in touch with Marianne Moyaert, the editor-in-chief of the Currents of Encounter series. My thanks to both of them for their suggestions and support. I also thank Ingrid Heijckers-Velt for her help and guidance through the publication process. I am ever grateful to Mrinalini Sebastian for kindly reading and checking my manuscript for grammar, coherence, and clarity. I cannot say how indebted I am to Immanuel Vivekanandh for the powerful cover image. It fits perfectly with the book's theme.

I could not have written this book without the spiritual support of the faith community to which I belong, the Episcopal Church of the Resurrection, Richmond Hill, NY. I am also grateful for the prayers and encouragement of many caring elders in my life, including Rev. Christopher and Sarah Solomon, Rev. Gideon Jebamani, Bishop Lawrence Provenzano, Fr. Winfred Vergara, and Prof. Jim Kodera.

My parents taught me to think critically. I am truly grateful to my *amma* and *appa*, Elizabeth Victoria and Samuel Jacob, for filling our home with unbounded love and generous freedom that encouraged their children to question assumptions and challenge conventions. I also thank my sister, Beulah Ezhilselvan, who, along with her husband, Joshua Ezhilselvan and their lovely son, Jerry, has been a constant source of motivation in my academic journey. I am

ACKNOWLEDGMENTS   XIII

blessed to have wonderful parents-in-law, Jeyaseelan David and Jessie David, who go out of their way to support me.

This whole enterprise would not have been possible without my beloved friend and life partner, Amirthaseeli Jeyaseelan. It was her love and wisdom that gave me the enthusiasm and energy to do this project. Together, we are delighted and proud of our children, Raphael and Matthew (who was born exactly three days after I submitted the final manuscript to the publisher). I thank God for giving me these three lovely people who make my life beautiful and my endeavors meaningful and fun.

PART 1

Dalit Bodies and Divine Possessions

∵

Missing

Do not search in my words
for anything that could give you
a high.

Ash of half-burnt bone
lies strewn about in them.
And smoking ghosts of ancestors
long dead, or gone
missing.

Oozing from my fingers
is blood.
From the (cow) slaughter-block
stench of my lines
you'll know it.

Into great, grief-stricken howls
have dissolved
our songs and pictures
never to be found again
The light welling from our lamps
has been stifled
in terrible fires.

The 'dung-milk'
my ancestors were given to drink
is what I'm vomiting
as poetry/*theology*.

YAZHAN AATHI[1]

---

1 Yazhan Aathi, "Missing (*En Sorkalil Thedatheer*)," transl.Vasantha Surya, in *The Oxford Anthology of Tamil Dalit Writing*, ed. Ravikumar and R. Azhagarasan (New Delhi: Oxford University Press, 2012), 38–39. Text in italics mine. Note: Dung milk is a mixture of cow dung (or at times human shit) and water that is forcefully given to Dalits who are 'trouble-makers.'

Introduction: a Comparative Theology from a Dalit Perspective

In 2009–12, I served in the Church of South India (C.S.I) as the pastor of a semi-urban parish (or pastorate, as it is called) in Pondicherry that also had several 'branch' village congregations. During this time, it was my practice to accompany enthusiastic and evangelistic-minded city church members to share the gospel in the villages. In one such visit to a village called Kottaikarai, I met an old man named Kuppusamy and his wife, Muniyamma. As I generally did, I began sharing about Jesus and the salvation that he offers. However, in this case, surprisingly, Kuppusamy already knew about Jesus and even about the church that met in his village. He said that he liked the Christianity, which he came to know about after his daughter's marriage to a Christian. In fact, his wife said she even came to the church occasionally to attend the worship. Kuppusamy and Muniyamma then went on to speak about their religion, affirming their faith in the local goddess (Mariamman) whom they fondly and devotedly called *amma*. They spoke of her as the source and sustainer of everything that exists and asserted that it is the goddess who gave meaning and purpose in their life. When I left them after an hour long conversation, I have to confess that I was deeply disturbed and challenged.

Among other things in this encounter, I was particularly intrigued by the confident and passionate faith of this couple in their deity. Kuppusamy and Muniyamma were Paraiyar Dalits, a community who were formerly called, and are still viewed as Untouchables according to the caste system. As a liberation theologian and as someone aware of the relationship between Hinduism and caste, I was fascinated to see that this couple were able to assert that a 'Hindu' goddess was sufficient for them to face the struggles in their life, even as they respected and learnt from other religious traditions like Christianity. Kuppusamy and Muniyamma were proud and confident about their faith, even as they knew their discriminated and marginalized place in the caste society.

Of course, I cannot say that I was unaware of the significance of the liberative potential of other religious traditions. After all, I had done my fair share of readings on these subjects in the graduate school. Still, this encounter with Kuppusamy and Muniyamma disturbed me in the sense that now the universality of God's revelation and liberation were empirically real for me; they were not 'merely' in the books, but were speaking at/to me. There was something profoundly powerful in this conversation that reminded me that divine

© KONINKLIJKE BRILL NV, LEIDEN, 2020 | DOI:10.1163/9789004420052_003

6 INTRODUCTION

salvation was present and operative in ways beyond that I could imagine and preach. This rendezvous alerted me that oppressed people have different ways of imagining, worshipping, and speaking about God to survive, resist, and subvert unjust social structures like caste. This book is inspired, along with many other factors, by that meeting and conversation that I had with two simple people in a remote village in South India.

1 Dalit Religious Experience as a Source of Comparative Theology

Across the world, social structures are embodied. That is to say that social systems always find expression in the bodies of the members of the society. Nonetheless, in hierarchical societies, it is the bodies of those at the bottom—the ones who are marginalized and discriminated—which bear the brunt of social norms the most. In fact, I believe it can be claimed that social hierarchies that such systems usually promulgate are often forcefully *founded on* the bodies of the subdued. These graded social systems are carefully guarded and meticulously sustained, both consciously and unconsciously, either through violent or gentle ('non-violent') disciplining of oppressed bodies. Yet, these bodies are not merely passive recipients of injustice, for they actively challenge and resist oppression in a plurality of ways, ways that we may not even recognize as resistance. In other words, the bodies of the oppressed—individually and collectively—constantly discover possibilities of 'being,' drawing upon and dynamically interweaving a wide variety of available resources.

This book is about one such people—identified and treated as Untouchables, or Dalits as they call themselves now—who have been discriminated and dehumanized for several centuries. In spite of the criminalization of untouchability and several policies of affirmative actions in the Indian constitution,[2] anyone familiar with the Indian (or broadly speaking, the South Asian) situation will know that discrimination and injustice against Dalits is still rampant. In fact, it has been noted that in recent times there has been a significant statistical increase in the levels of violence against Dalits.[3] And apart from these explicit acts of violence against Dalit bodies, we also witness what may

---

2 For instance, Article 17 of the Indian constitution makes untouchability a criminal offense. Article 15 allows compensatory discriminatory measures for the welfare of the Scheduled Castes (Dalits) and other such marginalized communities. For more see, John C. B. Webster, *Dalit Christians: A History,* 2nd edition (Delhi: ISPCK, 1994), 132–142.

3 http://indianexpress.com/article/blogs/dalit-violence-gujarat-gau-rakshaks-2930876/. Accessed on September 27, 2018.

INTRODUCTION

be called non-violent and civilized forms of control that force Dalits to adhere to Brahmanical values and norms. I call these acts of violence and control on Dalits as 'disciplining' of the Dalit body *to be* an 'untouchable' and 'outcaste' body. I shall study and explain the significance of this 'disciplining' more in chapter two. For now, it suffices to acknowledge that Dalit bodies are marginalized, violated, and controlled in/by the caste society.

Yet, in this context of Dalit bodies being discriminated, assaulted, and controlled, one also notices several occasions and modes of Dalit resistance and affirmation. In this project, prompted by experiences such as my meeting with Kuppusamy mentioned above, I am interested in looking for religious modes of Dalit struggles for liberation, not just in my own tradition viz. Christianity, but also in other religious traditions.

This book is a comparative theologizing of embodied religious experiences in Hindu and Christian Dalit communities. To be more specific, I study, compare, and explore how embodied experiences of the divine—which I call "divine possessions"—among Paraiyar[4] Dalits who belong to Hinduism and Christianity can be interpreted as means of Dalit liberation and a resource for doing constructive Christian liberation theology. But first, to provide the proper background, I want to present a brief overview of caste, untouchability, and who the Dalits are.

2   Caste

Let me begin with caste. To offer a comprehensive picture of the caste system with all its complex history and ambiguous forms in an introductory chapter such as this is evidently impossible. Mindful of this reality, let me attempt to outline the basic features of the caste system and its infamous 'offspring' untouchability.

David Kinsley suggests that the caste system "[I]n essence ... is a social system that is composed of closed, endogamous groups most of which perform a traditional occupation and all of which are ranked in a hierarchical order."[5] Generally, caste is assumed to be founded in and authorized by the sacred Hindu texts. As B.R. Ambedkar (1891–1956), the famous Dalit leader, wrote, "Caste is a social system which embodies the arrogance and

---

4   A Dalit community in Tamilnadu, South India. More will be said below.
5   David Kinsley, *Hinduism from a Cultural Perspective* (Englewood Cliffs: Prentice Hall, 1982), 122.

8 INTRODUCTION

selfishness of a perverse section of the Hindus who were superior enough in
social status to set it in fashion, and who had the authority to force it on their
inferiors."[6] One of the texts that is commonly considered as the foundational text for caste is the *Purusha Sukta* hymn from the Rig Veda (ca. fifteenth
century BCE).

> As they divided the Purusa into many parts, what would become of his
> many parts? For what was his mouth, his arms, his thighs, and his foot
> named? His mouth turned into the Brahman, his two arms were made
> into the Kṣatriya (warrior), his two thighs to the Vaiṣya, and the Śūdra was
> created from his feet.[7]
>> Rig Veda 10. 11–12

Another famous text that is considered to be crucial for caste distinction
and the discrimination it generates is the Manu Dharma Sastra (ca. third
century CE).

> For the Sudra ..., the highest law leading to bliss is simply to render obe-
> dient service to distinguished Brahmin householders who are learned in
> the Veda. When he keeps himself pure, obediently serves the higher class,
> is soft-spoken and humble, and always takes refuge in Brahmins, he ob-
> tains a higher birth[8]
>> Manu Dharmasastra 9: 334

> Because of his distinctive qualities, the eminence of his origin, his obser-
> vance of restrictive practices, and the distinctive nature of his consecra-
> tion, the Brahmin is the lord of all the classes. Three classes—Brahmin,
> Kṣatriya, and Vaisya—are twice born; the fourth, Sudra, has a single birth.
> There is no fifth..[9]
>> Manu Dharmasastra 10: 3, 4

Such texts form the basis of the well-known 'caste pyramid' where the Brahmins, the Kshatriyas, the Vaisyas, and the Sudras are placed in a four-fold

---

6 B. R. Ambedkar, *Annihilation of Caste*, The Annotated Critical Edition (London &
   New York: Verso, 2014), 241.
7 Carl Olson, trans., *Hindu Primary Sources: A Sectarian Reader* (New Brunswick and London: Rutgers University Press, 2007), 24.
8 Patrick Oliville (tranl.), *The Law Code of Manu* (Oxford: Oxford University Press, 2004), 179.
9 Ibid., 180.

INTRODUCTION

hierarchical stratification, with the Untouchables placed outside and at the bottom of the structure. However, as Diane Mines suggests, caste was not always a fixed social structure. Like many other social systems, caste is a very complex category. She argues that caste

> ... is not a coherent system that exists all over India and by which all Indians abide. It is not a set of precut categories into which people place themselves like rungs on an immovable ladder. Nor is it an "ancient tradition" set beside more modern realities. Rather, caste is a changing constellation of values, actions, ideas, and organizing principles that most Indians engage with in one way or another in their daily lives. Caste is a product of complex histories and exists today in multiple forms.[10]

Therefore, we may say that caste is more than what meets the eye, and it is certainly not one monolithic structure of ranking. Moreover, it is also difficult to trace a linear and unambiguous history of caste, leave alone identify the exact moment of its origin.

From a historical-religious perspective, we can say that caste is "the result of a historical blending of two social systems, the *varna* system, which dominates Vedic religion and the traditional law books, and the *jati* system, which is only vaguely described in Hindu literature but which dominates Hinduism at the village level."[11] It should be noted here that both these systems may not have been hierarchical in their original forms, definitely not as we have it now. Nevertheless, through time these two systems became integrated into one, taking a hierarchical form, and in the process, ostracizing certain communities as outcastes and Untouchables.

When we consider the history of caste, we should remember that it is under the influence of colonialism and orientalism that it became consolidated, stabilized, and rigidified into a politically authorized frozen social structure. Nicholas Dirks, in his famous historical study of caste in modernity, *Castes of Mind*, maps how, influenced by European missionary and orientalist scholarship and aided by the wisdom of Brahmin pundits, along with their ethnographic surveys, the colonial administrators 'catalogued' and constructed the modern category of caste. Dirks argues that therefore,

---

10   Diane Mines, *Caste in India* (Ann Arbor, MI: Association for Asian Studies, 2009), 75.

11   Kinsley, *Hinduism from a Cultural Perspective*, 122.

> Caste is not some unchanged survival of ancient India, not some single system that reflects a core civilizational value, not a basic expression of Indian tradition. Rather, ... caste (... as we know it today) is a modern phenomenon, ... the product of an historical encounter between India and the Western colonial rule.[12]

Of course, Dirks does not mean that caste was simply a clever 'invention' of the British (as if it did not exist earlier). Dirks is neither unaware of the existence of social hierarchies in precolonial India nor is in favor of an egalitarian past. Rather, what he points out is that in the precolonial era, the "referents of social identity were not only heterogeneous; they were also determined by context," so that, identities, hierarchical as they may have been, were "part of a complex, conjunctural, constantly changing political world."[13] But, as Dirks notes, "it was under the British that 'caste' became a single term capable of expressing, organizing, and above all 'systemizing' India's diverse forms of social identity, community, and organization,"[14] and "was thus made out to be far more—far more pervasive, far more totalizing, and far more uniform—that it had ever been before ..."[15] By the end of the 19th century, caste had become an essential and fixed identity of every Indian subject.[16]

---

12   Nicholas Dirks, *Castes of Mind: Colonialism and the Making of Modern India* (Princeton and Oxford: Princeton University Press, 2001), 5.

13   Ibid., 13.

14   Ibid., 5.

15   Ibid., 13.

16   Speaking on the same matter, Sumit Guha argues that the construction of caste began from the sixteenth century when the Portuguese (who were the first to arrive in India) imposed their western racialized notions of purity and pollution and imagined a hierarchical institution among Indians based on the same categories. Guha, using Morton Klass' proposal that the concept of preserving purity of blood was a European concept, argues that "The term 'caste' ... mingled emerging European notions of 'racial' purity with Hindu notions of religious purity" which was based on more than " 'pure descent.' " Sumit Guha, *Beyond Caste: Identity and Power in South Asia, Past and Present* (Leiden: Brill Publications, 2013), 19–20. Similarly, Gita Dharampal-Frick, aware of the European and the racial origins of (the word) caste, notes that "this terminological usage ... is ... indicative of the fact that the distinctive societal ordering perceived in Indian society was being brought in line with similar European social divisions; India was thus being drawn closer to Europe, be it in the latter's own terms ..." Gita Dharampal-Frick, *Interrogating the Historical Discourse of Caste and Race in India* (New Delhi: Nehru Memorial Museum and Library, 2013), 5–6.

INTRODUCTION

3   Untouchability

Let me now turn to the most well-known offshoot of caste—untouchability. As S.M. Michael notes, the history of India runs parallel to the history of untouchability.[17] In that sense, one may say, in the words of Shrirama, "untouchability has been built into the sociocultural structure of" the "Indian civilization" and the "Hindu society."[18] However, as we saw with caste, we can say that untouchability also is an ambiguous concept and practice which several historians, anthropologists, and sociologists have tried to decipher over the years. Given the sheer quantity of these works, not to mention the myriad of complexities, it is not possible to consider them in detail here. Nevertheless, in order to provide a foundation for the upcoming chapters, let me offer in broad strokes a simple but hopefully helpful sketch of the theories of untouchability within the broader framework of caste.

In order to consider the theories of caste and untouchability, I want to use the typology proposed by the social anthropologist Robert Deliège. For Deliège, theories on caste and untouchability can be broadly classified into two categories: models of unity and models of separation. In the first type, Deliège notes, caste is perceived—at least for some scholars—to be a complementary, harmonious, and well-balanced system, that also necessitates untouchability. For instance, Declan Quigley opines that caste and untouchability came into existence because society needed Untouchables to perform the religious rituals and duties that were concerned with *asuras* (demons). In that sense, for Quigley, untouchability can be assumed to be a socio-religious necessity. On the other hand, J.H. Hutton is convinced that untouchability is "an altogether unnecessary evil" that cannot be justified and must be removed.[19] However, according to Hutton, though untouchability as a practice must be annihilated, caste itself could be retained, as it facilitates an occupation-based harmonious society. That is, Hutton considers caste as a system of functional unity, except for untouchability.

---

17   S. M. Michael, "Introduction," in *Dalits in Modern India: Visions and Values,* 2nd ed. (New Delhi: Sage Publications, 2007), 16. Also see, James Massey, *Dalits in India: Religion as a Source of Bondage or Liberation with Special Reference to Christians* (New Delhi: Manohar Publications, 1995), 39–66.

18   Shrirama, "Untouchability and Stratification in Indian Civilisation," in *Dalits in Modern India,* 47. I must point out here that "Hinduism" as a unitary religion evolved only during modernity, making claims of a *monolithic ancient* Hindu society—which I believe is Shrirama's view—problematic. More shall be said in chapter three.

19   Cited by Deliège. Robert Deliège, *The Untouchables of India,* trans. Nora Scott (Oxford and New York: Berg Publishers, 1999), 34.

In this camp, Deliège also includes the noted anthropologist M.N. Srinivas who believes that in spite of its apparent hierarchical nature, because of the necessity of co-existence in the society (especially in villages), there are possibilities and provisions for the Untouchables to use the caste system to their advantage. In other words, though critical of untouchability, Srinivas asserts that, notwithstanding their inferior position in the caste hierarchy and the discrimination that it eventuates, because of the strong communitarian nature of the Indian village societies, "the position of Untouchables cannot... be thought of" solely "in terms of exploitation."[20]

Perhaps the best known of the proponents of the unity model is Louis Dumont, who in his magnum opus, *Homo Hierarchicus*, has offered a helpful theorization of caste. According to him, the stability of caste rests on the opposition of the pure and impure (i.e. purity and pollution) in the society as embodied by different castes. The extremes of such purity and pollution is found at the two ends of the caste spectrum, among the Brahmins and the Untouchables, respectively.[21] In Dumont's words,

> It is clear that the impurity of the Untouchable is conceptually inseparable from the purity of the Brahman. They must have been established together, or in any case have mutually reinforced each other, and we must get used to thinking of them together. In particular, untouchability will not truly disappear until the purity of the Brahman is itself radically devalued ...[22]

In that sense, for Dumont, "the execution of impure tasks by some is necessary to the maintenance of purity of others. The two poles are equally necessary, although unequal."[23] In sum, we may say that the models of unity of caste basically "emphasized the inherently balanced character of the system and the interdependence of the castes," including the Untouchables.[24]

The other category of theories on caste and untouchability that Deliège identifies is based on separation and exclusion among the different castes, especially between the caste people and the Untouchables. One of the important

---

20 Cited by Deliège. Ibid., 36.

21 Cited by Deliège. Ibid., 38.

22 Louis Dumont, *Homo Hierarchicus: The Caste System and Its Implications*, trans. Mark Sainbury, Louis Dumont, and Basia Gulati (Chicago and London: The University of Chicago Press, 1980), 55.

23 Ibid., 55.

24 Cited by Deliège. Deliège, *The Untouchables of India*, 36.

INTRODUCTION

13

voices in this camp that Deliège acknowledges is that of Gerald Berreman. Berreman, comparing caste with race and other forms of exclusion and hierarchy across the world, argues that "castes are 'culturally distinct' entities," who "do not share a common culture ..."[25] Certain that this was particularly true in the case of the Untouchables, Berreman asserted that they "do not share the values of the rest of society or the Brahmanic foundations of the systems..."[26] Thus, for Berreman, the caste system is essentially a system of divided castes without any common or bridging qualities. Deliège acknowledges that the tendency to view Untouchables as an exclusive and separate category is particularly favored in ethnographic research. Agreeing with Michael Moffatt, he notes that because "most of the anthropologists who have worked on untouchability have tended to stress the segregation and destitution of Harijans, and ... the Untouchables' efforts to end the oppression they endure," many of these models have a leaning toward asserting the distinctiveness of their culture and religion.[27]

Deliège believes that both these models will have to be considered critically. He argues that, "[A]dvocates of the models of separation are ... wrong in wanting to reduce" caste "to a purely Brahminic theory that ... is wholly alien to the lower castes, and particularly to Untouchables. ... The ideology of caste extends well beyond the upper castes."[28] However, on the other hand, the pervasive hierarchy and discrimination across the caste spectrum, Deliège is quick to remind, "does not mean, as the 'models of unity' would have us admit, that Untouchables are content with their lot, that they enjoy a number of privileges and that, ... theirs is a rather enviable status."[29] Given this complexity, I believe we can agree with Deliège that caste and untouchability can be neither monolithically interpreted as a unifying system nor construed as a structure of exclusive and opposed groups. In that sense, we may say that caste has a complex complementary nature. However, contrary to the complementarity that Dumont visualizes, I will argue that such complementarity is *forced* by the dominant castes, especially in the case of the Untouchables. That is, the seemingly 'harmonious' and 'balancing' nature of caste is perpetuated by according "low ritual status" of impurity, "wretched economic conditions," and denial of "political power" to the Untouchables, thereby depriving and excluding them

25   Ibid., 42.
26   Ibid.
27   Ibid., 45.
28   Ibid., 48.
29   Ibid., 49.

from society.[30] In other words, the caste subject is created by the othering of the untouchable subject.[31]

Notwithstanding the difficulty in understanding the complex nature of caste and untouchability, the ground reality is quite plain and (certainly) gruesome.[32] In January 2017, a young girl named Nandini was brutally murdered in Ariyalur, Tamilnadu. Abducted, gang-raped and killed by four men, including her upper-caste lover who had impregnated her, Nalini's body was found drowned in a well after a fortnight.[33] In March 2017, the news about the suicide of Dalit research scholar Muthukrishnan (aka) Rajini Krish at the Jawaharlal Nehru University in New Delhi made the news. Though there was no suicide note found with the body, Muthukrishnan had posted on social media a few months earlier—based on his own experiences—about the caste based inequality and bias that exists in institutions of higher education in India, and how difficult it is for people from marginalized communities to survive, let alone thrive, in the academia.[34]

---

30 Deliège, *The Untouchables of India*, 50.

31 I shall return to this question of caste subject formation through the generation/creation of the untouchable subject in the next chapter.

32 It is pertinent to note here that social historians like Debjani Ganguly argue that studying caste with untouchability in mind does not offer a critical or a wholistic picture, especially since such views are colored by modernist-liberal attitudes that simply conceptualize caste as a pre-modern evil that does not have a place in modernity. Rather, caste is a way of living, she insists. Therefore, Ganguly suggests that "it is imperative to make a theoretical shift from the ideological (caste is oppressive) to the phenomenological (caste generates ways of living of which, no doubt, pain and oppression are a part) in conceptualizing caste." Debjani Ganguly, *Caste, Colonialism and Counter-Modernity: Notes on a Postcolonial Hermeneutics of Caste* (London and New York: Routledge, 2005), x. However, I believe I cannot agree with Ganguly completely. While Ganguly's contribution in offering "a resistance to the reified ways in which caste continues to figure in social scientific and nation-building discourses" should be lauded, I am afraid her argument seems to reflect—despite her assertion that she does not want to be "considered an apologist for the caste system" or her confession that she "cannot not begin with the proposition that the caste system is inherently suitable for modern India" since "to say anything otherwise is *risky*"—a privileged perspective which sees and 'justifies' caste as simply "many ways of living and dwelling." Ibid., 237 & 239. Emphasis mine. For those who are at the bottom and outside the caste structure and suffer because of it, and for those who are aware of the reality of untouchability through solidarity with those who suffer, caste will certainly appear different.

33 http://timesofindia.indiatimes.com/city/trichy/missing-girls-body-found-in-well-in-ariyalur/articleshow/56590309.cms. Accessed on September 27, 2018.

34 http://www.firstpost.com/india/jnu-dalit-student-suicide-when-equality-is-denied-everything-is-denied-wrote-27-year-old-j-muthukrishnan-3333050.html. Accessed on September 27, 2018.

INTRODUCTION

Though I cannot study these two incidents systematically and thoroughly here, I believe the purpose of mentioning them is obvious. These are not
isolated or infrequent episodes of injustice against the Untouchables. Rather,
these incidents have to be seen as paradigmatic of how caste and untouchability continues to operate today. They also remind us of the intensity of the
viciousness and inhumaneness of caste for the untouchable communities.[35]
There are, of course, more subtle manifestations of caste and untouchability which we will consider in the second chapter. But for now, before I move
further, I believe it will not be out of place to clarify, especially for the sake of
those who are quick to sympathize and patronize, that untouchability is more
than 'not being touched' or 'being segregated,' although such acts also continue. Untouchability is an epistemic and systemic evil that continuously evolves
and changes, finding new and subtle ways of dehumanizing some people as
Untouchables. It will be a grave mistake to look for and judge 'untouchability'
literally.[36]

---

35 Of course, I am not saying that all Untouchables or untouchable communities suffer or
have similar experiences. My point is to show that caste and untouchability are quite alive
and active. For more on atrocities against Dalits see, http://www.indiatimes.com/news/
india/11-major-incidents-of-violence-against-dalits-which-show-how-badly-we-treat-
them-258944.html; http://economictimes.indiatimes.com/news/politics-and-nation/
crime-against-scheduled-castes-steep-spike-in-gujarat-most-number-of-cases-in-up/
articleshow/53329482.cms. Accessed on September 27, 2018.

36 It has been my experience in the west that the mention of the word 'untouchable'
quite often invokes responses like, "Oh, but they are not *un*-touchable; I will be happy
to touch them," or "Can I give them some money?" On the other hand, there are also
views like, "Come on, caste is not practiced anymore" or "untouchability is dead" or
sometimes "you are just making this up," or even "how are Dalits able to come to the
United States then?" Such responses, I believe, imply a literal and simplistic understanding of 'untouchability.' Such misconceptions have also pervaded the academy.
For instance, (even a scholar like) Deliège, in one of his recent writings, has claimed
that "untouchability is dead" and the Dalits are simply resuscitating it for political
and economic ends. In fact, Deliège alleges that the use of the term Dalit is only a
strategy employed by Dalit activists and intellectuals to divide the society "in order
to claim further protective measures and privileges." Robert Deliège, "Introduction: Is
There Still Untouchability in India?," in *From Stigma to Assertion: Untouchability,
Identity and Politics in Early and Modern India*, ed. Mikael Aktor & Robert Deliège
(Copenhagen: Museum Tusculanum Press, 2010), 27. I strongly disagree with Deliège
since his entire thesis is built on the assumption that "untouchability is largely a problem of the past," and it is in fact "better to be a member of the Scheduled Caste" (the
constitutional name for untouchable communities) today. Ibid., 24. I am afraid Deliège
miserably fails to see and read the ground realities of caste and untouchability, especially from the perspective of the oppressed.

16   INTRODUCTION

4   "Dalit" Resistance

While acknowledging the gravity and versatility of the problem of untouchability, we should note that the (hi)story of the Untouchables is certainly not
limited to discrimination and misery. Rather, it is filled with resistance and
resilience. And perhaps the most significant assertive move in the history of
Untouchables is the decision to call themselves 'Dalits.'[37] Dalit—from the
Sanskrit/Marathi *dal* meaning broken or crushed—was chosen by Dalit activists and intellectuals to both aptly characterize their situation as well as to
assertively affirm their worth and dignity. The word goes back to Jyotiba Phule
(1827–1890), a Maratha reformer, who used the word in an "anti-Brahmanical,
anti-upper class, anti-patriarchal" sense.[38] Historian John Webster notes that
the Dalit leader Ambedkar (1891-1956) had also used 'Dalit' to refer to the plight
and brokenness of the Untouchables.[39] However, it was with the Dalit Panthers
(a political-activist party inspired by the Black Panthers in the U.S.) that the
term became popular in the 1970s. The Dalit Panthers' use of the term 'Dalit' included the "Scheduled Tribes, neo-Buddhists, the working people, the landless
and poor peasants, women, and all those who are being exploited politically,
economically and in the name of religion.' "[40] Gangadhar Pantawane, founder
and former editor of *Asmitadarsh*, a Dalit journal, captured this appropriately
when he said,

> To me, Dalit is not a caste. He is a man exploited by the social and eco-
> nomic traditions of this country ... He does believe in humanism. Dalit is
> a symbol of change and revolution.[41] (*sic*)

However, this expansive meaning of 'Dalit' did not last long and soon came
to exclusively denote the Untouchables. And importantly, since then, 'Dalit'
has become the signifier of resistance, and its usage is seen as a self-conscious
assertion of the agency of the Untouchables. In that sense, one may say that

---

37   Note that in this section (for the most part) I have intentionally used the term
      Untouchables till the portion on resistance and assertion to indicate the shift of seman-
      tics in Dalit history.

38   Ganguly, *Caste, Colonialism and Counter-Modernity*, 130.

39   John C. B. Webster, "Who is a Dalit?" in *Dalits in Modern India*, 76.

40   Cited by Webster. Ibid., 76. For more on the early usage of the word, see the chapter "Dalit—
      New Cultural Context for an Old Marathi Word," in Eleanor Zelliot, *From Untouchable
      to Dalit: Essays on the Ambedkar Movement* (New Delhi: Manohar Publications, 1998),
      268–292.

41   Zelliot, *From Untouchable to Dalit*, 268.

INTRODUCTION

'Dalit' embodies together both the reality of the brokenness experienced by the Untouchables and their ability and potential to assert themselves and work toward emancipation. And in broader terms, as pointed out by Anupama Rao, we may add that the transition of 'the untouchable' to 'Dalit' is the history of modern India. As Rao perceptively notes, "the emergence of the Dalit as a political subject has altered the social field and political practice of caste" as a system in modernity.[42]

Given the realistic and affirmative import of the term 'Dalit' and the hope of liberation that it encapsulates, Dalit scholars have used this term to identify/ recognize and describe social, political, and cultural expressions of dissent and reclamation of agency. Among such modes of resistance, the role of religion is definitely significant. Although the Hindu religion is blamed for generating and maintaining the caste system, we should note that it has also played a key part in helping Dalits to voice and display their protest and in serving as a path of/ for liberation. For instance, one finds in the bhakti poets several untouchable and lower-caste saints who spoke against caste hierarchy and distinctions.[43] Ravidas, the famous Chamar saint wrote,

A family that has a true follower of the Lord
Is neither high caste nor low caste, lordly or poor.
    Adi Granth 29

Who could long for anything but you?
My master, you are merciful to the poor;
   You have shielded my head with a regal parasol.
Someone whose touch offends the world
   You have enveloped with yourself.
It is the lowly my Govinda makes high-
  He does not fear anyone at all-
And he has exalted Namdev, Kabir,

---

42   Anupama Rao, *The Caste Question: Dalits and the Politics of Modern India* (Berkeley, Los Angeles and London: University of California Press, 2009), 27.

43   Here I have to acknowledge that using the term 'Dalit' in reference to bhakti religion is surely an anachronism, for obviously the bhakti saints did not use, and most probably were not aware of, the term 'Dalit.' Nevertheless, to revisit the songs of these saints that challenge caste (in its premodern form(s)) is a part of the Dalits' reclamation of their history of resistance. Also note that in this section, I have intentionally used the term Untouchables till the portion on resistance and assertion to indicate the shift of semantics in Dalit history.

Trilocan, Sadhna, and Sen.
Listen saints, says Ravidas,
   Hari accomplishes everything.
      Adi Granth 33

Oh well born of Benares, I too am born well known:
   my labor is with leather. But my heart can boast the Lord.

And, I born among those who carry carrion
   In daily rounds around Benares, am now
      the lowly one to whom the mighty Brahmins come
And lowly bow. Your name, says Ravidas,
   is the shelter of your slave.
      Adi Granth 38[44]

Another bhakti saint, Chokamela, from the untouchable Mahar caste sang,

O God, my caste is low; how can I serve you?
Everyone tells me to go away; how can I see you?
When I touch anyone, they take offense.
Chokhamela wants your mercy.
   Abhanga 76

The only impurity is in the five elements.
There is only one substance in the world.
Then who is pure and who is impure?
The cause of pollution is the creation of the body.
In the beginning, at the end, there is nothing but
pollution.
No one knows anyone who was born pure.
Chokha says, in wonder, who is pure?
   Abhanga 11

Pure Chokhamela, always chanting the name.
I am a Mahar without a caste, Nila in a previous birth.

---

44   Chamar is an untouchable community in North India. John S. Hawley & Mark
Juergensmeyer, *Songs of the Saints of India* (New Delhi: Oxford University Press,
2004), 24–32.

INTRODUCTION

19

He showed disrespect to Krishna; so my birth as a Mahar.
Chokha says: this impurity is the fruit of our past.

Abhanga 4[45]

Here the question arises whether untouchable and low-caste bhakti saints like Ravidas and Chokamela challenged caste explicitly? Perhaps not. In fact, in some cases, like Chokamela above, they even accepted their low estate as the "fruit" of their "past." Writing on this subject of bhakti and resistance in the hymns of Ravidas, John Stratton Hawley notes that Ravidas does

> ... not propose any religious legislation that would change the current social order. To the contrary, it often seems that he values his own lowly position as a vantage point from which the truth about everyone comes more clearly into view. His *bhakti* vision seems to be not so much that God desires to reform society as that he transcends it utterly, and that in the light of the experience of sharing in God, all social distinctions lose their importance.[46]

In that sense, none of these saints necessarily challenged the caste system itself, and their songs did not help others to challenge the caste system. They spoke about their low status, but always in a devotional mode that acknowledged their situation but without making efforts to change it. Their songs reflected their anxiety to show that their condition need not and should not become a hurdle to experience God. Hence, it is not surprising that bhakti traditions are not always favored in the struggles for Dalit emancipation. One of the most well-known critiques was Ambedkar who felt that bhakti was unhelpful to the Untouchables.[47]

---

45   Zelliot, *From Untouchable to Dalit*, 5–6.

46   Ibid., 17.

47   There is the story of Ambedkar discouraging his (first) wife from making a pilgrimage to Pandharpur—a sacred site devoted to Chokamela. He is claimed to have said, "What of that Pandharpur which prevents its devotees from seeing the image of God? By our own virtuous life, selfless service and spotless sacrifice in the cause of downtrodden humanity we would create another Pandharpur. (As reported by Ambedkar's biographer, cited by Zelliot, *From Untouchable to Dalit*, 12)."

    Ambedkar was referring to the fact that though Chokhamela was an untouchable who was close with Vithoba (an incarnation of Vishnu), Untouchables cannot enter into the temple; the most that they could reach was the tomb of Chokhamela. He argued with his fellow Untouchables who went on pilgrimages to Pandharpur, "The appearance of Tulsi leaves around your neck will not relieve you from the clutches of the money lenders. Because you sing songs of Rama, you will not get a concession in rent from the landlords. You will not get salaries at the end of the month because you make pilgrimages every year to Pandharpur. Ibid., 11."

Nevertheless, bhakti can be recognized as a means of Dalit agential assertion. For as Hawley and Juergensmeyer note, through the bhakti of the untouchable saints "Untouchables are able to map out their relation to other aspects of Indian society in a manner that is clearer and more satisfying to them than the conceptual grids through which others are apt to see them."[48] In other words, given that the untouchable bhakti saints have orchestrated and displayed their agency in relation to God through their hymns i.e. their ability to be subjects who can create their own dignified identity by virtue of being children of God as opposed to being objectified by the caste system as outcastes and Untouchables, the saints do serve as inspiration and exemplars of Dalit assertion. In conclusion, we can agree with Zelliot that the "bhakti movement and its literature is still a reservoir of living ideas" which should be "revived" for "participation in the recognized higher intellectual culture" and "become once again a theme of inspiration ... from the past."[49]

Another, perhaps more explicit and popular challenge to caste by Untouchables was made possible through Buddhism. In the nineteenth and twentieth centuries, many Untouchables turned to Buddhism. One of the pioneers of this movement in the late nineteenth century was Iyothee Thass Pandithar (1845–1914), a leader of the Paraiyar Dalit community who argued that the "Pariahs were once followers of the Buddhist dharma," and that they should return to their original religion.[50] In 1898, he formed the Sakhya Buddhist Society at Madras, South India, which "rejected the rituals, beliefs in the supernatural, and traditions of Brahmanical caste Hinduism and replaced them with Buddhist ceremonies ..."[51] Though it was not as popular or influential as the later Dalit Buddhist movements, it is important to acknowledge that, given its anti-caste commitments, (Tamil) Buddhism had been an important avenue of resistance and liberation for the Dalits even in the nineteenth century.

However, the most well-known engagement of Dalits with Buddhism was led by B.R. Ambedkar. Dissatisfied with Hinduism, Ambedkar called his fellow Dalits to leave the religion. He said,

---

In any case, Ambedkar's popularity and his disdain for Chokhamela could possibly be one of the reasons for the decline in the popularity of Chokhamela among Dalit liberation movements in India. However, it should be noted that Ambedkar was favorable toward Kabir and Tukaram, (non-Dalit) low-caste bhakti saints. See Ibid.; Valerian Rodrigues, ed., *The Essential Writings of B. R. Ambedkar* (New Delhi: Oxford University Press, 2004), 7.

48 Hawley & Juergensmeyer, *Songs of the Saints of India*, 21.

49 Zelliot, *From Untouchable to Dalit*, 26.

50 Iyothee Thass, "A Unique Petition," in *The Oxford Anthology of Tamil Dalit Writing*, 221.

51 John C. B. Webster, *Religion and Dalit Liberation: An Examination of Perspectives* (New Delhi: Manohar Publications, 1999), 30.

INTRODUCTION 21

Choose any religion which gives you equality of status and treatment. We shall repair our mistake now. I had the misfortune of being born with the stigma of an Untouchable. However, it is not my fault; but I will not die a Hindu, for this is in my power.[52]

In his rather long search for a new religion,[53] Ambedkar was convinced that the Buddha had a social message that was relevant for the situation of the Untouchables. Ambedkar believed that, "on a careful review of the rules of Chaturvarna the Buddha had no difficulty in coming to the conclusion that the philosophic foundations on which the social order was reared by Brahmanism were wrong if not selfish," and therefore the Buddha had "rejected Brahmanism as being opposed to the true way of life."[54] Hence, Ambedkar believed that Buddhism will be the best alternative for the Dalits who were Hindus and suggested that they should convert to Buddhism to be freed from the shackles of caste.[55] In the process of studying and proposing Buddhism as liberative for Dalits, he not only "found that in many ways Buddhism satisfied the criteria he had developed" regarding religion, but "also used those criteria to reinterpret Buddhism for his own people's benefit."[56] In other words, the Buddhism that Ambedkar proposed was, so to speak, 'tailor-made' for the Dalits. This distinctive form of Buddhism that Ambedkar proposed and practiced is popularly

---

52 Cited by Arundhati Roy, "The Doctor and the Saint," in Ambedkar, *The Annihilation of Caste*, 52.

53 Though Ambedkar made his decision to quit Hinduism in 1935, he embraced Buddhism only in 1956, a few months before his death. Rodrigues, *The Essential Writings of B. R. Ambedkar*, 12 & 17.

54 Ibid., 214–215. Chaturvarna is the fourfold varna classification as Brahmins, Kshatriyas, Vaisyas and Sudras.

55 While Ambedkar's views on Hinduism is too well-known, it is important to remember that he also considered and rejected other religions like Christianity, Islam, Sikhism and Jainism. See "The Condition of the Convert" in Vasanth Moon, comp., *Dr. Babasaheb Ambedkar: Writings and Speeches*, Vol. 5 (Bombay: Government of Maharashtra, 1987), 470–473; Anthoniaraj Thumma, *Dalit Liberation Theology: Ambedkarian Perspective* (Delhi: ISPCK, 2000), 50.

56 Webster, *Religion and Dalit Liberation*, 51. For Ambedkar, religion is a "social force" that "may help or harm a society which is in its grip." See, Vasanth Moon, comp., *Dr. Babasaheb Ambedkar: Writings and Speeches* Vol. 3 (Bombay: Government of Maharashtra, 1987), 23–24. Ambedkar insisted that a religion (Hinduism, in his case), which is a "code of ordinances" that "tends to deprive moral life of freedom and spontaneity" must be rejected. On the contrary, he suggested that a "true religion" is one which is based on the principles of "liberty, equality and fraternity." It is on this basis that he rejected Hinduism and chose Buddhism. Ambedkar, *The Annihilation of Caste*, 306 & 311.

22 INTRODUCTION

known as Navayana (lit. new vehicle) Buddhism and continues to be an important form of Dalit resistance.

While considering how religion has played a critical and liberative role in Dalit liberation, one must also acknowledge the place of Dalit religious traditions that are part of Hinduism. Though these traditions were earlier rejected by Dalit activists and intellectuals as being oppressive and superstitious, in the recent decades there has been a significant turnaround among Dalits in their attitude toward such traditions. One of the pioneering voices on this subject, Abraham Ayrookuzhiel, suggested that

> Though the traditional religion of the Dalits is ambiguous in character, there are positive aspects to it such as its community-orientation and people-centeredness. ... Though the traditional world-view of the Dalits is beset with beliefs about magic, spirits, gods and goddesses causing evil, appeasement of ancestral spirits and gods in rituals, spirit possession and exorcism etc., they have egalitarian, community-centered and people-oriented rituals in their heritage like common sacrifice.
>
> There are gods like Pottam Teyyam of the Malabar Pulayas who calls for righteousness and divine retribution. There is a large amount of folk-songs, poems of Dalits and backward classes, saints, who condemn caste, ritualism, pilgrimage, priest-craft and calls for worship of God in spirit and truth. These could form the common body of the Dalit religious heritage irrespective of their religious affiliation in order to reinterpret the past and reconstruct the future.[57]

In other words, Ayrookuzhiel perceptively alerted Dalits to the abundant wealth of resources that are available in the Dalit religious traditions. Thankfully, his proposal to use Dalit religious sources for reflecting and theologizing on Dalit liberation has been heeded and employed by several Dalit scholars and theologians, including Theophilus Appavoo, Sathianathan Clarke, and Joseph Prabhakar Dayam.[58] In this lineage, I can say that this project

---

57　Abraham Ayrookuzhiel, *Essays on Dalits, Religion and Liberation* (Bangalore: CISRS, 2006), 127–8. Pulayas are a Dalit caste in Kerala, South India. It is worth noticing Ayrookuzhiel's unfavorable attitude towards beliefs and rituals in the Dalit religious traditions. I, on the other hand, claim that such elements of these traditions need not and, in fact, cannot be rejected when considering them for Dalit liberation.

58　Theophilus Appavoo, "Dalit Religion" in *Indigenous People: Dalits—Dalit Issues in Today's Theological Debate*, ed. James Massey (Delhi: ISPCK, 1994), 111–121. For a systematic study of Theophilus Appavoo's practical theology see, Zoe C. Sherinan, "Dalit Theology in Tamil Cultural Music: A Transformative Liturgy by James Theophilus Appavoo," in *Popular*

INTRODUCTION

is yet another attempt to identify and engage Dalit religion as a means of imagining and enacting resistance, and as a resource for doing constructive theology.

5   A Note on Ethnography

Along with the scholarly resources used in this book, because this is a people-centered project, my research is complemented by ethnographic field study of divine possessions in Tamil Hindu and Christian Paraiyar Dalit communities in Tamilnadu, South India. As John Van Maanen observes, "ethnographies are portraits of diversity in an increasingly homogenous world. They display the *intricate* ways individuals and groups understand, accommodate, and resist a presumably shared order."[59] In that sense, I believe that the findings of the ethnographic research will enable me to understand and interpret in a nuanced manner how divine possessions help Dalits to face and negotiate the caste system. However, it is important to note that ethnographies are "inherently *partial*—committed and incomplete."[60] In fact, as Van Maanen reminds us

> Ethnographies are shaped ... by the specific traditions and disciplines from which they are launched. These institutional matters affect the current theoretical position an author takes (or resists) regarding such things as the origins of culture, its characteristic forms, and its consequences ... Such pre-text assumptions help determine what a fieldworker will find interesting and hence see, hear, and eventually write.[61]

Christianity in India: Riting Between the Lines, ed. Selva J. Raj & Corinne G. Dempsey (Albany: State University of New York Press, 2002), 233–253 & Zoe C. Sherinan, *Tamil Folk Music as Dalit Liberation Theology* (Bloomington and Indianapolis: Indiana University Press, 2014). 119–166. Sathianathan Clarke, *Dalits and Christianity: Subaltern Religion and Liberation Theology in India* (Madras: Oxford University Press, 1998), 46. Joseph Prabhakar Dayam, "*Gonthemma Korika*: Reimagining the Divine Feminine in Dalit Christian Theo/alogy," in *Dalit Theology in the Twenty-First Century: Discordant Voices, Discerning Pathways*, ed. Sathianathan Clarke, Deenabandhu Manchala and Philip Vinod Peacock (New Delhi: Oxford University Press, 2011), 137–149.

59   John Van Maanen, *Tales of the Field: On Writing Ethnography* (Chicago and London: The University of Chicago Press, 1988), xiv. Emphasis mine.

60   James Clifford and George E. Marcus, ed., *Writing Culture: The Poetics and Politics of Ethnography* (Berkeley, Los Angeles and London: University of California Press, 1986), 7.

61   Van Maanen, *Tales of the Field*, 5.

Therefore, I have to acknowledge that the ethnographic research in this project is also influenced by the requirements and commitments of the theological field.

By engaging in ethnography, Natalie Wigg-Stevenson notes that "ethnographic theologians ... acknowledge and accept that there is no theological 'view from nowhere' that we can access, and that all theological claims are embedded in and produced by certain contexts, practices, and systems of power and privilege."[62] In other words, through ethnographic research, the subjective and contextual dimension of all theologies is acknowledged, thus debunking claims of objectivity. This "posture of epistemological humility...," of ethnographic theology, "invites its reader into an ongoing theological conversation more than it tries to convince its reader of a theological argument."[63] In that regard, I hope that my ethnographic research will also critically inform and shape the constructive comparative theology of liberation that I intend to develop, facilitating further conversations in Dalit theology and comparative theology.

However, even as I acknowledge its significance for this book, I have to confess that I employ ethnography only to *supplement and critically enhance* the information available through the existing literature on divine possessions in Hinduism and Christianity (particularly but not exclusively) pertaining to Dalits. In that sense, I have to admit that this book may not manifest the traits of a conventional ethnographic work. Rather, I consider my research as a multisited ethnographic approach which I owe to Joe Arun who has employed this methodology in his study of changing Paraiyar identities. Even though most anthropological studies have focused on a single site/space/place, Arun argues that since the "empirical reality today is ... governed by trans-national mobility and virtual communications, and the changing social, territorial and cultural emergence of group identity by migration" leading to constant reconstruction of histories and individual and collective identities, "studying a single site would hardly provide us with a complete understanding of the subject we want to explore."[64] In that sense, he proposes that "we have to locate our study in more than one site, and ... see the reality from one to the other."[65]

Following this approach, I studied divine possessions among Paraiyars in multiple sites during the Summer of 2016. Hence, though my principle study

---

62 Natalie Wigg-Stevenson, *Ethnographic Theology: An Inquiry into the Production of Theological Knowledge* (New York: Palgrave-Macmillan, 2014), 170.

63 Ibid., 170.

64 Joe C. Arun, *Constructing Dalit Identity* (Jaipur: Rawat Publications, 2007), 18.

65 Ibid., 18.

INTRODUCTION

was in Vichur[66] and Periyapalayam[67] (villages on the outskirts of Chennai, South India), I also looked at possessions in other places in Tamilnadu. And because of the nature of the multi-sited approach, I am also able to include my earlier research that I had conducted on Dalit religion in the villages of Kottaikarai and Pulichapallam (near Pondicherry, South India).[68] Further, the use of a multi-sited approach facilitates the incorporation of ethnographic research conducted by other anthropologists and religious scholars without much difficulty.

6   Paraiyars—a Glance

In this section, let me offer a brief description of the community that I focus on in this book viz. the 'Paraiyars.' Also called as Paraiyans or Pariahs, Paraiyars are one of the prominent Dalit communities in Tamilnadu.[69] It must be acknowledged that it is very difficult to identify the actual origins or the premodern history of the Paraiyars. However, Clarke identifies that, broadly speaking, four theories may be helpful in understanding the early history of the Paraiyars. The most commonly known version is the linking of the state of the Paraiyars to the law of Manu. Referring to Abbe Dubois and Oliver Cox, Clarke notes that according to this view, "Paraiyars ... are the descendants of those persons and groups that had been expelled from the caste system because of transgressing caste rules and social regulations. The offspring of parents who marry hypogamously—a lower caste male marrying a higher caste female— eventually became the Dalits" (in this case, the Paraiyars).[70] A second theory that tries to reconstruct the history of the Paraiyars is related to the *parai*, the

---

66   Vichur is a village located near the industrial town of Manali, outside Chennai with a population of about six hundred thousand. https://villageinfo.in/tamil-nadu/thiruvallur/ ponneri/vichoor.html. Accessed on March 20, 2017. Though Dalits are the majority in the village there are also dominant caste people like Reddiyars.

67   Periyapalayam is a temple town outside Chennai also with a population of about six hundred thousand. Periyapalayam which was once predominantly a Dalit village is now a bustling town made popular because of the Periyapalayathamman temple. https://villageinfo.in/tamil-nadu/thiruvallur/uthukkottai/periyapalayam.html. Accessed on April 3, 2017.

68   This research was conducted for a Paper that I presented at a Conference on Dalit Theology and Dalit activism in Bengaluru, South India. Joshua Samuel, "Dalits and Conversions" (Paper presented at the 'Interfacing for Emancipation' conference, Bangalore, India August 5–10, 2010).

69   The other Dalit communities in Tamilnadu are the Pallar and the Chakkiliyar.

70   Clarke, *Dalits and Christianity*, 66.

Dalit drum. According to the proponents of this view (like Robert Caldwell, an Anglican Bishop and linguist), the name Paraiyar is derived from the *parai*, and because of the Hindu notion of pollution associated with the *parai* which is made of (dead) cow hide, the Paraiyar also came to be considered as a polluted caste. Thirdly, Paraiyar, as some Tamil historians have claimed, are the original inhabitants and rulers of the Dravidian/South Indian land who were defeated and enslaved by the Aryan Hindus.[71] Finally, Clarke refers to the theory that the Paraiyar were excluded and segregated as outcastes "through an overall process of territorial augmentation."[72] While these theories may have several discrepancies which cannot be considered here, we may agree with Clarke's inference that

> i) The Paraiyar are an ancient people, perhaps even the aboriginal or original inhabitants of South India. ii) The Paraiyar are a culturally distinct community with the drum as a key symbol of this particularity. iii) The Paraiyar are an economically oppressed and culturally marginalized community, primarily because their particular heritage was not in conformity with the traditions of the Hindu caste communities.[73]

As a part of this overview, I believe it is germane to note that Paraiyars are also known for their resistance. One can see that, especially since the nineteenth century, there have been several leaders and movements who have inspired and symbolized Dalit liberation. For instance, in the second half of the nineteenth and early twentieth century there was a strong movement of religious conversions among Paraiyars who challenged caste oppression in Hinduism by changing their religion. One such well-known religious conversions is known as the mass movements, which I will revisit in detail in chapter five. Around this same period there was also a strong (but lesser-known) Paraiyar Buddhist movement led by Iyothi Thaas Pandithar, which was mentioned earlier. On the political front, during the first half of the twentieth century there were leaders like Rettaimalai Srinivasan (1860–1945), a pioneering Dalit journalist and leader, and M.C. Rajah (1883–1943) who was a member of the Legislature and a prominent spokesperson for the Dalits.[74] At present, one may identify

---

71   Because in Tamil *la* and *ra* are interchangeable, Paraiyar can also be read as Palaiyar i.e. the "ancient or original people." Ibid., 68.

72   Ibid., 69.

73   Ibid., 70–71.

74   For a glimpse of notable leaders in Paraiyar history see, Ravikumar and R. Azhagarasan, ed., *The Oxford* Anthology *of Tamil Dalit Writing*, 211–233.

INTRODUCTION

Thirumavalavan, the leader of the Viduthalai Chiruthaigal Katchi aka Dalit Panthers Iyakkam (Liberation Panthers Party), as a force to reckon in the Indian political arena.[75] To conclude this section, we may say that Paraiyar history is marked both by the reality of oppression and struggle for emancipation.

7   Location of the Comparativist

Speaking of Paraiyar Dalits, I want to acknowledge here that I myself am one i.e. a Paraiyar. I am from North Tamilnadu where Paraiyars are the majority Dalit community. My father hails from a small village called Kaiveli in the border between Tamil Nadu and Andhra Pradesh, while my mother is from Vadapathi, a village to the south of Chennai. In many ways, this book was inspired by my own identity as a Paraiyar Dalit. My research and writing were a search for my own (hi)story which was eroded and erased by the dominant stories of caste and colonialism. While history is always ambiguous, relative, and incomplete, for communities that were treated as 'non-human' and denied any sense of worth or dignity, (re)claiming their past becomes essential.[76]

However, I am not just a Paraiyar Dalit. I am also a Christian Paraiyar Dalit. I am told that my great grandparents embraced Christianity as adults in the early part of the twentieth century. There could be many reasons why someone chooses another religious tradition. As we shall see, Dalits chose Christianity both for spiritual and socio-political reasons, and it has certainly proved to be helpful (even if there are shortcomings as Indian Christians continue to practice caste). But embracing Christianity through the work of missionaries in the colonial era also meant leaving and cutting their ties with their old religious traditions in Hinduism. But did Dalits leave their past entirely in obedience to the missionaries? Have Dalit Christians snapped their relationship with the religions of their ancestors completely? This book asks such questions and more. As said earlier, raising and struggling with these questions is a way of (re)searching and reconnecting with my past.[77] In that sense, this work is part

---

75   For a methodical study of the politics of Thirumavalavan and his party see, Hugo Gorringe, *Untouchable Citizens: Dalit Movements and Democratisation in Tamilnadu* (New Delhi, Thousand Oaks and London: Sage Publications, 2005).

76   Let me clarify here that I do not speak of identity in an essentialist sense. That is, I do not believe that Paraiyar history or identity is monolithic, fixed, or pure, and does not completely define who I am. All identities are constructed, ever changing and intersecting with each other, and do not define an individual or a community entirely.

77   My ancestors were worshippers of some of the deities that are mentioned in this book.

28INTRODUCTION

of my ongoing quest for what it means *for me* to be a Dalit in the twenty-first century.

8   Layout of Chapters

The book has three parts. The purpose of the first part—comprising of this Introduction and the first two chapters—is to lay down the groundwork for the comparative study and constructive theology ahead. In the first chapter, I will offer a basic theological framework for a comparative theology of liberation by incorporating the fundamental components of comparative theology and Dalit liberation theology. In each case, I will describe 1) the basic method and fundamental features of the discipline and 2) the issues and new directions that have been identified by scholars in recent times. From these individual investigations of comparative theology and Dalit theology my objective is to dialogically and critically integrate the basic method and the positive elements of the two disciplines into a 'comparative theology of liberation.' Such a comparative theology of liberation will be, as I shall argue, an embodied, people-centred, non-identitarian and inter-religiously liberationist theology.[78]

The second chapter will deal with preparing the theoretical framework for the later chapters. In this section, I will identify the significance of the Dalit body within the caste context by engaging anecdotes and Dalit literature in dialogue with Judith Butler's and Michel Foucault's theoretical conceptualization of the body. Following this, using feminist and womanist scholarship on the body, I shall go on to suggest that the bodies of the oppressed (like Dalits) are sacramental by virtue of their brokenness. Building on this 'privilege' of the Dalit bodies, I point out that such sacramentality becomes particularly visible during moments of embodied divine experiences or "divine possessions." Finally, based on these suggestions, I will propose that it is possible and relevant to construct a comparative theology of liberation by comparing embodied divine possessions in Hindu and Christian Paraiyar Dalit communities.

In the second part of the book, we turn to the study of divine possessions among Hindu and Christian Paraiyar Dalits in Tamilnadu, South India. There are four chapters in this part. In chapter three, because of the complex and

---

78   For the sake of clarity, let me say that I am not 'comparing' comparative theology and Dalit theology in this book. As mentioned earlier, I am comparing divine possessions in Hindu and Christian Dalit communities. What I am attempting in the first chapter is to propose a comparative theology of liberation by critically interweaving the disciplines of comparative theology and Dalit theology.

INTRODUCTION

29

ambiguous relationship of Dalits and their religious traditions with Hinduism, I will offer a brief history of the 'construction' of Hinduism as *a* religion in modernity under the influence of orientalism and the aegis of colonialism. Here, I will make the case that if we critically re-view and move beyond the Sanskrit and Brahmin centric Hinduism of modernity, it is possible to consider Dalit religions as continuous with and a part of Hinduism, without compromising the distinct resistive and assertive dimensions of the former. Based on this argument, I will sketch and critically evaluate the liberative significance of Dalit goddess traditions within the broader framework of goddess traditions of Hinduism.

In chapter four, I begin by mapping the essential elements of divine possessions. In the second section, the different aspects of divine possessions among Paraiyars will be presented by incorporating data both from the existing scholarship and my own ethnographic research. The final part of the chapter will be an interpretative and reflective summarization of Hindu Dalit possessions.

The fifth and sixth chapters follow the same basic structure as the previous two chapters, except that the focus will be on divine possessions in Christian Dalit communities. In order to locate Christian Dalit divine possessions within the larger framework of Dalit Christianity, in the fifth chapter, I will give an overview of the history of Paraiyar Dalit Christians and the issues faced by them. In the second section, because this book also situates itself within Dalit theology, I will carefully look at the prominent interpretations of God in the discipline, including criticisms posed against them. I end the chapter by highlighting a new trend in Dalit theology, viz. the focus on the Dalit body as a hermeneutical tool.

Keeping in line with this new turn in Dalit theology, in the following chapter, I will map embodied experiences of the divine in the form of possessions among Christian Dalits. I will look at its meaning for Christian Dalits by using existing scholarship on this subject and listening to Christian Dalit voices through ethnographic research. The primary focus is on the ecstatic experiencing of the Holy Spirit (also known as Holy Spirit anointing or Holy Spirit baptism) among Christian believers during charismatic worship. However, to acknowledge alternative understandings of divine possessions among Christians, I refer to instances of Marian possessions—moments when Mary (the mother of Jesus) possesses her devotees—and the embodied experiencing of the divine through the sacraments.[79] The concluding section of the chapter will be a preliminary interpretation of possessions.

---

79   In this book, I focus only on the sacraments of the Protestant church.

30   INTRODUCTION

Part three is the comparative and constructive section of the book. In chapter seven, the inquiries and observations made in the previous chapters on Hindu and Christian divine possessions will be compared. However, before I begin comparing, I want to look at the complex and ambiguous hybridity and multiplicity of Paraiyar religion in South India. Based on this study, I will argue that comparison, in the case of Paraiyars, is not simply done between two 'mutually exclusive' religions, but rather between two 'overlapping' religions held together by the commonality of Dalitness. With this important observation, I enter into comparing divine possessions among Hindu and Christian Paraiyar Dalits. It should be noted that the purpose of this comparison is not merely for the sake of seeing similarities and differences—although that is inevitable in a way—but to look for liberative elements during these moments. Based on this, I will interpret Dalit divine possessions, both Hindu and Christian, as hidden transcripts and a form of infrapolitics that have affirmative, resistive, and emancipatory potentials. As a part of this liberative reading of possessions, I will argue that divine possessions help us to re-imagine and re-envision resistance and liberation in alternative ways.

Assuming and ascribing a liberative motif to the divine possessions, in the final chapter I turn to the concept of *kairos* to interpret them theologically. Although I shall consider its different usages (for instance, during the South African struggle against apartheid), I will focus on *kairos* as construed and conceptualized by Paul Tillich, and make the case that it is appropriate to interpret divine possessions as *kairos*. However, I will also argue that the theological concept itself can be enriched and enhanced when we critically and dialogically interpret possessions as *kairos*. To further deepen the theological significance of possessions, given the normative relation of the various *kairoi* in history to the Christ event (which Tillich calls as the great *Kairos*), I propose that Dalit divine possessions (as *kairoi*) could be interpreted as Christic moments. Let me acknowledge here that the use of Christian theological concepts to interpret Hindu Dalit possessions does not mean that I assume or seek to impose Christian universalism. Rather, as a Christian theologian I find the Christ symbol to be *appropriate* (as a Christian) as well as *expansive* (as an interreligious scholar) to interpret religious concepts and experiences beyond the Christian tradition.[80] Based on this understanding and using the framework of Spirit

---

80   I have to confess that I do identify myself as an (open) inclusivist theologian of religion (although some might consider my position more pluralistic). The inclusivist position in the theology of religions "believes that, because God is present in the whole world, God's grace is also at work in some way among all people..." in their respective religions, although, these religions "play a role preparatory to the gospel of Christ, in whom alone fullness of salvation is found." Clark H. Pinnock, "An Inclusivist View," in *Four Views on*

INTRODUCTION

31

Christology, in the last section, I will attempt to offer constructive theological interpretations. Firstly, I will demonstrate that divine possessions among Dalits as embodied Christic experiences enable us to imagine and speak of the symbol of God as immanent in the broken subjectivity of oppressed bodies. Further, using the conceptualization of God in process philosophy, I argue that such immanent presence of the divine in possessions can be perceived as transgressive *creativity* that diverges from, disrupts, and deconstructs oppressive and divisive 'normative' epistemic structures such as caste and gender (just to name a few), and opens up new, unique and distinct ways of being (human). Finally, I suggest that because of the transgressive, creative nature of God which initiates and facilitates new ways of being in the world, it is possible, relevantly and meaningfully, to envision the divine as the liberative and empowering ground of be(com)ing.

Salvation in a Pluralistic World, ed. Dennis L. Okholm and Timothy R. Phillips (Grand Rapids: Zondervan, 1996), 98. However, as it can be seen in the final chapter, my inclusivist position diverges much from this 'basic' definition of inclusivism and is conceptualized based on the pervasive and embracive grace of God as revealed in Jesus Christ that allows and acknowledges other independent divine revelations without them being bound to or limited by the Christ event. For a concise study of the different approaches in the theology of religions see, Paul F. Knitter, *Introducing Theology of Religions* (Maryknoll, New York: Orbis Books, 2011).

CHAPTER 1

Toward a Comparative Theology of Liberation

The purpose of this chapter is to lay out the interdisciplinary theological framework for the book.[1] Here I propose that comparative theology can be envisioned and expanded as a liberative theology when integrated with and interpreted through the lens of liberation theologies like Dalit theology. Such an interreligious theology, I believe, would ensure the integrity and efficacy of both comparative and Dalit theologies.

I shall begin this section with a brief introduction of comparative theology going on to underscore some problematic issues in relation to text centrism. In the next section, I will concisely summarize the key aspects of Dalit theology with special emphasis on recent suggestions and proposals in the discipline. The third step, stemming from observations and criticisms made within each of these two disciplines, will be a proposal for a Dalit comparative theology of liberation. The object of this exercise is that the ensuing product of such a dialogue would pave the path for constructive comparison between Hindu and Christian divine possessions among Dalits in the later chapters.[2] In other words, dialogue between comparative theology and Dalit theology in this chapter envisions and engenders a comprehensive comparative-liberation framework for later work.

1   Comparative Theology

In spite of being a relatively new academic discipline comparative theology has indeed made a significant impact in the area of interreligious engagement. What is comparative theology? In the words of Francis X. Clooney,

---

1   An earlier and embryonic version of this chapter was published as "Towards a Comparative Theology of Liberation: Exploring Comparative Theology's Relevance for Doing Indian Liberation Theology," *Interreligious Studies and Intercultural Theology* 1/1 (2017): 47–67.

2   A good example of such a critical methodological dialogue is Paul Knitter's liberationist theology of religions where he brings together the strengths of theology of religions and liberation theology to envision an interreligious liberationist theology of religions that is focused on justice to the poor and the oppressed. See, Paul Knitter, "Toward a Liberationist Theology of Religions," in *The Myth of Christian Uniqueness: Toward a Pluralistic Theology of Religions*, ed. John Hick and Paul F. Knitter (Maryknoll, New York: Orbis Books, 1987), 178–200.

Comparative theology—comparative and theological beginning to end—marks acts of faith seeking understanding which are rooted in a particular faith tradition but which, from that foundation, venture into learning from one or more other faith traditions. This learning is sought for the sake of fresh theological insights that are indebted to the newly encountered tradition/s as well as the home tradition.[3]

That is, in comparative theology the theologian who is rooted in a particular religious tradition ventures out to learn from another religious tradition. However, it is important to remember that the comparative theologian does not stay behind in the new tradition. Rather, having been enriched by her encounter, she returns back to her tradition, to critique and enhance it. It is equally important to remember that in none of these processes does the comparative theologian assume a know-it-all or militant attitude. On the contrary, the entire enterprise is to be undertaken as a spiritual task with reverence and vulnerability.[4]

It should also be noted that the emphasis is not on learning *about* other religions, but learning *with* other religions.[5] There is a deep engagement with the studied tradition so that the interreligious learning is not undertaken for the sake of 'investigating' the validity of that tradition or interpreting it from the perspective of Christianity (as in the case of theologies of religions). Rather, as John Thatamanil asserts, comparative theologians "wish to engage specific texts, motifs, and claims of particular traditions not only to understand better these traditions but also to determine the truth of theological matters through conversation and collaboration."[6] Bagus Laksana summarizes the task of comparative theology using the apt metaphor of pilgrimage as follows:

> ... at the heart of comparative theology lies a dynamic of fostering an ever richer and deeper sense of religious identity through the arduous journey of productive encounters with alterity, respecting a certain degree of irreducibility inherent in the religious others ... while refusing to succumb to the idea of the absoluteness of this alterity. In this respect, comparative theology shares the profundity of the pilgrims' sentiment

---

3 Francis X. Clooney, *Comparative Theology: Deep Learning Across Religious Borders* (Chichester: Wiley-Blackwell, 2010), 10.

4 Ibid., 60–61.

5 John J. Thatamanil, *The Immanent Divine: God Creation, and the Human Predicament: An East West Conversation* (Minneapolis: Fortress Press, 2006), 3.

6 Ibid., 3.

34   CHAPTER 1

and passion of reaching out to the Other (*God*) and other (*other religious traditions and communities*) as well as of going home refreshed by this very act of reaching out.[7]

1.1 *Interrogating Comparative Theology*

While comparative theology is certainly a promising discipline that has marked "a new stage in Christian theology's encounter with other religious traditions,"[8] it is important to note that there are issues and concerns that have been pointed out in recent scholarship to make comparative theology sensitive and responsive to historical injustices. For instance, John Thatamanil has called for the need for a comparative theology that is critical of the essentializing power of the category of "religion" by being aware of its genealogy in modern colonial history.[9] Michelle Voss Roberts has proposed the need for comparative theology to take the voices of the marginalized seriously.[10] Tracy Tiemier, in a related move, has suggested that it is important for comparative theology to become a theology of liberation.[11] There is no doubt that all these scholars serve as important signposts for this project.

While heeding to these critical voices, in this book, I point out that, from a Dalit perspective, there are three issues, related to the above mentioned observations, that need to be attended to by comparative theologians, and to which Dalit liberation theology could serve as a possible corrective. The three issues are: lingering Euro-Christian centrism, indifference to the agency of faith communities, and re-inscription of unjust hierarchical structures. However, it should be noted that these three issues that I name stem out of a common and prominent feature in comparative theology, namely the primacy of texts. In the following section, I will show how text centrism facilitates Euro-Christian supremacy, non-people-centered interreligious learning, and hierarchical stratification within religious communities.

---

7   A. Bagus Laksana, "Comparative Theology: Between Identity and Alterity," in *The New Comparative Theology: Interreligious Insights from the Next Generation* ed. Francis X. Clooney (London and New York: T & T Clark, 2010), 3. Italicized text within parenthesis mine.

8   Thatamanil, *The Immanent Divine,* 3.

9   John J. Thatamanil, "Comparative Theology after "Religion,"" in *Planetary Loves: Spivak, Postcoloniality, and Theology,* ed. Stephen D. Moore and Mayra Rivera (New York: Fordham University Press, 2011), 238–257.

10   Michelle Voss Roberts, "Gendering Comparative Theology," in in Francis X. Clooney (ed.), *The New Comparative Theology: Interreligious Insights from the Next Generation* (London & New York: T & T Clark, 2010), 109–128.

11   Tracy Tiemier, "Comparative Theology as a Theology of Liberation," in *The New Comparative Theology,* 129–149.

1.2 *Prioritization of Texts*

In naming and framing the fundamental elements of comparative theology, Clooney notes that, in his view, "the foremost prospect for a fruitful comparative theology is the reading of texts."[12] Even if he accepts that other ways of doing comparative theology is possible, Clooney is convinced that texts "remain the single-best resource ... for knowing religious traditions deeply and subtly."[13] Thus, it is not surprising that a majority of works in comparative theology seem to focus on texts and textual comparative study seems to be the more conventional method in this discipline. While at the surface such an endeavor, namely studying and comparing religious texts, appears to be innocent and exciting, the underlying (and hidden) dangers of prioritization of texts in comparative theology have to be considered carefully, especially since they re-strengthen unjust dynamics and relationships in and between religious communities. To this we turn next.

1.2.1   Lingering Western/Christian Supremacy

Tomoko Masuzawa, in her study of *The Invention of World Religions,* shows that the primacy of texts played a critical role in justifying European and Christian supremacy within the context of colonialism. Masuzawa notes that in comparison to Christianity, those religions with textual traditions studied by orientalist scholars "came to be recognized as a vast and powerful metaphysical system deeply ingrained in the social fabric of a particular nation, and in the psychical predilections of its individual citizens and subjects" and named as "world religions."[14] However, through this recognition, as Masuzawa points out, such text-based world religions became *"just another name for Christianity"* so that through them, Christianity and Christian supremacy "became available to men and women of faith as a new conceptual framework" allowing "the adaption of Christian absolutism to the modern reality."[15] In other words, the idea of world religions facilitated the translation and transposition of Christian supremacy (on) to other religions in colonized contexts.

---

12   Clooney, *Comparative Theology,* 58.

13   Ibid., 67.

14   In contrast to these world religions were the tribal or primitive religions that "had experienced little historical transformation" and would therefore "eventually and inevitably dissipate or disappear, through the process of assimilation, atrophy, or banishment." Tomoko Masuzawa, *The Invention of World Religions: Or, How European Universalism Was Preserved in the Language of Pluralism* (Chicago and London: The University of Chicago Press, 2005), 18 & 42.

15   Ibid., 119. Emphasis mine.

36   CHAPTER 1

These text-centric dynamics become clearer when we turn our attention to colonialism in India. Richard King, in his *Orientalism and Religion,* elucidates how orientalism was inspired by the Protestant preference for the 'text.' King observes,

> [P]rotestant emphasis upon the text as the locus of religion placed a particular emphasis upon the literary aspects of Indian culture in the work of Orientalists. Academics and highly educated Western administrators are already inclined towards literary forms of expression because of their training, and so it is not all that surprising to find Orientalists (both old and new) being drawn towards Indian literary materials as sources for understanding Indian culture...[16]

That is, it was the influence of protestant values that was behind the European scholars' preference for textual traditions over non-textual traditions.[17] Geoffrey Oddie, in his study of the role of protestant missions in the construction of Hinduism, has also identified the unquestionable link between the inclination to focus on texts, protestant missionary interests, oriental scholarship, and colonialism.[18]

Given this problematic history of text-centrism, it is necessary to question and be critical of the primacy of texts in comparative theology. And since most comparative theologians are from the west—although one needs to be critical about the (unspoken) claim that it is a discipline 'created' by the western academia[19]—one cannot but wonder whether it is the colonial-orientalist

---

16   Richard King, *Orientalism and Religion: Postcolonial Theory, India and the 'Mystic East'* (London and New York: Routledge, 2002), 101.

17   When this text-centric orientalism meshed with nationalistic uprisings for independence among the Indian elite class in the nineteenth century (of course, always under the watchful eyes of the colonizers), it resulted in the creation of a religion called Hinduism. Ibid., 96–117. We shall return to this in the third chapter.

18   Geoffrey Oddie, *Imagined Hinduism: British Protestant Missionary Constructions of Hinduism, 1793–1900* (New Delhi, Thousand Oaks, California & London: Sage Publications, 2006), 99–101. In fact, as Richard Davis points out, the very interest for learning non-European religious traditions was rooted in colonial motives. Richard Davis, *The Bhagvad Gita: A Biography* (Princeton & Oxford: Princeton University Press, 2015), 76.

19   This oversight can be seen when Clooney, in tracing the history of comparative theology, considers comparative theologians from the past and the present without acknowledging the comparative theological works of several Asian scholars including Keshub Chandra Sen, Brahmobandab Uppadhyaya, and A. J. Appasamy which long predated (and possibly even surpassed) the western scholarship. Clooney, *Comparative Theology,* 24–53.

Christian supremacy that encourages them to prioritize texts. Writing on this, Marianne Moyaert rightly observes that this "assumption that texts form the privileged locus from where we can fathom religions"—which is the theory of scholars like Clooney—"is a dubious one," since "lurking just around the corner is... the problem of the Christianization of religion."[20] Simply put, prioritization of texts is only a means of interpreting all religions using a Western-Christian lens, within a Western-Christian framework, and would go against comparative theology's aim to acknowledge the individuality and particularity of religious traditions.

1.2.2 Disregarding Agency of Faith Communities

Another problem one can identify in comparative theological projects in relation to the primacy of texts is the failure to see the broader meaning of religion and the failure to recognize the agency of the communities in which the studied religions are actually practiced. Even though texts play a key role in religious traditions, we know that religions do not and cannot exist (with)in texts alone. Rather, religious texts find meaning only when/as they are practiced, or to be more precise, lived—albeit in different forms and with varying levels of significance—*in* religious communities.

Naturally, this human/communitarian dimension of religion is also applicable to interreligious encounters, including comparative theology. Michael Barnes, in his analysis of Clooney's methodology, proposes that religion and hence interreligious encounters have to be seen in a wider sociopolitical framework, *(with)in the lives of the people.* He writes,

> ... no practice of comparative reading is ever done in a cultural and religious vacuum. Texts need to be read as part of the wider and more complex framework that makes up religious life—and that must include the buildings and artefacts and practices of faith and even the people who make up communities of faith.[21]

---

20   Marianne Moyaert, "Inaugural Address," given at Vrije Universiteit Amsterdam on November 1, 2014. (Unpublished). Also see, Marianne Moyaert, "Christianity as the Measure of Religion? Materializing the Theology of Religions" in *Twenty-First Century Theologies of Religions*, ed. Elizabeth J. Harris, Paul Hedges & Shanthikumar Hettiarachchi (Leiden & Boston: Brill Rodopi, 2016), 257.

21   Although Barnes' critical observation is very helpful, one cannot ignore his choice of vocabulary—"even the people who make up communities of faith"—when it comes to recognizing people as resources and agents of religious traditions. Michael Barnes, *Interreligious Learning: Dialogue, Spirituality and Christian Imagination* (Cambridge: Cambridge University Press, 2012), 21.

38   CHAPTER 1

Moreover, convinced that interreligious learning cannot be limited to texts, Barnes is candid that his

> ... version of comparative theology differs from that espoused by Clooney in that the examples, the starting points of reflection, are *embodied* in the lives of persons of faith and inscribed in the places of worship and artefacts that give voice to their faith—sometimes more eloquently than their words and conversation.[22]

Such people-centered interreligious learning becomes imperative especially when dealing with marginalized traditions, since several of them do not have textual foundations but exist predominantly in oral, iconographic, and mythographic forms.[23] Thus, given the richness of the embodiment of religion in religious communities and in their symbols of faith, especially in marginalized non-textual traditions, I agree with Barnes that interreligious learning cannot be limited to texts.

However, we should also note that the need for community centered, rather than text-centered, interreligious study becomes more compelling if we recognize that religious communities, and therefore, religious traditions, do not exist in fixed containers. That is, in spite of the visible demarcation between and within religions, in reality there has always been an inevitable interaction and overlap between (often neighboring) religious traditions because of the traffic of ideas and practices between religious communities.

Moreover, there is also the intersection of multiple identities in individuals and communities that affects religious identities. Writing on the problem of elitism in interreligious dialogue, Indian theologian Muthuraj Swamy alleges that "[T]he interaction of multiple identities in a human being or among human beings is a common factor that has often been ignored at the cost of emphasizing religious identities."[24] In other words, as Jeanine Hill-Fletcher notes, "[O]ur religious identities are not sui generis and unaffected by other dimensions of who we are; rather, our very understanding of the religious dimension of our identity is informed by the diverse features of our location and experience."[25] They intersect with other identities (gender, social, political,

---

22   Ibid. Emphasis mine.

23   Dayam, "*Gonthemma Korika,*" 139.

24   Muthuraj Swamy, *The Problem with Interreligious Dialogue* (London and New York: Bloomsbury, 2016), 169.

25   Jeanine Hill Fletcher, *Monopoly on Salvation? A Feminist Approach to Religious Pluralism* (New York: Continuum, 2005), 88.

economic, cultural etc.,) so that the overall composite identity of two individuals from (say two) different religious communities, could have significant similarities. A classic example which I would develop in the later chapters is the similarities between Dalit Hindus and Christians, who, though from different religious communities, are bound by their experiences of caste discrimination. In fact, in such cases one finds that multiple religious belonging is not uncommon.[26] But, this continuity between faith traditions and faith communities, I am afraid, cannot be considered properly and appropriately if the focus in interreligious encounters is limited solely to texts.

Finally, delving deeper into the issue of preference of texts with liberationist and post-colonial sensitivity, one discovers that it not only provides a distorted view of religion, but also denies the *agency* of the people concerned. That is, limiting religious traditions to texts is not just an intellectual limitation, but more than that: it is an act of injustice since it does not respect the way in which these scriptural and theological texts find meaning and purpose for those communities. When reading comparative theological projects of the above genre, one cannot but wonder whether it is the old colonial desire 'to study the ways of the oriental other' that sneaks up again in such projects. Therefore, I would suggest that it is necessary for all comparative theological projects to be conscious about this silencing of the voices and experiences of religious communities.

1.2.3   Perpetuation of Hierarchies

Finally, prioritizing texts for interreligious learning in comparative theology may also facilitate further marginalization and discrimination of oppressed communities and their traditions. To understand this better, let me turn to the construction of Hinduism in the colonial era.

As noted earlier, there was clearly a bias toward texts among orientalist scholars and the colonial administration. In this context, with its growing popularity in philological scholarship—and "the application of philological scholarship to the classification of religions," thanks to the likes of Max Müller[27]—Sanskrit became the most-preferred language among orientalists.[28] However, since learning Sanskrit (often) meant learning from Brahmin pundits, the religion that took shape in orientalist scholarship and colonial 'administrative

---

26   For more see, Joshua Samuel, "Practicing Multiple Religious Belonging for Liberation: A Dalit Perspective," *Current Dialogue* 57 (December 2015): 78–87.
27   Masuzawa, *The Invention of World Religions*, 207–209.
28   Davis, *The Bhagvad Gita*, 76–79. Davis accurately identifies this Sanskrit bias in the translation and promotion of Bhagvad Gita as the Bible of the Hindus.

records' viz. Hinduism, was a Sanskritic, Brahmanic Hinduism. At the same time, as King notes, "the oral and 'popular' aspect of Indian religious tradition was either ignored or decried as evidence of the degradation of contemporary Hindu religion into superstitious practices that bore little or no relation to 'their own' texts."[29] It is important to remember that such ignored oral religious traditions were (mostly) practiced by the lower castes, Dalits, and Tribals.[30] This meant that the textual bias of orientalist scholars in the colonial era that centered the Brahmanic and Sanskritic traditions only strengthened the already existing caste-based hierarchies.

Given this history of alliance between orientalist text-centrism and reification and re-inscribing of caste hierarchies, comparative theology's preference for texts and elitist choices, especially in relation to Hinduism, becomes a concern indeed. When comparative theologians, with very few exceptions,[31] continue to show disinterest in engaging with non-textual Dalit and other such marginalized traditions, it raises the suspicion that the discipline has also fallen prey to the old orientalist task of ignoring, and thereby, oppressing the marginalized people by siding with the dominant castes. This suspicion seems to be further validated when comparative theologians are silent on injustices related to their studied religious traditions, in this case Hinduism. Peniel Rajkumar identifies the tendency of western comparative theologians to overlook the evils of caste in Hindu-Christian interreligious engagements as the reflection of "colonial guilt."[32] Moreover, reflecting on Hindu-Christian interreligious dialogue, Rajkumar contends that "[I]f we continue to treat the issue of caste ... as 'untouchable' in the context of Hindu-Christian dialogue, we need to question whether dialogue has not become part of a 'conspiracy of invisibility' which 'refuses to see' and 'deliberately ignores' the issue of the oppression

---

29   King, *Orientalism and Religion*, 101.

30   An important feature of this 'hierarchicalization' of religious traditions as 'high' and 'low,' is based on the comparability with the "universalistic and proselytizing elements of Christian Theology." Ibid., 62–68.

31   A noteworthy example is Michelle Voss Roberts, who, in a section of her *Tastes of the Divine*, studies the various emotional expressions of fury in Dalit communities. However, it has to be noted that her predominant framework is still Brahmanic and Sanskrit-based and does not include religious traditions practiced among Dalits. Michelle Voss Roberts, *Tastes of the Divine: Hindu and Christian Theologies of Emotion* (New York: Fordham University Press, 2014), 117–155. For more, see my Book Review in *The Ecumenical Review* 68.1 (March 2016): 157–159.

32   Peniel Jesudason Rufus Rajkumar, "Re-Cast(e)ing Conversion, Re-visiting Dialogue: Indian Attempts at an Interfaith Theology of Wholeness" *Journal for the Academic Study of Religion* 26/2 (2013): 164.

TOWARD A COMPARATIVE THEOLOGY OF LIBERATION

of Dalits and Adivasis under the caste system."[33] Hence, I believe that comparative theology cannot pretend to be innocent and indifferent about its elitist preferences and its silence about injustices nor claim that this is unavoidable, given that such choices result in the strengthening of unjust structures.[34] The 'silence' of comparative theologians on issues of injustice could do more harm than good.

Having seen the problems inherent in comparative theology with respect to text-centrism, how does one address them? As a liberation theologian, I propose that engaging comparative theology in conversation with liberation theologies like Dalit theology can help overcome the problems posed by text-centrism. And, as we will see, such a dialogue with comparative theology will also broaden and deepen the liberative aims and prospects of Dalit theology. But first, let me give a brief critical introduction to Dalit theology.

2   Dalit Theology

Dalit theology—inspired and influenced by Latin American and Black liberation theologies[35]—began as an academic discourse in the early 1980s with the objective of challenging the then dominant Brahmanic-upper caste Indian theological discourses. While there may have been earlier Christian theological articulations on Dalit liberation, it is generally accepted that it was Arvind P. Nirmal who sowed the seeds of Dalit theology.[36] In what is considered to be one of the foundational texts of the discipline, Nirmal states that Dalit theology is a theology "about" the Dalits, "for" the Dalits and *"from"* the Dalits, "based on their own dalit experiences, their own sufferings, their own aspirations and their own hope."[37] In other words, the principal focus of Dalit theology will be—but not exclusively—the experience and the liberation of Dalits.

---

33   Ibid., 166. Tribal communities in India are referred to as Adivasis.

34   These are the reasons given by Clooney. See Clooney, *Comparative Theology*, 67.

35   See Clarke, *Dalits and Christianity*, 45; Peniel Rajkumar, *Dalit Theology and Dalit Liberation: Problems, Paradigms and Possibilities* (Farnham, Surrey: Ashgate, 2010), 53.

36   Considering that this is only an introduction and we shall enter into details and nuances of Dalit theology in the later sections and chapters, I will limit my focus to Nirmal.

37   Arvind P. Nirmal, "Towards a Christian Dalit Theology" in *A Reader in Dalit Theology*, ed. Arvind P. Nirmal (Madras: Gurukul, 1990), 58. As Nirmal himself has acknowledged, "[T]he Germs of this article was first presented at the valedictory function of the Carey society, United Theological College, Bangalore, in April 1981." "Acknowledgements," Ibid. Note: Carey society is the social and cultural body of the United Theological College community.

From this standpoint, making the Deuteronomic creed (Deuteronomy 26: 5–12) his base text, Nirmal posits, what could be called as, the five principles to guide Dalit theology. Nirmal insists that, to begin with, Dalit theology should be founded in historical consciousness about Dalit identity and roots. Secondly, it should always be a community-oriented and community-centered theology. Thirdly, Dalit theology springs out of the pathos experience of Dalits. Fourth, Dalit theology will be a theology of protest and agitation against caste oppression. Finally, liberation from oppression, rather than aspiring for comfort and luxury, is the goal of Dalit theology.[38] It would be relevant to note here that these five principles find expression in one way or the other in most Dalit theological reflections and projects.

Nirmal also emphasized the "methodological exclusivism" of Dalit theology, by which he meant that Dalit theology should never compromise its status as a counter-theology that seeks to subvert dominant and oppressive discourses.[39] However, Nirmal clarifies that "a methodological exclusivism does not imply a community exclusivism" but rather the need for Dalit theology to "shut off the encroaching" and assimilating "influences of the dominant theologies."[40] In that sense, Nirmal intended that Dalit theology should always be conscious of and maintain its distinctiveness as a counter discourse in opposition to the dominant theologies.

2.1   *New Directions in Dalit Theology*

With the dawn of the twenty first century, Dalit theology has been subjected to critical scrutiny in order to make it more relevant. James Massey—one of the first generation Dalit theologians—suggests that since "[T]he process of Dalit Theology had not discovered for itself any clear cut methodology" in its early years, there is a need for "the present generation of Dalit theologians" to "give concrete shape and form" to its method.[41] In a related note, Charles Singaram also claims that there is need for 'systemizing' Dalit theological method.[42] Just to clarify, I believe that what is meant here is not the absence of method in Dalit theology per se, but rather that pioneering Dalit theologians had not

---

38   Ibid., 60–61.

39   Ibid, 58–59 & A. P. Nirmal, "Doing Theology from a Dalit Perspective," in *A Reader in Dalit Theology*, 142–143.

40   Nirmal, "Doing Theology from a Dalit Perspective," 143.

41   James Massey, "Revisiting and Resignifying the Methodology for Dalit Theology" in *Revisiting and Resignifying Methodology for Dalit Theology*, ed. James Massey & Indukuri John Mohan Razu (New Delhi: CDS, 2008), 55.

42   Charles Singaram, *The Question of Method in Dalit Theology: In Search of a Systematic Approach to the Practice of an Indian Liberation Theology* (Delhi: ISPCK, 2008), 5–12.

intentionally and explicitly focused (much) on method. However, I agree that this methodological consciousness is especially important as Dalit theology is now entering into and engaging with new academic disciplines at a global level. Here, I highlight three methodological issues that have been identified as a matter of concern in Dalit theology recently, viz. Binarism, Identitarianism, and Christian-centrism.

2.1.1   Binarism

One of the major issues that has been identified in Dalit theology is the rigid oppressed-oppressor relation assumed between the Dalits and the non-Dalits i.e. the caste people. With the aim of confronting caste and reaffirming the dignity of Dalits, Dalit theologians sought to imagine and articulate a binary outlook that categorically portrayed the Dalits as the victims, and therefore, innocent and ontologically good. Based on these epistemological foundations, Dalits and their social, cultural and religious practices were epitomized as egalitarian and just. Such Dalit glorification resulted in the othering, debasing, and even criminalizing of caste people and their cultures. This black-and-white view can be best seen in Dalit theology's antagonistic relationship with Hinduism in general, and caste Hindus and their traditions in particular. Because of the seeming roots of caste and untouchability in Hinduism, caste Hindu cultures are seen as unjust, and hence, irredeemably evil, while their polar opposites—Dalits and their cultures—are perceived as inherently just and good.

Is this binary imagination helpful? Should Dalit theology continue such black-and-white outlook? Peniel Rajkumar acknowledges that it is indeed true that "focusing on binarism can give a suitable methodological framework that can free Dalit culture from the reification of 'inferiority' imposed on it by caste Hinduism ..." and the "inordinate accentuation of the positive dimensions of Dalit culture can also help to balance the 'history of vilification' directed against the Dalits."[43] That is, upholding Dalit people and their cultures as good and just can indeed help in countering the centuries-old tendency of categorizing (almost) everything associated with Dalits as evil and base. It is also justifiable that such bold and loud acclamations and assertions of innocence need to be made in order to assert Dalit agency and break through the wall of indifference and complacency to Dalit suffering among the caste people.

Nonetheless, we cannot overlook the fact that such binary thinking could create illusionary sense of empowerment and worse still, become

---

43   Ibid., 169.

counter-productive. Moreover, as Rajkumar warns us, such "bipolar methodology" would result in "ideological and theological ghettoization."[44] In other words, a strictly dualistic thinking with clear and fixed dividing lines between the oppressor and the oppressed, would isolate the Dalits from the caste people and their culture, and thereby affect solidarity building. Such a limiting view, as we shall see, is not only unhelpful but also unrealistic. But, what is more concerning is, as Rajkumar reminds us, that such a divisive outlook is "antithetical to the one important dimension of the purpose of Dalit theology, which is the breaking of structural boundaries."[45] Therefore, I agree with Clarke's suggestion that it is necessary for Dalit theology to challenge and transcend its bipolar outlook and acknowledge that

> Affirming the full humanness and gifted dignity of Dalits and all other subjugated peoples without denying the same fullness and giftedness to other human collectives is an ongoing challenge for Dalit theology. The healing of the self cannot take place without healing of the other in the intimately interrelated and mutually interconnected web of human community.[46]

2.1.2 Identitarianism

While binarism is in itself problematic, it is important to note that this oppressor-oppressed dualism is strongly related to the notion of 'identitarianistic homogeneization' of Dalits. In other words, Dalits are viewed and spoken of as essentially one people with the same and fixed identities. We saw earlier in this section the critical importance of Dalit identity for Dalit theology. However, careful observation would show us that in reality Dalit identity is anything but monolithic and fixed. Rather, what we see is a dynamic hybridity between the caste and the Dalit communities. As Clarke points out, hybrid or "soft boundaries that exist between Dalits and non-Dalits" is a good example of the often overlapping "inter-relatedness between the religious world of the caste communities and Dalit communities."[47] Further, we should also consider the internal diversities among Dalit communities. While the experience of discrimination against Dalits has been undeniably existent, as I mentioned in the introduction, it was by no means the same throughout the sub-continent.

---

44 Ibid., 169–171.

45 Ibid., 169–171.

46 Sathianathan Clarke, "Dalit Theology: An Introductory and Interpretative Theological Exposition," in *Dalit Theology in the Twenty-First Century*, 34.

47 Clarke, *Dalits and Christianity*, 126.

TOWARD A COMPARATIVE THEOLOGY OF LIBERATION

In other words, a fixed Dalit identity or essence, or even a uniform Dalit experience does not exist. Thus, as Y.T. Vinayaraj rightly points out, "[D]alit is not a unitary term," and therefore, "[T]he pluriformity of the Dalit world needs to be acknowledged."[48]

Again, from a practical point of view, the over-emphasis on a single Dalit identity also affects the applicability of Dalit theology. Vinayaraj warns us that "fixity of dalitness or essentialism posited in Dalit identity prompts Dalits to associate themselves with stereotypical roles ...," thereby impeding and ignoring creative and pioneering strategies and schemes that demonstrate Dalit agency, empowerment and resistance.[49] Therefore, I agree that

> ... Dalit theology has reached the limits of its preoccupation with identity politics. The backdrop of discovering and expressing the similarity and difference of the future of OUR world must be rethought. Broken and crushed identities cannot be mobilized or healed by presuming and posturing of a fixed, essential, enduring, and a common Dalit identity.[50]

Therefore, moving beyond identitarianism would project " 'Dalit' as an open and dynamic affirmation of brokenness" that "invites solidarity from others who commit themselves to breaking down all forms of dehumanization based on the caste system."[51] And better still, it would enable the Dalits to build transglobal solidarities enabling them to join "other subjugated identities in various parts of the world."[52] In that sense, I will assert that a non-binary and a non-identitarianistic outlook would present Dalit theology with new promises and possibilities in the struggle toward Dalit liberation.

However, it is important to acknowledge that questioning the fixity and counter-productiveness of Dalit identity does not mean neglecting its critical significance. As the Dalit ecumenical theologian, Deenabandhu Manchala suggests, Dalit identity is different from other identities based on caste, race or gender. According to him,

---

48 Y. T. Vinayaraj, "Envisioning a Postmodern Method of Doing Dalit Theology," in *Dalit Theology in the Twenty-First Century*, 99.

49 Ibid.

50 "Introduction," in *Dalit Theology in the Twenty-First Century*, 12–13. Uppercase in the original text.

51 Ibid., 13.

52 Ibid.

the Dalit identity is based on their (Dalits') shared vision of an ethical-
ly transformed Indian society. By acknowledging their predicament of
unjust suffering and oppression, they expose, confront, and counter the
injustice that lies at the foundations of India's social, religious, economic, and political structures. Hence, Dalit identity is counter-cultural and
ideological in nature and purpose. It affirms the dignity of every human
being and promotes alternative values of justice and equality that are absent in the dominant cultural traditions of the Indian society. The assertion of 'Dalit identity,' therefore, is the key ideological tool in their struggle for the birth of a new social order.[53]

In other words, Dalit identity is (or has to be) an expansive identity that includes the liberation of all and, in Manchala's words, one that "affirms the dignity of every human being." It is in light of these critical observations that it has
become necessary for Dalit theology to simultaneously be critical of a narrow
identitarian stance even while continuing to re-view and re-envision the possibilities offered by an expansive and inclusive Dalit identity.

2.1.3 Christian-Centrism

Finally, intertwined with binarism and identitarianism, the uncritical pinning
of the hopes of Dalit liberation almost entirely on Christianity is another concern in Dalit theology. There is no doubt that Christianity—especially Protestant Christianity—has played a paradigm-shifting role in Indian history. In
a context where sacred texts and spaces were denied access to Dalits by the
dominant castes, and their oppressed status was justified by some of those
texts, reading, owning, and interpreting the Christian scripture, and becoming leaders in the church has meant a lot to Dalits. Along with this underlying
spirit of gratefulness and excitement I believe that there is also, what might
be called, a strong—albeit inconspicuous—Barthian influence in most reflections of Dalit theology.[54] This is perhaps why, even though Dalit theologians

---

53   Deenabandhu Manchala, "Expanding the Ambit: Dalit Theological Contribution to
Ecumenical Social Thought," in *Dalit Theology in the Twenty-First Century*, 51. Text within
parenthesis mine.

54   I confess that this claim needs further research. But nonetheless, as in the case of Black,
Latin American, and Political liberation theologies, I believe that the Barthian essence
in the early phase of Dalit theology cannot be missed. That is, a careful reading of Dalit
theologians, in particular those of the first generation, shows that they reflected (to put
it in simple terms) Karl Barth's emphatic insistence on the singularity and the finality of the incarnation, even asserting it as *the* "critical principle" of Dalit ideology. See,
Arvind P. Nirmal, "Developing a Common Ideology: Some Theological Considerations,"

TOWARD A COMPARATIVE THEOLOGY OF LIBERATION

(especially those of the first generation) were critical of the presence of caste in the Indian Church, their reflections were theologically exclusive in relation to other religious traditions.[55]

It is understandable that in a context where they are threatened by Hindu fundamentalism and extremism, Dalit Christians have to stress their Christian beliefs and identity.[56] However, such exclusivist passion about Christianity is problematic, and even (as in the previous cases) counter-productive to the objectives of Dalit theology. Given the interreligious commitments of this book, let me clarify this claim in detail. Firstly, imagining and glorifying Christianity, especially Western-missionary Christianity as the hope of Dalit liberation will result in an uncritical stance toward western imperialism. For, we cannot easily overlook the fact that often colonizers and the Christian missionaries collaborated to subjugate, civilize, and control the colonized people. And in many cases, Christianity was imposed on the colonized by means of threat and

---

in *Towards a Common Dalit Ideology*, ed. Arvind P. Nirmal (Madras: Gurukul, 1989), 124–126. For the Barthian influence on other liberation theologies see the following: Black Theology—James H. Cone, *A Black Theology of Liberation*, Fortieth Anniversary Edition (Maryknoll, New York: Orbis Books, 2016), xxiii; Latin American Liberation Theology—George Hunsinger, "Karl Barth and Liberation Theology," *The Journal of Religion*, 63/3 (7/1983): 247–263; Political Theology of Jürgen Moltmann—Roger Haight, *Jesus: Symbol of God* (Maryknoll, New York: Orbis Books, 1999), 318–320.

55   But to be fair to Nirmal, it is worth noting that though he sounded like an exclusivist as a Dalit theologian, as a theologian of religion, he was quite radical and open to other religious traditions. Wesley Ariarajah recognizes this side of Nirmal when he remembers that Nirmal had courageously called for radically "examining our theological traditions and formulations in the light of specific dialogical experiences," rather than trying "to safeguard the uniqueness of Jesus Christ or the finality of Jesus Christ or the total commitment to Jesus Christ before entering into a dialogical situation..." S. Wesley Ariarajah, *Your God, My God, Our God: Rethinking Christian Theology for Religious Plurality* (Geneva: WCC Publications, 2012), 164. Further, we should be aware that, as his colleague and friend Eric Lott points out, "Nirmal himself never espoused an anti-Hindu stance per se." Eric J. Lott, "A Missionary's Dilemma: The Emerging Dalit Identity" *Gurukul Journal of Theological Studies*, Volume 24, No. 2, (June 2013), 11–12.

56   As I have argued elsewhere, such claims are similar to the "survival language" of the persecuted (minority) early Christians of the first century. Joshua Samuel, "Untouchable Bodies, Ecstasy, and Dalit Agency: Charismatic Christianity in a South Indian Village," (Paper Presented at 'World Christianity Conference,' Princeton Theological Seminary, March 15–18, 2019). Also see, Knitter, *No Other Name? A Critical Survey of Christian Attitudes Toward the World Religions* (Maryknoll: Orbis books 1985), 184. However, as we shall see in chapter seven, despite the exclusivist language, the lived reality of Dalit Christians is inherently pluralistic.

coercion.[57] Therefore, uncritical Christian centrism of Dalit theology could mean a silent, uncritical, and unconscious justification of the brutal programs of colonialism, thereby greatly weakening and even jeopardizing the Dalit cause for liberation. This narrow obsession with Christian-centrism could prove to be too costly at a time when Dalits are enthusiastically stretching out their hands to similar oppressed communities to build networks of solidarity.

Secondly, Christian-centrism also results in 'shortening' the history of Dalit liberation and limiting the resources of Dalit theology. That is, glorifying Christianity as the only hope for Dalits would mean not acknowledging the different ways in which Dalit communities have resisted and subverted the caste structures over the centuries. Thus, Christian-centrism narrows down the vision of Dalit theologians so that there is neglect of and indifference towards other religious traditions, including the religious traditions of Dalits themselves. As Clarke points out, this act of Dalit theologians "... turning their backs completely on their own religion and culture which has sustained them through centuries, may in fact be a collective act of avoidance: an attempt to evade and dodge their own identity and selfhood."[58] Thankfully, some good progress has been made in this area through the likes of Sathianathan Clarke, Theophilus Appavoo (aka Parattai), and Joseph Prabhakar Dayam in the direction of engaging with Dalit religious traditions.[59] However, as Clarke observes, "there has not ... been much constructive theologizing" involving Dalit religious resources, while "literal interpretations of biblical texts to address the complex reality of Dalits pathos" is more prevalent.[60]

Finally, Christian-centrism in Dalit theology has also meant overlooking the multiple religious belonging and hybridity that is prominent in contexts like India. In other words, compartmentalized understanding of religions has failed to acknowledge both the interreligious and intrareligious theological continuities. Writing on fluid boundaries, Clarke observes that "... elements of Dalit religion are still operative in Dalit Christian communities," even though "they are reluctant to admit it openly ..."[61] Thus, imagining rigid borders between

---

57   Susan Viswanathan, "The Homogeneity of Fundamentalism: Christianity, British Colonialism and India in the Nineteenth Century," *Studies in History*, 16/2, (2000): 221–222.

58   Clarke, *Dalits and Christianity*, 45–46.

59   Clarke, *Dalits and Christianity*; Parattai, *Dalit Samayam* (Madurai: Parattai Kalvi Mattrum Samuga Arakattalai, 2010); Dayam, "*Gonthemma Korika*," 137–149.

60   Clarke, "Dalit Theology," 31.

61   Clarke, *Dalits and Christianity*, 62. Similar observation was made by me in my earlier research on Dalit Christians. Samuel, "Dalits and Conversions."

Christian and Hindu Dalit communities is far from the reality. Moreover, as already mentioned, one should also be conscious of the hybridity that exists between Dalit religions and the caste traditions of Hinduism. Even though Dalit religion does have its distinct qualities, Clarke argues that

> [W]e cannot glorify Dalit religion as completely independent of and, thus, at all points contradictory to caste Hinduism. This binary structure of opposition subject-object, foreign-native, colonizer-colonized, self-other, and Hindu-Dalit, ... hardly does justice to the complexity of the relationship between caste Hindu and Dalit religion.[62]

In other words, in spite of their hierarchical relationship, Dalit religion and caste Hinduism overlap and mutually inform each other. Felix Wilfred, in his study of subaltern religions like that of the Dalits, calls this kind of religious hybridity as "creative ambiguity"—a distinct feature of subaltern religions—which facilitates resilience to survive and resistance to fight oppressive systems.[63] In sum, we can conclude that a Christian-centered exclusivist outlook does not reflect the Dalit situation, and therefore is unhelpful for Dalit theology.

3   A Comparative Theology of Liberation from a Dalit Perspective

Having seen the fundamental features and new methodological issues and concerns both in comparative theology and Dalit theology, in this section, let me highlight the ways in which the two academic disciplines can critically and constructively inform each other. This critical and constructive interdisciplinary dialogue I choose to call, "A Comparative Theology of Liberation." Though this comparative theology of liberation is from a Dalit perspective, I believe that it could also be paradigmatic of other such interreligious liberation theologies.[64]

---

62   Clarke, *Dalits and Christianity,* 126.

63   Felix Wilfred, *The Sling of Utopia* (Delhi: ISPCK, 2005), 146.

64   Other such works include, Aloysius Pierris, *Fire and Water: Basic Issues in Asian Buddhism and Christianity* (Maryknoll, NY: Orbis Books, 1996); Adam Barnes, "A Comparative Spirituality of Liberation: The Anti-Poverty Struggles of the Poverty Initiative and the Tijaniyya Sufi of Kiota" (PhD diss., Union Theological Seminary, 2016). And, as already mentioned, Michelle Voss Roberts' work is also a comparative liberative theology.

50   CHAPTER 1

3.1   *People Centered Theology*

To begin with, I propose that the people-centeredness of Dalit theology can
help to address the problematic roots and consequences of prioritization of
texts in comparative theology. Writing on the nature of Dalit theology, Nirmal
explains that

> Dalit theology is a theology by, for and of an oppressed people. It is there-
> fore a people's theology. The primary datum for doing this theology is
> people themselves. The word "people" here becomes a theological cate-
> gory, a theological concept. It is both a theological concept and a socio-
> logical reality.[65]

Thus, rather than general and universalistic theologizing, "[T]heological affir-
mations in Dalit theology are grounded in people's experiences."[66] Moreover,
Dalit theology insists that the Dalit experience is also a community oriented
experience. Once again turning to Nirmal, we see that

> [T]he question of identity and roots is inseparably bound with the sense
> of belonging to a community. In our search for Dalit theology it is well-
> worth remembering that what we are looking for is community-identity,
> community-roots and community consciousness. The vision of Dalit the-
> ology therefore, ought to be a unitive vision—or rather a "community"
> vision.[67]

Taking the cue from Dalit theology, my proposed comparative theology of liberation chooses to be centered (up)on peoples' experiences *in* the communities. However, as the Dalit experience is not limited to one tradition/commu-
nity viz. Christianity/Christian community/ies, Dalit comparative theology of
liberation would be a people centered enterprise that is concerned with (and
about) 'people' belonging to (two) *different* religious traditions—Christianity
and Hinduism. This means that, as comparative theology suggests, there is
deep interreligious learning that happens, only that it is not *between* 'texts' (of
two religious traditions) here but rather *among* the 'people' of two religious
communities. Of course, in the case of Dalits the absence of sacred texts that
speak of their religious experiences further necessitates this move. However,
as already warned, this people-centered approach need not be seen as a mere

---

65   Nirmal, "Doing Theology," 139.
66   Ibid., 140.
67   Nirmal, "Towards a Christian Dalit Theology," 60.

TOWARD A COMPARATIVE THEOLOGY OF LIBERATION

compulsion but as imperative to recognize the agency of the people belonging to the studied religious traditions. It studies texts as they are embodied and practiced in faith communities. This way I believe that comparative theology would be able to acknowledge religious traditions as lived human experiences rather than as mere abstract texts.[68]

While on the subject of people centered interreligious learning, we need to pay attention to a new development in Dalit theology. While caste and untouchability have been studied in depth, it was not until recently that, thanks to the insightful voices of feminist and postmodern scholars, the critical importance of the Dalit body was recognized. Evangeline Anderson-Rajkumar, one of the pioneers of body theology from a Dalit feminist perspective, asserts that "[T]he earth's body, the woman's body, and Dalit's body prove to be reference points that can be the locus of new ways of theologizing, for new womanist theologies to be born."[69] Y.T. Vinayaraj, another important proponent of Dalit body theology, suggests that "[I]n the epistemic shift that Dalit theology envisions, the body cannot be a side issue but must be recovered as the pivotal point of reference."[70] Accordingly, in the next chapter, I seek to consider the embodied nature of caste-based discrimination and Dalit resistance. For now, I believe it suffices to state that engaging in interreligious learning *among* and *within* the faith communities—which in this case are the Dalits—will entail focusing on Dalit bodies as the sites of comparison and the center of theologizing. In other words, I am proposing that Dalit bodies in (two) different religious traditions can become resources for comparison instead of texts. *Dalit bodies* will be *the texts* in this comparative theology.

3.2 *Non-Othering Theology*

Secondly, the critical and constructive dialogue between comparative and Dalit theologies is also helpful in working toward a non-othering theology. We observed how in Dalit theology, on the one hand, strong (bi-)polarizing tendencies reveal a triumphalist and an essentialist notion of Dalit identity. On the other hand, we also saw that the identity question remains crucial for the marginalized Dalits and there is a critical need for it to be recognized as inclusive

---

68   While I do not want to force ethnography as an obligatory task for doing comparative theology, I believe that there must be some recognition and acknowledgment of how religious traditions, including textual traditions, are experienced by the faith communities.

69   Evangeline Anderson-Rajkumar, "Turning Bodies Inside Out: Contours of Womanist Theology," in *Dalit Theology in the Twenty-First Century*, 214.

70   Vinayaraj, "Envisioning a Postmodern Method," 100. I shall return to the work of Vinayaraj again in the chapter six.

and expansive. Thus, there seems to be a tension between making use of the affirmative aspects of Dalit identity, even while not allowing identity to become an essentialized attribute that reifies divisions and hierarchies. Amidst this methodological *impasse*, I find comparative theology's understanding of identity and margins helpful.

Comparative theology encourages the theologian to move across the religious borders in order to learn from other religious traditions with a spirit of humility and vulnerability. However, this learning process is not a tension-free experience, given the home commitments of the theologian and the (at-times-unsettling) teachings and practices encountered in the new tradition. In other words, in spite of the (self-identified) rootedness of the comparative theologian in one tradition, having been influenced by the new tradition, she now 'bears the marks' of more than one tradition. Thus, the comparative space is a space of dialectical relationship i.e. a space of "yes" and "no," a space simultaneously *between* and *inclusive of* the two traditions, that generates a dialectical identity. Clooney notes that it is because of this 'in-between' identity that comparative theologians are often marginalized in their own community.[71]

Taking the cue from comparative theology, I believe that we can re-visualize marginal(ized) space as an in-between space which is inclusive of the 'other' (tradition) rather than as an exclusive or a binarizing space. Writing on this subject, post-structuralist feminist theologian Diane McDonald reminds us that margins are not spaces *wholly other* to the dominant space, but rather spaces that "call into question and subvert the binary structure upon which systems of oppression are built..."[72] In other words, margins cannot imagine themselves as the binary opposite of the oppressors or even (solely) as a challenge to oppressors and their discourses. Rather, the primary attribute and task of the margins is to subvert and dismantle the very attempt to reify binarizing and polarizing stances between the oppressor and the oppressed.

When we look at the Dalit context with such an understanding of margins, we are reminded that the Dalit identity itself—as an outcaste identity—is an in-between and inclusive space. In fact, according to the Manu Dharma Sastra, one becomes a Dalit—a *Panchama*, a *Chandala*, a *Svapaka*—because of 'unholy' mixing among the four classes.[73] And empirically speaking, it is well-known that Dalits are often the ones most subjected to violence for engaging

---

71 Clooney, *Comparative Theology,* 158.

72 Diane L. Prosser McDonald, *Transgressive Corporeality: The Body, Poststructuralism, and the Theological Imagination* (Albany: State University of New York Press, 1995), 141–142.

73 Patrick Olivelle, trans., *The Law Code of Manu* (New York: Oxford University Press, 2004), 181.

in intercaste relationships and marriages.[74] Thus, it appears that Dalit identity is anything but rigid and fixed. In other words, Dalitness is constituted, not necessarily (exclusively) by historical lineage or by hereditary (im)purity but by in-betweenness and inclusiveness that transcends and transgresses boundaries of separation, hierarchicalization, and binarization. Therefore, as a comparative theologian of liberation I believe that the marginalized Dalit identity (as the first generation Dalit theologians suggested) is certainly foundational, but only in so far as it serves as an inclusive and embracive in-between space that challenges and subverts any form of essentialization and polarization.

Based on the above discussion, let me conclude with a relevant methodological suggestion offered by post-structuralist feminist theologian Mary Fulkerson. In her work on problematizing heteronormativity and heterosexuality prevalent in feminist theologies, Fulkerson proposes that feminist liberative conversations seeking to revalidate the concept of *imago Dei* (image of God) will have to take place in the form of episodic narratives.[75] Based on this suggestion, I propose that recognizing and theologizing of diverse episodic narratives of embodied religious experiences—in this case that of the Dalits—is needed for a comparative theology of liberation that foregrounds the agency of people.

3.3   *Comparative Liberation Theology*

It has already been mentioned that comparative theology has to be cautious about furthering structures of injustice through its elite (text-centric) choices. Writing about the marginalization of women, Voss Roberts keenly notes that though they participate "in religious traditions and bear the names" of those traditions, "yet ... [they] have not been admitted into authoritative canons ... to the same extent as men."[76] She reveals that this tendency has also crept into comparative theology where men and their voices are frequently the preferred focus of theologizing. Hence, she believes that turning comparative theology's attention to marginalized people like women would help to interrogate and challenge the oppressive tendencies within. Moreover, she argues that giving

---

74   A more recent incident is the killing of Pranay Kumar. Kumar, who is a Dalit from the Madiga caste, was hacked to death in front of his (upper) caste wife, Amrutha Varshini. http://www.india.com/news/india/honour-killing-man-hacked-to-death-over-inter-caste-marriage-in-telangana-3325802/. Accessed on September 17. 2018.

75   Mary McClintock Fulkerson, "Contesting the Gendered Subject: A Feminist Account of the *Imago Dei*" in *Horizons in Feminist Theology: Identity Tradition, and Norms*, ed. Rebecca S. Chopp & Sheila Greeve Davaney (Minneapolis: Fortress Press, 1997), 109 & 111–115.

76   Voss Roberts, *Dualities*, 4.

54   CHAPTER 1

attention to the 'outsider within' will enable comparative theology to open up to "new subjects, genres, and goals for the discipline."[77]

In that sense, engaging the marginalized Dalit voices and experiences would certainly help comparative theology to expand its horizons, even while challenging caste discrimination and untouchability. Listening to the voices of Dalits would enlighten comparative theology about caste-based oppression in relation to Hinduism, and how "marginal subjects accommodate, survive, and resist hegemonies."[78] This evolution of comparative theology as a theology of liberation can enable it to "participate in the wider process of dialogue, functioning to promote interreligious theological knowledge, cultural understanding, and social justice."[79]

However, as Voss Roberts gently nudges us, this learning (from liberation theology) is not just unidirectional. She reminds us that liberation theologians can also learn from comparative theologians to "read the habits of the religious others—carefully, empathetically ... by paying attention to particularities."[80] This is precisely what is attempted here in this comparative theology of liberation where the trajectory of the liberative discourse is no longer controlled by Christianity alone. Although the liberation motifs in Christianity continue to inspire me, as a comparative theologian, I am also interested in learning the emancipatory potentials and methods in the Dalit religious traditions.

Finally, I believe that such an interreligious learning would also help us to widen our understanding of liberation. Sabah Mahmood in her book, *Politics of Piety*, challenges the dominance of Western-Christian modes of understanding agency and flourishing within feminist discourses, and points out that there is a plurality of alternative liberative discourses and praxis available in different contexts.[81] I believe this is true for other liberation discourses and, certainly for liberation theologies as well. For, far too often in Christian liberation theology—as we saw in the case of Dalit theology—there is a sense of superiority regarding its perception of resistance and liberation which suppresses liberative voices in other religious traditions in that context. My objective therefore, is to listen to these suppressed voices, suppressed by Christian liberation theology itself (which in this case is Christian-centric Dalit theology).

---

77   Voss Roberts, "Gendering Comparative Theology," 110.

78   Ibid., 126.

79   Tracy Sayuki Tiemier, "Comparative Theology as a Theology of Liberation," in *The New Comparative Theology*, 149.

80   Roberts, "Gendering Comparative Theology," 127.

81   Sabah Mahmood, *Politics of Piety: The Islamic Revival and the Feminist Subject* (Princeton & Oxford: Princeton University Press, 2005), 5–10.

Thus, one of the main tasks of Dalit comparative theology of liberation is to allow Dalit religious traditions to enlighten Christian theology in general, and Christian liberation theology/ies in particular, on the existence of alternative modes of resistances and liberation, and help them to envision new and creative modes of reclamation of agency and emancipation.

To conclude this chapter, summarizing the observations and suggestions made in the previous sections, let me offer a working definition of a Dalit comparative theology of liberation which will be described and demonstrated in the rest of the book: "A comparative theology of liberation from a Dalit perspective is a people-centered and non-identitarian theological project that engages in deep and respectful conversation(s) with the religious traditions of the Dalit communities in India, to identify, celebrate, and theologize new means and modalities of liberation and emancipation."

CHAPTER 2

Dalit Body—the Untouchable Sacrament

In the previous chapter, I proposed a Dalit comparative theology of liberation by integrating the salient features of the two disciplines. In this chapter, I seek to identify an appropriate comparative category in order to construct a liberative comparative theology in the following chapters of this book.[1] The purpose of this chapter is two-fold: First, to identify the critical significance of the Dalit body within the caste context, and second, to suggest a suitable comparative category for doing comparative theology.

This chapter will have three main sections. In the first section, using anecdotes of life experiences, and snippets from Dalit literature, I will attempt to 'read' and understand the dynamics of subjugation and discrimination of the Dalit body using the language of poststructuralist scholarship. In the second section, I shall highlight the theological significance of the body, stressing in particular the 'sacramental' significance (i.e. the ability to symbolize the divine in the world) of Dalit and other such oppressed bodies. Finally, insisting on this sacramental privilege of the oppressed body, I will introduce and propose that "divine possessions" in Hinduism and Christianity as experienced among Dalits can serve an appropriate comparative category. Let me note that the objective here is not to trace the theological/philosophical history of the body *per se*, but rather to (selectively) look at how the bodies of the oppressed, in spite of all the defamations and denigration, can provide a theoretical template for constructive theologizing. The theoretical and theological explorations begun in the sections below will be returned to, challenged, and developed further—all in the process of construction—throughout this project.

1   The Dalit Body

As already noted in the introduction, untouchability is, in a sense, at the heart of caste. However, I believe that it is through the construction and imposition of untouchability *on* 'the untouchable body,' that the caste society functions and sustains itself.[2] For, as Anupama Rao observes, "the Dalit body continues

---

1 By comparative category, I mean the religious concept or practice which is compared.

2 Note that I do not speak of a Hindu society but rather of a caste society. While I believe that the vedic *Purushasuktha* hymn has played a critical role in the creation/evolution of caste

© KONINKLIJKE BRILL NV, LEIDEN, 2020 | DOI:10.1163/9789004420052_005

DALIT BODY—THE UNTOUCHABLE SACRAMENT 57

to be the site of recurrent stigmatization, making it a historical and contemporary object of suffering."[3] Given its critical position within the caste framework, in the following section, let me offer a brief description of the significance of the Dalit body.

1.1   Bodies That 'Don't' Matter

To begin with, we can say that caste can be described—to use the words of Judith Butler—as an "exclusionary matrix by which subjects are formed" and that which "requires the *simultaneous production of a domain of abject beings*, those who are not yet 'subjects,' but who form the constitutive outside to the domain of the subject."[4] To put it simply, the caste system needs the 'outsider,' or perhaps more rightly, an 'outside,' the 'perennial other' to sustain itself. Within this framework of othering, the caste subject is *the* valid subject, the subject whose body alone 'matters.'

But who is the caste outsider, the caste other, the out-caste?[5] Butler's description of "the abject" appears to quite appropriately describe this category.

> The abject designates here precisely those "unlivable" and "uninhabitable" zones of social life which are nevertheless densely populated by those who do not enjoy the status of the subject, but whose living under the sign of the "unlivable" is required to circumscribe the domain of the subject. This zone of uninhabitability will constitute the defining limit of the subject's domain; it will constitute that site of dreaded identification against which—and by virtue of which—the domain of the subject will circumscribe its own claim to autonomy and to life. In this sense, then, the subject is constituted through the force of exclusion and abjection, one which produces a constitutive outside to the subject, an

---

   stratification, and caste practices are perhaps (more) concretely visible in Hindu traditions, I would also say that it is more complicated than that, as noted in the introduction. I also do not deem it appropriate to limit caste to the Indian society or context since caste now pervades across the globe.

3 Rao, *The Caste Question*, xiii.

4 Judith Butler, *Bodies that Matter: On the Discursive Limits of Sex* (London and New York: Routledge, 2011), xiii. Emphasis mine.

5 Note that I do not use the word 'Dalit' when referring to the *mechanism* of abjection and discrimination in the caste system. In other words, caste system does not create Dalits, it creates Untouchables. On the contrary, Dalits are self-assertive Untouchables. For more on the term Dalit, see the introduction and also James Massey, *Dalits in India: Religion as a Source of Bondage or Liberation with Special Reference to Christians* (New Delhi: Manohar Publications, 1995), 15–16.

58   CHAPTER 2

abjected outside, which is after all, "inside" the subject as its own founding repudiation.[6]

There are two levels in the politics of subject formation that can be identified
here. At one level, it is clear that the untouchable creates the caste subject, but
only because that which makes a person untouchable—the presumed conditions of unlivability and uninhabitability—is inside the caste subject and is
needed to make the caste person a valid subject. In other words, caste subjects
and outcaste subjects create and sustain each other, all the while maintaining
the hierarchy between them.[7] But on the other level, caste subject formation
is not always strictly 'person-al' i.e. requiring a simple explicit bipolar opposition between Dalit and caste individuals/communities. Rather,as Michel Foucault suggests, it is the 'exercise' of power on/in bodies—more than anything
else—that lies at the heart of such (valid/caste) subject formation at the cost
of others.

> The power exercised on the body is conceived not as a property, but as
> a strategy, that its effects of domination are attributed not to 'appropri-
> ation', but to dispositions, maneuvers, tactics, techniques, functionings;
> that one should decipher in it a network of relations, constantly in ten-
> sion, in activity, rather than privilege that one might possess; that one
> should take as its model a perpetual battle rather than a contract reg-
> ulating a transaction or the conquest of a territory. In short, this pow-
> er is exercised rather than possessed; it is not the 'privilege', acquired or
> preserved, of the dominant class, but the overall effect of its strategic
> positions—an effect that is manifested and sometimes extended by the
> position of those who are dominated.[8]

In that sense, as Athena Athanasiou states,

> Our bodies are beyond themselves. Through our bodies, we are implicat-
> ed in thick and intense social processes of relatedness and interdepen-
> dence; we are exposed, dismembered, given over to others, and undone

---

6 Butler, *Bodies that Matter*, xiii.
7 I am not speaking of caste in a Dumontian sense as a balanced and closed social system.
   Rather, I suggest that caste survives and flourishes through the unjust (continuous) creation
   of 'an other.' For more, see the introduction.
8 Michel Foucault, *Discipline and Punish: The Birth of the Prison*, trans. Alan Sheridan
   (New York: Vintage Books, 1995), 26–27.

DALIT BODY—THE UNTOUCHABLE SACRAMENT

by the norms that regulate desire, sexual alliance, kinship relations, and conditions of humanness. We are dispossessed by others, moved toward others and by others, affected by others and able to affect others.[9]

This reminds us that subject formations happen by embodied processes and practices. In other words, it is the (bodily) performativity that creates valid subjects, and "identity is performatively constituted by the very "expressions" that are said to be results."[10] Given that "[P]erformativity is ... not a singular "act,"" but "always a reiteration of a norm or set of norms, and to the extent that it acquires an act-like status in the present, it conceals or dissimulates the conventions of which it is a repetition,"[11] one can say that the caste system is also reified and re-inscribed through performativity. It is the performativity of caste that makes it a natural and '*norm*-al' way of life, so that when these norms are challenged, disturbance and discomfort ensues.

Take for instance the case in Hassan in South India where Dalits were never allowed inside the village Kariyamma temple. In March 2016, when the Dalits of the village decided that they wanted to enter the temple, there was an uproar and agitation among the upper castes. After some attempts at negotiations i.e. basically trying to ask the Dalits to give up their request, it was decided that it was better to cancel the festival itself.[12] The message is clear: Dalits cannot transgress their prescribed places in the society. Writing on such practices, Dalit writer Bama narrates how the places and positions of Dalit and caste bodies are always fixed. In her novel *Karukku* she writes,

> All the time I went to work for the Naickers, I knew I should not touch their goods or chattels; I should never come close to where they were. I should always stand away to one side. These were their rules. I often felt pained and ashamed. But there was nothing that I could do.[13]

---

9 Judith Butler & Athena Athanasiou, *Dispossession: The Performative in the Political* (Cambridge & Malden: Polity Press, 2015), 55.

10 Judith Butler, *Gender Trouble: Feminism and the Subversion of Identity* (New York and London: Routledge, 2007), 34.

11 Butler, *Bodies that Matter*, xxi. Also note the difference between performativity and performance. As Butler writes, performance is a "bounded 'act,'" whereas performativity "consists in a reiteration of norms which precede, constrain, and exceed the performer and in that sense cannot be taken as the fabrication of the performer's 'will' or 'choice.'" Ibid, 178–179.

12 http://www.thehindu.com/news/national/karnataka/to-deny-dalits-entry-upper-castes-cancel-temple-fest-in-hassan/article8379078.ece accessed on March 12, 2018.

13 Bama, *Karukku*, 2nd edition, transl. Lakshmi Holmstrom (New Delhi: Oxford University Press, 2012), 52. *Naickers* are an upper caste community in South India.

One can see that Dalits and caste people are 'expected' to be 'faithful' to their identities by (always) 'acting' in a certain way—standing at a particular place, at a specific distance, in a particular posture. After all these were the rules that the dominant castes enforced and the Dalits have internalized over several centuries. Any change or transgression is seen as a betrayal of who both parties are (supposed to be).

While considering these prescribed bodily places and performances, we must note that caste performativity needs both the caste and the Dalit body. Dalit Political theologian, Sunder John Boopalan, aptly names this correlative dynamic as the "grammar of the bodies." Conversing with various philosophers and theorists, Boopalan uses "grammar of the body" to refer both to the "socially conditioned rules by which bodies are habituated to 'speak,'" and "to the corporeal entanglements in which victims and survivors are caught up in shared social networks, in various kinds of 'body politics'..."[14] That is, the grammar of the bodies are the socially conditioned embodied performativities of a subject in relation to herself and to others. Furthermore, in the caste context, Boopalan notes that such "socially conditioned 'speech acts and body language' are means by which personal and social values are affirmed or denied," and "are not always fully conscious and intentional acts at the moment of their occurrence."[15] In other words, these acts—such as Dalits not being allowed to enter a temple or standing aside for the *Naickers*—are performed by the "force of exclusionary practices and norms ... through *subconscious 'encoded memory'*... stored in the human body,"[16] giving them an appearance of being natural. Any attempt to disturb this (seemingly) normal way of life creates chaos.

And yet, we know that *"exclusionary* practices and norms" are not the only means by which the grammar of/between caste and Dalit bodies operates. Bodily grammar is also actualized by means of co-option and assimilation. As already mentioned in the introduction, one of the primary manifestations of caste today is the incorporation of Dalit and other such subaltern cultures into the dominant Brahmanical epistemological framework. But the attempt to be like the upper-caste is/becomes tempting, not just because it is attractive but also because it appears to be the right and proper way of being. On this, P. Sivakami, in her novel, *Grip of Change,* portrays how the father of her lead character Gowri, a local Dalit leader, tries to imitate a Brahmin.

---

14 Sunder John Boopalan, *Memory, Grief, and Agency: A Political Theological Account of Wrongs and Rites* (Cham, Switzerland: Palgrave Macmillan, 2017), 89–90.

15 Ibid., 93–94.

16 Ibid., 93. Emphasis mine.

DALIT BODY—THE UNTOUCHABLE SACRAMENT

Stepping out after his bath, he wrapped the wet towel around his waist, faced the sun, and folded his hands. He began reciting the taraka mantram to seduce the Devi. 'Om Sarvasoori, Sankari, Chamundi, Rubi—destroyer of Taraka, protector of the devas ...'

Lately, after his bath, he had taken to chanting this mantram, a practice he had picked up from Vakil Venkatakrishnan, a Brahmin lawyer. Using three fingers, he took the thiruneer from a wooden box and applied it on his forehead in there broad strokes.[17]

What is to be noted here is that, as in the case of gender identity constructions of which Butler speaks, the caste cultural matrix "requires that certain kinds of 'identities' cannot 'exist'" and if they do, can "appear only as developmental failures or logical impossibilities..."[18] Hence, the need to and civilize and 'brahmanize' these identities. Moreover, as we saw earlier, such 'inclusion' and brahmanization— much like exclusion—often happens in the subconscious, and is both actualized in and by embodied performativity, thus reifying caste-based identifications. In that sense, we can say that untouchable (and caste) identity is constructed not only by exclusionary performativity but also by inclusionary performativity.

1.2 Disciplining the Bodies

While reflecting on bodily performativity, the subconscious control and enactment of the "encoded memory" within (all) bodies that both excludes, 'others' and includes/civilizes the marginalized, I want to consider, what could be called, the element of control. For, though the grammar of the bodies operates below the radar of the conscious, one cannot avoid questioning the ways in which the bodies are 'forced' to experience and enact a certain grammar within and without. How do the bodies of the oppressed, which in this case are those of the Dalits, respond (or are forced to respond) to these control mechanisms? How are these bodies 'disciplined' to follow a particular grammar?

On July 11th 2016, in the town of Una, Gujarat, four Dalit men were stripped and beaten by the members of the Shiv Sena (a Hindu political party) for skinning a cow in Gujarat. Though the victims tried to make the assailants understand that they were indeed skinning a dead cow, their pleas went unheeded. They were beaten in public, with someone even recording what was happening, before the victims were taken to the police station.[19]

---

17   P. Sivakami, *The Grip of Change* (Chennai: Orient Blackswan, 2009), 14.
18   Butler, *Gender Trouble*, 24.
19   http://timesofindia.indiatimes.com/city/rajkot/4-Dalits-stripped-beaten-up-for-skinning-dead-cow/articleshow/53184266.cms Accessed on March 14. 2018.

This incident is a good example of the reification of the grammar of the bodies through violence. The assault on the four Dalits is not just a punishment for skinning a (dead) cow—the quintessential symbol of Brahmanism. Rather, the beating and humiliation that they were subjected to is a warning for them and to others (in India) not to disturb the norms framed by the nexus of Brahmanism and Hindu nationalism. After all, according to the Hindutva ideology, protecting the cow doesn't have anything to do with safe-guarding life but rather about re-inscribing Brahmin supremacy. In that sense, punishing the four men was a way of disciplining an entire society and a nation to follow the Brahmanical-caste norms. And this was accomplished through re-confirming and reasserting control and subjugation over the most oppressed and vulnerable bodies of all, the Dalits.

Such disciplining becomes even clearer and pronounced in the raping, lynching, and murdering of Dalit women. While these acts of violence should certainly be seen as gender based—since controlling and killing women are seen as paradigmatic acts of control[20]—as Ruth Manorama, a Dalit activist explains, in rape and murder, "Dalit women's bodies are used as the battleground for the caste war. The attacks on our bodies are used to teach a lesson to the larger community."[21] Thus, by punishing *a* Dalit body—a Dalit women's body—caste and gender 'transgressions' are kept in check, even while caste supremacy and patriarchy, are reasserted.

Of course, this type of disciplining is not singular to India. One of the most obvious examples is the use of violence to control and subjugate people of color, especially African-Americans in the United States of America.[22] Each lynching and each shooting of a black body is a reassertion of white supremacy. Hence, episodes of violence on oppressed communities are not simply

---

20   For instance, during the partition of the Indian subcontinent in 1947, women were at the center stage; they were raped, abducted and killed by men, both on the Indian as well as the Pakistani sides, to vent their anger and prove their nation's superiority. For more see, Urvashi Butalia, *The Other Side of Silence: Voices from the Partition of India* (Durham: Duke University Press, 2000), 87–152.

21   Transcripts from http://www.democracynow.org/2015/9/29/a_voice_for_dalit_women_in. Accessed on September 26, 2016.

22   On the criminalization of black bodies see the chapter "Black Body: A Guilty Body," in Kelly Brown Douglas, *Stand Your Ground: Black Bodies and the Justice of God* (Maryknoll, New York: Orbis Books, 2015), 48–89. On lynching of black people in the past and new forms of lynching see M. Shawn Copeland, *Enfleshing Freedom: Body, Race, and Being* (Minneapolis: Fortress Press, 2010), 117–121 & James H. Cone, *The Cross and the Lynching Tree* (Maryknoll, New York: Orbis Books, 2012), 163–166. Also see, Michelle Alexander, *The New Jim Crow: Mass Incarceration in the Age of Color Blindness* (New York: New York Press, 2011).

DALIT BODY—THE UNTOUCHABLE SACRAMENT

incidents of inflicting injury on or killing of an individual or a group, although that dimension cannot be underplayed. Rather, violence on the oppressed is always a way of reminding and re-inscribing the 'prescribed' and 'accepted' grammar of the bodies. It can therefore, be called a disciplining act, and as Foucault says, "a political tactic."[23]

However, disciplining need not always involve violence. In this age, violence is generally shunned, and therefore violent means of maintaining the grammar of the bodies is not preferred. Writing on the political technology and control of bodies, Foucault perceptively observes that

> ... subjection is not only obtained by instruments of violence, or ideology; it can also be direct, physical, pitting force against force, bearing on material elements, and yet without violence. It may be calculated, organized, technically thought out; it may be subtle, make use neither of weapons nor of terror and yet remain of a physical order.[24]

In other words, violence is not favored or (even) required to keep the normative relationality of the bodies alive. Rather, there is a need to have subtler means of disciplining. Let me explain how this works in the case of the Dalits with an anecdote.

While working as a Pastor in South India, I would often take off to the 'beef market'—a place that was in the outskirts of the city—to buy beef. One day, one of the church members—whom I know to be a Dalit—came to me when I was alone and lovingly volunteered to buy beef for me through one of his subordinates at work. I was touched by his kind offer to help me (and save me the long travel), but I thanked him and said that I can manage it myself since it wasn't too difficult a job for me. However, after some hesitance, seeing my obstinacy, he confessed that his objective was not so much to help me, but rather to keep me away from the beef market. He was worried that me going to the beef shop—a dirty and degrading place associated with Dalits—was beneath my dignity as a pastor. He was concerned that I would lose my face if the church people saw me in the beef shop and be humiliated if people came to know that I and my wife (who is not a Dalit) ate beef. For him—and as I discovered, for many others—association with beef, at least in public, was disgusting and inappropriate. I, as a Pastor, a person of good standing in the society, cannot be 'seen' in a beef stall.

---

23   Foucault, *Discipline and Punish*, 23.
24   Ibid., 26.

64 CHAPTER 2

In this anecdote, unlike the earlier incidents where violence was used to discipline Dalit bodies to reassert caste and patriarchy, the Dalit body is disciplined in a rather different way. The subject in this case encountered no threat or any physical assault but was simply (and gently) chided to 'behave' in the right manner and keep in mind that he is always being 'observed.'

Here, I find Foucault's analysis of the "panopticon" helpful to unpack the watching, chiding, and disciplining of the Dalit body exemplified by the above anecdote. In the panoptic mechanism, Foucault points out how the bodies to be disciplined are in "a state of conscious and permanent visibility that assures the automatic functioning of power," even as the concerned body is not able to see and recognize the source or the direction of observation.[25] Further, underscoring its polyvalency,[26] Foucault notes that panopticism

> ... automatizes and disindividualizes power. Power has its principle not so much in a person as in a certain concerted distribution of bodies, surfaces, lights, gazes; in an arrangement whose internal mechanisms produce the relation in which individuals are caught up ...[27]

Thus, in the panoptic system, there is no need for any violent impositions or threats or punishments. In fact, there is no need for a visible hierarchy. One does not even have to see or know the observer.

> He who is subjected to a field of visibility and who knows it, *assumes responsibility* for the constraints of power; he makes them play spontaneously upon himself; he *inscribes in himself the power relation* in which he simultaneously plays both roles; he becomes the principle of his own subjection.[28]

The fear of my Dalit parishioner is perhaps more understandable now. For him, and I am sure for others, to be associated with beef meant the betrayal of oneself as a Dalit and consequently, the necessity of living with the shame attached to it. What is important here is the fear of being 'seen,' of being observed. Like in the panopticon, one is always seen or *could* be seen; no one knows. Therefore, (perhaps) it is easier to be careful and self-disciplined or rather to allow the 'self' to discipline itself—"to alter behavior"[29]—in order

---

25   Ibid., 200–201.
26   Ibid., 205.
27   Ibid, 202.
28   Ibid, 202–203. Emphasis mine.
29   Ibid, 203.

DALIT BODY—THE UNTOUCHABLE SACRAMENT

to be the valid subject that one needs to be. However, it is important to note that to be observed is not merely to be corrected, but also to play "a positive role ... to increase the possible utility of individuals,"[30] as it is stressed by the functional motifs of the caste system. In other words, the panoptic effect in a caste context, assures increased productivity since it upholds normative caste (predominantly brahmanic) ideals which serve the powers of global capitalism. As Foucault notes,

> The body is... directly involved in a political field; power relations have an immediate hold upon it; they invest it, mark it, train it, torture it, force it to carry out tasks, to perform ceremonies, to emit signs. This political investment of the body is bound up, in accordance with complex reciprocal relations, with its economic use; it is largely as a force of production that the body is invested with relations of power and domination; but on the other hand, its constitution as labour power is possible only if it is caught up in a system of subjection ...; *the body becomes a useful force only if it is both a productive body and a subjected body.*[31]

Therefore, the grammar that regulates bodies, particularly the bodies of outcastes like Dalits—those casted out—often, though not always, has a larger functional purpose as foregrounded by some theories of caste.[32] However, unlike Foucault's observation, the term 'functionality' here should not be seen merely in terms of an increased and better productivity, although that too is generally true. Rather, we should recall that in a caste context, functionality also takes the (though not always explicitly visible) form of maintaining *dharma*, the global and cosmic order of stability as prescribed by some strands of Hinduism.[33]

We shall return to the disciplining of the Dalit body and its different modalities of resistance later in the book. But at this point, I believe it suffices to note that Dalit bodies are watched, controlled, and disciplined within the caste system to be either othered or to be co-opted. With this preliminary

---

30   Ibid., 210.

31   Ibid., 25–26. Emphasis mine.

32   See the section on caste and untouchability in the Introduction.

33   Here I refer to dharma in the narrow but popular sense of the word. According to this view, it is believed that it is the duty of every Hindu to maintain the dharma of varna (See the Introduction). However, contesting this popular conception, Hindu liberation theologian Anantanand Rambachan argues that to enable the well-being of all creatures is the real meaning of dharma. Anantanand Rambachan, *A Hindu Theology of Liberation: Not Two is Not One* (Albany: State University of New York Press, 2015), 185.

key observation, let me move on to the theological dimension of this project. I want to raise the question as to how one can speak about dehumanizing political technologies on the body in relation to God. What is the relationship between the Dalit bodies and the divine within the framework of caste and how do they experience the divine?

2 Theological Significance of the Dalit Body

So far, using post-structuralist lens we have seen how marginalized and discriminated bodies, such as those of the Dalits, are regulated through unconscious (often self-inflicted) disciplinary measures. In this section, I want to explore how the body has been viewed and interpreted in the history of Christian theology in general. I also intend to interrogate if the oppressed body has any distinct meaning so that it can be used as a theological symbol. But in trying to map the role of the body in Christian theology I believe that two important clarifications are necessary. First, I have to confess that what scholars usually refer to regarding the presence of the body in Christian history and what is presented here in this section is representative of a Euro-centric Christianity.[34] Second, as already noted at the beginning of the chapter, the aim of this section is not to give a detailed and a full-blown theological/philosophical history of the body. Rather, I only want to show that the body has a prime place in Christian theology, and more importantly, how oppressed bodies can serve as a key symbol for constructive theologizing.

2.1 *Body in Christianity*
As feminist theologians of the body have observed, it is true that Christianity has not been kind to the "body" in general.[35] However, notwithstanding this

---

34 That is, these historical appraisals of the body in general assume a Euro-Christian perspective, thereby entirely neglecting the non-European Christianities across the world, such as African, Chinese, and Indian Christianities, and their interpretations of the body in their contexts. I understand that this is deeply problematic and myopic, and I acknowledge that when we write Christian history from these alternative locations, (conceptualizations of) the body might look very different.

35 A clarification has to be made here regarding the use of the term 'body.' I am aware that, as Margaret Miles rightly elucidates, it is preferable to use 'body' rather than '*the* body' since the latter, more often than not "connotes either the male body of traditional scholarship, or a generic entity that no one has ever seen or touched." Nevertheless, in this book, for the sake of clarity and easier understanding, I choose to use definite article when referring to body. See footnote 6 in Margaret R. Miles, *Bodies in Society: Essays on Christianity in Contemporary Culture* (Eugene, Oregon: Cascade Books, 2008), xi.

DALIT BODY—THE UNTOUCHABLE SACRAMENT

dominant view, we have to acknowledge that, historically, there is actually an ambiguous attitude toward the body in the Christian tradition. In the early church period, the body was given a prime place principally because of the strong belief in 'bodily' resurrection. Nonetheless, because of the influence of Greco-Roman dualism, there was a strong inclination to discipline the body in order to make it worthy of eternity. Though it was felt that the soul needed the body to experience and receive knowledge about God, the body was clearly not held on the same plane as the soul. The Middle Ages saw the prominent presence of women mystics who were also known for their explicitly embodied erotic construal of their relationship with Christ. Nonetheless, as held by the likes of Aquinas, it was believed that it was "the intellective principle that determines 'man' as a species," and hence "the body has no part in the operation of the intellect."[36] During the Reformation, the body was given more importance with the celebration of marital relationships of the clergy, albeit with strong emphasis on conjugal purity. But, the theologies of reformation in general, directly or indirectly, insisted that "every traditional concept of the body had to be abandoned and replaced by a 'utilitarian' rather than a 'sacramental' view."[37]

It was after the Enlightenment, however, with the stress on reason that we see a more concrete relegation of the body (and also nature/earth) to an inferior position. Now, the body became a lifeless object that could be scrutinized and controlled by the mind. It is worth noting that this move to degrade the body was also closely related to "the regulation and taming of nature" and "the taming and training of the outer world of alien societies through a project of colonization."[38] Today, in spite of the strong critique from postmodern and feminist scholars, the derogatory attitude toward the body still continues to be predominantly present in our societies. The conventional view seems to be that bodies are merely containers within/on (and from) which the superior mind acts. Thus, even from this brief glimpse of the history of body, I believe that it is safe to conclude that, notwithstanding its ambiguous place in Christian history, due to the continuing influence of Greek philosophical dualism and the resulting patriarchal, misogynic attitudes, the general Christian stance is that "all that is truly worthy lies *beyond* the body."[39] No wonder then, for

---

36 Ibid., 15–16.

37 Frank Bottomley, *Attitudes to the Body in Western Christendom* (London: Lepus Books, 1979), 145.

38 Bryan S. Turner, "The body in Western Society: social theory and its perspectives," in *Religion and the Body*, ed. Sarah Coakley (Cambridge: Cambridge University Press, 1997), 23.

39 Ibid., 17. Emphasis mine.

Christian theology too "the body is a contested site—ambiguous and sacred, wounded and creative, malleable and resistant—disclosing and mediating 'more.'"[40]

Yet, we know that the foundations of the Christian faith lie in the incarnation—"a very earthly, fleshy, physical way to connect with one's God."[41] Set within the context of marginalization and objectification of certain bodies—bodies of women and those of a certain orientation or composition—Jesus' body can be seen as an embodied subversion of and resistance to the body politic of the Roman empire. The enfleshed resistance of the incarnate one begins with his conception where the "unclean" one—the body of the still unmarried Mary—"becomes the site of incarnation."[42] During his ministry, Jesus, through his embracive hospitality of sinners and the marginalized, shows that the kingdom of God is a "warm, fleshy, all-encompassing body."[43] Even at the time of his death, the body of Jesus unites within itself everyone, by offering itself as the food and drink of the world both at the table and on the cross. But this self-giving body could not be held captive by the life-denying force (of death) and was raised to life by God "to give and receive hospitality again, to eat and drink and enjoy friendship and to provide a perpetual, eternal source of nourishment to those to whom he gives his spirit and who become his body on earth."[44]

In fact, recognizing the centrality of the body in incarnation implies that the human body can and must be seen as a sacrament. Sacrament, as Edward Schillebeeckx understands, is "a divine bestowal of salvation in an outwardly perceptible form which makes the bestowal manifest."[45] Based on this conception, Schillebeeckx asserts that "the man Jesus, as the personal visible

---

40 Copeland, *Enfleshing Freedom,* 56. I have to acknowledge here that, given the brevity of the section, I have not done an extensive study of body in Christian theology by engaging with a wide range of scholarship. For further reading let me suggest, Margaret R. Miles, *The Word Made Flesh: A History of Christian Thought* (Oxford: Blackwell Publishing, 2005), and (for a general (male) view), Frank Bottomley, *Attitudes to the Body in Western Christendom* (London: Lepus Books, 1979). Also see, Part 3 on "Embodiment" in Ola Sigurdson, *Heavenly Bodies: Incarnation, the Gaze, and Embodiment in Christian Theology,* transl. Carl Olsen (Grand Rapids, Michigan: William B. Eerdmans Publishing, 2016).

41 Lisa Isherwood and Elizabeth Stuart, *Introducing Body Theology* (Sheffield: Sheffield Academic Press, 1998), 16.

42 Ibid., 59.

43 Ibid., 60.

44 Ibid., 61.

45 Edward Schillebeeckx, *Christ the Sacrament of the Encounter with God* (London: Sheed and Ward, 1977), 15.

DALIT BODY—THE UNTOUCHABLE SACRAMENT 69

realization of the divine grace of redemption, is *the* sacrament, *the primordial sacrament*."[46] But as Schillebeeckx reminds us, this actualization of redemption always proceeds as in any "human encounter *through* the visible obviousness of *the body*."[47] In that sense, we can say that the incarnation becomes sacramental only as much as it is (in) the body.[48]

But what does this mean for the bodies of the followers of Jesus? How do they 'experience' incarnation event? Margaret Miles reminds us that,

> Understanding the Incarnation maybe much more a matter of feeling the presence of Christ in one's body than of being able to explain the Incarnation philosophically or theologically. Christianity, understood not primarily as a nexus of ideas but as concrete participation in a body—the Body of Christ—provides a very strong formulation of the centrality of physical existence, as do the doctrines of creation and the resurrection of the body.[49]

In other words, what Christians believe comes not (only) from some documents written in the past or what ecclesiastical authorities prescribe and suggest in the present, but from how they experience the enfleshment of God in Jesus Christ in their (own) bodies as a community of faith. Thus, the body is indeed central to the Christian faith in terms of understanding and experiencing the incarnational event. However, as Isherwood and Stuart suggest, the body is not only significant in terms of understanding or experiencing the incarnation event. Rather, they argue that

> Bodies are the divine presence on earth, they are sacramental ... All the created order pulsated with divine reality and needs no transformation to make it so. ... Those committed to an incarnational religion should surely be committed to (and worship) the power, the passion, the pain, the sorrow, the joy and the mystery and majesty of *the human body and the body of creation*.[50]

---

46   Ibid. Emphasis mine.

47   Ibid.

48   We should note here that Schillebeeckx dualizes the "inward man" and the outer body when he says, "Human bodiliness is human interiority in visible form," which I don't agree with. Ibid., 15–16.

49   Miles, *Bodies in Society*, 14–15.

50   Isherwood and Stuart, *Introducing Body Theology*, 149. Emphasis mine.

That is, it is not only the body of the incarnate one which is sacramental, but all bodies re-present God as sacraments. Every human and creaturely body, as much as they are habitats of divine life, constitute and pulsate with divine sacramental essence. Here, it is important to note that the sacramentality of the body comes not from elsewhere, but is inherent in creation itself, which for Christians is re-affirmed by the incarnation. However, conceiving the body as a sacrament does not mean the glorification and romantization of the 'perfect' body—understood as the flawless, 'healthy' body. Rather, acknowledging the sacramental nature of the body "is a celebration or mourning of things as they are, it is part of the process of divine becoming."[51] Hence, I believe we can agree with Shawn Copeland who suggests that because "[T]he body constitutes a site of divine revelation" it can be called a "basic human sacrament.""[52]

2.2 Sacramentality of the Dalit Body

Even if all bodies are by themselves sacramental, I believe that there are some bodies that reinforce, more appropriately, their sacramental essence and meaning. Recalling that, for the Christian tradition, it is Jesus Christ who is the primordial sacrament, Christian theology cannot ignore the elements within his sacramental nature. In other words, as the central medium of God's revelation, Jesus Christ is the *normative* sacrament for Christians.[53] But we should remember that what constitutes the sacramentality of Jesus Christ are not just his life and works but also his death and resurrection. In the words of James Cone, "the paradox of a crucified savior lies at the heart of the Christian faith."[54] And because our focus is on a *crucified savior*, and because the cross stands at the center of the Christian faith, it is impossible to look away from the sociopolitical meaning and relevance of the cross (of Jesus) then and now.[55]

Writing on the crucifixion in the Roman Empire, New Testament scholar, Brigitte Kahl notes,

> ... the core visual program of a crucifixion is quite stable. What needs to be shown is not just the execution of a criminal but the *elimination of a*

---

51   Ibid.

52   Copeland, *Enfleshing Freedom*, 8.

53   On Jesus as the symbol of God and the sacramental understanding of Jesus' symbolism see, Haight, *Jesus Symbol of God*, 12–15. Also see, Roger Haight, *Dynamics of Theology* (Maryknoll, New York: Orbis Books, 2001), 69–71.

54   James H. Cone, *The Cross and the Lynching Tree* (Maryknoll, New York, 2012), 1.

55   Note that I am not entering into a theology of the cross here. Rather I am only pointing out how and why the sacramentality of the body can be more relevantly and appropriately extended to certain groups of people.

DALIT BODY—THE UNTOUCHABLE SACRAMENT

rebellious, transgressive other and the restoration of the proper order of the world. ... it is not human cruelty played out but the sacred violence of divine retribution. A fundamental threat to the divine and human order of the world is eliminated, for everyone's benefit.[56]

Thus, the cross was a *statement.* It was a statement of warning given by the Roman Empire to either follow the 'sacred' imperial hierarchical order or face the consequence of brutal death. The cross also signified failure, the failure of the rebel who tried to challenge the Roman imperialism. Either way, the cross was the symbol of/for the fallen people. And it is because the cross is a symbol of those at the bottom of the socio-political ladder who had dared to transgress the law of the empire that it continues to be relevant beyond its historical context.

Speaking from the perspective of Black people in the U.S., James Cone reminds us of the similarities between the cross of Jesus and the lynching tree.[57] Black feminist theologian, Kelly Douglas also argues for the similarities between the "lynched class" and the "crucified class of people" during Jesus' time.[58] Thus, as the Asian theologian C. S. Song insists, reflecting about Jesus and his cross should point and drive us toward the "crucified peoples" of this world.[59] But this similarity between the crucified Jesus and the crucified people is simply not a coincidence. Rather, as Douglas argues,

Jesus' identification with the lynched/crucified class is ... intentional. It did not begin with his death on the cross. In fact, that Jesus was crucified signals his prior bond with the 'crucified class' of his day. [60]

Therefore, the resemblance between the experiences of Jesus and the oppressed people is a deliberate way of God showing his solidarity with them. Based on a similar premise, Jürgen Moltmann suggests that by dying on the cross, Jesus' suffering—and in him God's suffering—is identified with the suffering of all those who suffer unjustly in human history viz. "the weak, the poor and, the sick."[61] Reflecting along the same lines, Jon Sobrino posits that

---

56   Brigitte Kahl, *Galatians Re-Imagined: Reading with the Eyes of the Vanquished* (Minneapolis: Fortress Press, 2010), 158. Emphasis mine.

57   Cone, *The Cross and the Lynching Tree,* 3.

58   Douglas, *Stand Your Ground,* 174.

59   C. S. Song, *Jesus: The Crucified People* (New York: Crossroad, 1990), 215–216.

60   Douglas, *Stand Your Ground,* 174.

61   Jürgen Moltmann, *The Way of Jesus Christ: Christology in Messianic Dimensions,* Transl. Margaret Kohl (New York: HarperSanFrancisco, 1990), 151–157.

"[W]hat God's suffering on the cross says in the end is that the God who fights against human suffering wanted to show solidarity with human beings who suffer, and that God's fight against suffering is also waged in a human way."[62] Hence, Sobrino rightly identifies the victims of the world as the "sacramental" location of God's "revelation."[63] For it is in those lives that one can witness the revelation of God. Agreeing with Sobrino I will assert that even though all bodies can claim to be sacraments, it is the bodies of the marginalized and oppressed peoples, by virtue of their proximity and similarity to the broken body of Christ, that can truly (and fully) be the sacrament of God. And, because the body of Jesus is not only the broken and crucified body, but also the risen body, we may find redemptive meanings in the bodies of the oppressed.[64] Discriminated and dehumanized bodies find ways to resist and flourish within the labyrinth of unjust social structures.

This is certainly true of the Dalit bodies as well. Even though the Dalit body is watched, controlled, humiliated, subjugated, violated, and killed, it also creatively and (one can add, strategically) challenges, resists, and subverts domination and oppression. It is based on this premise that I believe Dalit bodies to be brimming with the message of salvific and liberative grace of God. And it is in this sense that we can assert that the Dalit body, as the broken and crucified body, is truly the sacrament of God. We will return to these themes later in the book. But, the key question we should raise now is this: what does the sacramental significance of the Dalit body mean for doing comparative theology? To this we turn next.

3   Choosing a Category for Comparison

One of the fundamental aspects of doing comparative theology is to choose a category for comparison. This means selecting a concept or theme that is common to the two chosen religious traditions. After this, selected texts on

---

62   Jon Sobrino, *Jesus the liberator:* A Historical-Theological Reading of Jesus of Nazareth, Transl. Paul Burns and Francis McDonagh (Maryknoll, New York: Orbis Books, 1993), 245.

63   Ibid., 251–252.

64   I am aware of problems and concerns surrounding the redemptiveness of innocent and unjust suffering of oppressed people. However, I find Cone's assertion helpful in this regard when he says, "I find nothing redemptive about suffering in itself. ... What is redemptive is the faith that God snatches victory out of defeat, life out of death, and hope out of despair, as revealed in the biblical and black proclamation of Jesus' resurrection." Cone, *The Cross and the Lynching Tree*, 150.

the concept in each of the traditions will be studied carefully and then engaged in a comparative and constructive dialogue with each other. It is only by using a common and relatable category that we can do any sort of comparison across religious traditions. However, we should note that choosing a common comparative category, as helpful as it is, does pose a major problem. That is, because each religion has its own specific language and cultural expression, more often than not what we see as similar concepts or concerns in (any) two religions may not actually be so. In other words, we cannot simply assume that concepts or motifs mean the same across religious traditions. In some sense, it is precisely because there are differences we engage in comparative studies.

Given the differences and in order to facilitate comparison, it is necessary that we identify a "vague comparative category" at the beginning of a comparison project. Taking the cue from Robert Neville, Thatamanil notes that "no comparison is possible unless vague comparative categories can be specified because ideas expressed in their own terms are incomparable."[65] Choosing and using a vague comparative category involves three important elements. First, we need to identify a concept (or theme) that appears in both the traditions. The comparative category should have some (at least a minimum) level of commonality across the compared traditions. Secondly, however, the element of vagueness acknowledges and allows differences in the understanding of that concept in the two traditions. In fact, there might not only be different interpretations, but also contradicting interpretations of the concept. It is these differences and opposing claims that make comparison a worthwhile act. Finally, because the category is vague, it is possible for us to re-view the category itself during the comparative study. That is, as we engage in a close study of the category within the traditions and as we compare them across religious traditions, we get a clearer and enhanced understanding of the compared category. Keeping these observations in mind, let me turn to selecting and introducing the vague comparative category for this project.[66]

3.1 Divine Possessions as Vague Comparative Category

As I consider a suitable comparative category for this book, I believe it is imperative that I take into consideration the various arguments and proposals made in the previous chapter and sections. Let me summarize them in the following two points. First, we noted that text-centrism in comparative theology

---

65 Thatamanil, *The Immanent Divine*, 14–16.

66 Let me note that I am only introducing the comparative category. More detailed description of the comparative category will be offered in the following chapters.

poses several problems such as Euro-American Christian supremacy, denial of agency of communities, and perpetuation of unjust social structures like caste. Therefore, I proposed the need for a comparative theology of liberation that centers the experiences of those who are marginalized like Dalits. Second, in the previous section of this chapter, I mapped out the significance of the Dalit body within the caste matrix. I noted that, in a sense, the caste system is kept alive by controlling and disciplining the Dalit body. Keeping these observations in mind, for this comparative theology, rather than use religious texts as resources for comparison, I want to turn to the body which "is the medium through which the person as essential freedom achieves and realizes selfhood through communion with other embodied selves."[67] And because the focus in this book is on the Dalits, I want to make the Dalit body the "subject of concern."[68] But, if we treat Dalit bodies like texts, what is it that we actually want to compare? What is the vague comparative category?

Recalling the sacramental potential of the Dalit body described in the earlier section, for this comparative project, I want to identify a category in which the liberative presence of God becomes conspicuously present in the Dalit bodies. Thus, focusing on moments or occasions when the sacramental essence becomes clearly, ecstatically, and (as we shall see in the later chapters) disruptively visible, I choose rapturous experiences of the divine in the bodies of Dalits as the category for comparison. During these moments, which are popular in Hinduism (as in Shamanic traditions), a deity comes upon a devotee and uses her body as a medium to communicate with other devotees. Such trance-state ecstatic experiences are generally known as 'divine possessions.'

While this is the case in Hinduism, in Christianity too, we find ecstatic experiences of the Holy Spirit among believers during, what is popularly known as, charismatic worship. During these moments of worship, like in Hindu possessions, the believers enter into a state of rapture and receive the divine Spirit in their bodies. Such Spirit-filled believers then display exaggerated movements of the body, often accompanied by speaking in strange languages (known as speaking in tongues or glossolalia) or giving special messages to those who are gathered (prophesy).

These ecstatic experiences of the divine which are popular among (but certainly not exclusive to) Dalits, experienced in Dalit bodies in Hinduism and Christianity will be my vague comparative category. Though certainly there are differences between the two phenomena, for the sake of better clarity, I will

---

67   Copeland, *Enfleshing Freedom*, 24.

68   Ibid., 3.

DALIT BODY—THE UNTOUCHABLE SACRAMENT

use the term 'divine possessions' to describe the experiences of the devotees and believers in both the traditions.

However, I acknowledge that there is a major problem with using divine possessions as a comparative category for Christianity, especially since it is not a Christian category. In fact, when I first shared the idea of Christian divine possessions, the suggestion was met with discomfort, since 'possessions' in Christianity is often related to demonic or evil spirit possessions. Nonetheless, I believe that the choice of such a comparative category is based on some convincing grounds. Firstly, we have to remember that the usage of possessions in a positive sense, i.e. in relation to God, is not entirely new to Christianity. In fact, the concept of Spirit possession is a common terminology in Spirit Christology. Tillich, for instance, describes that it was because Jesus' "spirit was 'possessed' by the divine Spirit" he is the Christ, "the decisive embodiment of New Being for historical mankind."[69] More recently, using the lens of shamanism, Pieter Craffert argues that what Jesus went through during his baptism by John the Baptizer at the river Jordan was a "Spirit-possession experience."[70] Therefore, I believe I am not suggesting anything novel or transgressive in using divine possessions to describe the presence and activity of the divine Spirit among Christians.

Secondly, the proposal to use divine possessions as a comparative category is not an end in itself. The definition of divine possessions as a comparative category is not fixed. We have to remember that what I have chosen here is only a vague comparative category which means that we would keep re-viewing and conceptually revising the comparative category through the course of this book. In fact, as we shall see in the following chapters, divine possessions is not an appropriate term for the divine embodiment experiences among devotees in Hinduism too. Though anthropological scholarship has used this term for long, my ethnographic research has shown that it is yet another example of western (academic) misinterpretation of non-western cultures and religious experiences. Hence, we can say that it is precisely because of its 'vagueness' that it is possible for us to enter into a more nuanced and deeper understanding of "divine possessions" in the later chapters.

To sum it all up, we can say that in this book, Dalit bodies serve as the texts for comparison, and divine possessions as embodied in Hindu and Christian Dalit communities serve as the vague category/concept/phenomena of

---

69   Paul Tillich, *Systematic Theology*, Volume III (Chicago: The University of Chicago Press, 1963), 144.

70   Pieter F. Craffert, *The Life of a Galilean Shaman: Jesus of Nazareth in Anthropological-Historical Perspective* (Cambridge: James Clarke & Co, 2008), 215ff.

comparison. Now, having established that the Dalit body is a valid and relevant resource for doing comparative theology, and having finalized a 'working' and tentative comparative category, viz. divine possessions, let us now turn to the task of 'setting up' the poles of comparison in the second part of the book—divine possessions in Hindu and Christian Dalit communities.

PART 2

Divine Possessions among Hindu and Christian Dalits

∴

CHAPTER 3

Dalits and Hinduism

In the next two chapters, we will look at divine possessions among Hindu Dalits. However, before engaging in this study of possessions, I believe it is necessary to map the characteristics of Dalit religion(s) and its complex relationship with Hinduism. Given the history of marginalization of Dalits, it is indeed important to be aware of both the ambiguous place of Dalit religion with(in) Hinduism as well as its distinctness. As we shall see, these observations will be helpful when we try to identify how self-affirming agency and liberative resistance find expression among the Dalits in divine possessions. Hence, this chapter will be dedicated primarily to the study of the genealogy of Hinduism, and its politically turbulent and yet definite relationship with Dalit religious traditions.

I begin this chapter by mapping in brief the history of the evolution of Hinduism as *a* religion in modernity. Here I will also present the distinct features of Dalit religions to show how they stand apart from the dominant caste Hindu traditions. The following section will be a close look at the goddess traditions among the Paraiyar Dalits of South India. But, because of the relationship between Hinduism and Dalit religions, I will situate the Dalit goddesses within and in relation to the goddess traditions of Hinduism. In the final section, I will present a critical appraisal of the liberative interpretations of Dalit religious traditions offered by Dalit scholars, suggesting the need for new ways of understanding the emancipatory potential of these traditions.

1   Dalit Religion and Hinduism

Dalits have a very strained relationship with Hinduism. In general, caste Hindus have kept the Dalits out of the Hindu society denying access to their sacred texts and spaces. And as Kancha Ilaiah argues in his popular and controversial book, *Why I am not a Hindu?*, it is possible that many Dalits and Dalitbahujans[1] have possibly never even heard of the name "Hindu," let alone identify themselves as one.[2] It is also important to note that there has been a strong

---

1   A generic (and unifying) name for caste communities immediately above the Dalits who are considered to be low in the social hierarchy.

2   Kancha Ilaiah, *Why I am not a Hindu: A Sudra Critique of Hindutva Philosophy, Culture and Political Economy* (Calcutta: Samya, 2002), 1.

© KONINKLIJKE BRILL NV, LEIDEN, 2020 | DOI:10.1163/9789004420052_006

movement among Dalits, particularly among Tamil Dalits that Buddhism, and not Hinduism, is their true ancestral religion.[3] Thus, it seems that Dalits or their religious traditions do not fall within the bounds of Hinduism. Nevertheless, in spite of this reality, we cannot easily separate or severe Dalit religion from the larger umbrella of Hinduism. But, in order to understand the complexity that marks the relationship between Dalit religious traditions and Hinduism, we need to first carefully look at the genealogy of Hinduism and the various factors that influenced its evolution.

1.1   *The Modern Birth of Hinduism*

As historical and religious scholarship in the late twentieth century have shown us, Hinduism is not an ancient religion in the literal sense of the word. As John Stratton Hawley notes, though some variations of the word *Hindoi* were used by Greeks and later by Muslims in the pre-modern era, it was not employed as a particular religious identity.[4] In any case, it was not a name that was known or used by Hindus themselves in the precolonial era. Rather, as already mentioned in the first chapter, Hinduism is a relatively new religion that was 'constructed' in the 18th and the 19th centuries by combining several diverse traditions through the influence of western orientalist scholarship and Christian missionaries under the careful eye of colonialism.

However, before we move to the construction of Hinduism, we should also be aware of the construction of the category of religion. Brent Nongbri, in his concise historical appraisal of the evolution of the category of religion in his book, *Before Religion*, writes,

> ... religion does indeed *have* a history: it is not a native category to ancient cultures. The idea of religion as a sphere of life separate from politics, economics, and science is a recent development in European history, one that has been projected outward in space and backwards in time with the result that religion appears now to be a natural and necessary part of our world.[5]

Nongbri reminds us here that religion is not a *sui generis* category that existed in human history forever. Neither is it an 'essential(-ized)' human identity that

---

3   Though this is not well-known in the academic circles in the west, scholars in India strongly argue for the plausibility of this position. Thass, "A Unique Petition," 221.

4   John Stratton Hawley, "Naming Hinduism," *The Wilson Quarterly* (Summer 1991): 22.

5   Brent Nongbri, *Before Religion: A History of a Modern Concept* (New Haven: Yale University Press, 2013), 7.

DALITS AND HINDUISM

simply takes different names and forms (such as Christianity or Hinduism). Rather, though the word itself is old, religion as an essentialized category as we see it today only became consolidated in the context of reformation and colonialism.[6] Writing on this subject, anthropologist Talal Asad argues that "[I]t was in the seventeenth century, following the fragmentation of the unity and authority of the Roman church. ... that the earliest attempts at producing a universal definition of religion were made."[7] Asad also notes further that the construction of the category of religion is closely related to the development of its "Siamese twin," viz. the category of secularism. Within this framework, religion was viewed as the sacred private space in contrast to the profane public space of secularism.[8] Moreover, this evolution of "religion" as a category also coincided with the 'discovery' and subjugation of new lands and peoples by European colonial powers. Nongbri points out that this new encounter with new cultures meant that the European colonizers, in order to understand the natives better, had to understand and 'catalogue' the colonial subjects, particularly based on their faith.[9] In other words, religions and religious identities were created, at least in part, for a more efficient colonial rule.

This tendency to create categories among the natives for the sake of ruling them seems to be glaringly obvious in the case of Hinduism. Let me explain this with an example. In 1772 when Warren Hastings was appointed as the governor-general of India, he recommended "that the British colonial administration should seek to govern the territories under its control not according to the British law but rather according to the laws and customs of the local traditions."[10] In other words, Hastings encouraged the British colonial officials, missionaries, and scholars to engage in the study of local customs and practices. These new breed of interested inquirers, under the impression that the laws of the Hindus were contained in Sanskrit texts, took to studying Sanskrit with the Sanskrit pandits, who were mostly, though not exclusively, Brahmins.[11]

During these interactions, when these European officials, scholars, and missionaries came across texts like the Bhagavad Gita, they assumed that it was the 'Bible' of the Hindus, since "[T]he *Brahmans* esteem this work to contain

---

6   Ibid., 85.

7   Talal Asad, *Genealogies of Religion: Discipline and Reasons of Power in Christianity and Islam* (Baltimore and London: The John Hopkins University Press, 1993), 40.

8   Talal Asad, "Reading a Modern Classic: W. C. Smith's "Meaning and End of Religion,"" *History of Religions,* 40/3 (Feb. 2001): 221.

9   Nongbri, *Before Religion,* 85–131.

10   Richard Davis, *The Bhagvad Gita: A Biography* (Princeton & Oxford: Princeton University Press, 2015), 76.

11   Note: In this chapter, I use both terms Brahmin and Brahman synonymously. Ibid., 77.

82   CHAPTER 3

all the grand mysteries of their religion,"[12] That is, the colonial administrators assumed that the Gita was probably the most sacred book for the natives because it was important for the most 'educated' and 'elite' Hindu class, viz. the Brahmins. However, it is important to note that it was not just innocent intellectual curiosity that was behind the translation of the Gita. As Davis declares, "[F]or Hastings and the East India Company, the translation of the Bhagavad Gita *was a political act,*"[13] for in the words of Hastings, " '[E]very accumulation of knowledge and especially such as it is obtained by social communication with people over whom we exercise dominion founded on the right of conquest, is *useful to the state.*' "[14] In other words, "The *Bhagavad Gita* and other classical works from Sanskrit were taken as evidence for forming British judgments about contemporary India," especially in terms of religion.[15] And these judgments became extremely crucial when the census was conducted by the colonial administration. This meant that every native was put into a 'religious box,' and all those who did not fit into the category of Christianity or Islam or Buddhism and worshipped deities (even remotely) related to that of the Brahmins were 'pushed' into the category of Hinduism.[16] In conclusion, we may say that colonial assumptions played a pivotal role in the creation of Hinduism as we see it today.

Secondly, the European missionaries also played a catalytic role in framing notions about Hinduism. Certainly the main objective of the missionaries was the conversion of natives to Christianity. However, along with evangelization, the missionaries also studied and wrote about the religions of the natives, thus influencing the construal of Hinduism. Geoffrey Oddie, in his *Imagined Hinduism*, observes that the missionary construction of Hinduism happened in at least two phases. In the first phase, as new protestant missionaries landed in India and encountered the religion(s) of the natives, they were often shocked and disturbed by their beliefs and practices. But as they 'studied' the religious traditions of the locals they became convinced that the natives practiced a religion that was fundamentally centered on the (Sanskrit) religion of the Brahmans but eventually became corrupted as it moved away from this center. In the words of Oddie, in this first phase the missionaries assumed "the absolute centrality of the brahmans" and proposed that the "idea of pantheism

---

12   Quoted by Davis. Ibid., 79. Brahmans is another way nineteenth century Europeans referred to the Brahmins.

13   Ibid., 83. Emphasis mine.

14   Quoted by Davis. Ibid. Emphasis mine.

15   Ibid., 93.

16   Nongbri, *Before Religion*, 109–113.

DALITS AND HINDUISM

(a brahmanical teaching)" was " 'the essence' of the Hindu system."[17] This was especially the perspective of early missionaries like William Carey and William Ward.[18] In the second phase, as the missionaries became more informed about and involved with the grass-roots level issues and concerns, there was a much more critical and conscious evaluation of the Hindu religious system.[19] For instance Robert Caldwell observed,

> ... the use of the common term 'Hinduism' is liable to mislead. It is true that certain general theosophic ideas are supposed to pervade all the Hindu systems, and that theoretical unity is said to lurk beneath practical diversity. But this representation, though in some degree correct, is strictly applicable only to the mystical or metaphysical systems. Practically, the Hindu religions have few ideas and but few practices in common; and the vast majority of their votaries would be indignant at the supposition that their own religion, and the detested heresy of their opponents, are after all one and the same ... The term 'Hinduism,' like the geographical term 'India,' is a European generalization unknown to the Hindus.[20]

Nonetheless, in spite of this awareness of the diversity within Hinduism, given the lingering effect of the first phase of interpretations, Brahmanic Sanskrit centered Hinduism retained its privileged place.

Thirdly, the impact of oriental scholarship in the construction of Hinduism as a religion cannot be emphasized enough. Oddie points out that orientalism influenced the creation of Hinduism in two ways. First, Oddie notes that "the idea of Indian religion as a unitary system was bolstered by ... the 'doctrine of the linguistic unity of India.' "[21] Secondly, related to this presumed linguistic unity was also the conviction that "Sanskrit texts contained all that was worth knowing of ancient Indian customs and religion."[22] To put it simply, Orientalists assumed that there was a broad and single Indian religion that was founded upon and knit together by sacred texts in Sanskrit. We may recall from the previous chapter that, as pointed out by King, this obsession with Sanskrit stemmed out of the interest of Orientalists in written texts, which in turn was

---

17   Oddie, *Imagined Hinduism*, 343.
18   Ibid., 149–151, 156 & 170–175.
19   Ibid., 344.
20   Quoted by Oddie. Ibid., 285–286.
21   Ibid., 98.
22   Ibid., 99.

84   CHAPTER 3

rooted in the protestant bias toward 'the written word(s).'[23] That is, orientalism strongly facilitated the centralization of Brahmin and Sanskrit traditions
while relegating the oral traditions to the margins within, or more precisely, as
Hinduism.

Finally, the role of Indian upper-castes—especially Brahmins—in the construction of Hinduism cannot be overlooked. King succinctly captures the
Indian-Brahmin influence when he writes,

> There is, of course, a danger that in critically focusing upon Orientalist
> discourses one might ignore the importance of native actors and circum-
> stances in the construction of Western conceptions of India. Here per-
> haps we should note the sense in which certain elitist communities with-
> in India (notably the scholarly brahmana castes) exerted a certain degree
> of influence upon the Western Orientalists, thereby contributing to the
> construction of the modern, Western conception of 'Hinduism.' The high
> social, economic and, to some degree, political status of the brahmana
> castes has, no doubt, contributed to the elision between brahmanical
> forms of religion and 'Hinduism.'[24]

Oddie also agrees with King when he notes that Brahmin influenced and biased "views ... implied that the so-called 'religion' of 'the vulgar' or common
people, including oral traditions and low-caste religious movements, was ...
inferior, derivative, less-interesting, or of little value, and certainly not the 'real
thing,' "[25] and hence, worthy of being ignored at best or demonized at worst.
Thus, Brahmins played a significant role in creating a Hinduism that was centered around them(selves). But, we should also note that this Brahmin contribution was often apologetic. That is, in a context of fetishization of their
culture and demonization of their religious values, it is not surprising that
much of the early Indian response was reactionary and defensive. Writing on
the history of Hindu nationalism, Christophe Jaffrelot notes that most of the
19th century Indian (upper caste) intellectuals

> ... regarded the West as a threat. They were inclined to reform their tradi-
> tions along modern lines but not to the extent that they would abandon

---

23   King, *Orientalism and Religion*, 101. King refers to the centrality of the Bible as *the* Word
      of God in the protestant tradition(s). See the section on issues in comparative theology in
      chapter one.

24   King, *Orientalism and Religion*, 102.

25   Ibid., 99.

DALITS AND HINDUISM

or even disown them; in fact they often wanted to reform these traditions in order to save them.[26]

Thus, the Brahmins defended, reformed, and revived their religious traditions, in the face of western interference, to reify and construct *a* Brahmin-centric religion called Hinduism.

Therefore, summing up, it seems apparent that Hinduism was never one unified religion. As Heinrich von Stietencron declares,

> ... the term "Hinduism" is a relatively recent one. Not only is the term modern, ... but also the whole concept of the oneness of Hindu religion was introduced by missionaries and scholars from the West. ... Historically, the concept of Hindu religious unity is questionable when applied to any period prior to the nineteenth century. Both the religious practice and the theological doctrine of important Hindu religious traditions go against it.[27]

Similar views are also held by the well-known Historian of Religion, Robert Frykenberg, who claims that, "There has never been any one religion—nor even one system of religions—to which the term 'Hindu' can accurately be applied. No one so-called religion, moreover, can lay exclusive claim to or be defined by the term 'Hinduism.' "[28] Hence, I believe it would be appropriate to say there was no one religion called Hinduism before the colonial era, and the Hinduism that we have today is a relatively newly constructed religious category in which the Brahmanic traditions were given primacy and into which the traditions of the lower castes and the Dalits were forcefully assimilated—only to be marginalized. This is precisely the reason why several Dalit and Dalit-Bahujan scholars argue against considering their traditions as a part of Hinduism.

1.2   *The Unity of Traditions within Hinduism*

Nonetheless, I believe that Hinduism cannot be simply considered to be a brand new political cocktail of different traditions. Though Hinduism is not *a*

---

26   Christophe Jaffrelot (ed.), *Hindu Nationalism: A Reader* (Princeton and Oxford: Princeton University Press, 2007), 7.

27   Quoted by Nicholson. Andrew J. Nicholson, *Unifying Hinduism: Philosophy and Identity in Indian Intellectual History* (New York: Columbia University Press, 2010), 197.

28   Cited by Will Sweetman. Will Sweetman, "Unity and Plurality: Hinduism and the Religions of India in Early European Scholarship" in *Defining Hinduism: A Reader*, ed. J. F. Llewellyn (New York: Routledge, 2005), 81.

86   CHAPTER 3

religious category in the conventional sense (like following a leader or having a set of doctrines or belief(s) centered around a particular deity or a group of deities), Gavin Flood notes that the unity of Hinduism is "more in the sense of prototype theory."[29] That is, in spite of the vast and perhaps even irreconcilable diversity among traditions within Hinduism, Flood points out that "there are nevertheless prototypical forms of Hindu practice and belief."[30] According to Flood,

> [P]rototype theory ... maintains that categories do not have rigid boundaries, but rather there are degrees of category membership; some members of a category are more prototypical than others. These degrees may be related through family resemblance; the idea that 'members of a category may be related to one another without all members having any properties in common that define the category.'[31]

For Flood, this is a good description of Hinduism since "[S]ome forms of religion are central to Hinduism, while others are less clearly central but still within the category."[32] In any case, Hinduism can be said to be a religion that is not rigidly centered around a single set of beliefs or a person, but rather exists in diverse forms while still maintaining an unbreakable (inter-)relationship with one another. There are certain traditions that are more powerful or 'central' than the others, but nevertheless all are related to each other and are mutually influential.[33]

So what are the prototypical aspects of Hinduism? Let me briefly highlight three aspects of Hinduism that bind the diverse traditions together. To begin with, one of the main continuities between the Hindu traditions is the interrelatedness of the deities. Any student of Hinduism would agree that the myths of Hindu deities are all interwoven, even if they appear to be radically different and the different (caste) communities that worship them are separated from one another.[34] Even if the Brahmanical deities often appear to be more

---

29   Gavin Flood, *An Introduction to Hinduism* (New York: Cambridge University Press, 1996), 7.

30   Ibid.

31   Flood's definition is based on the work of George Lakoff. Ibid.

32   Ibid.

33   Ibid.

34   Scholars like Lawrence Babb have shown that caste communities and their religiosities are never completely separated from one another. In fact, seemingly opposing and contradictory traditions complement one another. Lawrence Babb, *The Divine Hierarchy: Popular Hinduism in Central India* (New York: Columbia University Press, 1975, 211.

DALITS AND HINDUISM

powerful and important in Hinduism, nevertheless, their myths, beliefs, and practices are influenced by the non-Brahmanic/non-Vedic deities, just as it often happens the other way around. In other words, there is a common thread that connects almost all Hindu deities and their traditions. This does not mean that all the deities are related to by every (caste) community in the same way, but rather that no deity or the deity's tradition could be understood in a compartmentalized manner.[35]

Secondly, there are some main concepts within Hinduism that can be found across all the Hindu traditions in the sub-continent (eg.: *karma, moksha, and dharma*). Almost all Hindu communities seem to acknowledge (whether they benefit from it or not) that they are what they are because of the past *karma*, thus desiring to be freed from its bondage. While many of these communities—especially Dalits and Dalit-Bahujans—may not be familiar with, or at least may not be interested in, the philosophical or theological explanations of these beliefs, and could have been forced to believe in them, they nevertheless believe in the cycle of rebirth. Flood summarizes this when he claims that, in spite of its diversities, Hinduism can be essentially "... characterized as belief in reincarnation (*samsara*) determined by the law that all actions have effects (*karma*), and that salvation is freedom from this cycle" (*Moksha*).[36] Hence, we may agree that there are at least some common beliefs for all Hindus.

Thirdly, there is the continuity of caste. Of course, caste in its present form is an invention of modernity and colonialism.[37] However, even in its existence as *varna* and *jati* in the precolonial era, we have to agree that caste was present across the subcontinent. For example, while the experience of the Brahmins and the Dalits were surely not the same across the sub-continent, still they held their respective positions at the extreme ends of the social spectrum. There was of course, as Kinsley notes, certainly fluidity for *jatis* to move between the *varnas*.[38] But, we need to remember that this mobility was neither a taken for granted option nor something easily available, especially for the Dalits and the lower castes. In other words, in spite of the complexities, *varna* and *jati* wielded their power, and caste was/is a common and connecting socio-religio-cultural factor among the different communities of the Hindu society.[39] Considering these proto-typical factors together, I believe we can

---

35   This shall become more lucid in the following section on Dalit goddesses.

36   Flood, *An Introduction to Hinduism*, 6.

37   See the section on caste in the Introduction.

38   Kinsley, *Hinduism from a Cultural Perspective*, 123.

39   Note that here our focus is on Hinduism. Of course, caste is also practiced in other religious communities.

conclude with Flood that Hinduism "is not purely the construction of western Orientalists attempting to make sense of the plurality of religious phenomena within the vast geographical area of South Asia ... but ... is also a development of Hindu self-understanding; a transformation in the modern world of themes already present."[40]

What does this mean for this comparative theology of liberation project done from a Dalit perspective? First, the complex genealogy of Hinduism alerts us to the highly political processes through which its many diverse traditions, especially those of the lower castes and Dalits, became subsumed under a Brahmanic-Sanskritic umbrella. This means that we cannot simply treat Hinduism as a monolithic Sanskrit-texts centered religion—a common misconception across the world. Second, we are reminded that there is a prototypical continuity between the diverse traditions of Hinduism, which includes the Dalit and other non-brahmanic traditions. Hence, notwithstanding the political history, the traditions of the Dalits cannot be simply severed from Hinduism. They would have to be referred as Hindu traditions.

Thinking beyond this project, I will strongly suggest that any interreligious work engaging Hinduism should be conscious of both the problematic genealogy and the complex prototypical nature of Hinduism. However, when we treat Dalit religious traditions as a part of Hinduism, caution is necessary. For, as I have mentioned in the previous chapter and as we shall see in chapter five, assimilation is a major strategy of the propagandists of Hindu fundamentalism. In fact, calling Dalits as Hindus could be easily misunderstood and even (mis)used as a tool to oppress Dalits and deny the particularities of their traditions, especially those aspects that challenge and resist caste oppression, and curtail their freedom to choose a religion of their choice.[41] Therefore, considering these grave political and social implications, in the next section, I will identify, albeit briefly, the distinct features of the religious traditions of the Dalits.

1.3   Distinct Features of Dalit Religion

In this section, I will offer a general, broad-stroked picture of *Hindu Dalit* religion by summarizing the studies made by Dalit scholars. Note that I stress 'Hindu Dalit' to differentiate it from what I call 'Paraiyar Dalit' religion which

---

40   Flood, *An Introduction to Hinduism*, 8.

41   This is often the ideological ruse employed by Hindu nationalists and fundamentalists to convert 'back' and keep Dalits within Hinduism and thrust down brahmanic upper-caste practices on the Dalits. Ankur Barua, *Debating 'Conversion' in Hinduism and Christianity* (London & New York: Routledge, 2015), 185–191. More will be said on Hindu fundamentalism and conversions of Dalits in chapter five.

DALITS AND HINDUISM

89

is more specific to the Paraiyar Dalit community and goes beyond Hinduism (or any one religious tradition). We will look at the hybrid nature of Paraiyar religion in chapter seven before we engage in comparison. For now, let us look at Dalit religion in relation to Hinduism.

To begin with, we need to be aware that Dalit religion is definitely not monolithic. As mentioned in the introduction, "Dalit" is a name embraced by the many untouchable communities in South Asia to consolidate and assert their identity. Therefore, it is only natural that the religious traditions are diverse. For instance, the tradition of the Paraiyars, which is my focus in this book, is different from that of other Dalit communities such as the Mahars and Chamars. In fact, differences must be expected even among the Paraiyars according to region, local practices, and so on. Nevertheless, there are several similarities among the religious traditions of the Dalits which set them apart from the dominant caste traditions of Hinduism. Notwithstanding its brevity, I believe that this (even if generic) (re)presentation of Dalit religion is needed, especially in a context where Dalits are looked down as "very bad theologians, and their religious knowledge, very superficial."[42] It is even more necessary given the aforementioned inclination of Hindu fundamentalism to colonize Dalit and other lower-caste religions and cultures. In that sense, I confess that the following section is motivated by the objective of countering casteist and Hindu fundamentalist objectives.

Firstly, it is obvious that Dalit religion is the religion of the 'outside(rs).' Given that Dalits have to still live in segregated areas in villages, Dalit deities and their traditions practiced by them also exist in these outcaste spaces. We can say that this 'outcasteness' of Dalit religion serves two important purposes. First, Dalit religion plays a crucial role in the "orchestration" of the subjectivity of the Dalits within this outcaste space through a "creative emancipatory resymbolization of their own religious particularities," in spite of their oppressive situation.[43] Second, Dalit religion also acts as a system of protection for the Dalits who are made vulnerable by violent casteist regimes. Clarke observes that by living with the Dalits in their 'colony,'[44] the Dalit deity (which in this case is the Ellaiamman) "shields and polices the geographic, social, and cultural space ... from the continuous colonizing proclivity of the caste peoples."[45]

---

42   Robert Deliège, *The World of the 'Untouchables': Paraiyars of Tamilnadu* (Delhi: Oxford University Press, 1997), 251.

43   Clarke, *Dalits and Christianity*, 125.

44   Dalit settlements in villages are typically called colonies. Previously, they were (and in some places, still are) called *ceris*.

45   Ibid., 102.

Thus, we can say that Dalit religion both facilitates the continual re-creation of Dalit subjectivity and guards the Dalits from the intrusion and aggression of the upper-castes.[46]

Secondly, Dalit religion is rooted in relatable human (hi)stories. That is, Dalit religion is generally not based on sacred scriptures but rather on anthropocentric myths that exist in the form of oral traditions. Moreover, these myths also strongly indicate that most of the deities were real human persons who had met violent ends or had violent experiences in their lives. Wilfred elucidates that Dalit deities,

> ... do not descend from above but ascend, as it were, from beneath the feet of the society. The deities are often historical persons who were in conflict with the unjust system of casteist and feudal society and its laws and injunctions. They are persons who transgressed, for example caste norms, or fought against injustice, or defended their community against the onslaught of the upper castes and dominant castes.[47]

Moreover, these mythographies also serve to imbibe emancipatory values in the Dalit communities. As Clarke asserts, by re-viewing and re-visiting these myths Dalits are able to see both in their deities and in themselves, the potential, not only to reassert their dignity in the midst of the challenges posed by the caste system, but also to re-affirm their ability to resist and challenge them.[48] In other words, the narratives of the sufferings and the deification of the Dalit deities closely relates with and creatively inspires the Dalits to think beyond and against their oppressive situation.

Finally, Dalit religion is also distinct in terms of its "tacitness and subtlety that ensures the survivability of dimensions of subaltern religion within an overall context of dominating forces."[49] I believe that this attribute is important to note since Dalit religion is often—because of the reality of oppression—expected to be rebellious and revolutionary. However, Dalit religion doesn't necessarily meet these hopes of dramatic uprisings or insurrections. Rather, there appears to be complicity, submissiveness, and even resignation in Dalit rituals like possessions or drumming or sacrifices. Nothing explicitly political going on here, one might think! However, Wilfred warns us that just because Dalit religion doesn't openly speak of overturning the caste structure, "[T]hey

---

46   Ibid., 101.

47   Wilfred, *Sling of Utopia*, 142.

48   Clarke, *Dalits and Christianity*, 107.

49   Ibid., 129.

DALITS AND HINDUISM

are not merely structure-maintaining devices, or mere symbolically projected utopia, but ... an important means which offer new energies in their *actual* struggles against the continued oppression of the dominant castes and classes."[50] In other words, the distinctness of Dalit religion is precisely in using creative and industrious ways of resistance under the guise of seeming passivity.

Having briefly seen the distinct features of Dalit religion, in the next section, I want to turn to the goddess traditions among the Paraiyar communities in South India and their place amidst the complex web of the goddess tradition(s) of Hinduism. It is within the context of the traditions of the Hindu Paraiyar goddesses that I want to consider my comparative category, divine possessions, in the next chapter.

2 Hindu Dalit Goddesses

It is generally accepted that Paraiyar have "a particular veneration for female deities"[51] and that they play a prominent and significant role in their religio-cultural world. However, as pointed out in the previous section, given that Dalit religions are part of the larger umbrella of Hinduism, Dalit goddesses cannot be studied without taking into consideration the larger (inter-connected) goddess traditions of Hinduism. Below, I give a brief and general overview of goddesses in Hinduism.

2.1 *Goddess(es) of Hinduism*[52]
In his book, *Hindu Goddesses,* David Kinsley observes that "[N]o other living religious tradition displays such an ancient, continuous, and diverse history of goddess worship" as Hinduism.[53] Beginning from the pre-vedic period, several Goddesses have evolved and appear as different persons. But in spite of the seeming multitude of goddesses, it is generally believed that all of them are embodied together in the "Great Goddess." During the Vedic times, she was worshipped in the form of a number of deities such as Pṛthvī (Earth), Aditi (the unbound one), Uṣas (dawn), Nirṛti (destruction) and Vāc (speech). But,

---

50 Wilfred, *Sling of Utopia*, 156.
51 Deliège citing Stephen Fuchs. Deliège, *The World of the 'Untouchables,'* 252.
52 Note: When using Tamil or Sanskrit terms in this and other sections, I have used Tamil and Sanskrit lexicon transliteration only when citing other authors. That is, in my own use of Tamil/Sanskrit words (eg.: Mariamman), I have used simple English transliteration.
53 David Kinsley, *Hindu Goddesses: Visions of the Divine Feminine in the Hindu Tradition* (Berkeley and Los Angeles: University of California Press, 1988), 1.

92   CHAPTER 3

perhaps the more popular representations of the Goddess are Durgā and Kālī, as the śakti of the gods i.e. as the spouses of the Trimurthis (Vishnu, Siva, and Brahma)—Lakṣmī, Pārvatī, and Sarasvatī, as the seven mothers (Sapa-mātṛikās), and more commonly, as local or regional icons and aniconic forms, such as stones and trees. Finally, the Goddess also appears as natural phenomena (rivers) and, male and female mediums (devotees) possessed by a deity.[54] But, as Flood warns us, the Great Goddess is quite

> ... a contradictory and ambivalent figure in Hinduism. On the one hand she is the source of life, the benevolent mother who is giving and over-flowing, yet on the other she is a terrible malevolent force who demands offerings of blood, meat and alcohol to placate her wrath.[55]

In other words, the Great Goddess and her many manifestations cannot be simply portrayed in a singular way. She is a calm and benevolent mother to her devotees. But she can also take fierce forms when her anger is kindled.

The two most important texts in the Great Goddess tradition are the Devibhagavatha Purana (ca. fourteenth century CE) and the Devi-Mahatmaya (ca. seventh century CE), which is a section of the Markandeya Purana. Let me offer a glimpse of the latter here. Devi-Mahatmaya is basically constructed around three different myths involving the Great goddess. Each of these myths narrate her victory over (male) demons, and her greatness, not just over creatures, but even over the gods. Even the male gods, who are usually presented as more powerful than their female counterparts (and their spouses) depend here on the Devi to overcome evil in the universe.[56] In these myths, the Devi is

---

54   Flood, *An Introduction to Hinduism*, 175–179.

55   Ibid., 174.

56   In the first myth, Vishnu is asleep stretched out on his serpent, Sesa. Two demons—Madhu and Kaitabha—arise from the wax in Vishnu's ear and torment Brahma. He pleads with the Devi so that she could release Vishnu from his sleep (as it is through her power he is under the spell of sleep). When the Devi revokes her power, Vishnu awakens. However, the two demons ask to be slain where the earth is not covered with water. Therefore, Vishnu kills the demons on his thighs and creates the universe from their bone marrow. The second myth is about the killing of another demon Mahiṣāsura. A fiery splendor (*tejas*) came forth out of the gods and joined together to create a goddess who defeats Mahiṣāsura and his armies. The third myth is about the killing of the demons Śumbha and Niśumbha. First, the Devi killed the demon generals Caṇḍa and Muṇḍa, thus, receiving the name Cāmuṇḍā. After this, the sakthi of the gods came forth as seven goddesses, who, together with the sakthi of Candika, killed Śumbha and Niśumbha. Once again, the greatness of the Goddess(es), the Devī(s) is celebrated. Thomas Coburn, *Encountering the Goddess: A Translation from the Devī-Māhātmya and a Study of Its Interpretation* (Albany: State University of New York Press, 1991), 32–39, 39–48, 48–73.

DALITS AND HINDUISM

praised as the gracious and powerful creator and ruler of the world by and in whom everything exists. Thomas Coburn notes that she is even considered as the absolute Supreme Being—equivalent of Brahman—by her devotees.[57] The hymn also urges the devotees to worship her both regularly as well as during festivals, thereby consolidating the worship of goddesses as a prominent form of religiosity.

From a Dalit point of view it is important to note that the Great Goddess may not have always been a Brahmanic goddess. Rather, as Flood notes, the traditions of the Great Goddess could go back to the pre-Aryan, pre-vedic culture. It is possible that several low-caste and local goddesses unified and evolved into the Great Goddess, and it was only later that she became assimilated into the Brahmanic sphere.[58] Coburn also seems to agree with Flood when he places the origins of the Great Goddess in the pre-Aryan period, pointing out that the goddess cults were probably a part of the religious world view of the pre-Aryan Indus valley people that were later combined with the Aryan traditions.[59] As the Brahmanical synthesis and the Sanskritization of the various religious traditions happened, the Goddess was also included into this Aryan mainstream. In that sense, the Devi-Mahatmaya is possibly a remnant of a non-brahmanic pre-Aryan past when the Goddess enjoyed her place as the supreme cosmic power whose identity and glory was shared across several (goddess) traditions.[60] In conclusion, observing this history and the broad range of traditions covered by the Great Goddess, we can agree that,

> The Goddess, on the edges of the brahmanical world, is incorporated into orthoprax, puranic worship and her tantric worship becomes brahmanized ... Hindu Orthopraxy contains the Goddess within a brahmanical structure. However, on the edges of brahmanical authority among the lower castes, the tribals, and in the tantric middle ground between the high and low castes, she maintains a wild independence as a symbol of the reversal of brahmanical values.[61]

Keeping this broad and universal presence and influence of the Great Goddess in mind, we can assert that the Dalit goddesses also share (in) her identity.

---

57   Ibid., 122–148. Brahman is the equivalent of ultimate reality taught mainly (but not exclusively) by the Vedanta schools of Hinduism.
58   Flood, *An Introduction to Hinduism*, 180–181.
59   Coburn, *Encountering the Goddess*, 15.
60   Ibid., 14–18.
61   Flood, *An Introduction to Hinduism*, 175.

94 CHAPTER 3

And, based on this assertion, in the following section, we will examine how the Great Goddess manifests herself as the goddesses of the Paraiyar Dalits.

2.2 Paraiyar Goddesses

Before we enter into the study of Paraiyar goddesses below, let me make two important clarifications. First, I want to note that the objective here is not to give a detailed account of the religion of the Paraiyars or their goddess traditions since such work has already been done.[62] What I give here is a general overview of the Paraiyar goddesses even while simultaneously underscoring the complexity within and among the traditions of the goddesses. Second, I want to acknowledge that Paraiyar goddesses and most Dalit goddesses are considered to be *grama devatas/deivangal* (village goddesses). This means that although they can also be seen in areas within cities and towns (that are usually predominantly Dalit, like slums), Dalit goddess traditions are more explicitly practiced in rural areas. Hence, in this text, my focus will be—mostly though not entirely—on the Dalit goddesses worshipped in rural spaces.

When I began this project, my primary objective was to study the tradition of the goddess Mariamman, who is considered to be a Dalit goddess, or at least a goddess with Dalit links. One of the most popular Hindu myths on Mariamman is the Renuka myth which I present here.

Renuka, a Brahmin woman (and one of Brahma's daughters) was married to a rishi.[63] Every day she went to the river to fetch water, where, because of her chastity, a pot of water would get churned out on its own. One day she saw two gandharvas[64] making love and was sexually aroused. At that moment the miraculous pot broke indicating that she had lost her chastity as a loyal wife. When her husband discovered this, he was enraged and called his son to kill her. She ran for her life and hid with an old Paraiyar woman in a Paraiyar settlement. But her son, under the instruction of the father, followed her there and in his anger killed both his mother and the old woman. Appreciating his son's obedience, the rishi granted him a boon. But the boy used this boon to bring his mother back to life. However, in his excitement he mixed up the head of his mother with the body of the Paraiyar woman and raised her to life. This woman, with a Brahmin head and a Paraiyar body, became the goddess Mariamman.[65]

---

62   One of the most reliable and comprehensive description of Paraiyar religion, especially the Paraiyar goddess Ellaiamman, has been done by Clarke, *Dalits and Christianity*, 71–96.

63   A *rishi* is a Hindu sage/teacher who generally (though not always) lives a secluded life (in some cases with his family) away from the society.

64   Heavenly beings.

65   Paraphrased from Kinsley, *Hindu Goddesses*, 200–201. Also see, Eveline Masilamani-Meyer, "The Changing face of Kāttavarāyaṉ," in *Criminal Gods and Demon Devotees: Essays*

DALITS AND HINDUISM

In this story we are able to see the unmistakable Dalit 'element' in the body of the goddess as she embodies both the Brahmin Renuka (at the pinnacle of the caste ladder) and the Paraiyar woman (at the bottom, or in fact, outside the caste society) within herself. Though my aim is not to learn about Mariamman but about Dalit interpretations of her, nonetheless, let me offer a general picture of the goddess.

To begin with, we must note that Mariamman is not exclusively a Dalit goddess. She is, in many places, a village goddess. Kinsley observes that as the village goddess, Mariamman "represents the order of the cultivated field and the security of hearth and home," and is "civilized, orderly and refined realm of the village ..."[66] However, Kinsley is quick to point out that she can also be the angry mother (of the village) who is not slow to reprimand her children. In that sense, Mariamman is indeed the perfect blend of gracious benignity and protective wrath.[67]

The location of the goddess, often, though not always, is along the boundaries of the village, thus making her a guardian angel for the village, demarcating the boundaries and protecting it.[68] Moreover, in many places she is seen only with the head placed directly on the ground, implying that the body is buried under the ground. This is to show that her body is (rooted/grounded) in the village or the village soil/land. The villagers live (up)on the body of the goddess, or simply, the land and the people are the 'body' of the goddess.[69] Thus, Mariamman is perceived as a mother who carries her children (the whole village, with the land and every flora and fauna) in her body, providing for and protecting them. This iconic representation and imagination of the goddess as the village also denotes that the authority of the Goddess is restricted to the village and that each mother takes care of her own village.[70] Within this mother-children relationship in the village, the villagers also have responsibilities like offering sacrifices, performing rituals, and celebrating festivals. There is a participatory role played by each inhabitant of the village for the welfare and protection of the village.[71]

---

on the Guardians of Popular Hinduism, ed. Alf Hiltebeitel (New York: State University of New York Press, 1989), 9. In another version of this story, the Paraiyar woman's head is united with Renuka's body and becomes the goddess Ellaiamman or Yellamma. See, Henry Whitehead, *Village Gods of South India* (Calcutta: Association Press, 1921), 116.

66   Kinsley, *Hindu Goddesses*, 203–204.

67   Ibid., 204.

68   Ibid., 199.

69   Ibid., 198–199.

70   Carl Olson, *The Many Colours of Hinduism: A Thematic-Historical Introduction*, (New Brunswick, New Jersey: Rutgers University Press, 2007), 308.

71   This is strongly related to the portrayal of land as female. In Tamil, *'thai man'* (motherland or land as mother) is a common figure of speech.

96   CHAPTER 3

Finally, in spite of this village centeredness of Mariamman, she also has a universal reach. Her temples and festivals are more popular than those of other (Paraiyar) goddesses in Tamilnadu. For instance, the festival in Samayapuram is now one of the most popular Hindu festivals in the region attended by devotees from across the world.[72] These festivals are marked by drumming, sacrifices, processions of the goddess through the streets, and divine possessions. I will return to the Mariamman festivals in the following chapter.

Interestingly, in the midst of my study of the Mariamman tradition, I learned that it is not so easy to exclusively focus on only one tradition, in this case the Mariamman tradition, particularly in a rural Dalit context. For instance, in Vichur, Mariamman is the 'village goddess' who is worshipped by all (caste) communities. Her temple is at the place where the *ur* (the caste village) meets the *ceri* (the Dalit colony/hamlet). When I enquired about the Dalit deities in Vichur, I was directed to Nagathamman and Sithalamman whose temples were clearly within the *ceri* part of the village.

So did this mean that Mariamman was not a Dalit goddess? Not really. As Rani, the village priestess and *saamiyadi* (divine medium) for the local goddess, Nagathamman, pointed out, in spite of their different locations and constituency of devotees, these goddesses were just sisters.[73] Any question about the differences of the goddesses is usually met with a long mythical story that would finally end with them as sisters in a complicated sibling relationship. The same phenomenon is also recorded by Clarke when he notices much overlapping and ambiguity about the names and traditions of the Dalit goddesses. Each Dalit settlement could have one or more goddesses, all, either closely or remotely, related to each other, often as sisters (or sisters-in-law, as I was told in one case).[74]

---

72   http://www.samayapurammariammantemple.tnhrce.in. Accessed on April 3, 2018.

73   S. Pilavendran, a scholar on folk religions, points out that "Mariamman is addressed by different names—Nagamman, Naga Muthumari, Nagatha, Nagasuwari, Nagavalli, Naguliamman." Similarly, Sitalamman and Mariamman are interchangeably worshipped given their ability to heal small/chicken pox. K. Pilavendran, "Nattar Theivangalin Thiriburuvakkangal," in *Sanangalin Saamigal* ed. D. Dharumarajan (Palayamkottai: Folklore Research Center, 2006), 96–98. Translation from Tamil by me. Also see, Kinsley, *Hindu Goddesses*, 211.

74   Clarke, *Dalits and Christianity*, 71–72. It is pertinent to note here the fivefold classification of Paraiyar deities made by Moffatt viz. the chosen god (*ista deivam*), household god (*viittu deivam*), lineage god (*kula deivam*), hamlet god (*koloni deivam*) and, village god (*kiraama deivam*), who are also often (if not always) related to one another. Michael Moffatt, *An Untouchable Community in South India: Structure and Consensus* (Princeton: Princeton University Press, 1979), 221ff. Also see Clarke, *Dalits and Christianity*, 72–75.

DALITS AND HINDUISM

Similarly, Periyapalayathamman of Periyapalayam, who was a Dalit goddess before but now a popular goddess (for all caste people) across India, also shows herself in many names and forms. For instance, as Mofatt notes, in Endavur which is about forty miles away from Periyapalayam, Periyapalayathamman appears as "a form of Mariamman."[75] And, in Periyapalayam, when I tried to meet a devotee of Mariamman or Periyapalayathamman, I was taken to Soorya, a young man from Vadamathurai in the outskirts of Periyapalayam, who is possessed by Angalaparamesuwari (aka) Angaleswariamman or Angalamman. Even though he was sure about the particular name of the goddess who possessed him, he and other Paraiyar devotees with him saw the different goddesses (Periyapalayathamman or Mariamman or Angalamman) only as different manifestations of a single (divine) power.[76] As a matter of fact, this seems to be one of the special features of Mariamman. In his research on folk religions, Chellaperumal, a scholar of folk religions, suggests that Mariamman, like other folk deities, simply takes different names and forms in different places, suggesting the possibility that she can be considered as a 'generic' deity.[77] In other words, as Richard Brubaker observes, there is no fixity for the manifestations of

---

75   Moffatt, *An Untouchable Community*, 231.

76   It is pertinent to note that though Aṅkaḷapramēcuvari is not seen as a Dalit goddess by scholars like Eveline Meyer, in this case Soorya, a Paraiyar, is possessed by this goddess. Eveline Meyer, *Aṅkaḷapramēcuvari: A Goddess of Tamilnadu Her Myths and Cult* (Stuttgart, Germany: Steiner Verlag Wiesbaden GMBH, 1986), 85–104.

77   A. Chellaperumal, "Thamizhaga Naattar Theivangalin Panbukkoorugalum Panmuga Thanmaigalum," in *Sanangalin Saamigal...*, 50. Similar observation is made in the same volume by K. Ramapandi citing K. Lurdu when he says that folklore deities have fluid identities that change according to the community. K. Ramapandi, "Naatarvayamaakath Theivangal," in *Sanangalin Saamigal*, 147–148. Translations from Tamil by me. Here I want to note that although I use folklore research in this work, I want to maintain a cautious distance from them for two reasons. Firstly, I believe that folklore scholars assume a pan-non/anti-brahmanic group of religious traditions, thereby collapsing the distinctiveness among them. Given the caste dynamics among non-brahmin castes and traditions, especially in relation to Dalits, I am suspicious of such generalization. Secondly, I am also not convinced of the clear-cut divide between Aryan and Tamil religious traditions that is popular in this field. For me, this seems to reveal the influence of Dravidian and Tamil nationalist politics in South India. Dravidian and Tamil nationalist politics in Tamilnadu became popular in the mid-twentieth century primarily as a challenge to Aryan/Brahmin and Sanskrit/Hindi (and in some cases, North Indian) cultural and political dominance. For more on Dravidian and Tamil politics see, Ingrid Widlund, *Paths to Power and Patterns of Influence: The Dravidian Parities in South Indian Politics* (Uppsala, Sweden: Uppsala Universitet, 2000) & Sumathi Ramaswamy, *Passions of the Tongue: Language Devotion in Tamil India, 1891–1970* (Berkeley: University of California Press, 1997).

98   CHAPTER 3

the goddesses in any one way.[78] Therefore, I realized that to try to understand the religious experiences of the Paraiyar Dalit community by simply focusing on one goddess would be not just impossible but also imprecise, since there is no rigid compartmentalization among goddess traditions.

While the possibility of pinning down and focusing on one Paraiyar tradition seemed evasive, I discovered that it actually opens up an expansive and inclusive understanding of God, which even transcends the 'sister' traditions. When my research associate and I went to speak to the *saamiyadi* (the religious functionary who is possessed by a deity) in Vichur, we were advised not to reveal our Christian identity, since that could make her less open. However, to our embarrassment, the *saamiyadi* discovered who we were. But, contrary to our fears, she did not turn us away. We were thoroughly surprised when she announced that '*amma*' (mother, referring to the goddess) had revealed who we were and that 'we came from God and were sent by God.' She then proceeded to give us a '101' lesson on religious pluralism, concluding that there is only one Supreme Being and that we are all her children, and hence there is no reason for us (i.e. the two interviewers) to be embarrassed or feel unwelcomed in the sacred place. While I will return to this anecdote again in the later chapters, I believe that even at the surface level, we get a general picture of the basic conceptualization of God among the Paraiyars. Clarke also makes a similar observation that

> At a conceptual level, the Paraiyar believe in one supreme, omnipresent Spiritual Being, (that which is, or He/She who is) or *Sakti* (Divine Power). All the priests and the devotees who were interviewed asserted that even though they worshipped various goddesses called *amman* (Mother), these were only manifestations of one Supreme Being.[79]

Therefore, in the midst of all the ambiguity of the manifestations of the Dalit goddesses, I believe we can say that there is a deeper and broader and inclusive understanding of the divine. This doesn't mean that all the traditions are the same and that their myths and religious practices can be simply universalized or generalized. Rather, I believe that this complex interconnection among their deities challenges and encourages me to pay closer attention to the web of religious beliefs and expressions that empower the Dalits in the midst of caste

---

78   Richard L. Brubaker, "The Ambivalent Mistress: A Study of South Indian village Goddesses and their Religious Meaning" (PhD diss., University of Chicago, 1978), 61. I will come back to Brubaker's important work later in this chapter.

79   Clarke, *Dalits and Christianity*, 71.

DALITS AND HINDUISM

discrimination. This is especially helpful given that my objective of studying these traditions is to examine the liberative aspects of Dalit religiosity in relation to theology, which will be my focus in the next section.

3 Dalit Goddesses and Liberation

Using Dalit goddess traditions as a resource for liberation theology is not a novel idea. Although many scholars have written on this subject, let me point out just two works here. One of the seminal works in this area is the already much cited landmark text *Dalits and Christianity* by Sathianathan Clarke. For Clarke, the goddess Ellaiamman, who (as mentioned in the previous section) is closely associated with the goddess Mariamman, symbolizes Paraiyar resistance in two ways. Firstly, she acts as a symbol of iconic resistance by *being present* among the Paraiyar communities in their *ceri*. To be precise, Ellaiamman is not *in* the (middle of the) community. Rather, Ellaiamman—literally, mother at/of the borders—is right at the boundaries of the Dalit colony. This is no co-incidence, claims Clarke. The goddess is intentionally placed there, or, as the villagers believe, has chosen to stand there, to protect the Dalits from caste aggression and transgression. Thus, for the Paraiyars, "the goddess presides over the colony and safeguards its perimeters" and "is an iconic representation of the resistance of the Paraiyar to the conquering tendencies of the caste Hindu world," which has "constantly threatened" them.[80] Thus, within the ever-present (often visibly) well-laid out caste structures of the village, Ellaiamman stands as a guardian who "protects the boundaries of and for the Paraiyar."[81]

The other significant way Clarke identifies the goddess as a symbol of resistance is through emancipatory mythographies by re(-)membering and re-reading (liberative meanings into) the Renuka–Mariamman myth mentioned earlier. This myth, we may recall, is about a Brahmin woman who finds refuge with a Paraiyar woman, both of whom are murdered, but are raised back to life as Dalit deities with mixed up bodies. Clarke points out that this myth brims with "themes and mythological characters" so that it is "utilized with a view towards, reinterpreting the collective identity of the Paraiyar in an affirmative way."[82] There are three liberative motifs that Clarke recognizes in this myth. First, Dalits are seen as a helping community, despite their vulnerable status in the caste society. Second, the story reminds us that Paraiyars (and other

---

80   Ibid., 101.
81   Ibid., 102.
82   Ibid., 107.

Dalits) are often at the end of undeserving and unjustifiable violence. And finally, the myth asserts that the Paraiyar understanding of divinity cannot be disassociated from their brokenness and suffering. Therefore, re-visiting and re-interpreting myths and re-weaving mythographies helps the Paraiyars to re-imagine and re-present themselves not only as victims but also as agents who identify with and embrace the 'other' in their brokenness, even while experiencing and generating divine power within and through that brokenness.[83] However, at this point in his monograph, Clarke consciously decides that it is more appropriate for him to use another symbol of Dalit resistance—the drum—to do constructive theology.[84] Nonetheless, in spite of this decision to engage with the drum rather than Ellaiamman, there is no doubt that Clarke has pioneered new ways of acknowledging and celebrating the liberative and theologizing potential of the goddess Ellaiamman and her traditions.

Another (more recent) example of Dalit goddess traditions being used for doing liberation theology—though in a different context—is (the also earlier mentioned) Joseph Prabhakar Dayam's essay, "*Gonthemma Korika*: Reimagining the Divine Feminine in Dalit Christian Theo/alogy." Proposing that Dalit religious spaces have rich resources for articulating Dalit liberation theology, Dayam claims that "revisiting these contested sites of unorthodox religious experience and imagination provide fertile fields for the recovery of the divine feminine."[85] Dayam focusses on Gonthemma (or Gonthelamma), a goddess worshipped predominantly by the Malas, a Telugu speaking Dalit community in South India. The summary of the myth of Gonthamma, a colloquial rendering of the story of Kunti, the mother of the Pandavas (the five sons of Pandu) in the Mahabharata,[86] is as follows: When the Pandavas came to know that she had an illegitimate son in Karna, wanting to appease their anger and protect their honor, they pursued Kunti to kill her. Kunti, who was aware and afraid of the caste norms of her society, smartly chose the safest place of refuge possible, the hamlet of the Malas. She knew her sons, who were Kshatriyas, would not follow her there for fear of polluting themselves. When Yudhishthira, the eldest of the Pandava brothers, found that he could not enter the untouchable space, he cursed his mother. However, his curse, instead of destroying Kunti,

---

83   Ibid., 107.

84   Clarke believes that him not being situated within the academic discipline of feminist theology and his inability to substantially engage with the voices of Dalit women justify his conviction that the drum is a "safer and a more neutral symbol to work with in doing constructive Christian theology." Ibid., 141.

85   Dayam, "Gonthemma Korika," 138.

86   One of the two epics of Hinduism, the other one being Ramayana.

DALITS AND HINDUISM

turned her into a Goddess of the Malas. Thus, Kunti became Gonthemma, literally, Kunti amma (mother)—amma being a general term of respect used for mothers and all women—and is worshipped by the (Hindu) Mala communities in Andhra and Telengana.[87]

Dayam notes that there are two ways in which this tradition of Gonthemma can inspire liberation theology. Firstly, using the Telugu poet Gurram Joshua's depiction of Karna as a symbol of Dalit resistance, Dayam notes, "[F]rom the point of view of the Dalits, for Kunti to reclaim her motherhood and become Gonti, she had to take the road that leads to the habitat of the un-belonged" i.e. the Dalits.[88] It was her way of showing her Kshatriya sons that neither Karna nor the Malas were no longer un-belonged. It was an act of breaking down the barriers between belonging and un-belonging that are constructed under notions of purity and pollution which form the bedrock of the caste system. But, as Dayam asserts, it is only when Kunti decides to be(come) associated with the un-belonged and partake in their pain and pollution that she becomes divine. Dayam asserts

> For the Dalits, the divinity of the 'wholly other' lies in choosing to belong to the Dalit self by becoming one with the community and getting polluted in the process... In the Dalit imagination of the divine and the practice of the ritual, the dichotomy of purity and pollution is not only dismantled, but pollution is privileged as the necessity in the divine human interaction and the life-giving and life-saving acts of the divine. To be divine is to be polluted.[89]

Secondly, Dayam observes that Gonthelamma is both the hospitable and the terrifying mother. She is hospitable precisely because she was the recipient of the Mala/untouchable hospitality. Dayam observes, "Having received such hospitality, she opens up her sacred space to the community and the strangers. Thus, she symbolizes the sheltering grace of the divine embodied and manifested in the community."[90] Therefore, she sustains and cares for the entire community and provides for their needs. At the same time, her fiery side becomes visible when she possesses her chosen devotee to express her demands and chide and correct the community when she is displeased. However, as Dayam notes, "though possessions tend to conjure up the horrific, they are

---

87   Ibid., 139.
88   Ibid., 144.
89   Ibid., 144–145.
90   Ibid., 145.

occasions of divine hospitality... She invites the community to participate in the divine life."[91] We will return to possessions in the next chapter. Overall, Dayam's assertion is that the Dalit goddess Gonthelamma is a goddess of the Dalit community who defies the 'sacred' order of the Indian society which lies at the heart of the caste system and the practice of untouchability. She subverts the accepted norms of purity and pollution by reversing their value. To be sacred for Gonthelamma is to become polluted. Seeing parallels between this and the subversive acts of Jesus Christ, Dayam suggests that Gonthemma and other Dalit goddesses can become significant resources for doing Christian liberation theology.

Now, it is important to remember that both Clarke and Dayam approach their goddesses from a Christian liberationist perspective, and therefore, are looking for messages of hope and liberation for the Dalits. While I do agree with many of their observations and in fact build on them (as a liberation theologian myself), I want to look more deeply and carefully at the Dalit goddess traditions before searching for liberative motifs in them. As we shall see in the next section, while some strands of the Dalit goddess traditions and their practices do support a Dalit liberationist reading, there are also several ambiguities which we cannot ignore.

3.1 The Ambivalence of the Goddess(es) and Its Impact on Liberation Theology

Richard Brubaker, in his doctoral dissertation, calls the South Indian goddesses like Mariamman and Ellaiamman, "ambivalent mistresses." While Brubaker's work captures the ambivalence of the goddesses and the ambiguity of their traditions elaborately in all their complexity, let me only summarize those arguments that are related to the objectives of the book. Firstly, Brubaker notes how in most villages in South India, the goddess often manifests herself as a complex mixture of good and evil, life and death and, sickness and healing. Observing the correspondence of the above polarities to each other—good, life, and healing vs. evil, death, and sickness—Brubaker writes that the village goddess is

> ... the one who manifests herself in epidemic disease, who guards against it and keeps it at bay, who inflicts it upon her people in wrath, who joins her people in fighting and conquering it, who suffers it herself; she it is who invited its appearance and then struggles against it; she enters

---

91   Ibid., 146.

DALITS AND HINDUISM

people's bodies by means of it, but sometimes heals it by taking it upon herself; she uses it as a means to enhance her own worship. ....[92]

Thus, the goddess is a complex divine symbol who embodies all aspects of existence within herself. This may remind us that the village goddess is the epitome of feminine power, similar to what we saw in the Devi-Mahatmaya. But, as Brubaker notes, in everyday life, unlike the Devi-Mahatmaya, the village goddess is an ambivalent deity, who is not (only) the 'good' goddess who kills the 'evil' demon. In some sense, she is the evil asura herself for the villagers when she embodies and gives diseases. This, Brubaker insists, does not merely show the ambivalence of the village goddess, but "rather emphasizes how multidimensional her ambivalence is."[93]

Secondly, Brubaker points out that even the myths about the goddess may be very ambivalent. The Renuka myth (which, as we saw, is quite similar to the Gonthamma myth), seen by Clarke as emancipatory, is only one of the many myths about Mariamman (and Ellaiamman). Most of these myths do not necessarily highlight the agency or the resistance of the Paraiyars. In one myth, a girl who was killed by her brothers on adulterous grounds becomes the Mariamman.[94] In another, a Brahmin woman who was deceived into marriage by an untouchable (pretending to be a Brahmin), kills both him and herself in her fury. But this 'suicide victim' is transformed into a goddess after her death while the one she had killed, viz. the untouchable husband, becomes an ashura who guards her temple.[95] In another story, the goddess is a woman who is cheated by a *mleccha* (a foreigner), who has the same status of an untouchable in the caste structure.[96] In all these stories, Brubaker notes the commonality and the critical place of "male lust and female wrath."[97] He points out that it is precisely the politics surrounding female sexuality and forbidden social/sexual relationships (with an ashura or an untouchable or a *mlecca* or a *gandharva*) that is the reason for the ambiguity of the goddesses. However, for Brubaker, the village goddess is not concerned about the status of women or oppressed people in her community, and hence he argues that,

---

92   Brubaker, "The Ambivalent Mistress," 382–383.
93   Ibid., 383.
94   Ibid., 87–88.
95   Ibid., 90–91.
96   Ibid., 96–97. Clarke does mention other myths. But, in all these versions, Mariamman is seen to favor the Paraiyars. For more see Ibid., 108 & 134.
97   Ibid., 90.

[T]he goddess is not a champion of women's rights, nor a symbol of their suffering and revenge. She is not the deified embodiment of female protest and self-assertion.[98]

Now, while I agree in general with his thesis concerning the ambivalence of South Indian village goddesses, I have to disagree with his proposition that these goddesses and their traditions do not embody resistance at all.[99] Nevertheless, I also agree that neither the iconic representation nor the myths of these goddesses, particularly those like Mariamman or Ellaiamman, can be simply seen as emancipatory in themselves given their ambiguity. Of course, this does not mean that I undermine or deny the liberative faces of the Dalit goddesses or the emancipatory aspects of their traditions, especially as interpreted by eminent scholars like Clarke and Dayam. Rather, what I suggest is the need to ask if there are moments when the resistive elements of Dalit religions become (more) concretely explicit and visible. I want to explore the ways in which Dalit goddesses, notwithstanding their ambivalent nature, conspicuously communicate to and speak through the Dalits, empowering them to resist and subvert the caste system. The next chapter seeks to address this question.

---

98   Ibid., 122.

99   I believe that several scholars would agree with me. For example see, Cynthia Ann Humes, "Power in Creation" in *Breaking Boundaries with the Goddess: New Direction in the Study of Saktism*, ed. Rachel McDermott and Cynthia Ann Humes (New Delhi: Manohar Publications, 2009), 328–329 & Tracy Pintchman, *The Rise of the Goddess in The Hindu Tradition* (Albany: State University of New York Press, 1994), 213.

CHAPTER 4

Divine Possessions among Hindu Dalits

In the previous chapter, I noted that interpreting Paraiyar religious traditions as liberative, while certainly possible, has its difficulties. As pointed out in the last section, iconic representations of the goddesses which signify the protection of the vulnerable Dalits and myths that portray the inclusive and transgressive qualities of the goddesses, as powerful as they are, cannot be singled out. As Brubaker reminds us, we need to be aware of the ambivalence of these goddesses and their traditions. It is keeping these issues in mind that I suggest the need for a more explicit expression of the liberative presence of the divine (though not entirely free of ambiguity) among the Paraiyars, particularly as embodied in the devotees.

My objective in this chapter is to basically identify and look closely at those moments when the goddess becomes ecstatically embodied in the chosen devotees. As mentioned in chapter two, these divine embodiments, a significant feature of Hindu Dalit religiosity, are called "divine possessions" (also referred to as simply "possessions" in this book). Thus, the major portion of this chapter will be devoted to the close study of divine possessions and its many underlying components as experienced in Paraiyar Dalit communities. In the first section, I will give a general introductory picture of divine possessions. The second section will be a mapping of different dynamics and nuances of the phenomena where I will draw upon the existing scholarship on possessions and my own ethnographic research. In the final section, I will offer a preliminary interpretative reflection of possessions in order to prepare the ground for comparison with Christian divine possessions in the seventh chapter.

1   Divine Possessions: an Overview

Acknowledging that "playing host to the deity" (to use the words of Paul Younger)[1] is an important aspect of the Paraiyar goddess traditions, in this section, I want to give a general picture of divine possessions. Based on what is established in this section, I would argue in the subsequent chapters that these possessions can be interpreted as liberative and subversive, thereby becoming

---

1   Paul Younger, *Playing Host to the Deity: Festival Religion in the South Indian Tradition* (New York: Oxford University Press, 2002).

© KONINKLIJKE BRILL NV, LEIDEN, 2020 | DOI:10.1163/9789004420052_007

106   CHAPTER 4

a possible resource for doing liberation theology. The material in this chapter shall also be compared and engaged in conversation with similar or parallel embodied experiences among Christian Dalits, ultimately developing into a comparative and constructive theological imagination.

However, before I move ahead, I believe it is necessary to recall that although my focus is on the Paraiyar Dalits in the villages of Vichur and Periyapalayam, because of the interconnectedness of Dalit religious traditions with other Hindu goddess traditions and the fact that possessions are a common and integral aspect of many non-Brahmanic traditions, I have included research and studies on possessions in non-Brahmin traditions in various places. In fact, the non-Brahmanic dimension of possessions, as we shall see, has its political significance, which can be used as a means for identifying Dalit resistance. Moreover, the scarcity of written resources on divine possessions among Dalits, I believe, justifies this broader mapping of possessions. Therefore, in the following section, even though the primary focus will be on Dalit possessions, I shall also interweave 'non-Dalit' possession narratives to present and strengthen my case.

1.1   *Divine Possessions*

What are divine possessions? Simply put, divine possessions are those experiences in which a devotee is filled by a deity so that he/she becomes a representative and spokesperson of the deity. During possessions, the deity comes upon a chosen individual and makes her the medium to communicate with the gathered devotees. As Clarke notes, "[B]ecause the power of the goddess is manifested and communicated through this individual, he or she is regarded and treated as a divine agent who participates in the power of the deity and mediates this divine power to people who come to them."[2] This, we must remember is a basic definition of divine possessions. As we shall see, this phenomenon of a person being chosen and used by a deity has several nuances and dynamics at various levels which have to be studied carefully. But before we enter into a detailed study in the next section, let us first look at the different types of divine possessions.

1.2   *Types of Possessions*

Scholars use different typologies to classify divine possessions. For instance, anthropologist Karin Kapadia categorizes possessions into three types. First, there are possessions that are temporary i.e. those that are spontaneous when

2   Clarke, *Dalits and Christianity*, 76.

DIVINE POSSESSIONS AMONG HINDU DALITS

107

a person is unexpectedly possessed either by a deity or by a *pey* (evil spirit). Then, there are those possessions that are considered to be institutional or "hierarchized" and "inherited" in a village community. Finally, Kapadia identifies those possessions that happen when wearing an *alaku* i.e. metal or spear objects that pierce the body of the devotee.[3]

Although this classification is appropriate and helpful, nonetheless, from my own research (and keeping in mind the objectives of this book), I choose a different and perhaps, a simpler way of classifying and understanding possessions as explicated by Clarke. Clarke classifies possessions as enduring and transitory, where the former refers to those that are experienced periodically and regularly by religious functionaries known as *saamiyars* (god-persons), whereas the latter refers to those possessions that happen during festivals and are experienced by *saamiyadis* (god-dancers).[4] However, (both) these classifications do not mean that the categories are (rigidly) mutually exclusive. Rather, as we shall see, there are several commonalities between the two that they "sometimes blur from one category into another in practice."[5]

1.2.1   Enduring Possessions

Enduring possessions involve those possessed persons who are active and functional throughout the year, even if their possessions become particularly prominent during festivals. Stephen Inglis, in his study of possessions among the Velar community,[6] notes that "possessed dance is the 'central focus' of a festival or 'necessary for any festival' where the possessed person serves 'as a temporary mouthpiece for a deity during the festivals.' "[7] The possessed persons prepare themselves appropriately to receive the deity with the expectation that they are going to be possessed. However, unlike Clarke's classification, Inglis and Kapadia identify these enduringly possessed persons as *saamiyadis* and not *saamiyars*. Similarly, both in Vichur and Periyapalayam, these possessed persons were not referred to as *saamiyars* but rather as *saamiyadis* or

---

3 Karin Kapadia, *Siva and Her Sisters: Gender, Caste, and Class in Rural South India* (Boulder, San Francisco & Oxford: Westview Press, 1995), 126. It is important to note that Kapadia also identifies benign and violent possessions, which will be mentioned later, not as separate categories, but as types of temporary possessions.

4 Clarke, *Dalits and Christianity*, 87–89.

5 Kapadia, *Siva and Her Sisters*, 126.

6 Velars are a community of potters. It must be noted that Inglis focuses only on the Velars and not on one particular deity in his study.

7 Stephen Inglis, "Possession and Pottery: Serving the Divine in a South Indian Community" in *Gods of Flesh Gods of Stone: The Embodiment of Divinity in India*, ed. Joanne Punzo Waghorne and Norman Cutler (Chambersburg: Anima Publications, 1985), 91.

108   CHAPTER 4

kurisollugiravargal (Soothsayers) i.e. those who tell the future, which is an important component of being possessed. I was told that even people from other
villages came to them to be healed, get answers for family problems etc. In
fact, often the possession only happened when the devotees came to see these
religious functionaries.

Apart from these *saamiyadis*, there are also the *kodangis* (literally, the an-
nouncer) who are possessed and speak on behalf of the deity. Inglis suggests
that *kodangis* are specifically soothsayers who usually "set up shop in the market to 'sell' their wisdom to the masses" and are different from the *saamiyadis*.[8]
While this was Inglis' experience, when I asked for a *saamiyadi* in Chekanur, a
village outside Madurai, South India, I was taken straight to the *kodangi*, implying that in the eyes of the devotees, *kodangi*, *saamiyadi*, and *kurisollugir-
vargal* are all divinely possessed and not necessarily different from each other.

One of the most significant aspects of these possessions is that they are
also institutionalized. That is, these possessions re-inscribe social and political
hierarchies that exist in the community apart from indicating "the superior
moral virtue and purity of the person who is possessed."[9] Most of these institutionalized possessions happen during the annual village festivals, so that
the importance of the person and his/her caste or sub-caste community is reasserted in the presence of everyone. This is why Kapadia chooses to describe
them as "hierarchized"—"where deities and possessed are ranked: The higher
deities are incarnated in the wealthiest men, and the lower deities are incarnated in less wealthy men."[10]

While I am not sure if I can agree with this class-based understanding of
possessions, given the unmistakable intersectionality of caste, gender, and political power,[11] I do agree that Kapadia alerts us to an important issue here, viz.
that possessions are not necessarily egalitarian; everyone and anyone cannot
be possessed. In fact, as Eveline Meyer points out, it is only the institutionalized possession that is encouraged and induced. For instance, in her study,
Meyer notes that it is the *pucari* who *must* be possessed. If others are possessed
it is usually stopped immediately, since "the power of the goddess might harm
a person" or in some cases, "the person may be possessed by another (maybe

---

8   Inglis, "Possession and Pottery," 91.
9   Kapadia, *Siva and Her Sisters*, 130.
10   Ibid., It is specifically men, since, as we shall see, in Kapadia's research, it is men (not
       women) who are generally possessed.
11   Although Kapadia only speaks of class hierarchies at this point, she does write about the
       influence of caste and gender in possessions elsewhere in the same work. Kapadia, *Siva
       and Her Sisters*, 136–137, 148–155, 157–160, 249–253.

DIVINE POSSESSIONS AMONG HINDU DALITS

conflicting) force or deity."[12] In other words, we may say that institutionally accepted/acceptable possessions are preferred and permitted over the other spontaneous and temporary possessions.

Similarly, Diane Mines in her study of possessions in Yanaimangalam, observes that such institutionalized possessions have a great political significance. For instance, in the festival for Cutalaimatan,[13] a certain person of the Dhobi (*vannaan*) community has to be possessed for the festival to conclude. In fact, in his possessed state, this individual not only brings the curtain down on the festival but also asserts the agency of his (low-caste) community and the Paraiyar and the Pallar communities.[14] We shall return to this affirmative dimension of possessions later, but for now, I believe it is clear that enduring institutionalized possessions have a key role to play in the religiosity of the village.

1.2.2   Temporary Possessions

Temporary possession often happens during festivals when the devotees are gathered together. Within this type of possessions, one may note some fine differences. There are those who are possessed after preparation and those who are 'suddenly' possessed without any expectation or preparation. The first category is probably the most common, where the devotees prepare themselves to be filled by the deity. In fact, the preparation is done not just by the devotee but by the entire community. At the right moment and under appropriately prepared conditions, the deity comes upon the devotee and possesses him/her. We shall look at these preparations shortly.

---

12   Eveline Meyer, *Aṅkaḷapramēcuvari*, 258.

13   Cutalaimatan is one of the fierce Gods who live outside the village and are greatly feared, albeit reverently. As Mines notes, "Unlike the village goddesses and unlike Brahmanical deities, fierce gods are not paraded through the streets in processions, nor are they generally brought inside the house for worship... As unpredictable and unstable as anger itself, these gods may protect or attack." Diane P. Mines, *Fierce Gods: Inequality, Ritual, and The Politics of Dignity in a South Indian Village* (Bloomington and Indianapolis: Indiana University Press, 2005), 131. I have to note here that as much as I find Mines' research a useful resource for understanding possessions (even if it is not on goddess possessions), I am not convinced of the distinction she makes between village goddesses and fierce gods on the basis of benignity and aggression. In other words, I do not believe that village goddesses are just benign deities while the fierce gods like Cutalaimatan are unpredictable and violent. As we saw in Brubaker's research, goddesses themselves are both hot and cold, gentle and fierce, and thereby ambivalent. See the previous chapter on the ambivalence of village goddesses.

14   Ibid.,169–175.

But there are also possessions that happen *without* preparation. I was informed that there are cases when a person is possessed, even if she is not prepared, and in fact, even if she does not want to be possessed or even believe in the deity. The first kind often happens, again around the time of temple festivals. Recalling an occasion about a devotee who was unprepared, Kapadia notes that "on smelling the *sambrani* (incense) lit for the ritual, she had suddenly been 'overpowered by the *sami*,' the goddess Mariyamman ... "[15] But Kapadia points out that temporary possession "is normally not a one-time occurrence," since there is usually a 'history' of possessions either in the family or in the clan.[16] Thus, there is an already existing relationship between the deity and the devotee through the other members of the family, only that here the devotee is not prepared but the deity forces herself upon her/him. Hence, one may say that temporary possession is only a temporary and unexpected manifestation of an enduring possession in a family.

At times, possessions also happen outside conventional modes. Kondaivilai, an activist and leader of unorganized city cleaners and sweepers (generally known in India as municipality workers) in Madurai, identifies himself as an atheist. He is an ardent follower of Periyar, the well-known pioneer of the Tamil Dravidian self-respect movement. However, while visiting his village during a festival, as Kondaivilai recalled, he was possessed by his family deity, Kondaiamman. On another occasion, he had to accompany members of his organization (who were all Dalits) for a puja at the temple of a local goddess (whose name he could not recall) when they were starting a new program for the workers. Being an atheist and also remembering his earlier possession experience, he remained outside the temple. But, the moment he stepped into the temple and was given the *vibudhi* (sacred ash), he became possessed, much to the surprise of his friends and (as he said) to his own embarrassment. Kondaivilai claimed that he still could not comprehend how he, a passionate atheist, could be possessed by a deity, and that too in the temple of a different goddess. Kondaivilai stated that after this awkward and puzzling experience, he is reluctant to ever step into a goddess temple again. While there are many important details to be unpacked from this account, I believe it suffices to note for now that Kondaivilai's experience demonstrates that possessions do not necessarily follow rigid rules and regulations or, for that matter, classifications, but are rather spread across a wide spectrum of experiences.

---

15   Kapadia, *Siva and Her Sisters*, 127.
16   Ibid.

2   Divine Possessions: a Closer View

Having seen the different types of possession, in this section, I want to look more closely at the various elements involved within the actual experience of divine possession itself. I begin with the preparations that need to be done for possessions to happen. Then I shall examine both how possessions are perceived and understood by others in the community and how the *saamiyadis* experience it themselves.

2.1   *Preparing for the Possessions*

Divine possessions are, in a sense, orchestrated. Hence, preparation is crucial. Let me describe the different elements involved in the preparation for possessions in brief. Firstly, drumming plays a central role in ushering in divine possessions. Though there are different drums that are involved in ushering in divine possessions,often along with bells,the one that is worth noting in relation to our project is the Dalit drum—*parai* (or *dappu*). Clarke, who has studied the role of the *parai* in detail, describes it as follows.

> The parai drum is a circular, one-sided drum made out of calf leather. The face of the drum has a diameter of about two feet and it is tightly strung around a circular wooden frame carved from a tree trunk. The leather is tightly wrapped around the wooden frame by means of thin leather strips. It usually has a rope that is attached to it which is used to tie the drum around the waist of the drummer. This allows the drummer to utilize both hands to play the drum.
>
> The drum is a focal and fecund symbol for comprehending and interpreting the religion of the Paraiyar. It provides the differential with which to perceive their religious traditions.[17]

It is this drum that one comes across commonly in the preparation for possessions. In Vichur, for instance, drumming of the *parai* occupies a central place in inducing possessions. When the drum was played in a certain way, I was told, possessions came upon the chosen devotee.[18]

However, it is important to note that the *parai* may be absent in places where the influence of Brahmanism is stronger. For example, in Periyapalayam, which is now frequented by devotees of all castes and is a major pilgrim

---

17   Clarke, *Dalits and Christianity*, 110–111.

18   Of course, this does not mean that every drumming will end in possessions.

112 CHAPTER 4

center, I did not come across any drumming of the *parai*, at least in the main Periyapalayathamman temple. Nonetheless, other drums are used to facilitate possessions. For, as Clarke observes, there is "... the possibility of the existence of a hierarchy of sorts among the various kinds of drums utilized by the Paraiyar."[19] In any case, it may be said that some sort of drumming is key for divine possessions.[20]

Secondly, offerings are also important to prepare for divine possessions. In Vichur, bloody offerings i.e. sacrifices of chickens, and in some cases goats or buffalos, are a common feature. However, in Periyapalayam, which, as mentioned before, is now assimilated by the Brahmanic traditions, there are strictly no bloody sacrifices, at least within the temple premises.[21] But generally, in all Mariamman and related traditions, blood sacrifice is an integral part of possessions. Younger captures these preparations succinctly in his study of the Mariamman festival possessions in Guyana, where several thousand Indians (particularly from the lower caste and Dalit communities) migrated in the eighteenth century as indentured laborers.[22]

> For the members of the Madrasi temple of Canefield, the preparation started a month before the festival. The preparation involved making repairs, and repainting the seven buildings of the compound, and planning for the food, bedding, and ritual clothes for the 20 visiting ritual specialists. It also involved locating the three different kinds of drums, knives, pots, tree branches, and leaves needed in the worship. Ritual needs

---

19 Clarke notes that there are certain drums that are acceptable to the caste people while some are not: "The uDukkai and the bambai drums, on the one hand, are made of goat skin and are utilized by the priests and their immediate ritual assistants. These are considered to be less threatening to the caste people and are regarded with somewhat more respect in the various collective festivals. The *parai* and the satti drums, on the other hand, are made from cow hide and are utilized by specialized Dalit drummers who are not priests. The latter drummers are religious functionaries but their role is confined to drumming alone."
    Ibid., 110.

20 Of course, this does not necessarily mean that every occasion of drumming will end in possessions.

21 There might be sacrifices outside the temple in the nearby villages, although it was claimed that they were not "recognized" by the temple authorities.

22 Indentured laborers are workers from former European colonies who offered to work in another colony. Indentured labor was a prominent feature of colonialism. For more, see David Northrup, *Indentured Labor in the age of Imperialism 1838–1914* (Cambridge: Cambridge University Press, 1995) & Madhavi Kale, *Fragments of Empire: Capital, Slavery, and Indentured Labor in the British Caribbean* (Philadelphia: University of Pennsylvania, 1998).

DIVINE POSSESSIONS AMONG HINDU DALITS

(tender bananas, etc.) must be provided for more than a hundred distinct worship events. Offerings of numerous cocks and goats are provided for the sacrifices.[23]

It is important to note that, notwithstanding the geographic distances and specificities, what Younger observes in his research in relation to sacrifices and possessions is quite applicable to the South Indian context: offerings, especially blood sacrifices are necessary to set the stage for possessions.

While these preparations are indeed important, what is perhaps more essential for divine possessions is the devotion of the devotees. When I visited the Periyapalayam temple, preparations were underway for the annual festival celebrated in the Tamil month of *Aadi* (mid-July to mid-August). There were many devotees who were praying, fulfilling vows, or simply present in a mood of devotion. I also noticed that there were several people, especially women, who were dressed only in neem leaves in fulfillment of their vows. All these, as we can recognize, are expressions of devotion toward Periyapalayathamman. In fact, as Kapadia notes, it is precisely this aspect of devotion that sets Dalit and lower-caste traditions apart from the Brahmanic traditions. She points out that even though devotion (bhakti) is not alien to the Brahmin traditions, there, "devotion is in a controlled, ritualistic manner."[24] But, in the non-Brahmanic traditions such as in Periyapalayam, devotion is understood in a moral sense. For,

> Much credit redounds to the possessed person, for she (or he) is seen to be pure (*suttama*) enough for the deity to "enter." This state of "purity" (*suttam*) is synonymous with "purity of heart" or spiritual virtue, and it carries status. ... People who are often possessed by a deity are generally regarded with special respect: They have been hallowed and made the embodiment of the Supreme Deity whether female or male.[25]

Therefore, it is evident that, as important as other preparations are, it is the devotion of the devotee that is crucial in prompting divine possessions.

Oon the subject of devotion, we have to pay particular attention to the element of purity that Kapadia alludes to. When I was conducting interviews on possessions in Madurai, Sahayam, a field researcher and Dalit activist, suggested that women are usually possessed when they are sexually 'pure' i.e. beyond

---

23   Younger, *Playing Host to the Deity*, 136.
24   Kapadia, *Siva and Her Sisters*, 125.
25   Ibid., 128.

sexual desires. This pure condition is supposed to be reached post-menopause, and therefore considered a favorable period for being possessed. Since, by this time these women are also advanced in years, their old age adds more respect in the society. Sahayam also made the interesting point that it is because of this reason that they take off their blouses[26] to indicate that they have transcended all (sexual) desires. Notwithstanding the element of possible exaggeration, this conversation does indicate that devotion and purity are closely linked to another issue viz. the sexuality of women. That is, it is women who are sexually 'pure,' those who are chaste, who are capable of being possessed. Moreover, apart from (or rather, in relation to) this criterion of sexual purity, it is worth noting that Sahayam also mentioned that a strong mind and body facilitates possessions for women.

> *"Strongana pengalukku saami varum, weakana pengalukku pey varum."*
> (For strong women, the god/dess will come ;
> A weak woman will only receive evil spirits).

Even though I am not very sure about the causal relationship between menstruation/age/strength and possessions, or even sexuality and possessions— since men and women of all ages are possessed—I have to say that staying 'sexually pure' does seems to be critical for possessions among women.

Turning to the case of those who are not devoted and those unprepared, there may be other factors that initiate possession, although, these may also be applicable for 'conventional' cases of possessions. Kondaivilai, who as I mentioned earlier is an atheist and someone who is neither interested in possession nor eager to be possessed, noted that along with drumming, the smell of certain flowers like *kadhambam, marikozhundhu,* and *sevvandhi* can facilitate possession. Added to these sensory stimulators, he observed that memories of torture and affliction can also create the conditions for possession.

I noticed that such psychological prompting can also happen through constant (annoying) questioning. During our conversation, as he was recalling his family history and the violence of caste, all of a sudden, at one point, Kondaivilai almost snapped and snarled at me:

> *summa nondi nondi kettukuttu irundha vandhurum!*
> If you simply keep pestering and pushing me, it (possession) will come!

---

26   A shirt worn by Indian women under their saree to cover their breasts.

DIVINE POSSESSIONS AMONG HINDU DALITS

I remember that there was a brief moment of uncomfortable silence after this remark when it looked like Kondaivilai could become possessed. As I and my research associate waited with bated breath, he continued his talking, going on to describe how possessions 'feel' like in his body which I shall turn to shortly.

Finally, there is one more component in the preparation that should not be overlooked, viz. the role of the community. In fact, it can be said that there can be no possessions without a/the community. Theophilus Appavoo emphatically observes that "the *'Sami'* will come only when all the (caste) members of the community are present. If anyone is possessed when the whole community is not present, the possession is not *'Sami,'* but *'Peyi'* (devil)."[27] Even though this dichotomization between good and evil possession based on the gathered community (not to mention the emphasis on the presence of the whole community) might be a bit overstretched, I believe that Appavoo is right in stressing the essentiality of the community for possessions. Kapadia also emphasizes the critical importance of the crowd and compares it with an orchestra conducted by the *pusari* (i.e. the priest) who induces the chosen devotee to enter into the state of possession. She writes,

> He whips it (the crowd) into an emotional frenzy in order to cause the devotees to enter a state of trance and become possessed. The crowd shouts into the very ears of the man who is to be possessed; it deafens him, very deliberately, in a carefully orchestrated uproar, seeking to excite him so that his limbs start trembling. Once his legs are quivering, his whole frame is soon shuddering, and in a moment, the man is possessed...[28]

Although I am suspicious of the undertones in this anthropological attempt to 'objectively explain' the phenomena of possessions devoid of divine involvement, I do agree with Kapadia that "[I]f the crowd was not present, possession would probably not occur."[29] Hence, I will say that the crowd, or more precisely the community, plays a crucial role in divine possessions. Now, having seen these various factors that prepare the ground for divine possessions, let me turn next to the actual event of possession itself.

2.2 *Experience of Being Possessed*

In this section, I want to address two questions: 1) What are the bodily expressions of possessions as seen by others? 2) What is the experience of possession

---

27   Appavoo, "Dalit Religion," 117.
28   Kapadia, *Siva and Her Sisters*, 139. Text within parenthesis mine.
29   Ibid.

like for the possessed person herself? In other words, I am looking at possessions from two different perspectives, from the perspective of those who witness them, and from that of those who experience it themselves i.e. how they feel and experience it in their bodies.

To begin with, possession is seen as a state in which the individual loses control of herself or rather is controlled by the deity. Kapadia recalls a description of possession by a woman in Aruloor where she had conducted her research.

> When someone becomes possessed they lose control over their bodies. They begin to twitch and vibrate, this becomes so violent that they may injure themselves. This is because they are no longer in control—they no longer even know what is happening: It is the *sami* who is in control.[30]

Most descriptions of possessions also underscore the importance of dancing. In some cases, this possessed dancing is (relatively) less violent. Kapadia notes that in one case, the possessed person,

> ... suddenly went rigid, his eyes becoming huge and staring, almost popping out of his head. He started jerking his hands, legs, and head, sticking out this tongue from time to time. His possession was not very violent, nor did he "dance" as such; instead he seemed to find it difficult to move at all.[31]

Notwithstanding the aggressive movements, Kapadia names the above phenomena as benign possessions. On the other hand, on some occasions, the possession dancing could be really violent. For instance, writing about an occasion of violent possession, Kapadia observes,

> The most violent possession, however, was that of Selvam. It began while we were up on the Main Road, but we heard cries from the crowd below, by the shrine: "He's possessed! Watch out! Hold him! But Selvam was leaping about so wildly that no one could hold him... A woman reported: "Selvam suddenly started quivering—first his legs began to tremble, then his whole body, then suddenly, with a great yell, he sprang forward and danced from side to side. It was a very powerful possession—and a very good sign."[32]

---

30   Ibid., 127.

31   Ibid., 134.

32   Ibid.

DIVINE POSSESSIONS AMONG HINDU DALITS

In general, however, we can say that possessions are violent and involve incredible acts of power and strength. Witnesses who had seen the possessions of the *Kodangi* of Chekkanur pointed out that when possessed he would jump to a great height with violent convulsions, so that the garlands around his shoulders (which are offered by the devotees) would be shredded to pieces. In another case, those whom I interviewed in Periyapalayam, said that when the goddess Ankaleshwari came upon Soorya (whom we had already met in the previous chapter), he would leap and dance, and occasionally would even bite a rooster at the throat and drink its blood. When I asked Soorya about it, he couldn't remember any of this. He did not hide his surprise and even declared that he will never do it in a normal state of mind.

In some cases, as David Kinsley notes, there is even witness to spitting during possessions. Though this element is not present in all cases, and surely not in Tamilnadu to my knowledge, it appears to be common among the Madhiga Matangis in Andhra Pradesh and Telengana.[33] Kinsley points out that during festivals "possessed by the goddess, the Matangi will dance wildly, use obscene language, drink intoxicants, spit on spectators, and push people around with her backside."[34] Further, as William Elmore notes, as "she rushes about spitting on... she breaks into wild, exulting songs, *telling of the humiliation* to which she is subjecting the proud caste people."[35]

Lastly, another important element in possessions are the oracles. Even though all possessions may not include proclamations, generally speaking, devotees gathered around the possessed person would expect her to act as a divine medium. Although occasionally a temporarily/spontaneously possessed person can be used by the deity to convey her wishes, it is more common for an enduringly possessed person, either in a festival context or otherwise, to speak for/as the deity. All the possessed people that I spoke to and enquired about acknowledged that they were often approached by devotees to give their opinion or help them in the form of healing or exorcism.

A unique form of divine possessions is portrayed by Mines. In her research in Yanaimangalam, Mines notes that the possessions by the village goddesses (Yanaiyamman and her different manifestations as Muppatatiyamman and Mariamman among others) are not different from possessions in other places. However, Mines identifies that the possessions by the fierce God Cutalaimatan

---

33 Madhigas are a Dalit community in the Southern states of Andhra Pradesh and Telengana. Matangis are unmarried Madhiga women dedicated to serve the local goddess in her temple.

34 Kinsley, *Hindu Goddesses*, 207.

35 William Theodore Elmore quoted by Kinsley. Ibid.

(who was already mentioned in the previous chapter) is rather distinct. During the annual festival in the month of May, Vellalakantan, a *Dhobi* (Washerman), possessed by Cutalaimatan, walks around the village in his possessed state. What is significant here is that, as Mines keenly observes, "Vellalakantan's walk, the route he chose to take, and the actions he performed en route together articulated a discourse on village social and spatial relations."[36] I shall come back to this very important dimension of possessions in the last section.

Now, I turn to the second perspective in my study of possessions, viz. the 'self-described' experiences of the possessed persons themselves. I have to note here that this aspect of possessions is not easy to record or decipher. One of the main reasons for this is that, as all my interviewees said, no possessed person is able to give a clear description of these experiences. For, in almost all cases, the possessed devotees could not remember what had happened and what they knew about this moment only came from what the witnesses had told them. Nevertheless, a few of the possessed persons were able to share, albeit sketchily, how they felt during those moments, which I present below in brief.

Kondaivilai (of Madurai) said that possession experience is similar to being in a 'high' state one is when smoking *kanja* (marijuana). Interestingly, he described this experience "like being hit on the head with a log." Kondaivilai recalled that a possessed person feels "high" (like a lord) and "looks down on others like a *poochi* (an insect)." The experience is so intense that when the clothes of the possessed person come off, as it often happens, the devotee is completely unaware causing embarrassment later. In a sense, it seemed like, from Kondaivilai's point of view, possessions were not too pleasant an experience.

Rani of Vichur, on the other hand, said that being possessed was a very satisfying and happy experience. The same view was expressed by Soorya, although he added that after the possessions, his body felt very weak and tired, as if someone had beaten him up (*adichi potta maadhiri*). Interestingly, some Christian women in Vichur who were *saamiyadis* before their conversion to Christianity recalled that possessions were a depressing and oppressive experience. Most of these women claimed that it was only after becoming Christians that they were able to free themselves from "the chains of possessions" and "the bondage of the demon," referring to the (different) goddesses who possessed them.

From this brief mapping of divine possessions in this section, it is evident that these experiences are a complex phenomena. Nevertheless, I believe that the above portrayal of possessions provides reasonably sufficient

---

36   Mines, *Fierce Gods*, 172.

DIVINE POSSESSIONS AMONG HINDU DALITS   119

material for further reflection and interpretation. In the next section, I will come up with some initial inferences which will be developed further in the chapter on comparisons.

3   Divine Possessions: Inferences and Interpretations

In the previous section, I mapped out some of the fundamental features of possessions among Hindu Paraiyars within the larger framework of goddess traditions in Hinduism. Now, in this last section, I want to briefly identify and analyze the various dimensions of and issues within possessions that could serve as avenues for further interpretation. Let me note here that what is offered in this section are initial observations which will be revisited and developed in the later chapters, and hence, are important and critical for this project.

3.1   *Not 'Possession' but Grace*
I believe we have to begin with the conceptualization of divine "possessions" itself.[37] Patrick, a Catholic priest and a religious scholar, and the Head of the Department of Christian Studies at the University of Madras, pointed out that the translation of experiences of divine embodiment in devotees as "possessions" is rather inadequate and problematic. He noted that the (western) anthropological interpretations of these phenomena fail to fully grasp their depth and intensity. With this awareness, I noticed that in Tamil divine 'possession' experiences are spoken of by devotees as 'acts of grace.' In fact, the term "possession" is never used to denote the phenomenon that we are studying i.e. divine embodiment in devotees. Generally speaking, the term 'possessions' in Tamil (*pidithal*) refers to demon possession (*pey pidikirathu*). Rather, the term that is used by devotees and religious communities for divine possessions is *arul varuthal* (lit. descent of grace) or as Patrick noted, *aruluruthal* (springing of grace).[38]

I have to acknowledge that it was precisely this element of grace that stood out and was defined by these experiences. Every (Hindu) possessed person

---

37   However, while the term "possessions" is generally used to indicate being filled with/by the deity, some scholars such as Kapadia and Deliège include *pey pidithal* (demon possession) under this category. Kapadia, *Siva and Her Sisters*, 128–129 & Deliège, *The World of the 'Untouchables,'* 288–295. As it is obvious, in this project I have used the term in the former sense.

38   Although I never came across this term i.e. *aruluruthal*, I do believe that this term also captures the phenomenon that we are considering more appropriately than the English term "possessions."

that I interviewed said that they were chosen and filled with the power (*sakthi*) of the goddess through her grace. They believed that their whole bodies were manifestations of the grace of the deity. I believe that it is this aspect of grace that is emphasized when the devotees speak about *sami vaaruthal* (coming of the deity) and *arul varuthal* (coming of grace) synonymously. In fact, if there is no *arul* (grace) the possession is clearly demonic. Nevertheless, in spite of the limitation of the term "possessions," I shall continue to employ it in this book both for the sake of clarity and familiarity, but (now) with the awareness that those who experience possessions perceive them as acts and embodiments of divine grace.

3.2 *Interweaving of Traditions*

Secondly, because of the ambiguity and the interrelatedness of Hindu Paraiyar goddesses, possessions cannot be understood linearly or compartmentally. In other words, just as there is much overlapping of the traditions of the deities, especially among the goddesses, possessions by a deity of one tradition may also happen outside that particular tradition. For instance, a *saamiyadi* (possessed person) of Angalamman is usually possessed by the deity during *her* festival. But there could also be occasions when this deity visits the *saamiyadi* during a festival of another goddess.

Both in Vichur and in Periyapalayam, I was told that it is not unusual to have multiple possessions by different goddesses at the same time. It was also pointed out to me that all possessions do not necessarily happen within the same space such as a temple building or compound. That is, when the drumming and the sounding of cymbals and bells begin, not only do possessions happen among those who are gathered in that temple for that particular goddess, but may also happen in a very different place, by a very different goddess. Soorya, from Periyapalayam, said that the moment he heard the sounding of bells and drums (even if they were for another goddess), no matter how far he was, he would be possessed and immediately run to that spot in a state of trance. Therefore, though possessions are specific and particular to one goddess, they exhibit multiplicity and flexibility. In other words, divine possessions of one deity (say Angalamman) may happen during the festival for another goddess (say Mariamman). There is no rigid compartmentalization of possessions or goddess traditions.

3.3 *Background of the Possessed Devotees*

Thirdly, we need to raise the important question: "who are possessed?" That is, what is the background of those who are 'graced' by the deity? Of course, we won't be able to know the actual background of each and every possessed

DIVINE POSSESSIONS AMONG HINDU DALITS

person. But in my research, I was alerted to the fact that there are some common characteristics that are attributed to those who are possessed of which I have listed two here. John Jayaharan, a social analyst and activist, suggested that in his experience, often those who are possessed have experienced some sort of intense suffering. In many cases, the possessed devotees are victims of violence, abuse, or rape. In some cases, I was told, extreme poverty can also induce possessions. This is why, as Jayaharan pointed out, it is usually women, Dalits, lower castes, and the poor who are possessed. In other words, possessions are intrinsically connected to social and economic oppression and suffering.

This was also mentioned to me in a 'negative sense' in Vichur by the *saamiyadi* women who had converted to Christianity. They said that they were impoverished when they were *saamiyadis* in their earlier life i.e. when they were possessed by the Hindu goddesses. Moreover, possessions are also considered to be related to "morality." In Vichur, for instance, Sankar, a local leader of the Bahujan Samaj Party[39] alleged that only "immoral women" are possessed. That is, he believes that those women who have a pre-marital or extra-marital sexual relationship easily become 'victims' of the goddess and are possessed by her. Of course, this may not mean that all possessed persons are suspected to be immoral. Recall Sahayam's notion (mentioned in the earlier section) that only those who are 'sexually pure' and have transcended sexual desires are possessed by the *saami* (deity). While it is difficult to verify the authenticity of these claims,[40] what is important to note is that these perceptions indicate that sex and sexuality often play a significant role in these phenomena, or at least in interpreting them.

3.4 *Sexual Ambiguity*

Fourthly, speaking of sexuality, sexual ambiguity in divine possessions cannot be overlooked. Soorya, from Periyapalayam upon whom *Angalamman* comes, said that the deity was both male and female. And later (in private) one of the villagers who was accompanying me as I walked back from Soorya's house pointed out that this divine sexual ambiguity also has a telling impression on Soorya. My companion noted that owing to his possessions Soorya had become an *ali*, a common term used for transgender persons. In other words, the villager was telling me that Soorya did not fit into the normative gender binary categories: he looked and acted too feminine for a boy. Does this mean that

---

39   Bahujan Samaj Party, headed by the Dalit leader Mayawati, is a national party popular in the North Indian state of Uttar Pradesh,. http://www.bspindia.org accessed on May 20, 2018.

40   We cannot ignore the fact that these views about female sexuality come from men.

being filled by the goddess made Soorya (and perhaps even others) to transcend gender binaries and embody an ambiguous sexual nature?

While I am unable to confirm this element of queering[41] of the bodies of those who are possessed, I have to note that Kapadia also makes a similar observation. Writing on the practice of *alaku kutharathu* i.e. piercing the tongue or the cheek of a possessed person with a sacred spear, Kapadia notices that this act of piercing symbolizes the act of sexual penetration, only in this case it is not done by a male on a female, but the other way around. That is, the possessed man (Kapadia focusses on male possessions; I will turn to that issue shortly) becomes the female and allows himself to be pierced/penetrated by the (female) goddess.[42] Again, one may wonder whether this means that all those who are possessed embrace queerness? Probably not. But I believe what we can say is that it does point out that sexual ambiguity—at least in some cases—is a significant aspect of possessions that we cannot ignore.

3.5 *Body and Collective Memories*

Fifthly, we need to note the centrality of the body in possessions. Divine possessions are fundamentally and essentially about the human bodies, and in fact the body of the entire village. It is the bodies that engage with, respond to, and embody the divine in them. No matter what the interpretation of these phenomena are, that these are moments when the divine becomes embodied—even if momentarily—in the devotee cannot be denied. However, this emphasis on the primacy of the bodies does not mean the dichotomization of the body and the mind. During my visit to Chekanur, as I mentioned earlier, I was taken to the *Kodangi* who at that time was working in his village office. But he was kind enough to allot me some time and speak to me about his possessions. He began with the history of how his family had been chosen to become *Kodangi*s and *pusari*s (priests) of the local deity Peykala Karuppan.[43] This mythical story which went back several generations goes like this.

Peykala Karuppan is the local village deity of Chekanur. Years ago it was a much larger village that included the seven villages which are now noted for their own

---

41 While 'queer' is an umbrella term that includes gay, lesbian, transgender, and intersex identities, here I basically refer to non-conformity to normative sexual and/or gender categories. For more on queer terminology, see Patrick S. Cheng, *Radical Love: An Introduction to Queer Theology* (New York: Seabury, 2011), 3ff.

42 Kapadia universalizes it for all male possessions.

43 I had already spoken to the local Priest who was also from the Paraiyar community who also gave me the exact story.

DIVINE POSSESSIONS AMONG HINDU DALITS

temples. The village was then dominated by Kallars[44] *as it is now. But seven generations ago, the deity chose a Paraiyar couple (the Kodangi's ancestors) to be his priests in his temple. However, when the Kallars heard about this they were furious and could not accept the lowly Paraiyars as their priest. However, the leader of the Kallars decided to perform a test to check the validity of the claim of the Paraiyars. The test was to put their hands in a pot of burning hot wax. And when the Paraiyar man, trusting in Peykala Karuppan, put his hands into the burning hot wax, behold, it was not burnt.*

As the *Kodangi* was speaking these words, he began to twitch and turn, face first, and then his entire body. And tears started flowing down his face. The person sitting next to him, who was a *saamiyadi* of another deity, also began to weep. Others in the office, including those who accompanied me (discreetly) indicated to me that the *Kodangi* was beginning to be possessed. As I sat there nervously, worrying about embarrassing him in his work place if his possession reached its peak—not to mention my own fear of sitting next to a possessed man—and debating if we should simply leave and come back later, as suddenly as it had started, the *Kodangi* regained his composure and calmed down.

Reflecting on this, Balasubramanium Jeyapal, a Dalit scholar of journalism and the person who helped me to meet the *Kodangi*, pointed out that this was a classic case of collective memories that transcend generations and find embodied expressions in cultural myths and religious practices. That is, these memories of the past, particularly those that have to do with oppression and violence, which were shared across the community through generations as oral tradition, had now become intertwined with the body of the individual, and was finding an outlet through phenomena like divine possessions. Jan Assmann confirms this when he observes that collective memories that reconnect with the past "transmit a collective identity," which often find expression through religious rituals (like possessions).[45] Moreover, Assmann identifies that religious rituals, "as the oldest and most fundamental medium of bonding memory, ... include the universe of spirits and the dead."[46] This is precisely what we see in the myth told by the *Kodangi*. Therefore, it is possible to claim that collective memories of the (mythical) past find visible embodiment in the devotees during times of possessions. The mention of one particular event that happened many generations ago leads the person to experience that pain and respond to it in his/her body. Thus, the body, in a sense, contains, sustains,

---

44   A non-brahmanical dominant caste in South India.

45   Jan Assmann, *Religion and Cultural Memory*, transl. Rodney Livingstone (Stanford: Stanford University Press, 2006), 6–7 & 10.

46   Ibid., 11.

124

and ignites memories from the past that eventually manifest themselves as possessions.

3.6   Liberative Elements in Possessions

Finally, given that this is a project of liberation theology, I am interested in enquiring about the emancipatory significance of possessions, particularly with respect to caste and patriarchy. Attempting to know whether divine possessions could be seen as resistive and liberative, I was surprised to see the range of responses that I received. In Periyapalayam and Vichur for instance, nothing was mentioned about possessions as a means of resisting caste. In fact, in some cases, it seemed to perpetuate caste hierarchy. In Chekkanur, the Priest and the *Kodangi* reported that even though Paraiyars are chosen to be the priestly class in that village, there are only ten families that are given this honor. And importantly, these families lived like the upper castes and were forbidden from having any relationship with the other Paraiyar families who lived in the Dalit colony in the village. The only exception is marriage, in which case, those who enter into a conjugal relationship with any of these ten families had to go through a purifying ritual before becoming a full member of the priestly family. Thus, on the surface there seems to be no real emphasis on resistance to caste.

However, Kondaivilai insisted that possessions were indeed resistive and liberative. He recalled how, when his grandmother and mother became possessed, they spoke back to the caste people and abused them. According to Kondaivilai these are definitely acts of resistance and retaliation by communities that are otherwise trampled upon. He also further noted that it was not uncommon for Dalits in their possessed state to beat the dominant castes (*adipaargal*). He knew this for sure since his own mother used to beat the caste people with a broom. Given that being beaten with a broom is considered an insult in the Indian society, we may say that divinely possessed Dalits are emboldened (by the deity) to engage in practices that they otherwise would not and cannot imagine, leave alone enact. In a similar vein, Kinsley also observes that during possessions, the person embodying and speaking as the deity gets the courage to 'stand up,' 'speak out' and even 'verbally abuse' those in power.[47] It is no surprise then that, as anthropologist Karin Kapadia notes, "[T]his public display of otherwise 'uncouth' and wild behavior is *cherished* by the lower castes, who normally have to behave cautiously and deferentially ... in the presence of their landlords and paymasters."[48] In other words, possession can

---

47   Kinsley, *Hindu Goddesses*, 218–220.

48   Kapadia, *Siva and Her Sisters*, 149–150. Emphasis mine.

DIVINE POSSESSIONS AMONG HINDU DALITS

be seen as moments when the lower-castes and the Dalits openly assert themselves and challenge the oppressive realities of caste around them, even if in very covert and subtle ways.

Finally, as mentioned earlier, the Cutalaimātan possessions studied by Mines have social and spatial significance in regard with Dalit and lower-caste resistance. Mines notes that

> The walk Vellalakantan walked from the cremation-ground temple and the talk he talked as he walked *redefined* the spatial dimensions of this dominant ūr. His walk *included* those who were in other contexts excluded, and his talk—as well as story of Dhobis and others about him—*centered* those who were in other contexts relegated to the outsides and peripheries of the dominant ūr's livable space.[49]

In other words, when the Vellalakantan walks around the village in his possessed state, he 'maps' and talks through the village, in such a way that the marginalized and outcaste spaces of the village (like that of the Washermen caste and the Dalits) are not just included but also centered. Mines contrasts this with the possessions and festivals of the dominant castes who 'map' the village to order and regulate the space of the village according to the caste hierarchy.[50] James Ponniah, who has also studied the Cutalaimatan cult from a ritual perspective, makes a similar observation that, in the possessed state, the Dalit *saamiyadi* engages "in the production of contradictions and subversion of roles in the caste hierarchy."[51] Thus, we may say that possessions could be seen as acts of subversion and counter-action by the marginalized communities.

Now, on the issue of gender, the resistive element of possessions becomes ambiguous. For example, Kapadia notes that it is the men who are possessed more than women. She notes that for the villagers of Aruloor, possessions by the "Great Goddess Mariyamman" is "solely a male activity" whereas the women are almost always possessed by evil spirits, especially since they are the weaker and the vulnerable sex.[52] In other words, even though it is claimed that possessions are acts of resistance against caste, it doesn't seem to be the case when it comes to contesting patriarchy. However, in contrast to Kapadia's observation, Jayaharan pointed out that women are possessed more often

---

49   Mines, *Fierce Gods*, 172. Emphasis mine.
50   See the chapter "Who is the Ūr?" Ibid., 29–49.
51   James Ponniah, "Rituals and Ritual Power of the Broken People: A Debate Over Strategies," *South Indian Folklorist* 9 (2010): 37.
52   Kapadia, *Siva and Her Sisters*, 129–130.

since they are the ones who are abused and exploited generally. Because of the excessive injustices that they face, divine (and even evil spirit) possessions become a means of resisting and subverting the structures of patriarchy and misogyny for women. Moreover, recalling Sahayam's observation that 'strong' women are divinely possessed, and Sankar's comment that adulterous woman get possessed, one wonders if we can see a mutual correlation between strong (minded) women, sexual independence, and divine possessions. If that is the case, then I believe that we can indeed claim that possessions, as the embodied divine experiences of 'immoral' or undisciplined female bodies can be interpreted as acts of transgressive resistance.[53] Keeping in mind these opposing views, we may conclude that though possessions may not be always seen as explicit acts of resistance, they do embody creative subversion, at least in some contexts.

In this chapter, I have studied and established one of the poles of my comparative work viz. divine possessions among Hindu Dalits. First, I laid out the fundamental features and types of divine possessions. Then, I looked at the different elements within the phenomena of possessions, and how they are witnessed and experienced by Paraiyar Dalit and other non-brahmanic communities who identify as Hindu. And in the final section, I have offered an initial reflection about divine possessions considering the various issues and complexities within. These observations will set the foundation for further constructive interpretation when they are compared with Christian divine possessions among Dalits. This will be the focus of the next two chapters.

---

53   After all, it should be borne in mind that women's sexuality is controlled in the patriarchal Indian society. An adulterous woman then, is usually seen as a bold 'transgressive' person. In that sense, I believe that a woman affirming and attaining her sexual desires denotes, at least indirectly, the independent nature and the strong-mindedness of the individual. Hence, the view that strong minded, uncontrolled/able women are possessed. Note here that I am not tracing or arguing for the causal relationship between female sexual independence and possessions. Rather, since both require a woman to be 'strong,' I am merely pondering such a possibility.

CHAPTER 5

Dalit Christianity and Theology

The purpose of the next two chapters is to erect the second pole of comparison in this project, namely, divine possessions among Christian Dalits. However, before I enter into the study of possessions, I believe it is first necessary to be aware of the complex and much politicized history of Dalit Christianity. This will be presented in the first part of this chapter. In the second part, to prepare the ground for the study of divine embodiment in Dalit bodies, I want to consider the basic conceptualization and expressions of God in Dalit theology. Thus, this chapter will provide a background for the study of divine possessions among Dalit Christians in the next chapter.

1   Dalit Christianity

Although the main objective of this book is to study divine possessions among Dalit Christians in South India, I believe that it is necessary to see these phenomena within the overall context of Dalit Christianity, albeit limited to Paraiyar Dalits and Indian Protestantism. In this section, I begin with Paraiyar conversions in the early Protestant missionary period, moving on to the mass movements of the late nineteenth century and early twentieth century. In the final section, I will give a brief and selective presentation of the issues facing Dalit Christians today.

1.1   *The Beginnings*
When speaking of Dalit Christian history, it is typical to begin with the "Mass Movements" i.e. the large scale conversions of Dalits to Christianity that happened around the turn of the twentieth century. Although I agree with this conventional historical point of departure, I believe that Christian links with Dalits, Paraiyars in this case, are earlier than it is often believed. Therefore, I want to begin with the early decades of Protestant missionary work, in the first half of the eighteenth century, focusing on two mass conversions that were led by and centered around two individuals who have not received much attention.

© KONINKLIJKE BRILL NV, LEIDEN, 2020 | DOI:10.1163/9789004420052_008

128   CHAPTER 5

1.1.1   Rajanaiken of Tanjore (1700–1771)[1]
Rajanaiken was an officer in the kingdom of Tanjore who had received some
form of education, possibly through Catholic missionaries. As a person with
great thirst for matters relating to religion, he longed to read the Bible, which,
however, was not available in Tamil then. Meanwhile the Raja of Tanjore asked
Rajanaiken to go to Tranquebar to protect the crops in the region. During this
visit Rajanaiken got the opportunity to meet the Protestant missionaries of the
Tranquebar mission.

In 1706, the first Protestant missionaries Bärtholomeus Ziegenbalg (1682–
1719) and Henrich Plütschau (1676–1747) had arrived in the sub-continent, and
by 1714 Ziegenbalg had translated the New Testament. Since Rajanaiken was
interested in reading the Bible he bought a copy from the missionaries and
began studying it. He was particularly impressed by the story of the Roman
Centurion Cornelius (Acts 10). The translation for centurion in Zieganbalg's
New Testament was *"sevaikaran,"* the equivalent of Rajanaiken's position in
the army. Inspired by this comparison, Rajanaiken decided to serve Christ and
joined the Lutheran church in 1718.

In 1727, he negotiated with the king of Tanjore and invited Aaron (1698–
1745) who was then a catechist (but was later ordained as the first Indian
priest) to preach and establish a congregation in the town. This establishment
of a church in Tanjore is significant given that the Raja of Tanjore was earlier not favorable to the Christian missionaries entering his kingdom. By this
time, Rajanaiken had resigned his position in the army and become a full-time
evangelist. The Halle mission was so impressed with Rajanaiken's work that
they wanted to ordain him as a priest. However, at this point, the issue of Rajanaiken being a Paraiyar came to the fore, and the Indian Christians would not
approve a 'pariah' to be their priest. On these caste dynamics in the Protestant
church during this early period, Daniel Jeyaraj writes,

> When the question of ordination was discussed, the names of Savari-
> muthu, Rayanayakkan, and Aaron were suggested. Savaraimuthu and
> Rayanayakkan were Pariahs by birth and the stigma of their status as

---

1   Also known as Rayanayakkan. This section is compiled from Daniel Jeyaraj, "Indian Par-
    ticipation in Enabling, Sustaining, and Promoting Christian Mission in India," in *India
    and the Indianness of Christianity: Essays on Understanding —Historical, Theological, and
    Bibliographical—in Honor of Robert Eric Frykenberg*, ed. Richard Fox Young (Grand Rapids
    and Cambridge: William B. Eerdmans, 2009), 26–40, & James Massey, "History and Dalit The-
    ology," in *Frontiers of Dalit Theology* V. Devasahayam (Madras: Gurukul, 1996), 161–163.

DALIT CHRISTIANITY AND THEOLOGY

outside the caste system influenced the decision-makers... to choose Aaron, who was a Pillai, belonging to the Vellalar-Shudra community.[2]

Meanwhile, Rajanaiken and his family faced persecution from the Roman Catholics who were upset with his success in evangelism, and he even lost his father in one such attack. By the time he died in 1772, after 44 years of service as an evangelist and catechist, the foundations of Christian mission in the Tanjore region were well established. In conclusion, I believe it is pertinent to note that in spite of his pioneering role in establishing protestant Christianity in India, Rajanaiken, who could have become the first Indian Christian priest, has been long forgotten because of his outcaste status. As Massey notes, he is one of the "ignored and forgotten heroes of Indian Christianity."[3]

1.1.2   Maharasan Vedamanickam of Travancore (1772–1827)[4]
Tranvancore, a former kingdom in the southwest coast of India, now in the states of Tamilnadu and Kerala, is considered to be one of the few places in India where Christianity is as strong as Hinduism (if not more). Here, the foundations of protestant Christianity were laid by Maharasan Vedamanickam, a Dalit of the Sambhavar community (a sub-caste of the Paraiyars). Maharasan, whose ancestors were mostly agriculturalists from Tanjore, was born in the village of Mylaudy near Kanya Kumari. Even though his family worshipped Elanamanyan, a local deity, Maharasan later became a staunch devotee of the son of Lord Shiva, Subramanium (also called Murugan) who had married a low-caste gypsy woman, and built a shrine for the deity. However, his spiritual thirst to know and experience the divine more fully was unquenchable, and he was advised by a friend to visit Chidambaram, one of the sacred Saivite centers in South India. It is claimed that Maharasan set off to Chidambaram desiring to 'seek' *Brahman*, the Ultimate Reality according to the *Vedanta* traditions of Hinduism. It is not clear if Maharasan was a *Vedantin* i.e. one who was well-versed with the Vedas and believed that Brahman is the Ultimate Reality. But nonetheless, we may accept that he was seeking for a closer and fuller union with the divine.

However, when he actually reached Chidambaram in 1799, Maharasan was greatly disappointed with—what seemed to him—the lack of morality of the

---

2   Jeyaraj, "Indian Participation," 34.
3   Massey, "History and Dalit Theology," 178. After Rajanaiken's death, his wife was appointed to take his place as a catechist, probably the first woman leader in Indian protestant history.
4   This section is summarized from D. Monikaraj, "Biographical Musings I–Vethamanickam," in *Frontiers of Dalit Theology*, 207–230.

place. As he was resting in the temple frustrated, he had a vision of an eminent looking white man dressed in white who asked him to leave the place immediately. Confused by this vision, Maharasan left Chidambaram, and on his way back to Mylaudy stopped in Tanjore to visit his sister. It was here that he first heard the Christian gospel and was introduced to the Lutheran Missionary John Caspar Kohlhoff who baptized Maharasan as Maharasan Vedamanickam. Vedamanickam left Tanjore and went to Mylaudy where he started to preach the Christian message among his people. Soon there were about thirty converts—all of them Dalits—who formed the nucleus of the Christian community in that region.

Vedamanickam was joined by the Church Mission Society (CMS) Missionary Ringeltaube in 1806 who was sent to build on the Indian evangelist's work. After meeting Vedamanickam, Ringeltaube, in his letter to the CMS, noted that Vedamanickam had already prepared nearly 800 people for baptism. Soon a church was built and dedicated in 1809 on a piece of land that was donated by Vedamanickam. Vedamanickam was ordained in 1816 and made the leader of the Travancore Protestant mission. His work as the pioneer and leader of Protestant Christianity received laurels from many, including Bishop Thomas Middleton, the first Anglican Bishop of India. When Vedamanickam died in 1827, the CMS mission was already well established in the Travancore region. Thus, the foundations of the Protestant church in what is now a thriving center of Christianity was laid by a Dalit. It is interesting that at this stage of its history, the Travancore church seems to have been quite an inclusive community drawing members from all castes, led by the Dalits. However, as Monikaraj notes, this inclusive church became a castiest church when Ringeltaube's successors began focusing more on the Nadars (a lower caste Sudra community), eventually silencing and ignoring the Dalit contributions to Christianity in Travancore.[5]

Though I have not engaged in a systematic study of the early Protestant Dalit converts and their mission, nonetheless, the objective is apparent: to show that Dalit Christianity—particularly Paraiyar Christianity—is older than it is assumed to be; and to problematize the general silence about pioneers like Rajanaiken and Vedamanickam in Indian Christian history.[6] And, even if Rajanaiken or Vethamanickam do not seem to have led or inspired Dalits to challenge caste oppression (as far as we know), yet, in a book that foregrounds

---

5 Ibid., 230.
6 I certainly hope and would highly recommend that someone would take-up such research more seriously.

DALIT CHRISTIANITY AND THEOLOGY   131

silenced voices and Dalit agency and assertion, I do not think that studying about these Dalit Christian pioneers is in any way irrelevant.

1.2   *Mass Movements*

As witnessed above, Christianity in South India made its presence among and through the Dalits much earlier than it is often thought. Nevertheless, it was during the late 19th century that Dalit Christianity spread visibly and influentially. Known as "mass movements,"[7] these conversions changed the face of Indian Christianity, making it predominantly Dalit in composition.[8] In what is considered to be a standard definition of mass movements, Waskom Pickett notes,

> The distinguishing features of Christian mass movements are a group decision favorable to Christianity and the consequent preservation of the converts' social integration. Whenever a group, larger than the family, accustomed to exercise a measure of control over the social and religious life of the individuals that compose it, accepts the Christian religion (or a large proportion accept it with the encouragement of the group), the essential principle of the mass movements is manifest.[9]

Therefore, we can say that in mass movements, the two main components are the "group decision" to join Christianity and, the "group control" exerted by the local Dalit church leaders on the group to adhere to the Christian principles and the community's decision.

But, it is interesting to note that initially the missionaries did not pay much attention to the Dalits, Paraiyars in this case, nor were they interested in converting or helping them. One of the most popular approaches of the missionaries for the most part of the nineteenth century was the 'downward percolation' policy of evangelism that "targeted the high castes for conversion on the assumption that Christianity would then filter down through them to the far more numerous lower castes."[10] However, as Webster is quick

---

7   In this project, though mass movements also happened among other communities like the Chuhras, Chamars, Malas and Madigas, I intend to limit my focus to the Paraiyars. Webster, *Dalit Christians,* 40–41.

8   Though it is difficult to know the exact numbers, it is estimated that over 60% of Christians in India are Dalits. See, R. R. Patil & James Dabhi, "Introduction," in *Dalit Christians in India,* ed. R. R. Patil & James Dabhi (New Delhi: Manak Publications, 2010), 3–4.

9   Quoted by Webster, n. 2. Webster, *Dalit Christians,* 33–34.

10   Webster, *Dalit Christians,* 36.

132 CHAPTER 5

to note, this was more an exception than the rule and the Protestant missionary work was not "caste-specific."[11] Yet, more often than not, the missionaries remained skeptical about conversions among Dalits and were even reluctant to treat them as *conversions*. Speaking of the Paraiyars, G.E. Philips writes,

> When a missionary book or periodical tells of the admission of (perhaps) four hundred persons into the Christian church in a single district, that does not mean that there have been four hundred 'conversions' in the technical religious sense of that term.[12]

In other words, the missionaries were not willing to place Dalit conversions on the same plane as the conversions of other (upper-)caste communities.

Further, the missionaries were not too eager about offering help to the poor and oppressed Paraiyars either. Rather, the missionaries were worried that their 'acts of goodness' would be misused by Dalits. As Viswanath writes,

> Missionaries were fastidious examiners of their own motives and viewed the motives of would-be Pariah converts with extreme suspicion, anxious that impoverished adherents might be accepting Christ for merely "temporal" reasons as opposed to "spiritual" reasons'—for "loaves and fishes," as it were. In addition to the demands of their own faith and conscience, there was also the possibility that they may find themselves accused by their ever-watchful colleagues of sacrificing principle in pursuit of the worldly success and renown that came with a large flock.[13]

Moreover, as Webster notes, "[M]issionaries were reluctant to baptize in time of famine, and even in good times, lacked the kinds of resources necessary to alleviate the poverty of those Dalits who approached them."[14] Hence, we can say that that the missionaries were neither enthusiastic about converting Dalits nor about providing them the (much needed) material aid that the Dalits may have wanted.

Similarly, educational opportunities offered by the missionaries to the Dalits were also 'well-calculated' on the part of the former. Writing about the

---

11   Ibid.

12   Quoted by Viswanath. Viswanath chooses to specify these 'conversions' as "Pariah-missionary alliance." Rupa Viswanath, *The Pariah Problem: Caste, Religion, and the Social in Modern India* (New York: Columbia University Press, 2014),, 72.

13   Ibid., 59.

14   Webster, *Dalit Christians,* 58.

DALIT CHRISTIANITY AND THEOLOGY

education of Paraiyars of Chengalpet and Madras area, Dayanandan notes how, while the missionaries were usually generous about providing elementary level education, they were also extremely cautious about opening institutions of higher education for/among the Dalits. On the other hand, missionary educational institutions—especially those that offered English education—preferred the upper castes on the basis of the earlier mentioned "downward filtration" theory.[15] Also, the missionaries—but for a few exceptions—wanted to be on the good books of the upper-castes whose help they needed to do their work in India.[16] In other words, education was not simply 'given' to the Dalits, but, if anything, was made easily and 'preferentially' accessible to the caste Christians and Hindus by the missionaries, who "were flocking to their institutions," with the awareness that "English education 'would soon become the main avenue to social distinction, to wealth, and power.' "[17]

But, this missionary reluctance to convert, help, or educate the Dalits was more than about pleasing the upper castes. At least in the case of the Paraiyars, it was also based on contempt and condescension. For example, take a look at how Albert Clayton, a Methodist missionary, describes them in one of his letters back to England.

> In this letter, I will try to tell you something about this poor degraded man's enemies ... *Chief among the Pariah's enemies is himself.* On the one hand he is most easily imposed on, and on the other he often tries to gain some end with a sort of low cunning which is deplorably foolish. In many villages, the caste-people, the *respectable* people, knowing this take all sorts of advantage of the Pariah.[18]

Thus, the Paraiyars were considered to be inherently cunning and foolish. Based on this perception, the primary objective of education, if and when it was provided to the Paraiyars, was to 'civilize' them. However, education to civilize did not mean empowerment or emancipation. Rather, the purpose of a missionary taught (western) education was to make them 'obedient' and 'disciplined' serfs and servants. The missionaries were keen that the education of the Paraiyars "... should never be such as to make" them "*unfit* for life in the

---

15   Dayanandan, "Dalit Christians of Chengalpet Area," 34.
16   Adam Andrew will be a good example of someone who helped the Dalits. Ibid., 43–44.
17   Dayanandan citing William Miller, the most popular of Principal of the Madras Christian College, Madras. Ibid., 28.
18   Quoted by Viswanath. Viswanath, *The Pariah Problem*, 66.

134   CHAPTER 5

village" but should be focused on making them—in the words of the Methodist missionary William Goudie—"good servants" of the caste people.[19]

However, the reasons for Missionaries' disdainful stance toward Dalits and respect toward the upper castes was even deeper and more vicious. In her study of missionary views about the Paraiyars, Viswanath notes that missionaries in general considered caste to be a religious problem, rather than a political or social evil. This meant that they believed that the civil nature of the caste system was actually good, and *must be retained*. In other words, they believed that while the religious component of the caste system viz. its rootedness in Hinduism, had to be *eliminated*, it was important that the social ordering that caste embodied be *maintained* for the well-being of society. Thus, as Viswanath observes, the missionaries initiated and facilitated,

> ... a complex *translational* project, a project in which Hindu caste prerogatives and practices were reconceived, reformed, and ultimately reconciled with European notions of class and status. Caste was to be shorn of its heathenish trappings and allowed to flourish among newly converted Indian Christians in its "pure" class form.[20]

In other words, the missionaries wanted a more civil(ized) and 'reason-able' manifestation of the caste system.

> The problem, therefore, was not with hierarchical social divisions per se, which existed "throughout the world," but first, that caste was based on a false religion, and second, that individuals were not permitted to change their caste.[21]

Therefore, we may say that the missionary agenda—at least predominantly—was not to annihilate caste but to modify and turn it into a 'civil(ized) class' system. Hence, Viswanath is correct in contesting the general (mis)conception that the missionaries "promoted egalitarianism and incited Dalits to rebel against high-caste dominance," when she notes that,

> Pariahs antagonized their "superiors" not because of, but in spite of, missionaries. To the extent that Pariah Christians can be said to have remade

---

19   Ibid., 66–67. Emphasis mine.
20   Ibid., 52.
21   Ibid., 53.

DALIT CHRISTIANITY AND THEOLOGY   135

aspects of their social condition, it cannot be missionaries to whom those gains are credited.[22]

It is in this sense that we can assert that the mass movements can be seen as perfect examples—not of missionary benevolence but—of Dalit agency and assertion. Webster, in his analysis of the different stages of the mass movements and why they happened in some places and not in others, notes that

> ... it is necessary to begin an analysis of Dalit mass movements not with circumstances of social forces, but with people and specifically with leaders. Periah, Ditt, Venkayya and Alagan were leaders not just because they were the first to convert, but because they were also determined to lead the rest of their people to convert also. They were men who by virtue of their work or family connections had been exposed to the wider world beyond their villages and were open to new orientations and new lifestyles. ... Where such local leaders existed and accepted the Christian message, a mass movement could follow; where they did not or where their concerns lay elsewhere, then it could not. This is what gave the Dalit mass movements that arbitrary character which missionary contemporaries found so baffling.[23]

Clearly, then, it was the people and the leaders of the Dalit communities across India who, in spite of the reluctance of the missionaries to accept them, took the initiative in the mass movements to embrace Christianity. This acknowledgment is important if we consider the ever-present accusation that Christian Dalits are "Rice Christians,"[24] with—to use the words of Gandhi—the intellectual capacity of a cow[25] who can be easily lured by material benefits such as food, education and medical assistance.[26] On the contrary, what we are able to see is that the conversions of Dalits in mass movements were neither uncritical nor forced but were a conscious and deliberate expression of Dalit agency. Therefore, Dalits embracing Christianity (and Buddhism or Islam) is a witness to the ability of Dalits to act as subjects who can choose their future path and

---

22   Ibid., 57.
23   Webster, *Dalit Christians,* 56. Periah, Ditt, Venkayya and Alagan were leaders of the Christian mass movements among the Madigas, Chuhras, Malas and the Paraiyars respectively. Ibid., 41–52 & 56.
24   Webster, *Dalit Christians,* 58.
25   Ibid., 115.
26   Viswanath, *The Pariah Problem,* 74, 82–84.

136   CHAPTER 5

destiny. Moreover, what can also be learnt from the mass movements is that these intentional choices made by Dalits were not simply based on material reasons. We saw that this is another allegation made about Dalit conversions, even by missionaries, namely that they were not spiritual or religious enough. However, historians have pointed out that "[T]heir motivation was primarily religious in that accepting the truth of the Christian message was central to their decision."[27] Dayanandan succinctly captures the primacy of the spiritual aspect in Dalit mass conversions:

> They saw in Christ a God who cared for them; a good and innocent man tortured and killed. They heard that Christ was against all forms of oppression and stood by the poor. They were equally fascinated with the Old Testament characters, and while converting were proud to adopt names such as Abraham, Moses, David and Ruth. ... Even though the first converts could not read, it was extraordinarily gratifying for them to see that their children and grandchildren could read. They were no more without a book; they were now people of a book, a sacred book.[28]

Hence, the condescending view that there was no theological conviction among Dalits or that they were simply driven by materialistic motives is wrong and has to be challenged.[29] Beginning from Rajanaiken and Maharasan Vethamanickam to the mass movements, Dalit conversions were profoundly spiritual and conscious decisions in every sense of the word. I believe that this brief consideration of mass movements in relation to the criticisms posed against them becomes clearer and pertinent when we notice that some of these views

---

27   Webster, *Dalit Christians*, 56.

28   Dayanandan, "Dalit Christians of Chengalpet area," 45.

29   However, on the subject of the intentions of Dalit converts, Viswanath perceptively warns us that making motive "as the most relevant criterion for the evaluation of action" is itself problematic and limiting, given that the same standard is not/never used for conversions among other peoples. Viswanath, *The Pariah Problem*, 88. I agree with this argument since the problem of "motive" is never asked or raised, say in the conversion of a "white Christian male" to Hinduism or Buddhism. It is pertinent to note that the uproar about the materialistic interests of mass movements (which is also true of Dalit conversions today) was further triggered because of the political bearing that these conversions had. In his study of the political implications of the mass movements, Webster observes that they triggered off a "politics of numbers" in the sub-continent, since with the 1909 communal act which divided electorates based on religion and created proportionate representation in the government, the conversions and the numbers of Dalits became a crucial political decider. Webster, *Dalit Christians,* 73–74, 77.

DALIT CHRISTIANITY AND THEOLOGY

continue to influence and affect Dalit Christian conversions and religious affiliations even today, to which I turn next.

1.3 *Dalit Christianity Today*

Among several issues related to Dalit Christianity today, there are two that are important (and also interrelated) that need mentioning. The first challenge that Dalit Christians face is the constitutional rule that denies Dalits who have embraced Christianity (and Islam) affirmative action (popularly known as 'Reservations').

In 1932, the British colonial administration chose to use the term 'Scheduled Castes'[30] to denote untouchable communities (or depressed classes as they were called until then) on the basis of religion. Although the objective was to provide compensatory representation to deprived communities in education, employment and politics, the definition of scheduled castes did not include Christians.[31] And when the Indian constitution was drafted after the Independence, the same definition was adopted and the President of India was empowered "to specify the castes, races or tribes or parts of or groups within castes, races or tribes which shall ... be deemed to be Scheduled Castes."[32] Accordingly, in 1950 the President of India issued a Constitutional Order (known as the 1950 Presidential order), that "no person who professed a religion different from Hindu shall be deemed to be a member of a Scheduled Caste (*sic*)."[33] This communally biased order was based on the supposition that caste was not applicable to other religious communities, despite the petitions offered by non-Hindu religious representatives. Though, the presidential order was later amended in 1956 to include Sikhs and again in 1990 to include Dalit Buddhists,[34] after seventy years of independence, the pleas of Dalit Christians and Dalit Muslims have not been considered for reservations.

The other major issue—closely related to the former—that continues to affect Dalit Christians is the conversion of Dalits to Christianity. Because of the gravity of the issue, let me describe it in detail. However, in order to understand

---

30 The Government of India Act of 1935 defines Scheduled Castes as "such castes, races or tribes or parts or groups within castes, races, tribes, parts or groups that appear to the Governor-General to correspond to the classes of persons formerly known as the Depressed Classes..." Quoted by James Massey, "An Analysis of Dalit Christian Issue with Special reference to 1950 Presidential order," in *Dalit Christians in India*, 83–85.

31 Webster, *Dalit Christians*, 116–117.

32 Article 341 (1) of the constitution. Quoted by Massey. Massey, "An Analysis of Dalit Christian Issue," 85.

33 Quoted by Massey. Ibid., 86.

34 Ibid.

138 CHAPTER 5

the underlying dynamics of the politics of Dalit conversions it is necessary to familiarize ourselves with the fundamentalist ideology of Hindutva. According to Vinayak Damodar Savarkar (1883–1966), one of its most important proponents and who wrote an influential book on the topic,[35] Hindutva is an autochthonous notion of Hinduism as the common religion and culture of one people bound together within one geographic space. In that sense, Hindutva is the "Hinduness ..., the inheritance of the Hindu blood" that runs in every Indian irrespective of her caste or religion.[36] Thus, as Ankur Barua notes, "[I]n this territorial and racialized conception of *Hindutva*, the three essential elements are a common nation (*rāṣṭra*), a common race (*jāti*) and a common civilization (*saṃskṛti*) ... "[37] Further, according to this monolithic Hindu worldview, those who have changed their religion, like the Muslims and Christians, have to recant and be reverted back to their proper home, viz. Hinduism. Savarkar wrote,

> ... in the case of some of our Mohammedan or Christian countrymen who had originally been forcibly converted to a non-Hindu religion ... are not and cannot be recognized as Hindus. For although Hindusthan to them is Fatherland as to any Hindu yet it is not to them a Holyland too ... Their love is divided ... Ye, who by race, by blood, by culture, by nationality possess almost all the essentials of Hindutva and had been forcibly snatched out of our ancestral home by the hands of violence—ye, have only to render wholehearted love to our common Mother and recognize her not only as Fatherland (*Pitribhu*) but even as a Holyland (*Punyabhu*); and ye would be most welcome to the Hindu fold.[38]

But not all Hindutva propagandists would welcome the 'religious other' back to their 'original home.' For Gowalker (1906–1973), a follower of Savarkar, those who are not Hindus have to be treated, not as transgressors who can return back home, but as foreigners who have to banished from the 'home-land.'[39]

These foundational beliefs of Hindutva continue to play a significant role in India even in the twenty first century, especially under the reign of the

---

35 Vinayak Damodar Savarkar, *Hindutva: Who is a Hindu?* (New Delhi: Hindi Sahitya Sadan, 2005).

36 Vinayak Damodar Savarkar, "Hindutva: Who is a Hindu?" in *Hindu Nationalism: A Reader*, ed. Christophe Jaffrelot (Princeton & Oxford: Princeton University Press, 2007), 94.

37 Ankur barua, *Debating 'Conversion' in Hinduism and Christianity* (London and New York: Routledge, 2015), 179.

38 Savarkar, "Hindutva," 95–96.

39 "M. S. Gowalker" in *Hindu Nationalism,* 98.

DALIT CHRISTIANITY AND THEOLOGY

Bharatiya Janata Party, the political wing of the family of Hindu fundamentalist organizations (known as the *Sangh Parivar*). We can say that there are three ways in which Dalit conversions are opposed and thwarted by Hindutva ideologies. First, there are the usual outbursts of violence against those who convert to Christianity (or Islam) and those who propagate the Christian message. Christians, especially Dalit Christians, are often threatened, assaulted, and in some cases even killed for ditching their 'home tradition' for a foreign religion. It should be remembered that often both the agents and recipients of violence are Dalits, only that the former have come under the influence of Hindu fundamentalism. Secondly, conversions are contained through legal measures. Though India is a secular state with freedom to practice and propagate religion, some Indian states have passed ordinances against what is called as, 'forced conversions.'[40] Even if only 'forced' conversions are punishable, in reality such laws have been (mis)used to control the agency and the religious freedom of the vulnerable sections, particularly Dalits and Adivasis (tribal communities). Finally, anti-conversion tactics are also realized through acts of assimilation by claiming and wooing back those who have left the Hindu fold. This scheme goes back to the pre-independence period when the likes of Dayanand Saraswathi (1824–1883), the founder of the Arya Samaj (a Hindu reform movement), preached the need for 're-converting,' particularly the lower-castes and Dalits.[41] In recent years, this reconversion scheme re-presented itself as *ghar wapsi* (homecoming) ceremonies in which Dalits and Tribals were brought 'home' to Hinduism through purification rituals.[42]

While considering these challenges to Dalit conversions, we also need to ask why such opposition arises in the first place. Broadly speaking, I believe we can identify two reasons. First, there is the politics of numbers that continues to be a concern for Hindu nationalists. It is true that India doesn't follow the practice of communal electorates anymore, and therefore, there is apparently no reason to believe that the numerical strength of Hindus will be an issue today. Nevertheless, as Barua notes,

---

40   For instance, the state government of Tamilnadu passed 'The Tamilnadu Prevention of Forcible Conversion of Religion Bill' in 2002 by which anyone accused of converting through "force, allurement or fraudulent means" could be imprisoned. Though this ordinance was withdrawn on the eve of the Parliamentary elections in 2004, similar laws are still effective in Orissa, Madhya Pradesh, Arunachal Pradesh, Gujarat, Chattisgarh, and Himachal Pradesh. See, Barua, *Debating 'Conversion,'* 182.

41   "Introduction," in *Hindu Nationalism,* 10.

42   See http://indianexpress.com/about/ghar-wapsi/. Accessed on September 21, 2018.

140 CHAPTER 5

the voting pattern of large numbers of Scheduled Caste Hindus who have often moved away from nationalist parties which are perceived to be subject to upper-caste control, the general difficulties in consolidating Hindu unity across denominational, regional and linguistic divide, and other such factors have often led Hindu nationalists to project themselves as threatened minority.[43]

In other words, for Hindu nationalists, Dalits are always the much-watched group because of their unreliability. No wonder their conversion is a matter of concern. Secondly, the rhetoric against conversions also betrays the frustration about Dalit self-assertive subjectivity. We need to remember that for Hindutva ideology caste is an indispensable social structure that needs to be prioritized and centralized, which is often done by trying to redeem it as a necessary and a non-hierarchical social order. Further, it is also believed (as seen earlier)—not just by Hindu fundamentalists but also those with a pluralistic outlook like Gandhi—that Dalits are incapable of exercising agency and making decisions for themselves. By noting that the "motivation for murder" of Dalits and other such vulnerable groups is closely related to the *"murder of motivation,"* Peniel Rajkumar explains that

> The motivation that is sought to be 'murdered' is the motivation of the subaltern communities to assert their identity and renegotiate their status using the avenues of religious independence, education and economic independence.[44]

This murder of the self-assertive initiatives of the Dalits is even more understandable and discernable if we are aware that, "[R]eligious conversions ... can be interpreted to be one strategy whereby Dalits seek to pursue and secure release from the ... world vision of caste communities."[45] Therefore, we can conclude that it is because conversions to Christianity or any religious tradition are deliberate acts of reclaiming their agency and human dignity that conversions are a contentious issue for the Dalits.

---

43 Barua, *Debating 'Conversion,'* 199.

44 Peniel Jesudason Rufus Rajkumar, "Hunting Using Hoax: Dalits, Caste and the Conversion Debate in India," in *Mission At and From the Margins: Patterns, Protagonists and Perspectives,* ed. Peniel Jesudason Rufus Rajkumar, Joseph Prabhakar Dayam and I. P. Asheervadham (Eugene, Oregon: Wipf & Stock Publishers, 2014), 250–251. Emphasis mine.

45 Clarke as quoted by Rajkumar. Ibid., 255.

DALIT CHRISTIANITY AND THEOLOGY   141

So far I have given a glimpse of Dalit Christianity, attempting to portray the early Dalit roots of Indian Protestant Christianity, and its 'Dalitization' during the Mass Movements. Then, I looked at the discrimination meted out to Dalit Christians through the denial of compensatory aid and freedom to convert to and practice Christianity. Even from such a brief survey, I believe we can agree that, from the beginning, Dalit protestant Christianity was deeply influenced by socio-political issues, and despite its colonial connections, Christianity has played a crucial role in the struggle for Dalit emancipation. In the next section, I seek to investigate how the experiences of Dalits serves as a critical tool for doing Christian theology.

2   Dalit 'God-Talk'

Theology is basically God-talk. In other words, whatever theology is and does, one cannot deny that it concerns God. However, K. Wilson cautions us that the question of God differs for different contexts and communities. For example, in the case of Dalits, "the problem ...is not and has never been that of God" for "[t]hey reposed as much faith in God as any other community," but rather "[t]heir basic problem is the knowledge of their own self."[46] In that sense, the (Christian) Dalit quest(ion) of God is not necessarily about trying to 'know' (about) God but rather about exploring and deepening the self-knowledge of the community. Keeping this in mind, in this section, I want to present the various theological expressions about God, their problems, and the possible correctives suggested by Dalit theologians.

2.1   *The 'Broken' God*

For Arvind Nirmal, the pioneer of Dalit theology, (the Christian) God is a servant God. In his view, in contrast to the Hindu Gods like Rama who "is a killer God... and murderer of Dalits," as pointed out in the first chapter, Nirmal believes that

> ... the God whom Jesus Christ revealed and about whom the prophets of the Old Testament spoke is a Dalit God. He is a servant God—a God who serves. ... Servitude is innate in the God of the Dalits. Servitude is the *svadharma* of our God ...[47]

---

46   K. Wilson, "An Approach to Christian Dalit Theology," in *Towards a Dalit Theology*, ed. M. E. Prabhakar (Delhi: ISPCK, 1989), 50–51.

47   Nirmal, "Towards a Christian Dalit Theology," 64.

142   CHAPTER 5

Acknowledging that this conceptualization of God is an inference from the servant songs in Isaiah, Nirmal envisioned God as a "Servant-God... a truly Dalit Deity," who serves and suffers in this world like the Dalits, "full of *pathos.*"[48] Nowhere is this divine pathos more evident than in the incarnation, inspiring Nirmal to assert, "Jesus Christ... was himself a dalit..."[49] It is with this conviction that Nirmal goes on to re-visualize divine ontology by suggesting that "brokenness belongs to the very being of God."[50] By looking at the different phases in the life of Jesus—from his conception to his death—Nirmal traces, what may be called, the Dalit traits and experiences of Jesus. Moreover, as he points out, Jesus' "dalitness is best symbolized by the cross. On the cross, he was the broken, the crushed, the split, the torn, the driven asunder man—the dalit in the fullest possible meaning of that term."[51] Jesus becomes the forsaken one on the cross when he cries, "My God, my God, why have you forsaken me?" (Matthew 27: 46). Observing that "[T]hat feeling of being God-forsaken is at the heart of our dalit experiences and dalit consciousness in India," Nirmal concludes that "[I]t is the dalitness of the divinity and the humanity that the Cross of Jesus symbolises."[52]

Building on this, M.E. Prabhakar, a contemporary of Nirmal, points out that the forsakenness of Jesus is not the end of the story. Rather, because "even in Jesus' forsakenness God had not cast him off," the Dalits can be assured that in the "Dalitness of Jesus they will be strengthened and upheld for victory against the forces that dehumanise them."[53] He also notes that "[T]he cross and the resurrection are God's ways of protesting against the powers of the world and overcoming them," and therefore the Dalits "have to protest and their protest should be so loud that the walls of Brahmanism should come tumbling down."[54] Inspired by the Black theologian James Cone, Prabhakar goes on to suggest the imperativeness of resurrection for Dalit liberation. He writes,

> Our belief that God was in Jesus and defeated suffering will not be true unless Jesus rose again from the dead and is alive and present with us in our struggles for freedom. In the resurrection of Jesus we have received the vision of the divine future and the gift of a new humanity, without

---

48   Ibid., 64–65.
49   Ibid., 65. In that sense, we may say that Dalit theology is founded upon Dalit Christology.
50   Ibid., 70.
51   Ibid., 69.
52   Ibid., 69.
53   M. E. Prabhakar, "Christology in Dalit Perspective," in *Frontiers of Dalit Theology,* 414.
54   Ibid., 413.

DALIT CHRISTIANITY AND THEOLOGY 143

which we the oppressed (Dalits) cannot go forward, transcending and transforming the present, to move into the future, for the full realisation of our humanity, under God.[55]

In that sense, as Charles Singaram, a second generation Dalit theologian, has pointed out,

God is not simply identifying with the Dalits and passively enduring the rejection, sense of shame, the burden of the stigma of pollution and the sufferings. On the contrary, God is taking the side of the Dalits and educating them, enabling them to fight against the evil system. In this sense, God could be understood as a liberating educator and as an animator, who is always with the suffering community and leading them towards a new life, one filled with hope and a bright future.[56]

Thus, we may say that God is proactively involved in empowering the Dalits in their struggle against caste oppression. And the Dalits are particularly inspired and encouraged by the resurrection of Jesus the Christ by God to continue the struggle for liberation along with God. Prabhakar alludes to this when he writes,

Despite the victory of the cross and resurrection, the war against Satan (evil and suffering) will go on until the final victory is won by Christ, when he will come again (Second Coming). Until then Christians are called to be liberated servants of God in their present and the oppressed Dalits) "are called to fight against suffering by becoming *liberated sufferers* with God." (*sic*)[57]

While considering the centrality of suffering in Dalit theology, we should be aware that the redemptive value of Dalit pathos is another key concept that has to be given careful attention. As Peniel Rajkumar notes, Dalit theology with its strong rootedness in "[D]alit Christology," accentuates "the convergence of pathos experience of Jesus and the Dalits," thereby according a redemptive "messianic identity" to the Dalits.[58] Elucidating this important concept,

---

55   Ibid., 422–423.
56   Charles Singaram, *The Question of Method in Dalit Theology: In Search of a Systematic Approach to the Practice of an Indian Liberation Theology* (Delhi; ISPCK, 2008), 203.
57   Prabhakar, "Christology in Dalit Perspective," 423. Emphasis mine. The quoted text is from Cone.
58   Rajkumar, *Dalit Theology and Dalit Liberation*, 54.

144   CHAPTER 5

Prabhakar argues that because "[T]here is a tremendous thought that the untouchables (Dalits) suffer on behalf of the frail of the Indian community..., it becomes then a Dalit vocation for "redemptive suffering," to renew and liberate a new humanity out of the rigid oppressive caste society!"[59] Therefore, Dalit pathos not only facilitates their own liberative relationship with the God of Jesus Christ, the God of pathos, but also makes Dalits the *facilitators* of God's redemption for the oppressors.

Moreover, the Dalit theological imagination of God based on the primacy of pathos also stresses the *retributive justice* of God which suggests that God always 'sides' with the Dalits and 'fights' against their oppressors. Theopilus Appavoo, affectionately called 'Parattai,' in one of his songs refers to this vengeful attribute of God.

> *Aandavane nee enakku kotta, kallu kotta*
> *Akirama kaaranakku saatai mullu saatai*
> *Pazhivaangu saami, pazhivanghu saami,*
> *Ezha rathatha sindhura paavimela veesu un velichatha.*
> (My Lord, you are my rock fortress, but for the wicked one you are a thorny whip.
> Have your revenge on him who shed innocent blood, and cast your light upon him.)

To be fair to *Parattai,* his theology is not simply exclusivist that it shuts the door of grace or forgiveness on the non-Dalit oppressors. Rather, if anything, *Parattai's* theology is inclusive and reconciliatory in nature insofar as it finds practical expressions in rituals such as '*oru ulai.*[60] Nonetheless, the fact that there is a strong insistence on the retributive character of God because of Her solidarity with the oppressed has to be acknowledged. In sum, I believe that we can say that in Dalit theological imagination, God in Jesus the Christ is a co-sufferer with the Dalits, who is truly in solidarity with them, partaking in their Dalit experience(s), challenging, encouraging, supporting, and fighting with/for them to resist the oppressive structures that dehumanize them while offering redemptive messianic value to their suffering to liberate their oppressors.

---

59   Prabhakar, "Christology in Dalit Perspective," 423–424.

60   *Oru* (one) *ulai* (cooking) is an adaptation of the agape meal. It is a feast in which the whole community (inclusive of all castes) comes together to cook and share a simple meal in a common place. Sherinan, *Tamil Folk Music as Dalit Liberation Theology*, 133–140 & 144–145.

DALIT CHRISTIANITY AND THEOLOGY

2.2 *Problematizing Dalit God-Talk*

While undoubtedly these reflections have done invaluable service in foregrounding the experiences and the liberation of Dalits in Indian and global Christian theology, there are problems with these ways of imagining God that cannot be overlooked. Firstly, Rajkumar observes that the extremes of overemphasizing the "Victor-ization of God" in terms of God defeating the oppressors and the "Victim-ization of God" in terms of God's pathos have "not sponsored adequate impetus for transformation of the situation of the Dalits."[61] Taking up the task of interrogating these problems, Rajkumar reminds us that these imaginations of God are strongly influenced by the Exodus liberation paradigm encapsulated by the Deuteronomic Creed (Deuteronomy 26: 5–12) and the servant songs (which we saw earlier).

With respect to the Deuteronomic Creed, Rajkumar notes that "the 'Victorhood' of God which emerges from this paradigm is highly estranged in its conformity to Dalit experience,"[62] and in the words of Clarke, "... does not find a dominant place in Dalit thinking and acting."[63] Moreover, it has also been pointed out by Native American theologians that the Exodus paradigm is blind to the experiences of the Canaanites which are similar to that of the Native Americans and many other indigenous people across the world who were brutally exploited and massacred by colonialism.[64] Given the general notion that Dalits are claimed to be the *'adi'* people—ancient people who originally inhabited the subcontinent landmass[65]—Rajkumar warns that "the Deuteronomic paradigm would serve more the interests of the Aryan invaders" i.e. the ones who are presumed to have introduced the caste system, rather "than the Dalits."[66] Finally, this paradigm, Rajkumar suggests, also creates the problem of binarism (mentioned in the first chapter)[67] that oversimplifies oppression rather than discerning the complexities that constitute these structures. Such binarism of people groups as oppressors and the oppressed "has the potential to advocate replication of the strategies of the dominant without breaking the cycle of domination."[68]

---

61   Rajkumar, *Dalit Theology and Dalit Liberation*, 61.

62   Ibid., 62.

63   Cited by Rajkumar. Ibid., 63.

64   Ibid.

65   Massey, *Dalits in India*, 38–39.

66   Rajkumar, *Dalit Theology*, 64. Of course, the Aryan invasion theory has been challenged by Dalit theologians. See, Philip Vinod Peacock, "In the Beginning is also an End: Expounding and Exploring Theological Resourcefulness of Myths of Dalit Origins," in *Dalit Theology in the Twenty-First Century*, 75–84.

67   See the section on Dalit theology.

68   Rajkumar, *Dalit Theology*, 64.

146

CHAPTER 5

On the other hand, with the servant songs that have inspired the imagination of God as a servant and Dalit, Rajkumar notes that there are problems with respect to its practical efficacy in terms of helping Dalits to challenge and move out of their oppressive situation. On the contrary, it appears to run the risk of "romanticizing Dalit servanthood, which is both a product and continuing source of their oppression."[69] Therefore, Rajkumar argues that the "emancipatory potential" of the suffering people/God paradigm needs to be questioned, as should be the "masochistic resignation" that is often hidden within pathos Christologies.[70] In that sense, we can agree with Clarke that, "direct and uncomplicated theological application" of biblical images of the divine to the Dalit context is "restrictive, simplistic, and fragmentary."[71]

Along with the above mentioned shortcomings in Dalit theological imagination of God, we can also note the strong Jesus-centrism that overwhelmingly dominates Dalit God-talk. As Clarke notes, in Dalit theology the importance of Jesus is so over-emphasized that he has become "the theological eye of the needle through which all proverbial divine camels must pass."[72] While there is no doubt that any theological construction should be faithful to the '(hi)story' of Jesus of Nazareth and that his humanness and humaneness are certainly appropriate paradigms to comfort and inspire the Dalits, Clarke points out that there are limitations to the overemphasis on the person of Jesus and his *suffering* that cannot be ignored. He wonders,

> Can the assurance of co-suffering bring about a transformed reality where suffering can be overcome with the help of Jesus as the Christ? Must not the exalted and cosmic face of Jesus as Christ be exploited to actualize liberation from suffering for Dalits?[73]

Given these potentials of a 'Christo-centric (rather than a 'Jesus-centric') theology, Clarke observes that,

> [I]t is because of the cosmic dimensions of the Christ that suffering is not hopeless and final. This power is needed if Jesus Christ must be thought of as able, trustworthy, and relevant to aid suffering Dalits to move towards freedom and liberation.[74]

---

69   Ibid., 65.
70   Ibid.
71   Clarke, "Introductory and Interpretive Theological Exposition," 30.
72   Ibid., 31.
73   Ibid., 32–33.
74   Ibid., 32–33.

DALIT CHRISTIANITY AND THEOLOGY

In other words, Clarke reminds us that it is precisely the (universal) significance of the risen and glorified Christ that makes any liberation theology, including Dalit theology, liberative. To ignore this crucial dimension of Christology not only weakens Dalit theology, but worse still, could be implosive, in so far as it disassociates itself from the foundations of the Christian tradition and theology. Thus, Dalit imagination of God cannot be limited to Jesus but has to incorporate the 'Christ' dimension which is central and could be of significance for articulating Dalit emancipatory discourses.

Moreover, I also cannot help but wonder whether the Christian Dalit imagery/inations of God are too anthropomorphic. While there is no explicit mention of God as a person *per se*, I notice that there is a clear absence of a more complex construal or interpretation that transcends the 'object-ification' of God. In other words, I am afraid that the one who is apparently (and ultimately) portrayed as the Dalit God is 'a' God who 'hears' the cry of the oppressed, 'comes down' to be with them, 'comforts and fights' for them, and so on. While I agree that this 'personifying' imagination of God is very helpful from a liberation perspective, theologians cannot simply ignore the problems that are inherent in such conceptualizations of God. Without a critical re-visioning, the existing anthropomorphic imagination of God in Dalit theology is a slippery slope toward reifying the patronizing imperial imagery of a 'big bearded old (white) male God' sitting high up on a heavenly throne who comes down to help and save the Dalits.

2.3   New Trends in Dalit Theology: Re-Turning to the Body

Looking at these different conceptualizations of God in Dalit theology, their problems and directives related to them, I believe that there is an imperative need to ask whether there might be other ways of talking about God in Dalit theology. Keeping this question in mind, I want to acknowledge an important methodological turn in Dalit theology viz. the emphasis on the critical significance of the Dalit body. While, as in other liberation theologies, (Dalit) 'experience' has been the starting point of doing theology from a Dalit perspective, it is unfortunate that 'body' has not received enough attention in Dalit theological method.[75]

Although recently this subject is beginning to gain attention and voice, one cannot but wonder along with Dalit womanist theologians whether this

---

75   As mentioned in chapter one, Evangeline Anderson-Rajkumar is one of the very few theologians to speak of the Dalit body and Dalit women's body. See for instance, "Turning Bodies Inside Out: Contours of Womanist Theology," in *Dalit Theology in the Twenty-First Century*, 199–214.

neglect of body is rooted in the patriarchal and misogynist history of Christianity, especially since, like many other academic disciplines, Dalit theology is also dominated by men.[76] Or, given that the "'body' is generally hated and condemned in the Vedic traditions," and the broken "bodies of people, belonging to certain castes and sections are loathed even more,"[77] perhaps it was/is difficult for Dalit theologians to (re-)imagine the body as a theological source. Hence, I believe that Anthony Pinn's perceptive critique of black theology's (dis)engagement with the body is quite applicable to Dalit theology as well. Pinn notes that Black theology (in this case Dalit theology) is "... often a theology of *no-body*, a system of theological expression without an organized (re)presentation of *the body as body*."[78] Dalit Christian and theological history (presented in the earlier sections) has, in a sense, deliberately avoided any engagement with the Dalit body. This despite the fact that the struggles and violence experienced by the Dalits in the past and the present (as pointed out in chapter two) are deeply embodied.

Nevertheless, it is heartening to note that the methodological significance of the body is now being given more consideration in recent times. We may recall here the perceptive suggestion of Y. T. Vinayaraj that it is crucial to recover the Dalit body "as the pivotal point of reference" in doing theology.[79] Since Vinayaraj is one of the pioneering theologians to offer a systematic analysis of the relevance and significance of 'Dalit Body' theology, I believe it is necessary to listen to his insightful observations.

> Dalit theology emerges from the broken bodies of Dalits. Body as a theological method invites Dalits to have a fresh look at their bodies. Here, Dalits reject all the colonially imposed imprints/notions of their bodies. By affirming the new social meanings/imaginations of their bodies, Dalits reject the casteist traces inscribed onto their bodies and determinedly enter into new and unattached social relationships. This is the way to deconstruct and reconstruct the social body. Dalit habitus changes in accordance with this reflexive self-formation and a corresponding social formation.[80]

---

76 Ibid., 206.

77 Geevarghese Mor Coorilos, "Dalit Theology and its Future Course," in *Dalit Theology in the Twenty-First Century*, 172.

78 Anthony B. Pinn, *Embodiment and the New Shape of Black Theological Thought* (New York and London: New York University Press, 2010), 3. Emphasis mine.

79 Vinayaraj, "Envisioning a Postmodern Method," 100.

80 Ibid.

DALIT CHRISTIANITY AND THEOLOGY

Further, Vinayaraj notes,

> Dalit body as a theological method invites Dalits to review the historical construction of the social institutions that are built into certain discourses in certain historical contexts and to reconstruct them with new strategies and symbols. For transforming the existing social practices, it is imperative to develop an alternate sense of looking at themselves as active social agents in a somewhat open-ended society. Body as a hermeneutical key offers Dalits the experience of possibly new relations with other social groups at church, at home, and in the streets. Dalits acknowledge platforms such as church, civic organizations, democratic social movements, and political parties and hence, aspire for a dialogical and pluriform social existence in a dynamic future of subjectivities.[81]

That is, taking the body as a methodological key offers Dalits the possibility of, not only deconstructing the degrading attributes and objectifying performativities in the caste system, but also of re-visioning and re-creating new(er) subjectivities both for themselves and for the society at large.

It is clear—from even this brief glance—that focusing on the Dalit body offers rich methodological possibilities for doing Dalit theology. Therefore, as Geevarghese Mar Coorilos insists, I believe that there is no doubt that the future of Dalit theology must take the "[R]ecovery and retrieval of Dalit body politic" seriously.[82] Considering these new directions suggested by Dalit theologians pertaining to the Dalit body, in the next chapter, I turn to the study of visibly embodied divine experiences among Christian Dalits.

---

81 Ibid.

82 Mor Coorilos, "Dalit Theology," 172.

CHAPTER 6

Divine Possessions among Christian Dalits

I ended the previous chapter, by identifying and underscoring the significance of the body in Dalit theology. Taking the cue from these observations, in this chapter, I will engage in the study of 'embodied' divine possessions in Christian Dalit communities. My primary focus will be on what may be called, 'Holy Spirit possessions.'[1] By Holy Spirit possessions I mean the experience of Christian believers being filled or anointed or baptized with the Holy Spirit. During these moments, believers enter into a charismatic state of ecstasy which is often accompanied with, but not limited to, glossolalia (speaking in tongues) and prophecy.

However, even if this book is only concerned with the emancipatory potential of charismatic Holy Spirit possessions, I will also mention, albeit briefly, possessions related to Mary, the mother of Jesus, in the Catholic Church. And, apart from these possessions in which devotees normally enter into a trance-like state, I will also describe—again in brief—the possibility of considering sacraments as a way in which believers embody the divine. The final section will be, as in the case of Hindu divine possessions, a preliminary critical reflection to prepare the ground for comparison and constructive interpretations in the forthcoming chapters.

1 Holy Spirit Possessions

Before I move further, it may be appropriate to give some methodological clarifications about the make-up of this section. While considering Holy Spirit possessions, one of the basic things to remember is that, although such phenomena are generally identified with Pentecostal churches, it is not possible to limit them to one particular denomination or tradition. As Michael Bergunder points out, despite their distinctiveness, there are similarities between old

---

[1] This term was used by Lazar Matthew, a Dalit Pentecostal pastor in Chenganoor, Kerala, South India. Interviewed by V. V. Thomas. Because of its similarity, both in semantics and concept, to Hindu divine possessions, I have chosen to use it for my book. V. V. Thomas, *Dalit Pentecostalism: Spirituality of the Empowered Poor* (Bangalore: Asian Trading Corporation, 2008), 369. On theological justification for nomenclature, see the section on comparative category in chapter two.

DIVINE POSSESSIONS AMONG CHRISTIAN DALITS

fundamentalist Pentecostal churches (like The Pentecostal Mission) and independent Charismatic Churches in terms of giving importance to Holy Spirit ecstasy.[2] Furthermore, as we shall see, increasingly, mainline Protestant (and Roman Catholic) churches, are encouraging charismatic Holy Spirit worship. Because of the broad range of denominations considered in this chapter, for the sake of clarity, in general, I shall simply refer to all churches that involve Spirit-based ecstatic worship as 'charismatic churches.' In the following section, I will describe in stages, the various elements in a charismatic church service that are related to invoking and experiencing the Holy Spirit.

Secondly, it is also necessary to acknowledge that though my own research has been mainly limited to Dalit churches in rural areas, I also chose to include studies on urban slums. Even though there are significant differences between the Dalit situation in villages and cities, and in spite of the claims that caste does not exist in cities, as S. Anandhi points out, caste and caste based segregation does survive in urban centers in subtle and covert ways, and predominant constituents in the slums of North Tamilnadu—the broad region-of-focus in this book—are from the Paraiyar community.[3] It is based on this fact that I believe that it is necessary to look at Dalit charismatic worship both in the rural and urban areas. Finally, because of the limited resources that are available on Dalit charismatic Christianity, I have included studies on Dalit Pentecostalism in other parts of South India. Also, I chose to widen my geographical area of study to make it more representative. Therefore, while my research was primarily focused on churches in the outskirts of Chennai located within twenty five miles (approx.) of each other[4] viz. Full Gospel Church in Thannirkulam,[5]

---

2   Michael Bergunder, *The South Indian Pentecostal Movement in the Twentieth Century* (Grand Rapids, Michigan & Cambridge: William B. Eerdmans, 2008), 121. For more on the "family resemblance" and the differences between different Pentecostal churches see, Chad Bauman, *Pentecostals, Proselytization, and Anti-Christian Violence in Contemporary India* (Oxford & New York: Oxford University Press, 2015), 29–41.

3   S. Anandhi, *Contending Identities: Dalits and Secular Politics in Madras Slums* (New Delhi: Indian Social Institute, 1995), 30–31. More recently, Nathaniel Roberts, in his study of caste in Chennai slums, has also made a similar observation. Nathaniel Roberts, *To Be Cared For: The Power of Conversion and Foreignness of Belonging in an Indian Slum* (Oakland: University of California Press, 2016), 32.

4   I did try to visit the charismatic churches in Vichur and Periyapalayam, but because of my own status as an ordained minister of the C.S.I., I was 'pulled' to the denominational churches in both these places and was not able to go to these churches nor meet their pastors. While I did regret this move, as I shall point out later, it was a blessing in disguise as I was able to learn about an entirely different way of understanding divine embodiment.

5   This Church is part of a larger group of churches known as the Full Gospel church group, and is located in Thannirukulam, in the outskirts of Tiruvallur, a town about fifty miles from Chennai. According the pastor, the village is almost entirely populated by S.C.s (Dalits) along

C.S.I. Church in Vichur,[6] and E.C.I. Church Aranvayil,[7] I also draw upon my previous research conducted in villages near Pondicherry (mentioned earlier).

1.1   *Praise as Preparation*

In charismatic churches, the service usually begins with a 'Praise Time.' Praise time basically involves a lot of singing accompanied by vigorous clapping. In the Indian Full Gospel Church at Thannirkulam, the songs were sung with modern/western music (instruments) like key board and drums. Throughout the time there was continuous invitation and encouragement by Pastor Ambrose, to be joyful, enthusiastic, and present in the moment. The singing went on for about an hour. Although this is a distinctive feature of charismatic churches, I found the same pattern in rural mainline denominational churches employing charismatic worship. These churches also had a praise time, which was included within the actual service for about half an hour. It was evident that the congregation was clearly enjoying the praise time and even preferred it to the other liturgical portions of the service like the confession or the creed.

I can recall that this was also the case in the villages near Pondicherry (about 100 miles from Chennai) where I had conducted a study in 2010 (already mentioned in the previous chapters). During this research, I noticed that praise time involved a bass drum, and was undoubtedly the most engaging and enthusiastic part of the entire service. In fact, they insisted that we use the drum for worship.[8] There was considerable time given for singing upbeat songs with music and clapping led by a layperson. I also noticed that the level of participation in charismatic (village) congregations appeared to be inversely proportional to the literacy rate of the members. The congregants, most of whom did not have a formal education, showed greater involvement during praise time. In fact, I learnt that rather than using the Tamil 'Book of Common Prayer' of

---

with a few Vanniyars, who had settled down there to work in Tiruvallur. He himself had come nearly to Thannirkulam seventeen years ago, to establish a church there. According to him, he was one of the first Christian pastors to establish a church when the place was not safe or conducive for evangelism. But in the course of time the situation changed, and there are more churches in the village now.

6   The C.S.I. Church in Vichur is a small 'branch' church of Manali New Town Pastorate, meaning that the pastor stays in the town and (usually) visits the church once a month.

7   The E.C.I. Church in Aranvayil is part of the Evangelical Church in India, which is a mainline protestant denomination. Although, there are lot of similarities with other protestant churches like the C.S.I., the E.C.I. is more popular and prominent among the poor and the marginalized sections of the society.

8   Samuel, "Dalits and Conversions."

DIVINE POSSESSIONS AMONG CHRISTIAN DALITS

the Church of South India, the congregation preferred the praise time when they could sing or in some cases, just clap along with gusto.

The most defining aspect of this praise time is surely the music, particularly western music, which plays a key role in creating the right atmosphere and getting the people into the right 'mood.' As Chad Bauman, in his study of Indian Pentecostalism(s) writes, "Western influences are one element of Pentecostalism's appeal to the masses."[9] However, despite the enthusiastic singing and participation, it was clear that what was going on was only a preparation for something of greater importance, viz. to be 'filled' with the Holy Spirit; the time was not ripe for the outpouring of the Holy Spirit yet, it seemed. It was quite obvious that there was a specific time when the Holy Spirit would be invoked to fill the people in the congregation, and this wasn't it. Nonetheless, it is this praise time that prepares the believers for the much awaited and more important time of their worship.

1.2   *Receiving the Spirit*

The second phase of worship is the central and salient portion of the service. It is during this time that the believers receive and visibly experience the Holy Spirit in their bodies. In the Thannirkulam Church I noticed that the actual service began after the praise time with an opening prayer. After the prayer, Pastor Ambrose invited his congregation to join him in what he called "worship time"—differentiating it from the praise time—when there was again singing with music accompaniment. While this looked very similar to the previous session, the music and the singing now had something unique viz. ecstatic movements of the body and glossolalia (speaking in tongues).

Since this portion of the service is very important for this book, let me describe the scene a bit more in detail. As the singing began with a slow tempo, the members were constantly reminded to experience the presence of God moving in their midst. But, gradually the music and the singing reached a high tempo. The believers were already clapping, but at this point, they began jumping with a high level of exuberance. After this went on for some time, speaking in tongues i.e. glossolalia began. It was the pastor who first started to speak in tongues and was soon joined by other congregants. It seemed that while the pastor was in 'control' when he spoke in tongues i.e. stood in the same place, held the microphone firmly and spoke at an even tone and a loud-but-not-deafening volume, those in the congregation were euphorically jumping

---

9   Bauman, *Pentecostals, Proselytization, and Anti-Christian Violence in Contemporary India*, 86–87.

up and down—many of them on their knees—and praying and speaking at high decibels with excessive hyper-energetic body movements. The ecstatic jumping, vigorous clapping, praying, and speaking indicated that they were in a state of trance. Occasionally, the pastor also prophesied, at times in Tamil and other times as a translation of his glossolalia. On the other hand, the glossolalia of the congregants was not translated. While the entire congregation was engaged in this form of worship, the exhilarated and excited movements, praying, and glossolalia were more pronounced among women than men.

Let me make a few preliminary observations here. First, 'worship' time is basically a time of prayer. That is, it was evident that the pastor and the believers were anointed by the Holy Spirit only as they were speaking to God. Even though singing and music formed the background and played a key role, Holy Spirit possessions did not happen until they were consciously and corporately engaged in praying. Writing in an urban context, Roberts also confirms this when he notes that it is only as they were praying that the believers began to experience the power of the Spirit—"swaying, clapping, singing" eventually "creating a constant drone of incomprehensible chanting interspersed with ecstatic and often equally incomprehensible outbursts of glossolalia ..."[10]

Second, while prayer is the overall context and those in the congregation appeared to 'speak *to God*,' the pastor spoke both to God and to the people. As mentioned earlier, sometimes the pastor simply spoke in tongues, and at other times, he translated the glossolalia (i.e. what he spoke) to the people, and occasionally also prophesied directly in Tamil. In other words, the leader prayed as well as acted as a medium for the divine. Thus, there was a well ordered blending together of different activities—singing, clapping, praying, and speaking to the people—during the Holy Spirit possessions. While this was the case in the independent charismatic church, in the C.S.I. Church in Vichur, I observed that it was only the catechist i.e. lay leader who spoke in tongues. The pastor (who was present and did not speak in tongues) and the catechist told me later (with some regret) that although the believers also usually spoke in tongues, that particular Sunday, glossolalia was—for reasons unknown—absent.

Let me present a digressive but noteworthy anecdote here. In the E.C.I. Church in Aranvayil which I also visited, there was ecstatic and spirit-filled worship, but no glossolalia (including for the pastor). However, interestingly, in his sermon, the pastor said that learning to speak in English is glossolalia. When I asked him about this after the service, the pastor said that he learnt to speak in English the hard way, and therefore, according to him, English was the

---

10   Roberts, *To be Cared For,* 207.

DIVINE POSSESSIONS AMONG CHRISTIAN DALITS

real empowering glossolalia. While I do not think what the pastor said could be over-emphasized or generalized for all Holy Spirit possessions, nonetheless, I believe it does show that speaking in tongues in Dalit churches is also imagined and understood as speaking in a different language (like English).

Finally, I would add that the context of Holy Spirit possessions was disciplined, at least in two aspects. First, in all the churches that I visited, the pastor, who was the leader of the worship, had complete control over the entire congregation from the beginning to the end. The worshippers began when the pastor gave the word and ended when he asked them to. In other words, while the believers were allowed to

express their joy of the Spirit in their bodies as they wished, it was restricted to a particular time during the worship by the pastor. The second dimension of discipline was in terms of space. The ecstatic experiences of the believers were always within the church. At no time did the ecstatic anointed persons leave the church building. In fact, as I said earlier, given that all this happened within the overall context of prayer, almost all of them were on their knees.

1.3 *Interpreting Holy Spirit Possessions*

With these observations in mind, I want to look deeper at the phenomena of Holy Spirit possessions and ask what actually happens when a person is anointed/filled/possessed by the Holy Spirit. During my research, when I posed this question to the believers—both to those who were anointed by the Holy Spirit and those who witnessed it—and asked them to describe their experience of being filled by the Holy Spirit, I got a broad range of responses. Despite the several differences in the narratives, I was able to categorize them into three broad types.

The first set of responses that I received denoted the mysteriousness of the Holy Spirit possessions. When I asked my interviewees how they felt when they were filled by the Holy Spirit, one of the common answers was that it was *indescribable* and *unexplainable*. While these experiences might indeed be difficult to express in words, I realized that this response often came at the early stage of my interviews, and therefore it is possible that it is a classical problem encountered in ethnographic research, namely unfamiliarity and concerns about sharing information with the interviewer. Nonetheless, as a theologian, I regard the value of the mysteriousness of the experience as immensely valuable.

The second set of answers that I received regarding Holy Spirit possessions was more positive. For instance, Sudha whom I interviewed in Vichur said,

> When we are filled with the Holy Spirit there is a deep sense of joy and peace (*santhosham samadhanam*). It is a joy and peace that comes from

156 CHAPTER 6

> forgiveness of sins. The Lord has forgiven our sins. (*Aandavar engal paavangalai mannichittar*).

Thus, being filled with the Holy Spirit and experiencing ecstasy was joyful and peaceful, which comes out of God's mercy. But, the significance of this experience—of being filled with joy and peace in the Holy Spirit—is even more accentuated by the fact that it was often contrasted with divine possessions in Hinduism. When I asked Mercy, the wife of the village church Catechist in Vichur, what her thoughts were about the local goddess possessions, she was quite blunt when she said: "*Athu Sathan*" (That is Satan). Similar sentiments were expressed by Anitha, who had been a *saamiyadi* before. She recalled that she was always afraid and lived in depression, including being plagued by suicidal thoughts when she used to be possessed by the goddess. For her, the goddess was a *pey* (an evil spirit) and nothing more. But now Anitha was filled by the Holy Spirit and was no longer afraid. Her life was calm and blessed, and there was no turning back.

The final kind of responses regarding Holy Spirit possessions indicated that it was an empowering experience. As I sat with the pastor's wife in Thannirkulam waiting for the pastor to finish his after-church fellowships and meetings, I asked her what the Holy Spirit meant to her. Without hesitation, she remarked "*Parisuthavi vanthal odambil belan varum*" (When the Holy Spirit comes the body is strengthened/empowered). When I pressed her further why the Holy Spirit was so central to their worship, she declared that if the Holy Spirit didn't come, there would be no energy (*sakthi illa*). Later, when I discussed with the pastor about the Holy Spirit, he also described the experience in bodily terms using a personal anecdote.

> Yesterday I came back from a series of meetings feeling very tired and feverish. I was so tired that I even thought of asking someone else to preach. But then I changed my mind and decided that I should do it myself. Even this morning when I came to church I felt sick and my head was pounding. But when we entered into the time of worship, and as I was filled with the Holy Spirit and began to speak in tongues, I became strengthened in my body. I could experience deliverance then and there. I became strong... Holy Spirit is not a ritual—it is for freedom.

Thus, for the pastor, empowerment by the Holy Spirit can be understood and experienced primarily as strengthening and healing of the body. One could therefore say that experiencing the Holy Spirit is truly a bodily experience, an experience that energizes and revitalizes the body.

Finally, given the liberationist leanings of this work, I was (obviously) tempted to ask my interviewees whether Holy Spirit possessions had any emancipatory value, particularly in regard to caste injustice. When I posed this question to the interviewees, I noticed that almost none of them said that they were empowered by the Spirit to face or resist caste oppression. But neither did they directly say that the Holy Spirit did not help them. Rather, more often than not, a long-drawn answer was offered, of what Christianity had done for them, how their lives had become better after receiving Christ, how they had access to education, how they were better respected in their village now and so on. And, quite frequently, the conversation about Holy Spirit anointing would turn toward freedom from sickness, fear, depression, alcoholism, and the most popular of them all, evil spirits. Despite appearing unhelpful, I believe that the ambiguous and encoded answers of these Dalit Christians cannot be easily ignored. In fact, as I shall argue, it is precisely in and through these seemingly 'less-political' concerns and views that Dalits envision and enact their resistance to caste.

1.4   *After Holy Spirit Anointing, It Is Bible Time*

Finally, though my focus is on the Holy Spirit experiences, I believe it is important that I should mention another important element of charismatic worship. In the church at Thannirkulam, the Spirit-filled worship time was followed by 'memory verse time' during which children and youth came forward to recite memorized verses from the bible, with the girls and young women taking the lead. Then, came the sermon which went on for about an hour, again with extensive use of bible verses. Even during the communion, the pastor read more verses from the Bible, rather than offer a prayer of consecration. It was evident that, as significant as the rapturous Spirit-filled worship was, the Bible definitely played a crucial role in the service.

I believe that this importance given to the Christian Scripture is notable given that the bible has always played a key role in Dalit churches. Historically, in a context where (written) scriptures were out of reach of Dalits and used to discriminate against them and other Sudra communities, it is no surprise that the Dalits readily "accepted the Bible as their Book of Faith and Scripture" when it was offered to them.[11] The Bible, as Clarke notes, "fills a void" and "supplies the Subalterns with a frame of knowledge that they did not have to start with," even as it "challenges and supplants the Hindu vedas" on which caste is

---

11   Monica Melanchthon, "Dalits, Bible, and Method." https://www.sbl-site.org/publications/article.aspx?ArticleId=459. Accessed on January 16, 2018.

(supposed to be) based, providing "an alternate worldview" characterized by justice and equality.[12]

Given this reality, it is therefore not surprising that the Bible and the words of the Bible were spoken of as life-giving and life-sustaining resources both in the charismatic and non-charismatic churches. When I asked about embodied divine experiences in non-charismatic mainline churches in Pandur and Kannigaiper, the response was about the Bible rather than the Holy Spirit. In other words, God's presence, they said, is experienced and embodied through the words of the scriptures. And, in fact, even during the ecstatic worship time in charismatic churches when Holy Spirit possessions happen, the worship was barraged with Bible verses. That is, there was an integral connection between the Bible verses that were heard by the congregation, and the Holy Spirit experiences such as clapping, jumping, and speaking in tongues. Therefore, while the use of scripture is not the same as Holy Spirit possessions and cannot be seen as its alternative, I believe we can say that the scripture does play a pivotal role in the believers' embodied experiences of the divine.

Let me end this section by noting the two primary modes of Dalit engagement with the Bible. Firstly, Dalit use of the Bible involves emphasis on contextual interpretations and creative weaving of biblical stories. As Clarke observes, "there is a distinct mindset of generosity extant in the practice of retrieving universal axioms from the Bible, which is not devoid of imaginative contextual amplification in its application to human life."[13] Thus, Dalits enjoy a sense of freedom, perhaps unacceptable to a traditional ear, in 'spinning' stories and making meanings, joining even totally unrelated incidents or narratives but in a way that will make sense to and relate with their experience. Secondly, the Bible also takes on a symbolic value for the Dalits. I can explain this with an example. In many of my visits to villages I was often asked to pray for sick people by laying the Bible on the head of the sick person. Recalling a similar experience, Clarke suggests that the Bible becomes a "native talisman" for the Dalits with "its power to touch and to act."[14] In that sense, we may say that the Bible is not just a 'text' book, but a symbol in its own right that inspires and instills the power of God in the bodies of the believers. Thus, the Bible, for the Dalits, is both a text filled with a myriad of meanings and values that can be unearthed through imaginative and situational readings and a symbol that can

---

12   Sathianathan Clarke, "Viewing the Bible Through the Eyes and Ears of the Subalterns in India," 10. http://www.religion-online.org/showarticle.asp?title=2444. Accessed on January 16, 2018.

13   Clarke, "Viewing the Bible," 11.

14   Clarke, "Viewing the Bible," 5–7.

DIVINE POSSESSIONS AMONG CHRISTIAN DALITS

be creatively viewed and resourcefully used for finding relief from mundane problems.

2   Embodied Divine Mediation through *Avi Kattu*

Thus far I have focused only on Holy Spirit divine possessions. However, those who are familiar with Indian Christianity may be aware of possessions among Christian Catholic communities in which a devotee is used as medium by Mary, the mother of Jesus. In such possessions Mary comes upon one of the devotees to interact with other members of the community. Such possessions are found usually in places affiliated with Roman Catholic, and in a few cases, Orthodox traditions. Even though I did not study these phenomena in detail as they were not within the purview of my research, nonetheless, I believe it is necessary to acknowledge their existence. Keeping this in mind, I mention one instance of Marian possessions in this section.

In his article in the volume *Popular Christianity in India,* Richard D. MacPhail describes possessions by the Virgin Mary among Sudra communities in South India. He writes about a prayer community (*Cepakulam*) in Coimbatore, Tamilnadu, where a young woman named Philomena was chosen by the Virgin Mary to serve as a medium to speak to the devotees. MacPhail notes that the primary ritual that was used in the *Cepakulam* is called *avi Kattu* (lit. spirit binding), during which the devotees bring candles to offer to the *Mata* (Mother Mary).

The ritual began with testimonies by the participants who have been blessed or healed by the *Mata* (embodied in Philomena). This was followed by prayer requests made to Mary. Then as the devotees began reciting the rosary, and as she sang about the suffering of Jesus on the cross "quietly and mournfully," Philomena entered into a trance crying "I'm feeling giddy."[15] MacPhail notes that "[T]his appears to be a transition stage when Mother Mary's and Philomena's persons are in contention for—or comingled within—Philomena's mind and organs of speech. The process seems to be cooperative rather than a struggle."[16] Then she began to speak to the gathered group identifying those under the power of evil. Those who were thus identified were required to perform a ritual of lighting five candles denoting the five wounds of Jesus while others said their prayers. When Philomena finally came out of the trance, she collapsed,

---

15   Richard D. MacPhail, "Finding a Path in Others' World: The Challenge of Exorcism," in *Popular Christianity in India*, 146.

16   Ibid.

160   CHAPTER 6

physically and emotionally exhausted. In the words of Sagaya, the *uliyan* (servant), this exhaustion was because "she bears the burden of evil for the sake of others."[17]

Even if there are many important factors and dynamics in this account that need to be carefully considered, given that this is not my specific subject of study, let me only make a few observations here. First, we should note that unlike the Holy Spirit possessions that we saw earlier, these Marian possessions are rather solemn and definitely less ecstatic. Furthermore, they do not involve, strictly speaking, embodiment of God or Christ or the Holy Spirit; it is clearly Mary, the mother of Jesus who comes upon these devotees. Moreover, it should also be noted that these possessions are generally *not desired* by the faith community, unlike the Holy Spirit possessions that we saw earlier. MacPhail observes that in almost all cases, the families were worried about the future of the chosen vessels of Marian possessions, especially since these were women who were already married or with intentions of entering into wedlock.[18] Any news of being possessed by Mary would affect the prospects of a marriage, which in turn will be considered a disgrace and curse in the Indian culture. Nonetheless, this example shows that there are other ways in which embodied divine mediation happens among Christian communities, and is surely a topic for further research. In the following section, I shall consider two more ways of imagining divine embodiment among Christian Dalits.

3   Divine Embodiment through Sacraments

When I began my ethnographic research for this book, given that my comparative category is divine possessions, it was natural for me to turn to charismatic churches. And even when I met people from non-charismatic mainline churches to inquire about embodied experiences of the divine, I felt that their answers only betrayed the lack of embodied worship. That is, I could not find any traces of experiences that could be called divine possessions in their worship. However, interestingly, during one of my interviews, Patrick—the same religious scholar mentioned in chapter four who had warned me about the limitations of the term 'possessions' in Hinduism—also suggested that what I was studying need not be restricted to 'Holy Spirit possessions' (or even Marian possessions that we just saw). Rather, the divine can be understood to be

---

17   Ibid., 147.
18   Ibid., 144.

humanly embodied in the administration and the reception of sacraments, especially the baptism and the Eucharist. Taking this suggestion into consideration and recalling my conversations during my research, I offer a brief reflection of these alternative ways in which the divine may be seen as embodied in Christian Dalit communities.

Firstly, I noticed the enthusiasm and passion with which many respondents spoke about baptism and its significance for their life. There seemed to be a general view among Dalit Christians (both old and new converts) that I spoke to that they 'receive' Christ and his Spirit in their bodies during baptism. In other words, through baptism, God revealed through Christ and present as the Holy Spirit dwells 'within' the bodies of the believers. This was made clear to me especially in the context of demonic possessions and sickness among rural Dalit Christians. For example, during one of my previous studies, I was told how 'receiving/having' Jesus Christ after baptism, kept evil spirits and diseases at bay.[19] This indwelling of the divine through baptism, this new life embodying Christ, is made concretely visible by the act of Dalit converts receiving a new Biblical/Christian name.[20] In other words, baptism becomes the occasion when God in Jesus Christ comes *with-in* the Dalit converts and lives in their bodies, giving them strength and power over evil.

The second possible way that divine embodiment could be understood is through the sacrament of the Eucharist. I am reminded of one of my village parishioners, an old lady (whose name I cannot remember) and a new convert to Christianity, who sent word to me through the catechist (i.e. the local lay church leader) asking for the 'blood of Jesus' (*Yesuvin Ratham*), meaning the wine, because she was sick and weak. The catechist told me—with tears welling up in his eyes— that this poor old woman wanted to receive and experience God's healing and strength in her body. Though I was not aware of the theological significance of this request then—apart from the urge to fulfill my pastoral responsibilities—I can now see that the Eucharist signified, for this woman and other Dalits, a deep bodily spiritual experience. Similar notions were evident in my research interviews, for whenever I brought up the idea of embodiment and relation between the God/divine and the body, the conversation invariably turned to the Eucharist. I was told that it is through receiving the bread and the wine—the body and the blood of Christ—that God is

---

19   Samuel, "Dalit Conversions."

20   This practice goes back to the time of mass movements and even earlier, when the Dalit converts took biblical names to show that they are a new person in Christ. See, Dayanandan, "Dalit Christians of Chengalpet Area," 45.

'experienced.' While this was not surprising to hear in non-charismatic church-es, I noticed that even in the Pentecostal churches, where the emphasis is gen-erally on the Holy Spirit (experiences), Eucharist was taken seriously. After the service in Thannirkulam, while speaking with the pastor, when I brought up the subject of communion, he explained that it should be considered as the lit-eral consumption of the body and blood of Jesus, and thus capable of purifying and healing one's body. I am not sure whether the members (or perhaps even the pastor) were aware of the doctrine of transubstantiation of the Eucharist. Nonetheless, I believe that receiving the Eucharist *as* the body of Christ can be understood to be another way of receiving and embodying the divine in Dalit churches.

So far in this section, I have looked at different ways in which the divine is experienced in an embodied manner among Christian Dalits. I began with the conventional Holy Spirit possessions during which the divine is experienced with visibly-pronounced ecstatic body movements. Then, I looked at Mari-an possessions in which devotees act as a medium for Mary. Following this, inspired by the suggestion of one of my interviewees that divine possessions should not be limited to charismatic possessions, I also identified Baptism and the Eucharist as alternative forms of divine embodiment among Chris-tian Dalits. Even if such interpretations appear far-fetched, I believe that such expansive understanding of possessions cannot be ignored, not only for the sake of recognizing non-conventional ways of embodying the divine, but also to transcend and disrupt predictable and compatible comparisons in compar-ative studies. Nevertheless, in this book, I limit myself to interpreting and com-paring Holy Spirit possessions.

4 Christian Divine Possessions: Prospects and Possibilities

In the previous section, we have looked at various types—both conventional and non-conventional—and different dynamics involved in divine possessions in Christian Dalit communities. In the next section, I shall offer critical—albeit brief and preliminary—reflections on the above observations which will be revisited and expanded in the following chapter.

4.1 *Centering the Body*
One of the most fundamental and notable aspects of Holy Spirit possessions is the centrality of the human body in worship. Indian Christianity—particularly Protestant Christianity brought by European colonizers and missionaries—was heavily influenced by nineteenth century European values, especially

those pertaining to the body. The result was, as Leonard Caplan observes in his study of Protestant Churches in Madras (Chennai), the creation of a Christian community that was essentially "Westernized middle class... suited to a more controlled, dignified religious expression," marked by "excessive formalism or 'coldness' of worship."[21] In other words, generally speaking, mainline church traditions restricted bodily movements and expressions of devotion during worship.

Contrast this with the worship in charismatic churches and mainline churches which follow Spirit-filled worship. As pointed out in the earlier section, during the anointing of the Holy Spirit, believers express their faith and adoration to God and Jesus with relatively unrestrained bodily actions such as clapping, singing, speaking in tongues, and even jumping. As the British Pentecostal theologian Allan Anderson rightly notes, Pentecostal and charismatic worship is a complete spiritual experience for a person, which includes the "body, mind, and spirit."[22]

The significance of these visibly embodied ways of experiencing the divine cannot be underestimated. Anderson suggests that what we witness in these charismatic churches is "a more holistic and emotional spirituality" which "stands in stark contrast to the doctrinal, intellectual emphasis of the European, Enlightenment-influenced Christianity that prevailed well into the twentieth century."[23] Therefore, during charismatic worship, particularly when the believers are anointed by the Holy Spirit, we may say that there is a definite disruption of modernist dualistic conceptualization of the human as body and mind/soul as well as the denigration of the body, and a re-centering and re-valuation of the human body in relation to the divine. Taking the methodological suggestion offered by Dalit theologians like Vinayaraj, when we re-turn to the body, I believe that Holy Spirit possessions and charismatic worship can be seen as a powerful counter to imposed colonial religious epistemologies that privilege mind/soul over the body. Thus, the prominent place of the body during Holy Spirit possessions when it becomes a receptacle of/for the divine may be seen, not merely as another mode of Christian worship, but as a form of post-colonial protest to the body-controlling/disciplining colonial European religiosity.

---

21 Leonard Caplan, *Religion and Power: Essays on the Christian Community in Madras* (Madras: CLS, 1989), 97 & 98.

22 Allan Heaton Anderson, *To the Ends of the Earth: Pentecostalism and the Transformation of World Christianity* (Oxford & New York: Oxford University Press, 2013), 139.

23 Anderson, *To the Ends of the Earth*, 143.

4.2   *Dalit Religious Elements*

Speaking of challenging western dualistic epistemologies, we can also identify the presence of, what may be called, 'non-Christian' features in charismatic worship. By non-Christian I mean those aspects that connects these Christian communities, Dalit communities in this case, to their pre-Christian religious traditions, thus indicating the continuity between Dalit Christian charismatic worship and Dalit religions in Hinduism. Here, I mention three such Dalit religious elements in Dalit charismatic worship.

First, a closer look at the charismatic worship in these churches shows the importance of drumming during worship, especially to invoke the anointing of the Holy Spirit. The drumming sets the right mood for the believers to be filled with ecstasy and receive the Spirit. Of course, I do not say that the use of the drum is limited only to Dalit congregations. However, for the Dalits, the drum connects them in a distinct sense with their larger community. Even in cases where the *parai* (the Dalit drum) was not used, other modern forms of drums were used.[24] Dalit Pentecostal Theologian V. V. Thomas puts it appropriately when he says, "[B]eating the drum is part of major functions/festivals among the Dalits whether they are Christian or Hindu" and "brings out the 'silenced' self of the Dalits."[25]

Another important dimension of charismatic worship that is related to Dalit religion is the central role of the community. While it is true that the Christian church itself is basically a community of faith, what is meant here is the communitarian aspect of Holy Spirit possessions. Even if it is the pastor (or worship leader in the absence of a pastor) who leads and conducts the worship, in a sense, it is the community—clapping and praying with ecstatic movements—that ushers in the Spirit baptism. There is unmistakably a high level of participation and involvement throughout the worship. Even during the sermon, the pastor and the congregation continuously talk to each other, through questions and answer or by calling out and reading bible verses. And perhaps the most important manifestation of this community-centeredness can be witnessed during the love meal—a simple vegetarian South Indian meal with rice, *dhal*, and a vegetable—after the service every Sunday. Theophilus Appavoo notes that such dining together is an essential and a defining feature of Dalit traditions.[26] Therefore, we can agree with Thomas who asserts that

---

24   Local Christians call this (western) drum 'band.' Samuel, "Dalits and Conversions."

25   Thomas, *Dalit Pentecostalism*, 366–367.

26   J. Theophilus Appavoo, "Dalit Way of Theological Expression," in *Frontiers of Dalit Theology*, ed. V. Devasahayam (Madras: Gurukul, 1997), 284.

DIVINE POSSESSIONS AMONG CHRISTIAN DALITS

165

> Dalit worship is the expression of real democracy and equality. As one family they stand before God in worship. There is no social discrimination among the worshippers because all belong to one family. There is a celebratory form of worship and communal life that we see in Dalit Churches. This celebration and communal life is highly participatory.[27]

Even if such a claim cannot be universalized for all Dalit churches and at all times, I do agree that communitarian dimension is, in many ways, critical to create the atmosphere to invoke and embody the divine Spirit. Recalling the observations made in chapter four on the significance of community in divine possessions among Paraiyar Hindus, we may agree that there are similarities between charismatic worship and Dalit religious expressions.

Finally, and perhaps the best re-presentation of Dalit religiosity in charismatic worship is the element of ecstasy itself. We already noted how Dalit charismatic worship includes much singing, shouting, violent shaking of one's body, and jumping. Further, there are also instances of dancing that have been noted in similar contexts.[28] Writing on such visible euphoric embodiments of the divine among Christian Dalits, Thomas suggests that "[s]uch... personifications of the power of God," should "be understood as a continuation of their pre-Christian culture."[29] Therefore, it is perhaps not surprising that several of my interviewees indicated that they would rather prefer the ecstatic worship in their villages than the solemn services of the city Churches. Appavoo also makes a similar claim that it is the emotional and physical expressiveness that draws Dalits to charismatic Christianity.[30] Thus, in more ways than one, charismatic worship and ecstatic embodiment of the Holy Spirit among Dalits can be seen as a revival (and perhaps even renewal) of precolonial and premodern forms of worship.

4.3   *Divine-Human Agency*

Thirdly, we should be careful not to consider Dalit Christian divine possessions as merely momentary or 'out of the blue' events. One of the common condescending remarks made about charismatic Christianity is that it is only emotional with no space for the mind. However, Holy Spirit possessions are surely more than that. During my research, I was able to identify two basic elements in charismatic worship. First, the Christians in these churches are clear that

---

27   Thomas, *Dalit Pentecostalism,* 379.
28   Anderson, *To the Ends of the Earth,* 138.
29   Thomas, *Dalit Pentecostalism,* 370.
30   Appavoo, "Dalit Way of Theological Expression," 287.

these ecstatic experiences are from God. As many of them categorically stated, these are moments of divine grace; it is by God's benevolence and kindness that the Holy Spirit is sent upon them and they are able to embody these rapturous experiences. We may be reminded of Patrick's criticism in chapter four regarding the use of the term 'possession' to denote divine embodiments in Hinduism. Rather, as we saw, it is appropriate to understand possessions as the embodied visibilization of divine grace, and as the coming down of grace (*arul varuthal*) or the springing of grace (*arulooruthal*). Keeping this in mind, I believe we will not be wrong in claiming that the charismatic Dalit view of possessions is not too different.

Yet, I was also reminded that, as much as such anointing is by divine grace, they are also influenced and effected by human agency. As Leonard Lovett points out, "Spirit-baptism... is a radical encounter of the divine with the human spirit."[31] Therefore, the embodied and ecstatic experiencing of the divine will have to be seen (within the larger context of the church worship and life in the society) not only as an act of grace but also as the consequence of conscious imagining, reading, praying, and reflecting of the Dalits. We see this in the mutual interconnection between possessions and other elements of worship, such as singing, reading of the bible, and the sacraments.

This element of divine and human agency in Holy Spirit ecstasy becomes especially significant in a context where the integrity of Dalit Christianity and conversions has always been doubted and questioned by skeptical Hindu liberals and fundamentalists. The claim is that Dalit Christians have neither any spiritual motive nor the intellectual basis for their decision to be Christian or to worship. They were and are considered, as we saw in the previous chapter, as 'rice Christians' who jump religions for material benefits and 'cows' with no intelligence or agency. Against such allegations, the divine and the human aspect of rural Dalit charismatic Christianity suggests that it is not merely materialistic as it is often alleged, but rather spiritual (indicating that it is divinely initiated) and intelligent (i.e. consciously thought out and planned) in every sense of the word.

However, as Nathaniel Roberts warns, we should also be aware that this counterargument could in itself be problematic since such 'liberal' counter discourses (that defend Dalit conversions and Christianity against accusation of being materialistic) assume that worldly needs are separated from religious decisions and experiences. Rather, Roberts argues that it is often the material

---

31   Leonard Lovett, quoted by Shaibu Abraham, *Pentecostal Theology of Liberation: Holy Spirit & Holiness in the Society* (New Delhi: Christian World Imprints, 2014), 34.

DIVINE POSSESSIONS AMONG CHRISTIAN DALITS

circumstances of the believers, in this case the economic poverty of the Dalits, that plays a crucial and valid role in their worship, implying that the spiritual and the material are inseparable.[32] To put it simply, people are generally religious for both spiritual and material reasons. Thus, given that Dalit Christian experience, in this case charismatic in nature, is both initiated by divine grace and consciously and deliberately organized and orchestrated with (Dalit) human agency within their socioeconomic context, we may conclude that the validity or integrity of charismatic Dalit religiosity cannot be doubted or under-estimated.

4.4 Possibilities of Resistance and Liberation

As a liberation theologian, one of my primary questions is naturally regarding signs of resistance during Holy Spirit Possessions. Thomas suggests that through their Spirit-filled ecstatic worship, Dalits connect with a God who cares for them and transforms them. This presence of a caring God is particularly evident in glossolalia, the gift of speaking in tongues. Thomas captures this aptly when he writes,

> For many Dalits, prayer and speaking in tongues is an "unburdening" experience. The act of praying, which is quite often in a loud voice, is a kind of 'speaking out one's heart' before God as well as before co-worshippers. This brings a lot of relief. It is a kind of catharsis... speaking to God, a God who cares for the one who prays.[33]

In other words, for a people who were silenced, invisibilized, and ostracized, to pray aloud, to be filled with the spirit, and to speak out can surely be seen as occasions of release and relief. But moreover, as Yabbeju Rapaka, in his research on the influence of the Indian Pentecostal Church (I.P.C.) among Dalits of Andhra Pradesh, posits, glossolalia and ecstatic Holy Spirit embodiment not only signify catharsis but also resistance. He writes,

> The adherents of the IPC may have used glossolalia as a kind of *discourse of resistance* to the oppressive system of Hinduism, especially the caste system... Tongues may be seen as the language of faith community... which is marginalized by the powers-that-be... For many Dalits, tongues

---

32 Roberts understands the worship in slum churches (and slum religion in general) as a creative response to the caste and class issues that affect them. Roberts, *To be Cared For,* 152–184.

33 Thomas, *Dalit Pentecostalism,* 352.

168 CHAPTER 6

> could be considered personal therapy and empowerment… leading to a
> sense of derived agency, authority and self-worth.[34]

However, we should note that catharsis and empowerment are not limited only to glossolalia and ecstasy in Dalit charismatic worship. Taking a closer look at urban Dalit Christianity in the slums of Chennai, Roberts reminds us of other ways in which Dalit affirmation and resistance find expression, intertwined with Holy Spirit possessions. Firstly, he notes that apart from the euphoric worship and glossolalia, which were noticeable signs of slum "women's performance of divine power," there were also "critical junctures when the women's voices took center stage," such as in "voluntary prayers" i.e. prayers led by the congregants (mostly women) in turns.[35] These prayers, Roberts points out, were times when the women in the congregation passed the microphone among themselves exhibiting an element of control and self-assertion. Noting that such "torrent of inspired and often furious invocations of divine power" were "similar to," but far more powerful than "the ecstatic prayers…," Roberts suggests that it "was generally understood that the only ones capable of such feats were women."[36] According to him, these voluntary prayers can be considered to be emancipatory and resistive in terms of giving opportunity for the women to take the center stage and steer the direction and focus of the worship.

Another occasion (even if not as charismatic) identified by Roberts as self-assertive is the testimony time (*saatchi neram*). He noticed that the *saatchi neram* "provided slum women with a platform from which to condemn the injustices in their lives and to proclaim publicly that… they were indeed loved and deserving of love."[37] I can confirm Roberts' argument from my observation of the *Saatchi neram* in Thannirkulam where the women spoke boldly about and against the injustices that they faced both as women and as Dalits, albeit with a tone of gratefulness. I also noticed that it became an occasion for women to share with each other and the community their everyday struggles and suggest and offer mutual help and support. Therefore, assertive and affirmative actions of Dalit worshippers, especially women, are not limited only to glossolalia or ecstatic prayers, but rather find expression within the broader context of worship in the form of voluntary prayers and *Saatchi neram*.

---

34 Yabbeju Rapaka, "The Indian Pentecostal Church of God in Andhra Pradesh, 1932 to 2010: A study of Dalit Pentecostalism" (PhD diss., Regent University, 2011), 188–189. Emphasis mine.

35 Roberts, *To Be Cared For,* 207.

36 Ibid.

37 Ibid., 209.

4.5 *Reimagining Evil*

However, in spite of these confident and astute claims made by Thomas, Rapaka, and Roberts, it has to be acknowledged that Holy Spirit possessions do not explicitly reveal liberative motives. In fact, as sociologist Leonard Caplan deduced more than thirty years ago, the general disposition of the Pentecostal churches is opposed to liberation theology and the social gospel.[38] Although this has changed considerably over the years—as we saw in the case of scholars like Thomas or Rapaka—one may say that there is no concrete liberationist interpretation among the congregations itself. Certainly caste (or patriarchy) was neither explicitly acknowledged nor challenged.

Nevertheless, while caste itself may not be mentioned or spoken about, at least not openly, there may be other ways in which evil finds presence and expression. Let me mention just two here. As mentioned in the previous section, one of the major concerns for Dalit Christians is the threat of evil spirits. In his study of the subject, Caplan, suggests that in precolonial/pre-missionary India, popular notions of suffering and affliction were related to sorcery and evil spirit (*pey*). However, because missionaries, particularly protestant missionaries, were unable to fit these 'super-natural' concerns into their 'enlightened' worldview and address these problems, they simply ignored them as irrational and superstitious. And naturally the same 'reason-oriented' approach was also adopted by the Indian mainline churches.

It was in this context of protestant indifference that, as Caplan notes, the charismatic churches, particularly among the lower castes, took these indigenous beliefs and expressions of evil seriously and spoke about them.[39] This meant that, in the worldview of the charismatic churches, the language of evil spirits and demons became the popular means of expressing all forms of evil, including social and economic injustice. Therefore, it is not surprising that in my research on Dalit charismatic Christianity, systemic evils like caste or untouchability or gender were never explicitly mentioned, leave alone challenged. Rather, as I pointed out earlier, questions about these social hierarchies were responded with stories about, among others, the problem of evil spirits. And, in that context, it was perhaps only natural that liberation and emancipation were often spoken of in terms of exorcism. These divergent and circumventing responses, as frustrating as they could be at times for the interviewer, should not be disregarded. As Pentecostal theologian Amos Yong perceptively points out, the re-presentation of social and political evil using other worldly

---

38   Caplan, *Religion and Power,* 49 & 62.
39   Caplan, *Religion and Power,* 45–46.

170

terminology was a common strategy that can be seen in the early church. As a vulnerable and marginalized community, employing symbols and narratives involving demons and evil spirits to describe the oppressive Roman Empire was a practical and an effective means of resistance for the early Christians.[40] Therefore, by inference, I believe that it is possible to claim that the same strategy is used by Christian Dalits as well to speak about and against the caste system.

Another related way of expressing evil and liberation among Dalit Christians is through the language of sickness and healing. As mentioned before, often I came across people who would speak of physical healing when asked about social liberation. This doesn't mean that they are ignorant about their social position or have sunk into a resigned indifference about their plight. On the contrary, as Frank Macchia points out, bodily healing is believed to be "a means of achieving deeper solidarity with the oppressed and the suffering creation as well as with the Spirit of redemption at work in healing."[41] In other words, healing of bodies, Dalit bodies in this case, connects them with the global web of fellow suffering creatures, both in terms of health and social status. It is in this context that ecstatic embodiment of the Holy Spirit becomes relevant. Pentecostal liberation theologian, Shaibu Abraham asserts that "[T]he *charismata* equip believers to move beyond their ability in this world of spiritual as well as physical bondages, rescuing people through healing their body and mind and bringing them to the kingdom of God."[42] I beleive that such a liberative and solidarity oriented view of physical healing is applicable to most charismatic Dalit Churches. Based on the above observations, we may conclude that while caste is undoubtedly an evil reality that is ever-present around them, Christian Dalits generally do not seek to address it explicitly. Rather, as we saw, they use a different vocabulary—language of evil spirits and physical ailment—to represent and re-conceptualize this systemic evil.

Thus far, in this second part of the book, I have presented the two poles of comparison viz. divine possessions among Hindu and Christian Dalits. I first looked at the ambiguous place of Dalits within Hinduism, considering the construction of Hinduism in modernity even while acknowledging the theological connectedness and continuities with-in the larger Hindu traditions. In chapter four, I presented the phenomenon of goddess possessions in Paraiyar Dalit communities concluding with some initial reflections. In the previous

---

40 Amos Yong, *In the Days of Caesar: Pentecostalism and Political Theology* (Grand Rapids, Michigan: William B. Eerdmans, 2010), 145–151.

41 Frank Macchia, Quoted by Abraham, *Pentecostal Theology of Liberation*, 39.

42 Abraham, *Pentecostal Theology of Liberation*, 37.

DIVINE POSSESSIONS AMONG CHRISTIAN DALITS

chapter, I began with the history of Dalit Christianity, focusing on early conversions, mass movements, and current issues for Dalit Christians, following which I looked at Dalit theological conceptualizations of God, acknowledging recent critical observations and suggestions for broadening the relevance of Dalit theology. Taking into consideration the new trends in Dalit theology, particularly in relation to the body, in the present chapter, I engaged in the study of divine embodiment in Christian Dalit communities, not only those that are manifested in the form of charismatic anointing of the Holy Spirit (which is the primary focus), but also those that can be seen in non-charismatic and sacramental forms. I concluded the chapter with some initial inferences in regard with the Holy Spirit possessions. In the next part of the book, I turn to the final phase of this project: constructing a comparative theology of liberation.

PART 3

Possessions as Kairos: an Embodied Constructive Theology

∴

CHAPTER 7

Divine Possessions as Dalit Resistance

In the second part of the book, we looked at divine possessions among Hindu and Christian Paraiyar Dalits. We noted that Hindu divine possessions (as experienced by Dalits), among other things, are fundamentally acts of divine grace that involve collective (cultural) embodied memories of brokenness and suffering. Among Christian Dalits, we observed that charismatic Holy Spirit possessions as ecstatic embodied divine experiences reflect Dalit agency in subtle and cryptic ways within the context of oppression. After the tradition-specific focus of the last four chapters, in the final part of the book, I will engage in the task of constructing a comparative theology of liberation. In this penultimate chapter, I seek to compare and inquire whether these moments of divine embodiment in untouchable bodies could hold emancipatory motifs.

However, before engaging in this comparison, I believe it is necessary to understand how 'religion' is perceived and practiced among the Paraiyar Dalits. In other words, I want to look at Paraiyar religion, transcending religious boundaries, from an anthropological perspective and give a glimpse of the significant features of Paraiyar religiosity. In the next section, I will compare divine possessions among Hindu and Christian Paraiyar Dalits. Finally, based on the comparisons, I will argue that possessions can be seen as alternative and creative moments of resistance and liberation.

1 Paraiyar Dalit Religion

Though some salient features of Dalit religion were mentioned in chapter three, remember that what was presented there was specifically in relation to Hinduism. However, in this chapter we shall consider the nature of Paraiyar Dalit religion, not just within/as Hinduism, but as practiced by Paraiyars in general. That is, I want to note that Paraiyar religion includes and transcends any one religious tradition, in this case, Hinduism and Christianity. In a sense, the stress here is on the Paraiyar identity and experience. My objective of presenting Paraiyar religiosity in this chapter is to recognize the dynamic overlapping and commonalities in the religious conceptualization of Paraiyars and the rich complexities it creates, *before* we engage in comparing their specific religious traditions viz. Hinduism and Christianity.

© KONINKLIJKE BRILL NV, LEIDEN, 2020 | DOI:10.1163/9789004420052_010

176 CHAPTER 7

Anderson Jeremiah, in his book, the *Community and Worldview among Para-iyars of South India*, suggests that, even though their religious identities are important to the Paraiyars, there is a frequent if not continuous "drawing and re-drawing of religious boundaries."[1] This means "there is no discontinuity in the Paraiyar perception of the gods and the goddesses, but rather... a confluence of local Paraiyar and Christian worldviews, giving forth a polyphonic, highly functional and contextually relevant perception" of the divine,[2] which, as Jeremiah notes, is particularly conspicuous in Dalit conceptualizations of Jesus. Moreover, the needs of the community such as deliverance from sickness, evil spirits etc., take precedence over religious divisions and identities.[3] In other words, within the caste context, Paraiyars tend to live with multiple religious worldviews, using them, explicitly for physical and mental healing, and implicitly to negotiate with and navigate through the caste system.

However, in order to understand this multi-dimensional and utilitarian nature of Paraiyar religion, Jeremiah proposes the need for a "synergetic" view of religion, in which "[T]he focus... is on the centrality of human agency and not on supernatural, otherworldly occurrences or objects."[4] Calling this "[L]ived religion," Anderson notes that it

> ... presents itself as malleable, decentralized and unmediated, providing space for negotiation and subversion within a community. Religious symbols, rituals and practices are utilized to unsettle, redraw and challenge the existing cognitive and social boundaries.... [R]eligious belonging is employed to loosen dominant ideological predicaments, be they colonial, caste or institutional structures.... [L]ives are lived within the matrix of religion and therein expressed.[5]

Based on these insightful observations made by Jeremiah, we may say that Paraiyar religion cannot be viewed as a fixed and compartmentalized identity/ifier (as religious traditions are generally understood). Rather, there is a clear

---

1 Anderson H. M. Jeremiah, *Community and Worldview among Paraiyars of South India* (London: Bloomsbury, 2013), 151.

2 Ibid., 153.

3 Ibid., 79–83.

4 Ibid., Synergetic perspective, for Jeremiah, "implies the ability of individuals or communities to act collaboratively in order to produce meaningful and relevant results..." However, Jeremiah is quick to warn that this doesn't mean that "religion is simply a figment of human imagination or invention," but only "that the less visible world is experienced and shaped by human beings within the visible world." Ibid., 165.

5 Ibid., 166.

DIVINE POSSESSIONS AS DALIT RESISTANCE

and even deliberate interweaving of religious tenets to locate and respond to the questions and needs of the Paraiyars within the reality of caste.

While Jeremiah focusses on a rural context, as pointed out in the previous chapter, there are similarities between rural and urban expressions of Dalit religion. In his research on slum religion in Chennai, Roberts notes that the religiosity of Dalits in the city slums is an ambiguous and complex conglomeration of Hinduism and Christianity. As he points out, since, in the slums, people "lived within households in which, more often than not, someone else followed a different religion than they did,...Christians and Hindus were not distinct communities."[6] But such living in close proximity of Christians and Hindus also means that they could frequently and effortlessly move across religious boundaries.

However, as Roberts notes, the reason for this co-existence and fluidity of different religious identities is simply not a sociological necessity necessitated by proximity, but also theological. Arguing that "the basic assumption of slum religion" is "best characterized as *theological realism*, in so far as they regarded gods as real beings whose characteristics... were completely independent of anything humans might happen to think about them," he believes that the (Dalit) slum dwellers did not feel the necessity of a "worldly allegiance" to any one particular religion.[7] Moreover, given the strong sense of morality (such as refraining from alcoholism, domestic violence etc.,) among the slum dwellers, since "[R]eligions were... not just morally equal in slum dwellers' estimation but *identical*...," Roberts points out that "they did not conceptualize the choice between Christianity and Hinduism as a choice between competing moral systems."[8] Rather, as Roberts observes, the slum-dwellers followed a religion and

> ... worshipped gods, not for their own sake or for some distinct spiritual goals, but for the worldly benefits they provided ... Residents not only felt no need to apologize for putting worldly interests first but even denied that otherworldly goals had any special value.[9]

Thus, they believed that "human beings were under no moral obligation to engage in the inherently unequal relationship" with the deities, but "did so" only "because it was very straightforwardly in their interest."[10] It was the practical

---

6   Roberts, *To Be Cared For*, 153.
7   Ibid., 160.
8   Ibid., 164, 169–170.
9   Ibid., 156.
10   Ibid., 183.

efficacy of the gods—to heal, care, comfort, and protect them from the power of evil forces/spirits—all within the context of caste, that ultimately determined the choice of veneration of deities. This means that if a deity does not respond accordingly and usefully to their needs, the slum dwellers do not feel any remorse in changing their religious traditions. In that sense, the Dalit slum dwellers are not tied to one particular god or religious tradition but are free to change their views or subscribe to any religion according to their current needs. Hence, we may conclude that in an urban slum context, there is no fixed religious identity as such for the Dalits. Rather what we see is a dynamic and creative fluidity of religious affiliation and divine veneration *based on situational needs* allowing the possibility of multiple religious worldviews and identities to flourish among the Dalit slum dwellers.

Summing up what has been presented above and recalling related observations made in the previous chapters, we can identify four broad essential features of Paraiyar religion which have to be borne in mind when we engage in comparison. To begin with, we can notice that in Paraiyar religion, there is clear overlapping and multidimensionality that blends together different religious traditions (Hinduism and Christianity in this case). There is both conscious and unconscious synergetic interweaving of traditions by Dalits of different religions around their existential social reality of caste. In other words, as Jeremiah and Roberts have suggested, Paraiyar religion is a multi-faceted religious response to their socio-economic predicament. It is important to note here that this is not religious relativism. Nor does it signify comfort and ease about moving to other religious traditions. Rather, there is total commitment and subscription to one tradition, (often) even to the extent of criticizing another tradition.[11] This is especially true of Dalit Christians. For instance, we may recall that Christians in Vichur compared Hindu goddesses to evil spirits indicating their discomfort, and even animosity, toward Hindu traditions. And yet, Pentecostal theologians remind us that Dalit Charismatic Christianity is constantly engaging with and drawing from pre-Christian religion and culture.[12] Therefore, what we see in Paraiyar religion is a *simultaneous* firm rootedness in one's own tradition and a critical dialectical relationship towards other traditions. Hence, the rigid and compartmentalized understanding of religions and their comparison may not be applicable to the religions of the Paraiyars, and

---

11   Ibid., 157

12   Placing this within the framework of theologies of religions, we may say that Paraiyar Dalits, while making exclusivistic claims, in practice, embody pluralism in their lives. Samuel, "Untouchable Bodies, Ecstasy, and Dalit Agency."

DIVINE POSSESSIONS AS DALIT RESISTANCE

we may add, Dalits in general.[13] Consequently, a comparative theology of religious traditions among Paraiyars and other such oppressed people is unique in the sense that it does not—strictly speaking—speak of two different and disconnected traditions that are compared, but two interconnected traditions in dialectical relation with one other.

Secondly, we are also able to see the centrality of 'worldly interests' in Paraiyar religion. Rather than being centered around the idea that religion is based on doctrines and deities (with)in a separated private realm—a notion conceived in the context of colonialism and orientalism—the religion of the Paraiyars is based on mundane issues situated in the public sphere. As Roberts has pointed out, there are no qualms about openly acknowledging and involving materialistic interests in choosing deities and their traditions. And it is through this materialistic awareness and responsiveness that the Paraiyar religion negotiates the system of caste. Here we may (once again) recall the allegation that Dalit conversions are based on social and economic upliftment rather than spiritual reasons.[14] This criticism, as mentioned in chapter five, which goes back to the nineteenth century, was mainly propagated by Hindu reformers and nationalists, and continues to be a problematic issue even today. However, Paraiyar religion reminds us that religion is thoroughly situated within the material realities of life. In that sense, we may say that Paraiyar religion stands as a post-secular critique of modernist sacred/private-profane/public compartmentalized notions of religion.

A third important (and related) aspect of Paraiyar religion that must be considered is the centrality of physical and spiritual healing. As seen in the previous chapters, and as explicated by Jeremiah and Roberts in their works, rather than dealing with social issues explicitly, Paraiyar religion—Hindu or Christian—seems to be primarily concerned with issues like healing and exorcism. I believe I can vouch to this from my own work among Hindu Paraiyar Dalits and Paraiyar converts to Christianity. Moreover, moral values such as

---

13   Though, I have not addressed how religion is understood in other Dalit communities (Malas, Madhigas etc.,) in this work, given their marginal status, I believe it is possible to claim similarities with the Paraiyar religion.

14   One of the most well-known criticism of conversions of Dalits came from Gandhi, according to whom, "the Harijans... who had not the even the mind and intelligence to distinguish between Jesus and Mohammed and Nanak and so on..." had blindly and ignorantly converted to Christianity and Islam. Cited by Arundhati Roy, "The Doctor and the Saint," in B. R. Ambedkar, *The Annihilation of Caste,* The Annotated Critical Edition (London and New York: Verso Books, 2014), 134. As Webster notes, "In Gandhi's view, the Dalits were becoming Christians because of material rewards offered or hoped for... " Webster, *The Dalit Christians,* 115.

180   CHAPTER 7

refraining from alcoholism, domestic violence etc., were also well pronounced both within the context of Christianity and Hinduism, based on the strong belief that without subscribing to moral practices, divine guidance and support may not be possible. In fact, we may say that because morality and physical well-being are important for the Paraiyars, deciphering their moral and therapeutic language is critical to understanding the religion of the Paraiyars.

Finally, there is a conspicuous hierarchical relationship that exists between human beings and deities, in terms of the former depending upon the latter. Yet, what stands out in Paraiyar religion is the vulnerability of the gods and the critical significance of human agency and subjectivity. This becomes particularly evident in the dynamics surrounding conversion, where the continuation of reverence toward a particular deity or tradition is dependent on the ability and tendency of the deity/ies to help. When a devotee is convinced of a deity's potential there is total and unwavering allegiance. But when this (current) deity is helpless at a time of need and the devotee or believer finds that another deity could be helpful, there seems to be no problem at all in changing one's affiliation to the other. In a sense, we can say that the devotee wields control (over the deity). However, this must not be (mis)understood as loose and shaky faith (as the likes of Gandhi assumed). Rather, as the Dalit leader B. R. Ambedkar argued, there is nothing unnatural in an individual or a group choosing a tradition that empowers them over another religion that does not help them.[15] Moreover, we also saw that despite these 'choices' there is also a synergetic weaving of traditions and deities across traditions. Jeremiah and Roberts both suggest that this reflects the ability of Dalits to re-create their own faith trajectory/ies in accordance to their existential situation. Bearing these features of the Paraiyar religion in mind, let me now move on to the comparison of divine possessions in Hindu and Christian Dalit communities.

2   Comparing Hindu and Christian Possessions

In this section, keeping in mind the ambiguous and hybrid nature of Paraiyar religion, I want to compare Hindu and Christian divine possessions under three broad categories recapitulating on the findings made in part two of the book: 1) the setting in which possessions occur 2) experiences of the devotees/believers during the possessions and 3) the role of the deities. These

---

15   See the essay, "Away from the Hindus," in Valerian Rodrigues, ed., *Essential Writings of B. R. Ambedkar* (New Delhi: Oxford University Press, 2002), 228–230.

DIVINE POSSESSIONS AS DALIT RESISTANCE

comparisons will then be revisited in the following section to identify the resistive and liberative elements in possessions.

2.1   *Setting*

To begin with, even if seemingly unimportant, the significance of the space in which possessions happen cannot be ignored. As we noted, Hindu possessions generally happen in open spaces, even though often, they occur within the temple premises. And there is a lot of freedom for the possessed devotee to move around—walk, run, jump etc. And, at least in some contexts, the possessed walk around the village with a crowd of devotees behind them. Therefore, in general, we may say that Hindu possessions are not limited to a particular space. Rather, the possessed person has considerable freedom for 'mobility' to move around.

On the other hand, Christian possessions happens within a worship space, usually a church building. Even in the case of an open-air meeting, the Holy Spirit anointed believers do not have the same kind of mobility as in Hinduism. That is, possessions do not extend into the public/'secular' space. However, it is important to note that in Marian possessions, in some cases, the (female) devotees were also filled by Virgin Mary's power at home, i.e. in a non-religious space (meaning that it is not a church or chapel).[16] Of course, this is an exception rather than a rule, and not true for divine possessions among Dalits which we are considering here. For, in a Dalit context, possessions are dependent on the gathering of the community. Appavoo's maxim is worth recalling here: 'possession happens only when there is a gathered community.'

Regarding the frequency of occurrence of possessions, devotees are possessed (mostly) sparingly in Hinduism. However, it is important to remember that the regularity of possessions differs for institutional and enduring possessions. The former happens during festivals which are usually held on a yearly basis. The latter possessions happen whenever the devotees need the help of the *Saamiyadi*s (the religious functionary who is possessed). But in both cases, there is no frequent recurrence of possessions. However, in Christianity, Holy Spirit possessions happen more regularly within the context of worship and prayer. Even though all worship services or prayers may not involve charismatic embodiment of the Holy Spirit, it may be said that these phenomena are certainly more frequent and periodic in Christianity.

Thirdly, we must pay attention to—what can be called—the 'trigger' elements for possessions in both traditions. The most important trigger factor

---

16   MacPhail, "Finding a Path in Others' World," 143.

182   CHAPTER 7

appears to be music. And among the many musical instruments used, the drum certainly seems to play a central role. We may recall how the drumming of the *parai* (the Dalit drum) is crucial for ushering in possessions among Hindu Dalits. On the other hand, the *parai* is not used much in Christian worship (except festivals or functions). Though the *parai* has become popular as the quintessential symbol of liberation in Dalit theology and Dalit Christianity, it was hard to find the *parai* in the regular Christian worship itself. Notwithstanding the absence of the *parai*, there are other (modern) forms of drum(s) that do play an important role in the worship. We may recall the use of modern drums (the 'band') in rural Dalit Christian worship. The significance of this Christian interest in the drum, as observed earlier, lies in the connections with the indigenous (pre-Christian) religion and culture of the Dalits. Thus, the drum, in its various *avatars* is surely critical for both Hindu and Christian Dalits.

Apart from the drumming, in the case of Hindu possessions, it was pointed out that there are other triggering elements such as the smell of flowers. The strong fragrance of certain flowers is considered to be a powerful stimulus to usher in possessions. Further, sacrificing cocks and goats is also seen as essential for creating the conditions for possessions. But in Christian worship, there is no mention of fragrance as an inducer of possessions. The only exception could be the Marian possessions during which incensed wax candles are mandatory. However, we noted that there is a unique triggering factor in Christianity viz. the Bible. Bible verses were used extensively, not only by the worship leader, but also by the congregants throughout the service. Given the important role of the Bible in Dalit and Charismatic Christianity, it is possible to claim that citation of scripture is crucial in Holy Spirit possessions.

I also want to point out the aspect of control in possessions in both the traditions. It is easy to note that in Hinduism, possessions are often not ordered or controlled, and definitely not led by a leader. Among Hindu Dalits, one may say that possessions are entirely controlled by the deity and no one else. There was no one person or a group of persons who 'led' the possessions. Not even the religious leaders are in a position to decide when and how possessions happened or who could be possessed. On the other hand, in the Christian tradition, possession not only happens within a specific space and time, but is also controlled by a leader. We may even say that if (perhaps) the leader decides that there should not be (a time for) Holy Spirit possessions, there may not be any on that particular day.

However, a closer look reveals that even in Hindu possessions, control may be exerted in less explicit ways. While certainly there is no leader who holds a microphone and invites people to be filled by the divine among Hindu Paraiyars, the preparation in the form of drumming and/or the sacrifices create the

DIVINE POSSESSIONS AS DALIT RESISTANCE

optimal conditions for possession. In other words, these preparatory elements are fundamental and play a critical role, as Kapadia noted, in orchestrating possessions. Also, in institutional possessions, because possessions have social and political significance, there is much effort to see to it that they definitely happen. The priest and the community do 'keep a finger on the controls,' so to speak, in order to ensure a (useful) possession experience. Therefore, we may say that both Hindu and Christian possessions are skillfully controlled and co-ordinated, even while acknowledging that control is exercised to a lesser extent in Hindu possessions.

2.2 *Experiences of the Devotees*

The second broad area of comparison that I want to consider are the experiences of the Dalit devotees during possessions. To begin with, in both Hinduism and Christianity, the devotees entered a state of embodied ecstasy when the power of the deity came upon the chosen persons. In this enraptured condition, in Hinduism, there was rigorous shaking of the body, often (but not always) accompanied with oracles. In the case of Christian Holy Spirit possessions, the exuberant bodily movements were characterized by jumping, clapping, and generally, glossolalia. While there are some similarities between these two enraptured moments, it is evident that Hindu possessions are surely more demanding and painful. This is nowhere more evident than in the different bodily acts that are performed during the Hindu possessions. For, apart from the jumping and dancing, we should recall that there is often piercing of the body (*alaku*) and occasionally, drinking the blood of sacrificed animals. In the Holy Spirit possessions, this is clearly not the case. While there are of course the bodily expressions of the presence of the divine (like clapping and jumping), the bodily excitement in Christianity is certainly less since it is always controlled and disciplined by the worship leader, not to mention the restrictions placed by the tradition itself.

Secondly, there are some distinct aspects in the self-descriptions of possessions in the two traditions. Hindu possessions were frequently portrayed as emotionally draining. In some cases, the experience was described as similar to consuming *ganja* (weed). Another common opinion among the devotees was that possessions were physically tiring and exhausting. However, in Christianity, possessions were generally recalled as joyful and healing, and seen as peace-filled experiences despite the rapturous movements. Overall, it may be said that there is a more positive portrayal of the experience in Christianity.

Thirdly, we also observed that oracles play a crucial role in Hindu possessions. It may be recalled that the deity is often (except in the 'mass' temple festival possessions) invoked upon the *Saamiyadi* (the possessed devotee) to

184   CHAPTER 7

receive answers to a problem, blessings, or healing. In other words, possessions
are responsive to the needs of the community. In Christian possessions, though
there are occasional proclamations of oracles during possessions—such as the
interpretation of glossolalia and prophesying—in general, oracles are not the
main objective. Even in instances of oracles being given, usually understood as
prophecies in Christianity, the control rests with the leader.

Finally, it is necessary to be aware that Hindu possessions are seen as the
proof of (embodied) divine presence in the community. If a devotee (or the
usual *saamiyadi* in the case of institutional possessions) is not possessed, it is
interpreted as a proof of the deity's anger with the devotees and the community. This is not the case with Christian charismatic worship. The outpouring
or being filled with the Holy Spirit never seems to be a concern for the pastor
or the congregation. Even if there were no possessions that did not seem to
denote divine absence or anger.

2.3   *Role of the Divine*

Finally, I want to consider how the deities are viewed during possessions in
Hinduism and Christianity. While studying about Mariamman and the two
goddesses in Periyapalayam and Vichur—Periyapalayathamman and Nagathamman respectively—we learnt that deities, particularly goddesses, are
not single and mutually exclusive individuals in the Dalit worldview. Rather,
as we saw, all goddesses are related (often as sisters), and almost always seem
to mutually influence each other. It was also pointed out that the many *am-
mans* (like the Periyapalayathamman and Nagathamman) are perceived (only)
as different versions of Mariamman. We should remember that all this *unitive
ambiguity* (of many as one) is based on the notion that all the goddesses (and
the different deities) are symbolic expressions of one ultimate divine reality.

Among Christian Dalits, though, the focus is not on multiple deities, but
on one God. Even though there is a Trinitarian understanding of God among
Christian Dalits in the villages and in the slums (they seemed to be at least
familiar with the doctrine), it was driven by a strong Christological emphasis,
inspired and sustained by the presence and the guidance of the Holy Spirit. In
other words, there is an essential unity in the understanding of (the person of)
God as revealed in Christ. To put it simply, Christian Dalits believe in *one* God
as taught by the Christian tradition. Nonetheless, despite the particularities,
we need to remember that, given the overlapping nature of the Paraiyar religion (as noted in the first section of this chapter), there are surely continuities
between the understanding of God among Hindu and Christian Dalits.

When we consider the question of God, it is necessary that we attend to its
counterpart: the question of evil. Here we may note some stark differences

DIVINE POSSESSIONS AS DALIT RESISTANCE   185

between the two traditions. In Christianity, God is (generally) seen as the pure embodiment of good, while evil is usually identified and personified (specifically) as Satan or the devil—which often become visible in the form of evil spirits. On the contrary, in Paraiyar Hinduism, there seems to be a more complex and perhaps inclusive understanding of evil. As we saw in the third chapter, Brubaker points out that the (village) goddess is more than a protector or an emancipator. She is not the 'other' to the forces of evil and chaos, but an embodiment of good *and* evil. At a local level, she is simultaneously the power of being, the very ground on which life exists, the provider and also the one who sends diseases and epidemics. And at the universal level, Brubaker notes that the feminine power of the Goddess is the cosmic primal force of creativity itself which also includes the forces of destruction.[17] Also, in the same chapter we noticed that the Great Goddess is viewed as being-itself and as the divine creative power, viz. Brahman in whom all reality, including evil, exists.

It is worth noting that this fits with the Dalit cosmological view where the divine is imagined as *bhu shakthi* (Earth energy) that does not dichotomize good and evil.[18] Thus, I believe that it is possible to say that in spite of the diversity in the understanding of God, there appears to be a general underlying agreement in the Hindu Dalit traditions that the many divine figures are symbols of a higher being/power, constituted by forces that challenge and oppose which are included in this higher being (or, as I prefer to call it, the ground of being).[19] The goddess therefore, is a non-binary symbol of being-itself who points to and participates in its power (of existence), thus opening up new ways of imagining God.

However, apart from the differences in the dualistic and non-dualistic interpretations of the divine in Paraiyar Christianity and Hinduism respectively, what are also noteworthy are the multiple levels and diverse ways of imagining, viewing, and interpreting evil in possessions. Though there is little, if any, direct mention of caste and untouchability as evil in relation to possessions in both the traditions, as suggested in chapter six, it seems that there are other ways in which it is portrayed which can be applied for both traditions. For instance, in Hinduism, divine possession is an occasion and means of fighting against evil, but in different dimensions. A *Saamiyadi* (a possessed religious

---

17   See the section on the Ambivalence of Goddesses in chapter three.

18   M. C. Raj, *Dalitology: The Book of the Dalit People* (Tumkur: Ambedkar Resource Center, 2001), 224–226.

19   This conceptualization of God comes from Paul Tillich who will be one of my main theological interlocutors in the next chapter. Paul Tillich, *Systematic Theology*, Vol. I (Chicago: University of Chicago Press, 1973), 235.

functionary) is usually approached when a person is possessed by a *pey* (evil spirit). It is necessary to remember that within the Dalit goddess traditions, especially the Mariamman traditions, possession is seen as victory over the (male) demon(s) of the village. Moreover, we noticed in chapter four that possessions are also considered to be occasions of healing, both individual ailments as well as communal epidemics such as chicken pox. In Christianity too, Holy Spirit possessions are related to exorcism and healing of sickness in the body. Recall, for instance, how the body of the pastor was strengthened after Holy Spirit possession. We may also interpret the anointing and presence of the Holy Spirit as the affirmation of the defeat of Satan (the personification of evil in Christianity). Therefore, despite the apparent distinctiveness of the religious traditions, it seems that in Dalit religious thinking, even if caste is seldom mentioned openly as evil, it is understood in multiple levels, usually as sickness and evil spirits, and interpreted and resisted accordingly.

In this section, I have compared Hindu and Christian possessions with particular reference to Paraiyar Dalits based on the observations made in the previous four chapters. In the following section, I want to enter into the main question of the project namely, inquiring whether possessions in both the traditions—seen separately and together as Paraiyar religion—hold liberative and emancipatory meaning for the (Paraiyar) Dalits. But before I move to this task, let me first sum up the above comparisons with the question of resistance and liberation in mind.

Firstly, it is clear that possessions (which are considered here) are from and of the divine.[20] Be it Hinduism or Christianity, it is clear that possessions are acts of grace. For the devotees and believers of both the traditions, it seems plain that possessions are possible only because the deity intends and offers it to chosen people. And yet, we have seen that in either tradition, possessions are also based on human efforts. The religious communities, to recall the words of Kapadia, orchestrate and conduct their actions so that possessions happen positively and in a certain way. In some cases, possessions are also 'regulated' in such a way that the needs of devotees are met. But irrespective of the specificity of the different cases, I believe what does stand out is that possessions are jointly engendered and enacted both by divine and human agency.

Secondly, in relation to the subject of human agency, we need to take note of the centrality of the body in both Christian and Hindu possessions. It is important to remember that the bodies of the Dalits are vulnerable to discrimination, hatred, and violence. Moreover, their bodies are also in a sense

---

20   Given that there are also *pey* (evil spirit) possessions.

perpetually 'polluted,' and for caste Hinduism, unworthy of approaching the divine or hearing the words of the divine. It is in this context that I believe that the untouchable *Dalit body* attains significance when it is touched and filled by the divine. Both in Hindu possessions and Christian possessions therefore, the capacity of (the body of) the Dalit person to embody the divine, is critical.

Thirdly, studying possessions and divine embodiments in both the traditions, both individually and comparatively, one may note that there is no open challenge to the caste system within possessions. We may recall that there are instances in Hindu possessions when Dalits do get an opportunity to speak up. But whether such occasions are regular is questionable. It is also doubtful whether these minor and infrequent challenges unsettle—leave alone dismantle—the caste system locally. In general, we may say that there is no explicit resistance that is posed to the caste system. The same conclusion can be reached regarding the possession of Dalit women. But these absences, recalling our discussion of evil, also suggests that there might be other ways in which caste oppression is resisted through possessions. It seems that there are other means through which resistance finds expression, and that the caste system and its diabolic nature are re-imagined and re-expressed in a different register in the Paraiyar communities.

Finally, what is also evident in the comparison of possessions is that there appears to be complex and non-dualistic notions of God (and evil). As noted earlier, Dalit religion is a complex category that includes a conglomeration of religious identities. Because of this synergetic view of religion, deities across religious traditions are seen dialectically as both independent and related. This, as pointed out, is not simple/istic pluralism or relativism in which all religions are viewed as good. Rather, there is simultaneous rootedness in one religion (and one deity) even as there is flexible and multi-level inter-weaving of belief systems. Recall that there is continuity of interpretation of deities across traditions, even as the affiliations to those deities are specific and even passionate. Moreover, the divine (which is symbolized by the deity) is not completely separate from evil. Even as attempts are made to ward off evil, it is not the wholly other of the divine. In other words, binary conceptualizations of theodicy[21] are absent in Hindu Paraiyar religion, which, it should again be recalled, is not entirely separated from the Christian Paraiyar religion. What has also been identified in the comparison of both traditions is that evil finds expressions in different ways, as evil spirits, demons, and sickness, and is common to

---

21   What I mean here are the dominant views of theodicy in Christianity which assume that God cannot have any trace of evil, and therefore, place evil in polar opposition to God.

both Hindu and Christian Dalits. In other words, evil is (predominantly) given either symbolic or bodily meanings that are faced and resisted with the help of the divine. Since I believe that such re-symbolization of evil within Dalit theological imagination is significant, I shall revisit this subject in the concluding section, and again in the following chapter.

3 Possession as Liberation

Having compared the divine possessions in Hindu and Christian Paraiyar Dalit communities, we proceed to address the main objective of this chapter: To enquire if there are liberative elements in divine possessions. We already recalled that in general possessions do not challenge caste or patriarchy explicitly. Nonetheless, I believe if possessions are viewed with different questions and more openness, we will be able to identify the emancipatory potential of these phenomena. But before I do that, first I want to return to the significance of the Dalit body and the performativity of caste discussed in the second chapter.

3.1 Bodies That Want to Be Mattered

Using Butler's theorization of gender construction we saw that the power dynamics of the caste matrix creates and regulates the grammar of the bodies—both the caste and the 'untouchable' Dalit body—through (caste) performativity. And, with the help of Foucauldian analysis we noted that the subjection of these bodies to the caste norms and their productivity are integral to the maintenance of the caste system. Also, we observed that the bodies (especially of those who are oppressed) are constantly 'disciplined' both through violence and panoptic observation to sustain the technology of power of/on the bodies.

However, in spite of such established power matrices of the (caste) society, there is always opposition to oppressive power structures. Colin Gordon, in his introduction to Foucault's essays on *Power*, perceptively observes that "... resistance is an endemic fact in the world of power relations" and therefore, "[A]wakening ourselves to the real world of power relations is awakening ourselves to a world of endemic struggle."[22] Such persistent struggles (against caste) can indeed be seen among Dalits.

Consider for instance the Una incident (mentioned in the second chapter) in which four Dalits were publicly beaten for skinning a cow. This act of

---

22 Michel Foucault, *Power*, ed. James D. Faubion, transl. Robert Hurley et al. (New York: The New York Press, 2000), xx.

DIVINE POSSESSIONS AS DALIT RESISTANCE

violence on Dalits did not go unnoticed, and there was a huge uproar across the country and even across the globe, condemning it.[23] There were also protests in Una and many took to the streets to decry this act of violence. But perhaps the most significant form of protest happened when the Dalits in Una and other surrounding towns and villages declared that they will not remove cow carcasses—a job that is specifically forced upon Dalits—anymore.[24] Thus, caste based violence was opposed both explicitly and subtly—through collective (loud) condemnation and (silent) boycott.

As we know, such resistance through protests and visible dissent is found not only among Dalits but among all the oppressed communities across the world. The most well-known protests in recent times include the Occupy movement that challenged the disproportionate usurpation and accumulation of wealth by a few, and the 'Black Lives Matter' movement which questions white supremacy and privilege and re-affirms the dignity of Black bodies in a context of state sponsored violence and murder of Black people. Along with this, in the U.S. (where I live at present), we could also include several other organized forms of resistance such as protests against violence against the LGBTQ communities, the rise of white nationalism, and the detention and arrest of 'illegal' immigrants. The significance of these protests cannot be emphasized enough. As Foucault says, "[I]f societies persist and live, that is, if the powers that be are not 'utterly absolute,' it is because, behind all these submissions and coercions, beyond the threats, the violence, and the intimidations, there is the possibility of that moment when life can no longer be bought, when the authorities can no longer do anything, and when, facing the gallows and the machine guns, people revolt."[25]

Of course, it is worth remembering that revolts may not always result in a perfect situation or an egalitarian society. Often revolutions and rebellions could create counter-structures that are equally oppressive. Nonetheless, the significance of protests and street politics cannot be ignored or underestimated. Writing on the dynamics of protests and "street politics," Athena Athanasiou rightly notes that "public gatherings enable and enact a performativity of *embodied agency*, in which we own our bodies as 'ours.'"[26] If the dominant

---

23   http://www.dalitcamera.com/boston-chalouna-protests/ Accessed on September 24, 2018.

24   http://www.thehindu.com/news/national/other-states/dalits-protest-refuse-to-dispose-of-carcasses-in-gujarat/article8918558.ece. Accessed on September 24, 2018. For more see the Introduction.

25   "Useless to Revolt?" Foucault, *Power,* 449–450.

26   Butler & Athanasiou, *Dispossession,* 178. Emphasis mine.

190   CHAPTER 7

oppressive systems have not completely annihilated precarious lives and assumed absolute power, it is because of these open forms of resistance when
the oppressed (finally) own their bodies and are able to name and shame their
oppressors.

3.2   *Looking beyond Protests*

While protest politics remains key to challenging oppressive and dehumanizing structures, as Butler and Athanasiou warn us, speaking of, naming, and
protesting socio-political issues have their own flaws and catches. The politics
of recognition in liberal discourses ensures that the wrongs are merely named
at best or colonized and assimilated into the dominant language and discourses at worst. Therefore, Athanasiou suggests that it is necessary to "critically
address the violence of rendering a person unspeakable without reinstalling
a normative regime of speakability in the form of mere naming, bureaucratic
taxonomy, or formal recognition."[27] Thus, simply naming an oppressive structure and/or re-using 'conventional' language/discourse of/on resistance could
be(come) insufficient and misleading. Therefore, "[I]f available language fails
to capture atrocity, we are compelled to invent," or we may add, identify and
acknowledge "new idioms of "'saying,' 'hearing,' theorizing, and acting" in a
context of injustice.[28]

Here I find Sabah Mahmood's critique of conventional modes of resistance
and her advice to respect and accept alternative forms of religious resistance
and reclamation of agency helpful. But looking for and acknowledging these
alternative ways of understanding agency is not easy as,

> For those with well-honed secular-liberal and progressive sensibilities,
> the slightest eruption of religion into the public domain is frequently ex-
> perienced as a dangerous affront, one that threatens to subject us to a
> normative morality... This fear is accompanied by a deep self-assurance
> about the truth of the progressive-secular imaginary, one that assumes
> that the life forms it offers are the best way out for these unenlightened
> souls, mired as they are in the spectral hopes that gods and prophets hold
> out to them.[29]

Based on her study of the women's mosque movement in Egypt, Mahmod
suggests that we need to move beyond such conventional liberal notions of

---

27   Ibid., 133.
28   Ibid., 132.
29   Mahmood, *Politics of Piety*, xi.

DIVINE POSSESSIONS AS DALIT RESISTANCE 191

agency and resistance. Therefore, she asserts, "I have come to question our conviction, however well-intentioned, that other forms of human flourishing and life worlds are necessarily inferior to the solutions we have devised under the banner of "secular-left" politics—as if there is a singularity of vision that unites us under this banner, or as if the politics we so proudly claim has not itself produced some spectacular human disasters."[30] Further, because in the conventional liberal epistemology human agency is located in the "political and moral autonomy of the subject," Mahmood notes that liberation is generally imagined as enjoying individual freedom.[31]

However, Mahmood recognizes that since the 1970s several feminist scholars have focused on "... operations of human agency *within structures of subordination*," and "have sought to understand how women resist the dominant male order by subverting the hegemonic meanings of cultural practices and redeploying them for their 'own interests and agendas.' "[32] For instance, Janice Boddy, in her study of the *zar* cult—an Islamic healing cult involving spirit mediums largely practiced by women in northern Sudan—observes that rituals in such cults are a "kind of counter-hegemonic process ...: a feminine response to hegemonic praxis, and the privileging of men ..." through which the Sudanese women "use perhaps unconsciously, perhaps strategically," what in a liberal view might be considered as "instruments of... oppression as means to assert their value both collectively ... and individually ..."[33] Mahmood concludes that "[A]gency, in this form of analysis, is understood as the capacity to realize one's own interests against the weight of custom, tradition, transcendental will, or other obstacles."[34] In other words, there are instances when the oppressed find opportunities to express their dissent and assert their agency as subjects, *within* and *through* the structures of domination, and not outside or in opposition to these structures. Taking this cue from Mahmood, I want to look closely at this suggested possibility of the existence of alternative and creative counter-discourses of agential assertion, subversion, and liberation in oppressive contexts.

3.3 *Hidden Transcripts and Infrapolitics*
In order to study the less conspicuous modes of resistance and assertion of agency among oppressed communities, I turn to James C. Scott's theorization

---

30   Ibid., xi.
31   Ibid., 7.
32   Ibid., 6. Emphasis mine.
33   Quoted by Mahmood. Ibid., 7.
34   Ibid., 8.

192 CHAPTER 7

of the relationship between the dominant and the dominated in hierarchical contexts. In his study of *The Everyday Forms of Peasant Resistance*, Scott notes "... that power-laden situations are nearly always inauthentic; the exercise of power nearly always drives a portion of the full transcript underground."[35] Therefore, he argues that

> Allowing always for the exceptional moments of uncontrolled anger or desperation, the *normal* tendency will be for the dependent individual to *reveal only that part of his or her full transcript in encounters with the powerful that it is both safe and appropriate to reveal*. What is safe and appropriate is of course defined rather unilaterally by the powerful. The greater the disparity in power between the two parties, the greater the proportion of the full transcript that is likely to be concealed.[36]

Considering the open and hidden power dynamics and strategies between and among the dominant and the dominated as it is manifested in different contexts such as slavery, serfdom, and caste, in his analysis of *Domination and the Arts of Resistance*, Scott categorizes these political phenomena as "public" and "hidden transcripts." While the public transcript is the "open interaction between subordinates and those who dominate,"[37] hidden transcript "takes place 'offstage,' beyond direct observation by powerholders," and "... consists of those offstage speeches, gestures, and practices that confirm, contradict, or inflect what appears in the public transcript."[38] But Scott is also quick to point out that "[I]f the weak have obvious and compelling reasons to seek refuge behind a mask when in the presence of power, the powerful have their own compelling reasons for adopting a mask in the presence of subordinates."[39] In other words, it is not just the oppressed that (are forced to) have their own hidden transcripts, but also the oppressors who (have to) have their public transcripts in order to 'put on a brave face' in front of their subordinates. Scott suggests that hidden transcripts manifest three basic characteristics.

---

35 James C. Scott, *Weapons of the Weak: Everyday Forms of Resistance* (New Haven: Yale University Press, 1985), 286.

36 Ibid. Emphasis mine.

37 James C. Scott, *Domination and the Arts of Resistance: Hidden Transcripts* (New Haven: Yale University Press, 1990), 2.

38 Ibid., 4–5. Note that given the wide range of contexts that Scott draws from, I have used several similar terms to denote the subordinates and the ones who dominate.

39 Ibid., 10.

DIVINE POSSESSIONS AS DALIT RESISTANCE

> First, the hidden transcript is specific to a given social site and to a particular set of actors ... Each hidden transcript, then, is actually elaborated among a restricted "public" that excludes—that is hidden from—certain specified others. ... A second and vital aspect of the hidden transcript ... is that it does not contain only speech acts but a whole range of practices ... Finally, ... the frontier between the public and the hidden transcripts is a zone of constant struggle between the dominant and subordinate—not a solid wall.[40]

Thus each group—the dominant and the dominated—have their hidden transcripts, which Scott believes are in *"never in direct contact.* Each participant will be familiar with the public transcript and the hidden transcript of his or her circle."[41]

Looking from the perspective of the subordinates, Scott notes that there are different ways in which they relate with their superiors. The most common form of discourse is one of flattering, making use of the existing public norms to further their own interests. The other political tactic is the already mentioned 'hidden' transcripts. The other end of this spectrum of subordinate politics is the open expression of anger, defiance, and resistance visible in protests and rebellions. However, these moments—as powerful and necessary as they are—are too infrequent in most hierarchical contexts.

Apart from these, Scott identifies an intermediate means through which the subordinated work out their resistance. Calling them the "infrapolitics" of the subordinates, he defines them as the "... politics of disguise and anonymity that *takes place in public view* but is *designed to have a double meaning* or to shield the identity of the actors. ... partly sanitized, ambiguous, and coded version of the hidden transcript ... a wide variety of low-profile forms of resistance that dare not speak in their own name."[42] In other words, because "their vulnerability has rarely permitted them the luxury of direct confrontation," the subjugated people across the world have developed modes of resistance that are "disguised, muted, and veiled for safety's sake."[43] In that sense, we may say that infrapolitics is the 'pubic use' of hidden transcripts in a coded or cryptic form. Using this framework, in the following section, I want to argue that

---

40   Ibid., 14.

41   Ibid., 15. However, I have to note that I am skeptical whether the parties are always explicitly conscious about their familiarity with the transcripts.

42   Ibid., 19. Emphasis mine.

43   Ibid., 136–137.

194 CHAPTER 7

divine possessions among Dalits can be seen as infrapolitics of Dalit resistance and agential assertion.

3.4 Divine Possessions as Dalit Resistance: Reimagining Liberation

We noticed in our study of divine possessions that they are complex phenomena whose dynamics and motifs cannot be narrowed down to simple categories, including those that are emancipatory or liberative. Scott too appears to be doubtful in acknowledging possessions as a form of protest. Though he recognizes that "[S]pirit possession and cults of possession... represent a quasi-covert form of social protest for women and for marginal, oppressed groups of men for whom any open protest would be exceptionally dangerous,"(sic)[44] Scott is skeptical about viewing them as explicit forms of resistance. As he notes,"Whether or not it is plausible to call such acts protest is nearly a metaphysical question, for "it is experienced as involuntary and as possession, never directly challenging the domination at which it is aimed."[45] Hence, we may say that what we see in spirit possessions are not acts of open and conscious resistance or explicit attempts for emancipation like in the case of protests or marches. Rather, possessions appear to be (generally) unrelated, at least directly, to socioeconomic issues, not seeking to make a permanent change or alter the power relations among the concerned communities. Nonetheless, in spite of this ambiguity, I believe that it is possible to see possessions as, to use Scott's vocabulary, a form of infrapolitics. Based on this premise, I want to identify how resistance and liberation are envisioned and experienced by the Paraiyar Dalits during divine possessions.

Firstly, the element of speaking is of considerable significance in both Hindu and Christian possessions. As Karin Kapadia and other scholars have noted, during possessions, Dalits—whose speech is normally curtailed and controlled by the dominant castes—are able to be loud, bold, and authoritative in the presence of the dominant castes. We may recall that in some instances possessed Dalits even tend to abuse the caste people. Moreover, though rare, as one of the interviewees, Kondaivilai, said, there is even the possibility of Dalits beating caste men (and rarely women) during possessions. In fact, given the holy status of the possessed Dalits, despite the embarrassment, the caste people permit and even prefer Dalit arrogance and authority, something that would be unthinkable at other times. It is perhaps one of the few occasions when the caste people would come to the Dalits in

---

44   Ibid., 141.
45   Ibid., 142.

DIVINE POSSESSIONS AS DALIT RESISTANCE

the Dalit *ceri* (the segregated Dalit part of the village) to listen to them and follow their instructions.

Though the same may not be claimed for Christian possessions among Dalits, we noted that Holy Spirit possessions also provide Dalits an opportunity to speak up, even if within the same religious community and controlled by a worship leader. V.V. Thomas suggests it is precisely because of the significance of these ecstatic Spirit experiences which allow the (usually) silenced Dalits to speak out that they prefer to join Pentecostal and charismatic churches in large numbers.[46] Further, we may also recall Robert's observation that anointing by the Holy Spirit is especially important for women—to speak, to share their joys and concerns, to pray for each other, and above all, to organize emancipatory schemes for their community.[47]

Along with the speaking, possessions—both Christian and Hindu—involve rigorous movement of the bodies of the devotees. As mentioned in the earlier chapters, there is swaying, jumping, clapping, dancing, and in some cases, even possessed walking. Scholars of Afro-Caribbean traditions like Haitian Vodou which emerged in a context of colonialism and slavery argue that enraptured bodily movement was and still is an important form of countering structures of injustice and oppression.[48] Given their similarities, it is possible to understand the significance of ecstatic embodied worship for the Dalits who generally have to "behave cautiously and deferentially" in front of the caste people.[49] Thus, through these counter "speech-acts" (to recall a phrase from chapter two) Dalits force the dominant castes to count them as human.

Secondly, the significance of speaking and acting during possessions lies also in its cathartic value for those who are possessed. We saw that among Hindu Dalits possessions offered the space for venting anger and frustrations from oppression. This is especially true for Dalit women who are often victims of both caste and gender based violence. Divine possessions serve as a means of releasing pent-up feelings of discrimination and humiliation for women. In the case of Christianity, we may recall the suggestion of Pentecostal theologians that it is because of their cathartic nature that Dalits and other lower castes lean toward Holy Spirit possessions and charismatic worship. Moreover, we also identified that catharsis becomes clearly conspicuous during glossolalia.

---

46 Thomas, *Dalit Pentecostalism*, 353.

47 Roberts, *To be Cared For*, 207.

48 For instance see, Margarite Fernández & Lizabeth Paravisini-Gebert, *Creole Religions of the Caribbean: An Introduction from Vodou and Santeria to Obeah and Espiritismo* (New York and London: New York University Press, 2011), 22–23.

49 Kapadia, *Siva and Her Sisters*, 149–150.

By speaking in tongues, the Dalit believers were able to experience relief from their deeply ingrained hurt and humiliation of being a discriminated community.

However, it is important to remember that catharsis is also related to healing. In both traditions, we have seen that being possessed has therapeutic implications. In the Hindu tradition, the possessed person is regularly approached by sick people for cure. However, I did not come across situations where the possessed person herself was cured of any illness through possessions. Rather, as it may be recalled, those who are possessed actually felt weak. In Christianity, however, healing is experienced both by the one who is filled by the Holy Spirit and, if she were the leader, by the members of the congregation as well. In other words, Christian possessions have therapeutic value both for the individual who is anointed by the Spirit as well as for the community. But, it is worth recalling that possessions in both traditions were mainly concerned with the physical or psychological forms of healing. There was no indication of, what we may call, 'social' healing i.e. empowerment for liberation. Nonetheless, as pointed out in the previous section and in chapter six, physical ailments and healing of oppressed people are not entirely unrelated to their social standing and their attempts to counter domination. As Pentecostal theologian Abraham noted, and also as attested by scholars of shamanic traditions, healing during possessions may be seen as a means of re-imagining evil—including social evils such as caste and patriarchy—and re-visioning resistance.[50]

All this suggests the centrality of the body in possessions. Both in Hindu as well as Christian possessions, we have seen that it is through their *bodies* that the oppressed (re-)gain their voice, and find release and healing. In a context where the bodies of the Dalits are rendered untouchable and expendable, and where often resources—including basic amenities, let alone luxuries—are denied (often violently), the body is perhaps the only resource available for survival and resistance. No wonder, then, that all such experiences, like suffering, grieving, lamenting, assertion, or celebration depend on and are situated within the (Dalit) body. As a caveat, it is important to note here that the body should not be seen in isolation. As Sudhir Kakar points out, "[T]he Indian image of the body...emphasizes its intimate connection with the cosmos."[51] Also,

---

50   For instance, healing practices in the Afro-Caribbean tradition of Espiritismo facilitates the "reclaiming of the power of inner transformation of spirit in order to create the consciousness that will lead to a transformation of unjust social structures." See the chapter "Espiritismo: Creole Spiritism in Cuba, Puerto Rico, and the United States," in Fernández & Paravisini-Gebert, *Creole Religions of the Caribbean*, 248.

51   Sudhir Kakar, *Shamans, Mystics, and Doctors: A Psychological Inquiry into India and its Healing Traditions* (Chicago: The University of Chicago Press, 1982), 233–234.

we may recall that the inhabitants of a village, including all creatures, are part of the body of the deity. In that sense, the Dalit body is connected to and symbolizes the entire environment in which it is located.

Returning to the possessed body, we saw that the possessed Dalit body is significant in terms of carrying and transmitting collective and cultural memories. This is clearly evident in the Hindu Dalit possessions during which incidents from the past were recalled and re-created by the possessed devotee. In that sense, possessions are not simply impulsive outbursts but moments of re-membering and re-embodying memories of suffering (and resilience) in the history of the Dalits. Hence, one may say that possessions are occasions of re-visibilizing hidden (and forgotten) encoded memories in the bodies of Dalits across time (and space).

While it may not be possible to make similar claims regarding collective memories of the past in regards with Christian charismatic possessions, we cannot forget the argument of Pentecostal theologians that charismatic Christianity—particularly among Dalits—is a continuation and celebration of pre-Christian Dalit culture. If that is the case, we have to acknowledge that in Pentecostal forms of worship—especially during the anointing of the Holy Spirit—memories of the past are indeed remembered and re-enacted by Dalit Christians, although differently from their Hindu counterparts. This suggestion finds more credibility if we consider a similar argument made by the Hispanic theologian Samuel Cruz that Puerto Rican Pentecostalism is nothing but "Masked Africanism(s)." Noting the close relationship between Pentecostalism among Puerto Rican communities, Afro-Caribbean religions such as Santeria and Haitian Vodou, and the traditions of West Africa (from where the enslaved people in the Caribbean and the Americas hailed from), in his book *Masked Africanisms*, Cruz proposes that "[U]nderlying the religious/spiritual world view of the Puerto Rican people is an African religious foundation that is present, unconsciously perhaps, in the religious practices of contemporary Puerto Ricans," which becomes visible during spirit possessions.[52] Based on this observation, we may say that it is possible that even in Dalit Christian charismatic worship and possessions, cultural memories from the past generations are recollected and re-enacted by the Spirit-filled believers. As Sudhir Kakar notes, such "collective myth subscribed to by the community" which "attends to the individual elements ..." also "addresses the dominant ... conflict in the community," such as caste (and/or patriarchy).[53]

---

52 Samuel Cruz, *Masked Africanisms: Puerto Rican Pentecostalism* (Dubuque: Kendall/Hunt, 2005), 54.

53 Though Kakar believes that this is only "in some cases," and the conflict is "individual," I believe that, in a deeply connected community-oriented (caste) society like India, it

198   CHAPTER 7

Fourthly, when we consider possessions, we have to consider the 'politics of space.' We may recall the various struggles that Dalits face regarding where they live, work, travel etc. As I noted, Dalits possessing land, where they reside, and how they navigate their space in relation to the caste people have been rigidly controlled and regulated by caste. And in cases where Dalits have tried to cross their allotted (and, generally segregated) spaces, either literally or symbolically, and transgress the caste rules, matters turn violent. It is important that we view possessions against this background of restrictions.[54] In this context, a possessed Dalit, speaking, standing, or walking, or running, or jumping could be seen as an act of assertion of her right to live, stand, and move, and (simply) *to be*, within a space that is clearly demarcated according to caste. This aspect of reclamation of space becomes even more significant if we remember Diane Mines' study in Yanaimangalam where the possessed Dalit walks through the village re-mapping and reclaiming the space of the Dalits. After all, it is usually (if not always) the caste people who map the village space, drawing boundaries, and keep Dalits out. But here it is the possessed Dalit—the one who is mapped out—who maps the village and defiantly keeps the caste people out of the Dalit space. Therefore, for Mines, the resistive and liberative dimension of possessions is actualized not only when possessed Dalits speak and act boldly in the presence of the dominant castes, but also when they strategically and assertively move and walk through the village, reclaiming their space, geographically as well as ontologically, on behalf of all the Dalits in the village.[55]

What is further significant here is the (interconnected) use of the two important Dalit religious symbols viz. the goddess (in her various local and universal manifestations) and the drum (in its many forms). As noted in chapter four, drumming, especially the drumming of the *parai* in the case of Dalit goddesses, plays a critical role in inducing possessions. Thus, the assertion of agency of the goddess possessed Dalit body through the various ecstatic speech-acts such as shouting, giving oracles, dancing, or walking, is integrally connected to the assertive sound(ing) of the untouchable *parai*. But that is not all. Mines 'complicates' things further by pointing out that the deity and the drum are not the only crucial symbols in Dalit possessions. She points out that along the path charted by the divinely possessed person, the statue of the Dalit leader Dr. B.R. Ambedkar is placed as a symbol of spatial assertion.[56] In other words,

---

is not possible to separate the individual from the larger social issues. Kakar, *Shamans, Mystics, and Doctors*, 115.

54   See the sections "Bodies that Don't Matter" and "Disciplining the Bodies" in chapter two.
55   Mines, *Fierce Gods*, 185–187.
56   Ibid., 188ff.

DIVINE POSSESSIONS AS DALIT RESISTANCE

199

the icon of Ambedkar assumes the role of a religious symbol along with the goddess and the drum, to reaffirm the agency and the resistance of the Dalits beyond the moments of possession. It should be noted here that even though the Dalit goddess traditions (which is the focus of this book) do not necessarily or always involve a possessed person walking, I can say with some confidence that the symbol of Ambedkar is never absent from the religious topography in most Dalit contexts.[57]

Of course, the same may not be said about Christian possessions, at least *prima facie*. But we already saw in chapter six, the significance of the drum— in its various avatars—for Christian worship, particularly for Holy Spirit possessions. Further, it should be noted that the significance of Ambedkar as an icon of Dalit liberation transcends religious boundaries. For instance, in many villages, it is not unusual to see a statue of Ambedkar near a church.[58] Given the influence of the mass movements explained in chapter five, it should be borne in mind that it is not unusual, particularly in the villages outside Chennai, for Christianity and church to be understood synonymously with Dalits and Paraiyars. Therefore, in a sense, Ambedkar is the common and unifying quasi-religious symbol for Hindu and Christian Dalits. In sum, we may say that possessions, including the drumming, the ecstatic shouts, the movements of the possessed bodies, and the strategic positioning of the image/statue of Ambedkar, are important for the Dalits in their struggle to assert and claim their space to exist within the 'caste-mapped' village.

Finally, possessions can also be seen as (moments of) disruption and deconstruction of conventional (read, colonial-modernist) epistemologies. Firstly, as we have seen, possessions are not exclusively 'religious' events—religious understood as separated from the 'secular.' Rather, Dalit religious traditions which include the element of possessions are creatively built on both spiritual and material concerns. Devotion, veneration, and being possessed by a deity are not individualistic other-worldly experiences, but are strongly founded on and related to the needs of the community and the ability of the gods/ goddesses to help the devotees meet those needs. As Roberts learnt, without

---

57   The image of Ambedkar has become the quintessential symbol of Dalit resistance. To place a statue or photo of Ambedkar in a public space is seen as an act of Dalit assertion. For more see, Johannes Beltz, "The Making of a New Icon: B. R. Ambedkar's Visual Hagiography," *Journal of South Asian Studies* 31(2015): 254–265. http://www.tandfonline.com/doi/full/10.1080/02666030.2015.1094210?src=recsys Accessed on September, 25, 2018.

58   In most villages in South India, churches are usually located in the Dalit colony. And this was definitely the case in the villages that I studied.

these practical 'uses' of the deities, neither worshipping nor embodying them makes any sense to the urban slum Dalits. Moreover, as Roberts also observes, being possessed for the Dalits—be it in Hinduism or Christianity—is part of a larger network of dealing with and finding emancipatory responses to socio-economic problems. Therefore, what we essentially see in Paraiyar Dalit religion in general (as mentioned in the first section of this chapter), and divine possessions in particular, is the collapse of the simple and rigid compartmentalization of the religious and the secular.

Along similar lines, we also saw from Jeremiah's insightful study that Dalit religion is characterized by the synergetic weaving of different religious traditions. Dalit religion is a 'lived religion' where religious identities are constantly reconstructed within the caste matrix. Therefore, rather than being bound to their 'essential' religious identities, there is much fluidity across traditions. However, as suggested before, this is not some simple religious relativism, for each devotee or believer is rooted to her tradition even while actively interacting with and learning from the practices and symbols of another tradition. This, I believe can be said of possessions as well. We already saw the interconnectedness of different symbols—the god/dess, the drum, and the statue of Ambedkar during possessions. But, here I also want to point out that both in my earlier research conducted in the villages of Pulichapallam and Kottaikarai, I found that, alongside the statue of Ambedkar, the image of the Buddha was also often placed as a symbol of Dalit assertion.[59] Further, again speaking from my research, I believe that, along with these religiously diverse symbols of the goddess, the drum, Ambedkar and the Buddha, one could also include the church, where Dalits—both Christian and Hindu—find respite, healing, and empowerment.[60] Thus, we may say that, in divine possessions among Dalits, multi-religious and secular symbols are creatively and interconnectedly woven together to re-imagine and realize their liberation.

Furthermore, in Hindu possessions (though not in Christian possessions), we can notice the dis/re-ordering of gender and sex identities. Soorya's story and Kapadia's study mentioned in the chapter on Hindu possessions showed that there is a reversal and collapsing of gender identities for those who are possessed, although according to Kapadia, it is limited to the duration of possessions. Despite the problems that Kapadia alerts us to—that only men are

---

59   Buddhism has been an important critique of the caste system for many centuries, and particularly in the modern period it has been an avenue of liberation for the Dalits. It became even more popular with the conversion of Ambedkar to Buddhism. For more see, Introduction.

60   Samuel, "Dalits and Conversions."

possessed and gender hierarchies are retained—it is of no less import that these moments of embodying the divine unmask the complexity, ambiguity, and fragility of sexual identities suppressed by heteronormative assumptions.

Lastly, we also noted that there is a non-binary understanding of good and evil peculiar to Hindu possessions. The goddess does not stand opposed to the force(s) of evil (like in Christianity) but rather includes and embodies both good and evil. In other words, there is an expansive yet complex and ambiguous understanding of the symbol of God among Hindu Dalits which becomes particularly conspicuous around divine possessions. In that sense, we can say that Hindu Dalit possessions surpass and serve as a critique to popular Christian interpretations of theodicy.

3.5 *Possessions as Alternative Resistance*

Looking at these various facets of Hindu and Christian possessions—some common and others tradition-specific—I believe we can conclude that these are indeed moments and occasions of subversion, resistance, and agential assertion. Possessions suggest that the Dalits can and do reclaim their agency and affirm their dignity to live and flourish through their bodies, albeit in unconventional ways. Therefore, during possessions, as Mark Jordan suggests, we may say that just as "[B]odies are shaped by religious powers," they also "use religious discourses or practices to resist powers."[61] Also, we can assert that the Dalits, through these embodied experiences of the divine, have "performatively exposed and repossessed the norms of visibility and audibility..." despite the powerful presence of the structure of caste (along with others like patriarchy and heteronormativity).[62] In that sense, we may say that possessions (and the festivals in which they occur) are similar to carnivals, where "[N]ormal rules of social intercourse are not enforced," and there is "celebration of the body..."[63] Of course, it should remembered that carnivals have their limits, since after all, even if "[S]ocial power in carnival may be less asymmetrical ... reciprocal power is still in power; ... [C]arnival is disorder, it is a disorder within rules ..."[64]

But we know that possessions do not happen only in a carnivalesque context. Both in the Hindu and the Christian tradition, we noted that possessions often happen in an 'enduring' manner, be it for the *Saamiyadis* who are approached throughout the year or for the Christian believers who gather as/in

---

61 Mark D. Jordan, *Convulsing Bodies: Religion and Resistance in Foucault* (Stanford: Stanford University Press, 2015), 10.

62 Butler & Athanasiou, *Dispossesion*, 140.

63 Scott, *Domination and the Arts of Resistance*, 173.

64 Ibid., 176–177.

the church and are anointed by the Holy Spirit. Also, we have seen, with respect to Christianity, that possessions (understood as embodied experiencing of the divine) need not be limited only to Spirit or charismatic possessions, but may also include other modes of divine embodiment. In that sense, I would suggest that divine possessions can be considered as, to use the words of Scott, "everyday forms of resistance."[65] Scott points out that even though everyday (or 'ordinary') forms of resistance are similar to other forms of resistance in that they deny the attempts of the dominant to absolutize their aims and purposes, he notes that the former are different and more effective. He observes "[W]here institutionalized politics is formal, overt, concerned with systematic, de jure change, everyday resistance is *informal, often covert, and concerned largely with immediate, de facto gains*."[66] It is this method of resistance that is realistic and possible for most oppressed peoples, and possession can be considered as one such form of everyday resistance.

Such a conceptualization of resistance, Scott believes, challenges us to critically analyze conventional notions of resistance. Scott observes that generally "*Real* resistance ... is (a) organized, systematic, and cooperative, (b) principled or selfless, (c) has revolutionary consequences, and/or (d) embodies ideas of intentions that negate the basis of domination itself," in contrast to those that are "(a) unorganized, unsystematic, and individual (b) opportunistic and self-indulgent (c) have no revolutionary consequences, and/or (d) imply, in their intention or meaning, an accommodation with the system of domination."[67] However, Scott alleges that conceptualization of resistance as organized, systematic, selfless, etc., is flawed since the struggles of the oppressed transcend narrow ethical principles. In fact, as Scott insists, "intentions are inscribed in the acts themselves."[68] Hence, even if they are not revolutionary or moralistic, nevertheless, it is the everyday forms of resistance that are grounded in reality. As Scott (almost skeptically) concludes,

> The revolution, when and if it does come, may eliminate many of the worst evils of the ancient(/oppressive) regime, but it is rarely if ever the end of peasant resistance... The stubborn, persistent, and irreducible forms of resistance... may thus represent the truly durable weapons of the weak both before and *after* the revolution.[69]

---

65   Scott, *Weapons of the Weak*, 29–30.

66   Ibid., 33.

67   Ibid., 292.

68   Ibid., 301.

69   Ibid., 302–303. Emphasis in the original text.

DIVINE POSSESSIONS AS DALIT RESISTANCE   203

Hence, in agreement with Scott's expansive and radical understanding of resistance, given that possessions too do not seek to overthrow the system of (caste) domination nor are they systematic or organized, we can conclude that they are as, if not more, practical than political struggles. Also, recalling Scott's insistence on locating *intentions in the acts themselves,* we can say that the intention of everyday resistances like possessions is not to change or overthrow or to be 'morally/politically correct,' but rather survival. Real life resistance and liberation is the ability to exist, to have the courage *to be* in circumstances that deny that possibility!

Here, it is helpful to return to Mahmood's study of the women's mosque movement. Mahmood perceptively notes that in most discourses on struggles against injustice, liberation is seen through the dualist lens of "doing and undoing, consolidation and subversion,"[70] and agency "understood in its performative dimension: as a political praxis aimed at unsettling dominant discourses ..."[71] But, she suggests that, "the concept of agency should be delinked from the goals of progressive politics," thereby freeing it from its "incarceration ... within the trope of resistance against oppressive and dominant power."[72] Rather, Mahmood believes that agency is beyond the consciousness of the subjects, and is located and can be understood only *within* the particular systems as corporeal events. She concludes that

> ... it is best not to propose *a* theory of agency but to analyze agency in terms of the different modalities it takes and the grammar of concepts in which its particular affect, meaning, and form resides. Insomuch as this kind of analysis suggests that different modalities of agency require different kinds of bodily capacities, it forces us to ask whether acts of resistance (to systems of gender hierarchy) also devolve upon the ability of the body to behave in particular ways. From this perspective, transgressing gender norms may not be a matter of transforming "consciousness" or effecting change in the significatory system of gender, but might well require the retraining of sensibilities, affect, desire, and sentiments—those registers of corporeality that often escapes the logic of representation and symbolic articulation.[73]

---

70   Mahmood, *Politics of Piety,* 23.
71   Ibid., 21.
72   Ibid., 34.
73   Ibid., 188.

If we apply Mahmood's penetrating suggestions to the Dalit context and the phenomena of divine possessions among the Dalits, we can conclude that what we see during possessions is the embodied corporeal reassertion of Dalit agency in a non-liberal register. Keeping this in mind, in the next chapter, I venture to accomplish what I had intended when I began this project, viz. articulate a comparative theology of liberation.

CHAPTER 8

Envisioning an Embodied Comparative Theology of Liberation

Comparative Theology becomes properly theological when it takes up the constructive task of assessing the meaning, importance, and truth-value of the similarities discovered through comparison.[1]

∴

In this chapter, the comparative theology of liberation project reaches its climax. In the following pages, I will offer a theological interpretation of divine possessions by building upon the work done in the earlier chapters. The first section will be dedicated to making the case that divine possessions can be seen as moments of *kairos* viz. those opportune and optimal moments when God's empowering and transformative intervention is experienced at its best. In the second section, acknowledging the normative relationship that these moments have with the "Great Kairos" viz. the Christ event, and using the framework of Spirit Christology, I will argue that possessions—both Christian and Hindu— can be viewed as Christ(ic) moments, and underscore the various liberative and emancipatory theological implications encapsulated within possessions.

1 Possessions as *Kairos*

In this section, after giving a basic overview of the concept of *kairos*, based on the past theological and political use of *kairos* in history—particularly as articulated by the Protestant theologian, Paul Tillich—I will show that it is appropriate to interpret divine possessions experienced by Hindu and Christian Dalits as divine *kairotic* moments. But more importantly, I will also argue that viewing possessions as *kairoi* enables the possibility of broadening and enhancing the meaning and relevance of the concept itself.

---

1 Thatamanil, *Immanent Divine*, 170–171.

© KONINKLIJKE BRILL NV, LEIDEN, 2020 | DOI:10.1163/9789004420052_011

206 CHAPTER 8

1.1 Kairos

During biblical times, *kairos* was understood in the sense of a "decisive or crucial place or point, ... spatially, materially, or temporally."[2] It was used positively (as a favorable place or time) or negatively (as impending danger) or, even in a neutral sense (a situation that is decisive or that which forces an action or response).[3] In the Septuagint, *kairos* is used predominantly in the sense of a divine appointment (Job 39: 18; Numbers 23: 23; Daniel 2: 21).[4] In the New Testament, *kairos* is used in a temporal sense, as the special or right time to do something,[5] during which there is a perfect balance between divine grace, historical urgency, and human response/ibility.[6] It is in this sense that Jesus' first proclamation, "The *kairos* is fulfilled" (Mark 1: 15), should be understood, as should the early church's message on repentance and salvation.

Based on this biblical understanding, in the words of Robert McAfee Brown, "*Kairos* ... is a time of opportunity demanding a response: God offers us a new set of possibilities and *we* have to accept or decline."[7] In the twentieth century, *kairos* became popular during the struggle against racial apartheid in South Africa. The famous *Kairos Document* that came out during this time, which Brown calls "a *status confessionis*, a 'confessional situation,' "[8] challenged the church and the society to take a prophetic stand against all forms of discrimination, particularly based on race. The statement declared:

> For very many Christians in South Africa this is the *KAIROS*, the moment of grace and opportunity, the favourable time in which God issues a challenge to decisive action. It is a dangerous time because, if this opportunity

---

2 Gerhard Kittel (ed.), *Theological Dictionary of the New Testament*, Vol. III, trans. & ed. Geoffrey W. Bromiley (Grand Rapids: Wm. B. Eerdman, 1965), 455. It is well known that Kittel was a Nazi supporter and anti-Semitic. Let me note here that while I engage his scholarship, I am strongly against any form of anti-Semitism.

3 *Kairos* is often used as a compound adverb (*eukarios*—well-timed, opportune; *akairos*—ill-timed, inopportune) or as a compound noun (*akairia*—inappropriate time). Ibid., 462–463.

4 Ibid., 458–459.

5 Eg.: "He (Jesus) said, "Go into the city to a certain man, and say to him, 'The Teacher says, *My time is near*; I will keep the Passover at your house with my disciples.' "" (Matthew 26: 18); "*The time is fulfilled*, and the kingdom of God has come near; repent, and believe in the good news." (Mark1: 15). Emphasis mine. All Bible texts are taken from the New Revised Standard Version.

6 Ibid., 459.

7 Robert MacAfee Brown, ed., *Kairos: Three Prophetic Challenges to the Church* (Grand Rapids, Michigan: William B. Eerdmans, 1990), 3.

8 Ibid., 7.

ENVISIONING AN EMBODIED COMPARATIVE THEOLOGY OF LIBERATION 207

is missed, and allowed to pass by, the loss for the Church, for the Gospel and for all the people of South Africa will be immeasurable.[9]

In this document, (some) South African theologians committed to justice called for "a response from Christians that is biblical, spiritual, pastoral, and above all, prophetic."[10] They contended that such a pastoral, prophetic, and practical theology was needed at that hour (*kairos*) to purge and heal the South African society of the evil of racism, and facilitate transformation and reconciliation between the oppressors and the oppressed.

Inspired by the South African *Kairos Document*, theologians in Central America also came together to put forth a *kairos* statement on the prevailing conditions[11] and the needed response of the church.

> ... This is the Central American *Kairos*: a chance for grace in which the Lord calls us to take up the challenges of this historic hour. A chance for grace to create a new international order where right makes might and not vice-versa, where peoples who have been denied and humiliated through the centuries become free human beings, to live in sovereignty and self-determination where nations can live together in brotherhood and sisterhood without any Empire threatening them ...[12]

Soon a similar move was undertaken at a wider level, when theologians from South Africa, Central America, and Asia came together to issue a joint statement named, *The Road to Damascus*. Recalling the conversion of Paul on the outskirts of Damascus, it insisted that

> 85. What was revealed to Saul was that God was not on the side of the religious and political authorities who had killed Jesus. On the contrary, God was on the side of the One who had been crucified as a blasphemer, who had been accused of being possessed by Beelzebul, who had been handed over as a traitor, an agitator, a pretender to the throne of David and a critic of Temple. On the road to Damascus Saul was faced with this

---

9   *The Kairos Document: Challenge to the Church*, Revised second edition (Grand Rapids, Michigan: Skotaville Publishers, 1986), 1.
10   Ibid., 17.
11   The context in Central America was marked by poverty and violence, perpetuated both by the local military rule and capitalism. See, Brown, *Kairos*, 78–81.
12   Ibid., 94–95.

208 CHAPTER 8

conflict between two images or beliefs about God. He was stuck blind by it. It was his *Kairos*. ...

86. This *kairos* on the road to Damascus must be taken seriously by all who in the name of God support the persecution of Christians who side with the poor. The call to conversion is loud and clear.[13]

Turning to the American context, it is believed that the context of racial discrimination and violence against people of color, particularly black people, and their struggles to resist and assert their agency is the *kairos* moment. Writing on this, Kelly Brown Douglas notes that,

> ... this time in the life of the country is a *kairos* time. *Kairos* time is the right or opportune time. It is a decisive moment in history that potentially has far-reaching impact. It is often a chaotic period, a time of crisis. However, it is through the chaos and crisis that God is fully present, disrupting things as they are and providing an opening to a new future- to God's future. *Kairos* time is, therefore, a time pregnant with infinite possibilities for new life. *Kairos* time is God's time. It is time bursting forth with God's call to a new way of living in the world. It is God calling us to a new relationship with our very history and sense of self, and thus to a new relationship with one another, and even with God.[14]

In all these different contextual interpretations of *kairos*, we can say that there is a common underlying urge to acknowledge the historical crisis in each situation and recognize the possibilities of acting (together) to change that situation. Having seen the conceptualization and usage of *kairos* in (the above) historical contexts, in the following section, let me delve further into its theological depth using Paul Tillich as my interlocuter.

1.2 *Paul Tillich's Conceptualization of* Kairos[15]

We first come across *kairos* in Tillich's corpus in the post First World War context.[16] After the destruction wrought about by the war, Tillich and his

---

13   Ibid., 135.

14   Douglas, *Stand Your Ground*, 206.

15   Tillich's earliest use of *kairos* goes back to the 1920s when he was the member of the "*Kairos* Circle." One of his earliest essays is "Kairos" that appeared in *Die Tat*, Vol. XIV (1922), Heft 5. Reproduced in Paul Tillich, *The Protestant Era*, trans. James Luther Adams (Chicago: The University of Chicago Press, 1953), vii & 32–51.

16   During the First World War, Tillich volunteered as an army chaplain and served in Bieuxy (France) and in Verdun, where he "experienced horrific hostilities," as a result of which, in

colleagues believed that the conditions were finally conducive for the birth of a new culture of Religious Socialism. Religious socialism, for him, was the perfect situation where the "sacramental" and the "rationally critical" attitudes of the society (Christian German society in his case) towards a particular historical situation met together in the prophetic attitude, giving birth to a theonomous culture.[17] For Tillich, the evolution of such an ideal society seemed possible in the 1920s, and therefore, he believed that it was a moment of *kairos* for Europe and the entire world. It is in this context that, in his introduction to *The Protestant Era*, that Tillich defines *kairos* as "the moment in which the eternal *breaks* into the temporal, and the temporal is prepared to receive it."[18] However, Tillich warns us that *kairos* is not a "mere demand or an ideal," to be seen as "a momentary trend that is not reality, or as utopian," but as "the fulfilled moment of time in which the present and the future, the holy that is given and the holy that is demanded meet, and from whose concrete tensions the new creation proceeds in which sacred import is realized in necessary form."[19]

While his earlier writings such as *The Protestant Era* had a more visible political bent, in the third volume of his *Systematic Theology*, Tillich gives a more theological (and perhaps less explicitly political) reflection on the subject. Here he suggests that *kairos* is a mature moment, where "maturity means not only the ability to receive the central manifestation of the Kingdom of God but also the greatest power to resist it."[20] In other words, it is a moment when the acceptance and the rejection of the divine by the human in history are

---

March 1918, he ended with an acute nervous disorder. After the war, in a context where there were new explorations for restructuring the (European) social order, Tillich became interested in writing about religious socialism. In fact, it was his 'Socialist Decision' with its anti-Nazi sentiments that led to his suspension from his chair at the University of Frankfurt am Main, ultimately leading to his move to Union Theological Seminary in New York. As Tillich himself confessed, his thought was heavily influenced by the world wars, the rise and fall of Nazism, and his forced immigration to the United States. See, Werner Schüßler, "Tillich's life and works," in *The Cambridge Companion to Paul Tillich*, ed. Russel Re Manning (Cambridge & New York: Cambridge University Press, 2009), 5–6 & Paul Tillich, *The Protestant Era,* trans. James Luther Adams (Chicago: The University of Chicago Press, 1953), ix.

17   Mark Kline Taylor, *Paul Tillich: Theologian of the Boundaries* (London and San Francisco: Collins, 1987), 56–57. Sacramental attitude for Tillich is "defined by a consciousness of the presence of the divine" in all dimensions of life. By "rationally critical" attitude, Tillich refers to the dominance of critical reasoning that desperately strives to "restore the lost presence of the holy," but at the expense of ignoring the 'givenness' of the sacred. Ibid., 55–56.

18   Tillich, *The Protestant Era*, xix. Emphasis mine.

19   Taylor, *Paul Tillich*, 57.

20   Tillich, *Systematic Theology*, vol. III, 370.

210 CHAPTER 8

at their optimal best. Thus, in *kairos* human subjectivity both agrees and disagrees with divine subjectivity, and therefore is a moment of utmost tension. But, even though Tillich located *kairos* within history, he did not believe that *kairos* could be understood in a scientific empirical manner. He believed that it was inappropriate to look for demonstrable evidence of such mo(ve)ments in history. Hence, he argued that visible expressions of theonomy "... may not be proofs that are objectively convincing."[21] Because of this unassuming and indemonstrable nature of the moment, Tillich believed that a *kairos* moment can neither be empirically tested nor analyzed, but only observed through "involved experience."[22] In that sense, we may say that the only way of knowing a *kairos* moment in history is through (some form of) direct experience.

However, Tillich proposes that it is possible to identify such moments by correlating them to the normative moment, the center of history—the great *kairos* viz. the appearance of the New Being in Jesus.[23] Tillich notes that this great *kairos* did not happen in isolation but in an historical community and with historical continuity. As Tillich notes, "[T]he appearance of the Christ in an individual person presupposes the community out of which he came (viz. the Israelite community) and the community which he creates (viz. the church)."[24] In other words, the great *kairos* cannot be the center of history without these communities. It is precisely because of these historical continuities that Tillich accepts the possibility of other *kairoi* happening at different points in history.[25] Thus, for Tillich, there is a plurality of *kairoi*, all of which are manifestations of the kingdom of God in relation to the criterion of Jesus Christ. He writes,

> The fact that *kairos*-experiences belong to the history of the churches and that the "great *kairos*," the appearance of the center of history, is again and again re-experienced through relative "*kairoi*," in which the Kingdom of God manifests itself in a particular breakthrough, is decisive for consideration. The relation of the one *kairos* to the *kairoi* is the relation of the criterion to that which stands under the criterion and the relation of the source of power to that which is nourished by the source of power. *Kairoi* have occurred and are occurring in all preparatory and receiving movements in the Church latent and manifest.[26]

---

21 Tillich, *Protestant Era*, 48. Emphasis mine.

22 Tillich, *Systematic Theology*, vol. III, 370.

23 Ibid., 369–370.

24 Ibid., 136. (text within parentheses mine).

25 Tillich, *The Protestant Era*, xix.

26 Tillich, *Systematic Theology*, vol. III, 370.

ENVISIONING AN EMBODIED COMPARATIVE THEOLOGY OF LIBERATION 211

It is important to note here that, for Tillich, the critical relation with the Great *Kairos* is fundamental and critical for the other *kairoi* in history to qualify as *kairos* in the first place.[27]

While underscoring the significance of *kairoi*, Tillich also alerts us that they are not completely free of misrepresentation or falsification, and can be "demonically distorted and... erroneous."[28] Recalling the situation in the First World War Germany, he remembers that *kairos* was used "by the nationalist movement, which, through the voice of Nazism, attacked the great *Kairos* and everything for which it stands."[29] In that sense, it is possible for *kairos* to be misconceived and misused (like in the case of the Nazis). On the other hand, it is also possible for *kairos* to be ignored and overlooked, like in the case of the Great *kairos* of Jesus Christ.[30] Therefore, *kairoi*—including the great *Kairos*—need not be absolute moments, absolute in terms of perfection or reception in the society. And yet, they are special since "something happened to some people through the power of the Kingdom of God as it became manifest in history ..."[31] Hence, even as he accepts that in reality God and God's Kingdom are never absent in history, for Tillich, *kairoi* are unique in terms of their rarity and in terms of their ability to change the course of history. He asserts,

> The Kingdom of God is always present, but the experience of its history-shaking power is not. *Kairoi* are rare and the great *kairos* is unique, but together they determine the dynamics of history in its self-transcendence.[32]

Hence, we may say that *kairoi* are fragmentary and often episodic (moments) in history that nevertheless make a difference.[33]

While much of this deliberation on *kairos* was limited to *Christian* theology, in his last lecture, "The Significance of the History of Religions for the Systematic Theologian," Tillich made some penetrating observations on religious

---

27   As we shall see shortly, it is this vital relationship that will provide the crucial thrust for my constructive theology.

28   Ibid., 371.

29   Ibid.

30   Tillich notes that even if he was the great *kairos*, Jesus was rejected by many during his time. Ibid.

31   Ibid.

32   Ibid., 372. As Tillich says elsewhere, "[N]ot everything is possible at every time, not everything is true at every time, nor is everything demanded at every moment." Tillich, *The Protestant Era*, 33.

33   Tillich, *Systematic Theology*, vol. III, 140.

212   CHAPTER 8

diversity by asking "[A]re there *kairoi* in the general history of religions?"[34] Here, Tillich asserted that all religions *strive* to become "the religion of the concrete spirit," which would be constituted by three essential elements viz. "the experience of the Holy within the finite," "the movement against the demonization of the sacramental," and "the ethical or prophetic element," i.e. the "element of 'ought to be,'" which challenges the sacramental to be rid of the demonic.[35] In that sense, all religions constantly seek to *actualize* as religions of the concrete spirit, even if only momentarily—"here and there"—in their moments of *kairoi*.[36] As Tillich elucidates,

> We can see the whole history of religions in this sense as a fight for the religion of the concrete spirit, a fight of God against religion within religion. And this phrase, a fight of God against religion within religion, could become the key for understanding the otherwise extremely chaotic, or at least seemingly chaotic, history of religions.[37]

However, as always, Tillich is emphatic that these *kairoi* should be considered against the criterion of Jesus Christ and the event of the cross. For him, it is that which happened at the cross of Jesus that is fragmentarily manifested in other *kairoi* in other places.[38] In sum, we may say that while Tillich was willing to acknowledge the presence of *kairoi* beyond Christianity, (from a Christian theological perspective) he was also surely keen on 'measuring' them against the Great *Kairos* of Jesus the Christ, the center of history.

Having seen the meaning and theological significance of *kairos*, let me now sum up the basic features of *kairos*. To begin with, it is clear that *kairos* is initiated by God. It is an act of divine grace and love that acts upon and within creation in history to inspire people to act. But, even as much as *kairos* is offered by God, human agency is also essential. As we saw in the *kairos* documents, it is a time of response to a situation that demands or calls right action. It is a time of/for change. *Kairos* is also, as Tillich asserts, a historical manifestation of the kingdom of God. Even though God's kingdom is never absent from history, *kairoi* are unique in terms of both their continuity with the past and

---

34   Taylor, *Paul Tillich*, 317. It should be noted here that though Tillich did speak of multiple *kairoi*, it was not until his last lecture that he spoke more clearly and explicitly about *kairoi* in relation to religious diversity.

35   Ibid., 318.

36   Ibid., 319.

37   Ibid.

38   Ibid., 319–320.

ENVISIONING AN EMBODIED COMPARATIVE THEOLOGY OF LIBERATION 213

their consequences for the future. Tillich also reminds us that *kairoi* have to be considered in relation to the great *Kairos*, the Christ event. For a Christian theologian, this criterion is crucial. Further, if we consider the life, death, and resurrection of Jesus Christ to be life-affirming and life giving, and that he was committed to justice for the poor and the oppressed and was in solidarity with them in their struggles, then, we may—without much difficulty—say that *kairoi* are moments of resistance and liberation. In fact, this is precisely what is evident in the *kairos* documents that we saw earlier. Finally, we saw that the breaking in of God's transforming power also happens in non-Christian cultures and religious contexts, perhaps in different ways. In other words, *kairoi* understood as divine liberation cannot be limited to the Christian tradition, but could be recognized in all religious traditions. It is based on this possibility that I want to propose that divine possessions, inlcuding Hindu possessions, can be interpreted as *kairoi*. To this task I turn next.

1.3 *Possessions as* Kairoi *in/of the Margins*

What Tillich has suggested regarding the appearance of *kairoi* beyond the Christian tradition is, in a sense, a truism. After all, God is not just a God for Christians, but for all. Hence, surely *kairos* cannot be limited to Christianity. Emboldened by this basic assumption, I want to propose in the following section that it is justifiable to identify divine possessions in Hindu and Christian Dalit communities as moments of *kairos* by recalling the observations, comparisons, and conclusions from the previous chapters. Let me acknowledge here that using a Christian category to interpret a religious phenomenon in another religious tradition (Dalit Hinduism in this case) might have imperialistic overtones. Moreover, as it can be expected, there is no (exact) equivalent to *kairos*, at least as far as I know, in the Tamil language or among Paraiyar Dalits. Yet, given the apparent pan-religious nature of *kairos* and the possibilities that it offers, I believe we can use this concept meaningfully beyond Christianity, albeit cautiously and respectfully. Moreover, I will address this issue of interpreting a non-Christian phenomena using Christian vocabulary in the next section when I turn to Spirit Christology. With this caveat, let me point out how divine possessions can be viewed as *kairoi*.

First of all, like *kairos,* which are fundamentally moments of divine intervention, we should recall that possessions are also divinely initiated. In the study of possessions among Hindu Dalit devotees, it was pointed out that the deity 'comes upon' them and fills them with divine power *through grace*. This is why, in Tamil, possessions are called *arul varuthal* (lit. the coming of grace) or *arulooruthal* (lit. springing of grace). And this was the reason why, as it was suggested by Patrick, the term 'possession' is limiting and even misleading.

Similarly, the Christian Holy Spirit charismatic possessions are also expressions of God's grace. Therefore, given that possessions are basically instances when God graciously acts in and through the devotees/believers, we can say that divine possessions are moments of *kairos*.

Secondly, possessions also involve human agency. As much as they are inspired and caused by divine grace, we saw that the beliefs and the actions *of the devotees* and the community play a major role in the process of inducing possessions. In other words, for the divine to be embodied in the bodies of the chosen ones, it not only takes initiative from above, but also includes the agreement and involvement of the community. It is in this sense that what Tillich and others have elucidated regarding *kairos*—that it is not simply an otherworldly intervention but a historical reality realized in communities through their willingness to accept the divinely inspired transformation—is also applicable for possessions. Since they are jointly enacted both by divine and human agency, it is possible to further the case that possessions can be considered as *kairoi*.

Thirdly, though *kairoi* are influential and transformative, as we noted, they are basically momentary and fragmentary in terms of occurrence. This clearly seems to be the case with possessions in both the Hindu and Christian communities. Among Hindu Dalits, we can recall that most possessions are temporary and happen during temple festivals. But even in enduring possessions we saw that while the person could be possessed regularly (rather than only at a festival), the possession experience itself was episodic happening according to the needs of the members of the community. In Christian possessions, theologically speaking, though the presence of the Holy Spirit is more permanent, the momentariness of charismatic possessions is evident.

Finally, and more importantly, what makes possessions *kairoi* is their ability to encapsulate hope, resistance, and liberation for Dalits (albeit, in their momentariness). As pointed out in the last chapter, during the moments when their untouchable bodies are filled with divine power—through the presence of the goddess or the Holy Spirit—they become emboldened and empowered. Thus, possessions are embodied moments of transformation brought about by divine intervention (with)in human history through human subjectivity to challenge caste and affirm the agency and the subjecthood of the Dalits. Therefore, we could say that possessions—as *kairoi*—are embryos of social change that germinate with new possibilities of emancipation for the Dalits. And like all other *kairoi*, these periods of resistance and agential reclamation affect the future course of history.

Thus far I have attempted to argue that possessions have the traits of, and therefore can be considered as, *kairoi*. But this being a comparative project,

ENVISIONING AN EMBODIED COMPARATIVE THEOLOGY OF LIBERATION   215

I believe it is necessary that we also ask if the concept of *kairos* itself can be enriched by seeing it through the lens of divine possessions. In the following section, I want to argue that considering divine possessions as *kairoi* can offer new insights to deepen the understanding of this Christian concept. The objective is to challenge and expand *kairos* to make it relevant in a religiously pluralistic and oppressive context like that of the Dalits.

1.4   *Re-Visioning* Kairos *Using Divine Possessions*

To begin with, considering possessions as *kairos* moments emphasizes the centrality of the body. *Kairos* is usually placed as a theological concept within history as a time when the eternal and the infinite divine power (radically) changes the temporal and the finite. This is clearly the case in the Post First World War, South African, and other contexts with which *kairos* is generally associated. In these instances, *kairos* is seen as a social, cultural, and political revolution that will alter the course of history. And this is certainly the conventional understanding of *kairos*. However, what I think is overlooked in these conceptualizations of *kairos* is the critical presence of the body. As we have seen in this book so far, in oppressive and hierarchical societies, the fundamental and crucial problem is the regulation of the body through the dynamics of performativity (of caste and other such social structures). Therefore, to imagine *kairos* only as a counter-moment/discourse/structure to oppressive moments/discourses/structures is, I am afraid, to miss the real depth of *kairos*. Rather, in the *kairoi* we have identified in possessions, what we see are instances when divine power finds concrete embodiment in (the bodies of) the Dalits. In that sense, Dalit divine possessions (and the Dalit body) serve as a corrective to the popular notions of *kairos*.

Further, what makes these *kairoi* truly authentic and meaningful is the fact that divine power acts through bodies that are ignored, despised, and rendered untouchable. Speaking as a Christian theologian who is devoted to the great *Kairos* manifested in the crucified and broken divine-human body of Jesus of Nazareth, I believe that the embodiment of the divine in the possessed Dalit bodies proves the legitimacy of these *kairoi*. In other words, I claim that these broken and oppressed bodies are crucial for *kairos*. In fact, as proposed in the second chapter, we can say that it is the brokenness of these bodies that makes them sacramental. This means that not every moment of divine possession can be interpreted as a *kairos*. It is only those possessions during which the divine finds embodiment in crucified bodies—bodies marginalized, discriminated, and despised like that of the Dalits—that can 'truly' be a *kairos*. Let me clarify here that I am not denying a place for other dominant and privileged bodies in *kairos*. They can be allies and supporters in the struggle. But *kairos* itself—for a particular issue and cause—will have to be centered on and spring from the bodies of the victims and the suffering (such as those oppressed by caste, patriarchy, or racial discrimination). This could mean that there might be multiple *kairoi* happening at a time, depending on the problem or issue, moving centrifugally from the 'bodies that don't matter,' overlapping, intersecting, and allying with, and at times even mutually challenging (given their particular commitments) other *kairoi*. I believe that such plurality of *kairoi*, even in instances when they challenge each other, can be mutually enriching.

However, this embodied *kairos* cannot be understood in a narrow individualist sense. We can recall how possessions among Dalits always occur in the presence of and in (comm)union with the entire community. Moreover, as seen in the previous chapters, the (possessed) Dalit body is intrinsically linked to the whole village (geographical) space and the Dalit body refers not just to the human body but the entire local Dalit topography. Therefore, we can say that, while *kairos* is generally believed to be characterized by the intervention of God (*theos*) and response from the human (*andros*), in the *kairos* of Dalit possessions, we see the crucified *theos* and the crucified *andros* intersecting and interacting with/in the untouchable *kosmos* (body-space)—the crucified earth that is being exploited by human greed—to empower the Dalits. In that sense, Dalit *kairoi* are not merely theonomous moments, but rather—to use the words of Raimon Panikkar—"cosmotheandric" moments.[39]

Secondly, interpreting possessions as embodied *kairoi* reminds us that *kairos* cannot be understood or viewed (only) within institutional history. Nor may *kairos* be expected always to lead to a cultural and political revolution. We see that Tillich, as open as he was to multiple and diverse occurrences of *kairoi*, was biased toward their institutional (church) or political-cultural (religious socialism) manifestations. And in the other contexts that were considered (such as South Africa and Central America), we observed that the interpretations of *kairos* were predominantly in regard with political revolution and change. Of course, it has to be acknowledged that Tillich himself considered this notion of *kairos*—especially with regard to religious socialism—to be too romantic.[40] May be this is what Tillich meant when he argued that *kairoi* cannot be assessed on an empirical basis.[41] In that sense, perhaps, Tillich also might agree that to see *kairos* solely as institutional, social, political, or cultural (re)actions is too limiting and short-sighted.

---

39   Raimon Panikkar, *The Cosmotheandric Experience: Emerging Religious Consciousness* (Maryknoll: Orbis Books, 1993), 60–61.

40   This observation is made by Taylor. See Taylor, *Paul Tillich*, 54.

41   Tillich, *The Protestant Era*, 48.

ENVISIONING AN EMBODIED COMPARATIVE THEOLOGY OF LIBERATION   217

As a challenge to such understandings of *kairos*, I suggest that the interpretation of Dalit divine possessions as *kairos* is much more realistic and promising. From my study of possessions and their interpretation as *kairos*, I can see that there is multiple and a plurality of *kairoi* that are possible. They do not and need not occur at visibly (and explicitly) recognizable conducive historical moments. These *kairoi* may not (openly) disturb or topple unjust structures or challenge discriminatory practices. But, as noted earlier, possessions do challenge the caste system as hidden transcripts and infrapolitics, pushing and disturbing the oppressive powers in subtle and tacit ways. Transformation brought about by *kairos* is not about drastic change, but rather about empowerment to survive and be resilient in the face of oppression. Because marginalization and oppression is an everyday lived reality for Dalit bodies and they (have to) constantly find creative ways of being, resisting, and thriving *within* their (age old) religious and cultural rituals, in a sense, every moment is 'optimal' for resistance and transformation, and hence, every moment is indeed a moment of *kairos*. And, as we saw in the previous chapter, these moments of *kairos* are crucial for any revolution or rebellion, the ultimate *kairos* (we may say)—if it ever materializes—to happen. To neglect these moments of *kairoi* is to fall into the danger of invisibilizing alternative modes of resistance and assertion on the grounds that these are politically insignificant.

Thirdly, by seeing *kairos* through the lens of divine possessions, we find that there is disruption and deconstruction of dominant (which are often divisive and hegemonic) epistemic and social structures happening at multiple levels. First, in opposition to the conventional compartmentalized understanding of religion, we observed the synergetic interweaving of religious traditions (in this case Hinduism and Christianity) in/as Paraiyar Dalit religion which becomes particularly visible during possessions. Obviously, this does not mean that there are no distinct aspects to the possessions in the Hindu and the Christian traditions. As we have seen in the earlier chapters, there are clear differences between Hindu and Christian possessions. But what we can say is that there is certainly an ongoing mutual conversation and continuation across religious boundaries within the framework of Dalit religious possessions. Along with this, we also noted the erasure of the religious-secular divide in Dalit conceptualization and experience of religion that is symbolic of Paraiyar religiosity. Moreover, we also saw that—though only in Hindu possessions—the dismantling of gender binary norms. Therefore, I believe it is possible to claim that viewing possessions as *kairos* reveals new and radical ways of being that disrupt and re-present existing (and imposed) norms of the society.

Finally, imagining possessions as *kairos* helps us in arriving at a complex and yet a different and deeper understanding of social evil, resistance, and liberation. As we saw in the previous chapters, most Dalits who were interviewed did not speak of possessions directly in relation to caste. Rather they seemed to speak in a symbolic religious language which, as suggested in the earlier chapters, may be connected to the social oppression that they are facing. Thus, resistance and assertion of agency in *kairos* as possessions happens (more) at a symbolic level where caste evil is taken to a metaphysical level and described and challenged using symbolic language such as healing and exorcism. And liberation, as pointed out earlier, rather than involving political rallies and protests, manifests itself as a(nother) way of being and living within the caste society. Therefore, a *kairos* moment is marked not only by conspicuous political movements as it is conventionally understood, but also by (relatively less) disruptive phenomena like divine possessions when the oppressed raise their voices and assert themselves right under the nose of their (upper-) caste oppressors, and, on occasions, even belittling them with their approval.

In conclusion, we can contend that divine possessions among the Dalit communities are—to use Tillichian vocabulary—occasions when the demonic is resisted and a (new) theonomy becomes visibly pronounced, not just in (historical) time but in the whole Dalit body-space. Hence, I believe we can assert that divine possessions are moments of *kairos* when the eternal breaks into the temporal, when the cosmotheandric forces converge in the possessed Dalit bodies to creatively challenge the powers that threaten their being, giving them "the courage to be."[42] Thus, possessions are *kairotic* instances when the New Being (revealed in the great *Kairos*) is experienced again, concretely though fragmentarily in Dalit bodies, impacting the culture in which it appears, and thereby becoming yet another occasion when the Kingdom of God can be glimpsed in history.

2 Toward an Embodied Theology of *Kairos*

Having argued that divine possessions can be legitimately and relevantly seen as *kairos* moments, now I want to look at the theological essence in these moments. An integral aspect of this exploration will be the theological re-imagination and re-vision of immanence, creativity, and liberation, not just pertaining to Dalits but the oppressed in general. I begin this section by revisiting the criterion of *kairoi*, viz. the great *Kairos* of the appearance of New Being in Jesus as the Christ. Using the symbol of Christ as the theological pivot is particularly helpful in articulating

---

42   Adapted from Paul Tillich, *The Courage to Be* (New Haven: Yale University Press, 1956).

a theology of liberation (given that this is the objective of this book) based on the emancipatory motifs inherent in the Christ event. However, while making this Christological move, I believe it is necessary to demonstrate the inclusive and universal meaning and depth of the symbol of Christ. I intend to do this by using the framework of Spirit Christology to propose an expansive and yet faithful understanding of the symbol of Christ that will in turn allow me to offer liberative interpretations of possessions. Finally, using this Christological impetus as my theological locus, I will articulate a comparative theology of liberation taking into consideration the rich possibilities offered by divine possessions.

2.1   *Christ and* Kairoi

In the previous section we saw that *kairoi* will have to be seen in relation to the great *kairos* of Jesus, the Christ. As Tillich insists, the great *kairos* serves as the criterion and source of power for all other *kairoi* to make them instantiations of the appearance of God's kingdom in history. In other words, whatever promise any *kairos* might hold, it is possible only because of its relationship to the "center of history."[43] I agree with Tillich that it is imperative that, from a *Christian perspective*, every *kairoi* in history be accountable to this one great *kairos*. Hence, as a Christian theologian, I firmly believe that it is essential to measure and interpret the essence of the *kairoi* moments in reference to the life, ministry, death, and resurrection of Jesus the Christ.

That being the case, if we consider possessions as *kairoi*, then it becomes mandatory that they must also be interpreted in relation to the great *kairos*. This means that possessions—along with the promise and the potential that they embody—will have to be seen and interpreted through the symbol of Christ.[44] However, while it is natural to interpret *Christian* divine possessions through the normative lens of Christ, is it acceptable and appropriate to do the same for *Hindu* possessions? Will this turn to Christology impede or cause a strain in this comparative theology of liberation? Will Christ 'mess-up' the interreligious study done so far? Or is the inclusion of a Christian symbol to interpret a non-Christian religious experience an act of imperialistic assimilation? These questions, though not new, are nevertheless important ones, especially for a comparative project such as this. Therefore, relating Hindu possessions to Christ necessitates a convincing explanation as to why and how Christ can

---

43   Tillich, *Systematic Theology*, vol. III, 364. As seen earlier, Tillich qualifies the center of history not in literal (calendrical) terms, but rather in terms of serving as *the* pivotal and paradigm shifting moment in human history.

44   While I agree that there are other ways of theologically interpreting possessions (using the lens of pneumatology, for instance), I choose to use a Christological route.

220   CHAPTER 8

be employed as a normative symbol for interpreting non-Christian religious phenomena. In the following section, acknowledging that there are different ways of interpreting Christ as a universal symbol, I choose Spirit Christology as my theological locus.[45]

2.2   *Spirit Christology*

In simple terms, Spirit Christology is an interpretation of the person of Jesus, the Christ event, and, its historical repercussions and corollaries (which includes the church) through the divine Spirit.[46] In the words of Ralph Del Colle,

> Spirit-christology focuses on theological reflection on the role of the Holy Spirit in christology proper. It seeks to understand both "who Christ is" and "what Christ has done" from the perspective of the third article of the creed: "I believe in the Holy Spirit, the Lord and Giver of Life." … It proposes that the relationship between Jesus and God and the role of Christ in redemption cannot be fully understood unless there is an explicitly pneumatological dimension. In other words, the relationship between Jesus and the Spirit is as important to conveying the truth of the Christological mystery with its soteriological consequences as that of Jesus and the Word.[47]

In other words, Spirit Christology emphasizes the significance of the Holy Spirit in understanding the event of divine revelation in Jesus the Christ and the Spirit's centrality in the history of salvation. It is the Spirit that makes Jesus who he is—to recall Tillich—the bearer of the New Being.

> The divine Spirit was present in Jesus as the Christ without distortion. In him the New Being appeared as the criterion of all Spiritual experiences

---

45   Though there are many Christologies that can be used to argue for Christ's universal relevance, because the symbol of the Spirit is more relatable to the understanding of God in most religious traditions, I choose to use this Christological method. For other Christologies, see chapter six of Roger Haight, *Jesus: Symbol of God* (Maryknoll, NY: Orbis Books, 1999), 152–184. Also, see, Jaroslav Pelikan, *Jesus Through the Centuries: His Place in the History of Culture* (New Haven and London: Yale University Press, 1985) & Veli-Matti Kärkkäinen, *Christology: A Global Introduction*, 2nd edition (Grand Rapids, Michigan: Baker Academic, 2016).

46   Even if I may have used the terms before, let me clarify that I use 'Spirit' to denote the divine/Holy Spirit or the Spirit of God, while 'spirit' refers to the human spirit. For more on this difference see, Tillich, *Systematic Theology*, vol. III, 111–114.

47   Ralph Del Colle, *Christ and the Spirit: Spirit-Christology in Trinitiarian Perspective* (New York and Oxford: Oxford University Press, 1994), 3–4.

ENVISIONING AN EMBODIED COMPARATIVE THEOLOGY OF LIBERATION 221

> in past and future. Though subject to individual and social conditions his human spirit was entirely grasped by the Spiritual Presence; his spirit was "possessed" by the divine Spirit or, to use another figure, "God was in him." This makes him the Christ, the decisive embodiment of the New Being for historical mankind.[48]

Thus, the Spirit of God possessed Jesus in such a way that he was able to wholly embody and reveal the divine to the world. Because of this close interdependence between Christ and the Spirit in terms of their existence, identity, and function, it is possible to say that despite their distinctiveness, "the line between Christ and the Holy Spirit is blurred."[49] In fact, as G. W. H. Lampe asserts, Christ is "not other than the Spirit."[50] In that sense, it is because of the presence of the Spirit in its perfection, that Jesus attained a universal salvific nature that is applicable for all humanity.[51] And, as Tillich emphasizes, (as in the case of *kairos*), it is the presence of the Spirit in Jesus makes him the criterion for all experiences of the Spirit. The unbounded and unlimited experience of the Spirit in Jesus makes him "the keystone in the *arch of Spiritual manifestations in history.*"[52]

2.3 *Spirit Christology and Religious Diversity*

Having considered the basic elements of Spirit Christology, let me now turn to the question of religious pluralism. I want to begin with the basic assumption that, since the Spirit of God is the source and sustenance of all life, the power of creativity, it is necessary that the Spirit must also be present universally across time and space. If that is the case then, "the Spirit is spread abroad, and it is not necessary to think that God as Spirit can be incarnated only once in history" in Jesus the Christ.[53] This implies that the Spirit cannot be bound to any religious tradition or community, including Christianity. In that sense, "by recognizing that the Spirit is operative outside the Christian sphere," Spirit Christology "is open to other mediations of God."[54]

---

48 Tillich, *Systematic Theology*, vol. III, 144.

49 Clarke, *Dalits and Christianity*, 186.

50 G. W. H. Lampe, *God as Spirit: The Bampton Lectures, 1976* (Oxford: Clarendon Press, 1977), 118.

51 Haight, *Jesus*, 456.

52 Tillich, *Systematic Theology*, vol. III, 146–147. Emphasis mine.

53 Haight, *Jesus*, 456.

54 Ibid.

222 CHAPTER 8

However, even as Spirit Christology offers this possibility of seeing the presence of God's revelation in other religious traditions, it is important to recall the intrinsic relationship between the Spirit and the Christ. This means that the work of the Spirit in other religions cannot be separated from the work of Jesus the Christ. Karl Rahner captures this succinctly when he writes,

> Christ is present and efficacious in the non-Christian believer (and therefore in the non-Christian religions) through his Spirit... If the non-Christian can have a redeeming faith and if it is permissible for us to hope that this faith really exists on a wide scale, then such a faith is, of course, made possible and sustained by the supernatural grace of the Holy Spirit. And this is the Spirit who proceeds from the Father and the Son, so that as the Spirit of the eternal Logos he can and must, at least in this sense, be called the Spirit of Christ, the incarnate divine Word.... Since this Spirit always and everywhere sustains justifying faith, this faith is from the outset, always and everywhere, a faith that comes into being in the Spirit of Jesus Christ, who is present and efficacious in all faith...[55]

Thus, Rahner believes that the validity of the Spirit in non-Christian traditions is possible through Christ and his Spirit alone, encouraging him to assert that non-Christians are "anonymous Christians."[56] But, here one may question whether seeing Christ present in other religions has a limiting and assimilating effect on the functioning of the Spirit in them. In other words, is it appropriate to look for (the Spirit of) Christ in other religious traditions?

Here I find the Spirit Christologies of Gavin D'Costa and Jacques Dupuis very helpful. Speaking from a Trinitarian perspective, D' Costa suggests a Christocentric pneumatology which, while claiming that Christ is the ultimate truth criterion for understanding the Spirit, "does not preclude the universal workings of the Spirit, which 'blows where it will.'"[57] He believes that "the values, truth and insights possessed in Christ not only question, but are also enlarged and enriched through meeting people from other religions."[58] In a similar vein, Jacques Dupuis also insists that by combining the "punctual event of Jesus

---

55 Karl Rahner, *Theological Investigation*, vol. XVII, *Jesus, Man, and the Church*, transl. Margaret Kohl (New York: Crossroad, 1981), 46–47.

56 Karl Rahner, *Theological Investigations*, vol. XII, *Confrontations 2*, transl. David Bourke (New York: Seabury Press, 1974), 165.

57 Gavin D'Costa, *Theology and Religious Pluralism: The Challenge of Other Religions* (Oxford and New York: Basil Blackwell, 1986), 135.

58 Ibid, 133.

ENVISIONING AN EMBODIED COMPARATIVE THEOLOGY OF LIBERATION 223

Christ and the universal action and dynamic influence of the Spirit of God," it is possible to see that "while the Christ-event plays an irreplaceable function in God's design for humankind, it can never be taken in isolation but must always be viewed within the manifold modality of the divine self-disclosure and manifestation through the Word and the Spirit."[59] In other words, the other manifestations of the Spirit (and the logos, which Dupuis also considers) are inseparable from and mutually in dialogue with the Spirit in/of Christ.[60] As Knitter notes, for Dupuis, "what the Spirit is about in other religions may be genuinely different from what one finds in God's word in Jesus—never contradictory to, but really different from. To affirm the Spirit within other cultures and religions implies, therefore, that God has more to say to humanity than what God has said in Jesus."[61]

Let me pause here to acknowledge that though I have given a broad picture of Spirit Christology in conversation with several theologians, their Christological positions are not the same, particularly with respect to religious diversity. For instance, the Christology of Haight is pluralistic, whereas that of Rahner, D'Costa and Dupuis is inclusivistic.[62] I myself lean close to the inclusivist camp, and with respect to Spirit Christology I will say that I am particularly closer to the positions of D'Costa and Dupuis. I find their pneumetological Trinitarian Christocentrism helpful to balance the truth of God's universal and distinct presence in different religious communities with the normative significance that Christ has for me as a Christian theologian. I believe that such a broad 'Spirit' based understanding of Christ can enhance, rather than hinder, the ability of a Christian to see and understand God's salvific presence and acts in other traditions, even if they may not resonate with her own faith in Christ.[63]

In conclusion, we may say that there are four basic features of Spirit Christology that become clear with respect to religious diversity. Firstly, it emphasizes that the Spirit and Christ are integrally interrelated, and may be synonymously understood even if they have their distinct natures. Secondly, it acknowledges the universality of the Spirit as the creative and empowering presence of God across history. Thirdly, Spirit Christology insists that from the Christian

---

59 Jacques Dupuis, *Toward a Christian Theology of Religious Pluralism* (Maryknoll, New York: Orbis Books, 1997), 207.

60 But unlike D'Costa, Dupuis believes in a " 'marvelous convergence,' of all things and all religious traditions in the Reign of God and in the Christ-omega." Ibid, 390.

61 Knitter, *Introducing Theology of Religions*, 90–91.

62 For a brief but helpful presentation of the different positions in Spirit Christology see, Haight, *Jesus*, 446–447 & 454–455.

63 However, while I claim to be an (open) inclusivist, I understand that some readers might situate me as a pluralist or somewhere within the broad range between the two camps.

theological perspective, these multiple manifestations of the Spirit will have to be seen and interpreted in relation to and (according to some theologians) qualified by the Christ event. Finally, correlating and interpreting other manifestations of the Spirit through the (Spirit of) Christ does not limit or dominate them but rather mutually clarifies and enhances each other.

With respect to possessions, we may say that if the Spirit of Christ is actively present in all religions, then Christ is also actively 'present' in the possessions. In that sense, I believe that there is no reason why possessions could not be considered as Christic moments. Methodologically, I believe that this move— of seeing the presence of Christ in possessions—opens new but theologically accountable ways of understanding the presence of God during those moments.[64] And, as we learned from D'Costa and Dupuis, re-viewing the Christ event through these *kairotic* possessions help us to enhance and deepen our comprehension of Christ and the Christ event. Keeping this in mind, I turn next to my theological reflection of divine possessions as Christic *kairos* moments.

2.4 The Untouchable God in Untouchable Bodies: A Constructive Theological Imagination

If possessions as *kairoi* are related to and accountable to the Christ event, how do we speak of God in these moments? Driven by this fundamental question and helped by Spirit Christology, in this section, I will make the following arguments. First, considering the immanental dimension of the symbol of the crucified Christ, and given his solidarity with the poor and the oppressed, we can infer that the 'God-hosting' Dalit bodies also manifest divine immanence. Secondly, drawing upon the radically new possibilities that are made possible in the Christ event, we can say that during possessions we encounter God, not just as a creative force, but as transgressive creativity. Finally, the liberative motifs in possessions, viewed through the lens of Spirit Christology, enable us to envision alternative ways of imagining liberation and human flourishing.

2.4.1 Untouchable Divine Immanence

Christology emphasizes divine immanence. In the words of Clarke, "God as Christ symbolizes God as redemptively embracive of the world by becoming immanent."[65] Spirit Christology speaks of this immanence in terms of the presence of the Spirit of Christ. It is the Spirit in Jesus who made him the central medium of

---

64 Accountability is an important criterion for doing theology. For the three criteria for doing constructive theology see, Roger Haight, *Dynamics of Theology* (Maryknoll, New York: Orbis Books, 2001), 210–212.

65 Clarke, *Dalits and Christianity*, 186.

God's revelation and the norm of God's salvation. After the resurrection, it was the same Spirit who became synonymous with Jesus.[66] Also, in as much as grace is universal, God revealed in Christ is present and operative in all human communities as the Spirit.[67] In that sense, the immanence of God made possible in the incarnation as the Christ is also available and applicable for all people, in all religions and cultures, albeit in different ways, through the Spirit.

Given this universality of the immanence of God in Christ through the Spirit, one can say that God's immanence is also made visible in divine possessions. It was already pointed out that in Hindu possessions, the experience involved the *coming* of the goddess upon the devotees. We had also seen that this act of divine embodiment is not actually an act of 'possession' (taking control) as it is often wrongly portrayed and termed, but rather the springing or descending of grace (*arulooruthal* or *arul varuthal*). In the charismatic Holy Spirit possessions, it is evident that through grace divine power comes upon and fills the Christian believer. In that sense, the common feature of both Hindu and Christian possessions is gracious divine immanence.

To further re-imagine immanence during possessions, I believe that process philosophy/theology can serve as a helpful framework. In the words of Alfred North Whitehead, who suggests that, because God is "primordial" ("infinite") and "consequent" (affected by the world), God is not only the "lure for feeling, the eternal urge of desire," but is also "the presupposed actuality of conceptual operation, in unison of becoming with every other creative act."[68] Christ, in that case, perfectly denotes both these dimensions—primordial in terms of his divinity and consequent in terms of his vulnerable humanity. And if, "the whole point of the unique incarnation is to open up a new intimacy with the infinite,"[69] then we may say that what we see in possessions—where God both invokes and is invoked, initiates and is initiated, acts and is acted upon by devotees/believers—are moments of that (deeper) intimacy made visible.

Such deep intimacy and immanence between the divine and creation is not unheard of.[70] However, what is noteworthy about divine immanence in possessions is the aspect of embodiment. As noted in the earlier chapters,

---

66   Haight, *Jesus*, 450.
67   Haight states, inferring from Rahner, that "[G]race is God as Spirit." Ibid., 452.
68   Alfred North Whitehead, *Process and Reality; An Essay in Cosmology* (New York: The Free Press, 1985), 345.
69   Catherine Keller, *On the Mystery: Discerning Divinity in Process* (Minneapolis: Fortress Press, 2008), 151.
70   A good comparative theological work that argues for a dynamic non-dualism is Thatamanil, *The Immanent Divine*.

possessions have to be understood in relation to the body of those possessed. This being the case, given that the incarnation, in the most precise terms, is the embodied immanence of God—for any other assumption would mean slipping into gnostic heresies—possessions depict the immanent presence of God in a truly incarnational and therefore, Christic sense. In other words, if it is embodiment that is crucial for the incarnation of God in Christ and the divine immanence it encapsulates, then possessions can be said to be legitimate forms of experiencing and witnessing the immanence of God.

But this closeness between the incarnated body of God in Jesus the Christ and the possessed body (not to mention the correlation between the two bodies which we shall consider shortly), directs us toward an important attribute of embodied immanence in Christ. As Tillich emphatically observes, "only by taking suffering death upon himself could Jesus be the Christ, because it is only in this way could he participate completely in existence and conquer every force of estrangement which tried to dissolve his unity with God,"[71] thus implying that the suffering and crucifixion of Jesus are central to the Christ event. In other words, it is the brokenness of Christ that defines, realizes, and facilitates embodied immanence.[72]

In that sense, we may say that rather than understanding immanence in abstraction or in a solely embodied sense, it is in brokenness that the immanence of God is best revealed. While, in general, the body, as much as it "constitutes a site of divine revelation," can be considered as the "basic human sacrament,"[73] as I had posited in the second chapter when constructing the framework for using the Dalit body as a comparative category and had reasserted in the section on *kairos*, we can say that it is the *suffering and crucified bodies* that are truly (but not exclusively) sacramental, and therefore, symbolize divine immanence in an authentic manner.[74] In that sense, recalling that the term 'Dalit' means to be broken and crushed (not to mention humiliated and discriminated as untouchable), I will assert that the Dalitness of possessions makes them true (but not sole) moments of divine immanence. To make this assertion, I find Eboni Marshall Turman's bold proposal helpful. After her careful study of the

---

71   Tillich, *Systematic Theology*, vol. II, 123. It is necessary to note here that Tillich insists that Jesus did not become the Christ *because* of his death on the cross. Rather, the cross is "an expression of the New Being in him." Ibid., 123–124.

72   However, this does not mean that the suffering of Jesus was willed by God. Rather, as Haight suggests, what this implies is that the suffering and death of Jesus on the cross did play a defining role in attaining his normative status. Roger Haight, *Future of Christology* (London and New York: Continuum, 2008), 87–89.

73   Copeland, *Enfleshing Freedom*, 8.

74   There may be other ways of experiencing the divine such as in love.

problems pertaining to the place and role of black women in black churches, Turman argues that the body of the human Jesus (of Nazareth) is symbolized today by the bodies of black women, which may be analogously and expansively applied to Dalits. She says,

> Clearly, the ethical identity of Jesus Christ can be identified in the bodies of black church women who by *reaching*, renounce the restrictions that society has placed on their destiny and affirm the *inconceivable more* that is acting *in* their flesh; who by *standing* in their brokenness dare to include their reality as a determinant of *what ought to be* and thereby wrestle with the *tension* that inevitably accompanies the attempt to negotiate seemingly opposed identities; and who by swaying to the beat embody "fitting action" that suggests that the body must never be held hostage by the tension that arises from mediating between apparent opposites. Thus, in accordance with the logic of incarnation revealed in the Chalcedonian definition and as theorized in the doctrine of the incarnation as womanist mediating ethic, womanist incarnation ethics unapologetically concludes that Christ is *homoousious* with black women as to his humanity, and therefore appeals to the bodies of black women as the starting point for the black church to craft its resistance to intracommunal body injustice.[75]

Like the bodies of black women, who by virtue of their oppression and resistance re-present Christ in the same way as his humanity did two thousand years ago, the bodies of Dalits—both Hindu and Christian—can also be considered *homoousious* with Christ's human nature. Divine possessions enable us to see this possibility of Dalits and Jesus the Christ sharing the same substance.

Here one may argue that this limits the grace of God's immanent presence in the world. It also creates the impression that divine grace is biased towards certain groups of people viz. those that are historically oppressed. I agree that grace and the movement of the Spirit cannot be restricted or bound (which is the basic assumption on which this theological reflection is being constructed) and that oppression itself is not monolithic given the intersectionalities of social structures and systems (such as caste, class, gender, race, and so on). Nonetheless, even as I acknowledge these important warnings, I will (again)

---

75   Eboni Marshall Turman, *Toward a Womanist Ethic of Incarnation: Black Bodies, the Black Church and the Council of Chalcedon* (New York: Palgrave Macmillan, 2013), 171. *Homoousious*, lit. same substance, is used to refer to the same nature of God the Father and God the Son in the Trinity.

228   CHAPTER 8

say along with James Cone that since it is the *crucified* savior who is "at the heart of the Christian faith," to fail to see the parallels and the primacy of the crucified bodies is an act of (perhaps deliberate) theological "blindness."[76] Accordingly, Christian theology, including a comparative enterprise such as mine, is obligated to see, interpret, and experience Jesus the Christ through the experiences of the crucified (which in Cone's study are lynched black) bodies. In that sense, I believe it is right to perceive Dalit bodies as sites of Christic divine immanence privileged through their Dalitness and divine grace. Therefore, I will boldly assert (once again) that divine possessions show that Christic divine immanence is faithfully and authentically (but not solely) symbolized in Dalit bodies.[77]

2.4.2   Transgressive Creativity
The biblical foundations of Spirit Christology lie in creation. The combined and inseparable presence of the Spirit (Genesis 1: 2) and the Word (John 1: 1) in the creation narratives attests to this. It was the Spirit of Christ who was active in creation in the past. And, it is the same Spirit who continues to be operative with-in her creation in the present. As Haight elucidates, "God as Spirit ... indicates God at work, as active, and as power, energy, or force that accomplishes something ... God as Spirit is God present to and at work, outside of God's self, *in the world of God's creation.*"[78] Further, to speak of God's presence in creation, is also to acknowledge that the divine act of creation in and through Christ and the Spirit is not a completed, but an ongoing, activity.

Taking these fundamental aspects of God's vocation of creating further, I would assert that God's ongoing act of creation is not from 'out there' but from 'here-within.' Process philosopher Alfred Whitehead succinctly captures this when he writes,

> The true metaphysical position is that God is the aboriginal instance of this creativity, and is therefore the aboriginal condition which qualifies its action. It is the function of actuality to characterize the creativity, and God is the eternal primordial character. But, of course, there is no meaning to 'creativity' apart from his creatures,' and no meaning to 'God' apart

---

76   Cone, *The Cross and the Lynching Tree*, 1, 37–38 & 159. Cone makes this allegation against white theologians, especially Reinhold Niebuhr.

77   To further understand the prioritization of the poor and the oppressed and the questions it raises and the responses see, Jon Sobrino, *No Salvation Outside the Poor: Prophetic-Utopian Essays* (Maryknoll, New York: Orbis Books, 2008), 72–76.

78   Haight, *Jesus*, 447–448. Emphasis mine.

ENVISIONING AN EMBODIED COMPARATIVE THEOLOGY OF LIBERATION   229

from the 'creativity' and the 'temporal creatures,' and no meaning to the 'temporal creatures' apart from 'creativity from God.'[79]

That is, it is precisely creational subjectivity that qualifies and facilitates divine creativity. But, what is also evident in this divine creativity being rooted in creaturely creativity is the vulnerability of God. On this Whitehead notes,

> The consequent nature of God is the fulfilment of his experience by his reception of the multiple freedom of actuality into the harmony of his own actualization. It is God as really actual, completing the deficiency of his mere conceptual actuality.[80]

In other words, even if God is the original (or primordial) force behind and with all creation, God's work of creativity (and Godself, in terms of God's consequent nature) is completed only in creaturely subjectivity (and creativity). As Whitehead puts it, "God is completed by the individual, fluent satisfactions of finite act, and the temporal occasions are completed by their everlasting union with their transformed selves..."[81] Here, I find Thatamanil's proposal for a non-dualistic dynamic imagination of God providing better clarity on this subject. He stresses that

> God is neither immutable, absolute, nor unrelated. The world cannot be apart from divine creativity; divine creativity is inseparable from what it creates. Dynamic nondualism is deeply and irrevocably relational, even if peculiarly so, because creation is a relation that creates the terms of the relation.[82]

God therefore, can be imagined as ontological creativity in perpetual synergetic relationship with the creation, affecting it and being affected by it.[83] To put this in concrete and simple Christian terms, we can claim that God as creativity—as revealed, present, and functional in Christ and the Spirit—is a God of eternal and unending possibilities, made possible through a dynamic relationship with-in creation. As Robert Mesle points out, "God makes available and draws

---

79   Whitehead, *Process and Reality*, 225.
80   Ibid., 349.
81   Ibid., 347.
82   Thatamanil, *The Immanent Divine*, 205.
83   The notion of God as ontological creativity comes from Joseph Bracken and Robert Neville. Cited by Thatamanil. Ibid., 186–195.

us toward a range of possibilities that enable us to envision a world beyond the world already actualized, to choose forms of self-creativity beyond what the world alone made possible."[84]

Such a view of God as dynamic ontological creativity helps us to construe the deeper theological significance of possessions. As deduced earlier, possessions are moments of divine immanence embodied with-in broken (Dalit) bodies. But, in the individual study of Hindu and Christian possessions in chapters four and six, and the comparative interpretations in the seventh chapter, it was shown that these moments of immanence are filled with new possibilities of imagining new, or to be accurate, alternative ways of living and surviving in a caste society. In that sense, these are also moments of immanental divine creative activity, or to be more precise, divine possibilities operating in the possessed Dalit bodies. In fact, it is because of this creatively transformative dimension of possessions—in being periods of resistance and agential reclamation that affect the future course of history—that I was able to call these moments, *kairos*. However, it should be noted that possession as a creative moment is not simply God acting upon human subjects. On the contrary, we repeatedly saw that possessions—despite being experiences of grace *initiated by God*—are strictly based on divine-human coalition. It may be categorically said that without human initiatives possessions cannot happen. To put it theologically, human freedom is not curtailed by divine grace in possessions, but rather re-visioned and enhanced in the process.

Writing from the perspective of Spirit Christology, Tillich points out that Spiritual presence or the Spirit possessing a person does not entail destroying the "essential i.e. rational structure."[85] Similarly, Haight also asserts that the God in Christ present and acting as Spirit in us "should not be understood as a suppression of human talent but of God working within."[86] In that sense, we can say that during possession moments, we see divine and human creativity working together in Dalit bodies, so that human/Dalit "agency might be altered in a deeper and more abiding fashion."[87] Therefore, recalling the momentariness and fragmentary nature of possessions as *kairoi*, we can say that possessions are episodic but nonetheless effective times when God as dynamic creativity co-acting with-in human subjectivity becomes visible in Dalit bodies.

---

84   C. Robert Mesle, *Process-Relational Philosophy: An Introduction to Alfred North Whitehead* (West Conshohocken, Pennsylvania: Templeton Press 2008), 86.

85   Tillich, *Systematic Theology: Volume III*, 112.

86   Haight, *Jesus, Symbol of God*, 453.

87   Thatamanil, *The Immanent Divine*, 200.

ENVISIONING AN EMBODIED COMPARATIVE THEOLOGY OF LIBERATION   231

Finally, I would suggest that it is only because of this freedom (of momentariness?) that we are able to see in possessions, what could be called, 'transgressive creativity.' Possessions, as seen in earlier chapters, are multi-dimensional and multi-layered. First, there is the fact that in both Hindu and Christian possessions, Dalits stand and speak up, bold and aloud, accompanied by aggressive body movements, in a context where usually their voices are silenced and their activities are controlled. We also saw that in some possessions, there is walking and mapping of spaces in the village as an act of assertion. It was also pointed out that during these moments, there is a synergetic interweaving of religious practices and beliefs. Moreover, possessions also combine spiritual/religious and materialist concerns or, to put it differently, reveal the overlapping of the religious and the secular. And, we also observed the reversal, and in some cases even the disruption and queering of gender, sex, and heteronormative identities.

In sum, we may say, that possessions embody (in a literal sense) both *creative transgression*, in as much as (imposed) normative assumptions and structures are violated, and *transgressive creativity*, in terms of envisioning, enabling, and engendering new ways of *being* in untouchable (aka) transgressed (but also transgressing) bodies.[88] Speaking from a theological perspective, once again I see the Christic dimension vividly surfacing during these moments in these 'untouchable' bodies. Jesus, after all, is a "deviant"[89] transgressor in many ways: in his birth (Matthew 1: 18–19; Luke 1: 34), his life and ministry (Luke 13: 10–17; John 4), his crucifixion (Mark 15: 21–32), and not to forget, his resurrection (Matthew 28: 6; Luke 24: 5).[90] And, so is the community that he initiated (Luke 5: 30–32; Acts 10) and the kingdom he envisioned (Luke 8: 11–12). In that sense, we may say that divine possessions among Dalits reveal God in Christ as *dynamic transgressive creativity*, ushering in (even if fragmentarily)

---

88   We may recall that according to the Manu Dharma Sastra, Untouchables are the offspring of 'unholy' relationships between the *Sudras* and the higher castes. In that sense, every untouchable body is a transgressed body in itself. Oliville, *The Law Code of Manu*, 180–181.

89   Clarke makes this observation to argue for Jesus' Dalitness. Clarke, *Dalits and Christianity*, 201–208.

90   Jesus being born to an unmarried 'transgressive' woman and his closeness to tax collectors and sinners, not to forget his Samaritan episodes are noteworthy examples of Jesus' deviancy. And given that crucifixion was a form of death given to those who were rebels and lawbreakers in the Roman Empire, we may say that Jesus' life and death were indeed transgressive. For more see, Ibid.; Kahl, *Galatians Re-imagined*, 156–159. Note that I also add the resurrection as an act of transgression when Jesus breaches the bounds of physical death (symbolized by the stone covering the tomb) as well as the oppressive laws of the empire (symbolized by the Roman soldiers) in the resurrection narratives.

232   CHAPTER 8

unconventional and radically new ways of living in this world. The "transgressive corporeality" of Dalit bodies is indeed a true embodiment of transgressive divine creativity.[91]

2.4.3   Empowering Be(com)ing

Having reflected on possessions as moments that reveal God in Christ as divine immanence and transgressive creativity, in this final section, I want to turn to the question of liberation. For quite some time now, liberation theologians have emphasized the centrality of liberation in theology, particularly Christology.[92] Accordingly, to put it in basic terms, in Christ we see the liberating act of God made visible and possible to all people who are oppressed and marginalized. Because, in Jesus' life and work, but especially in his crucifixion and resurrection, the oppressed are able to see themselves, they have hope of freedom from the chains that bind and oppress them. Writing from the Black perspective, Cone perceptively portrays the relevance of Jesus the Christ to the oppressed. He says,

> The Crucified One is also the Risen Lord. Faith in the resurrection means that the historical Jesus, in his liberating words and deeds for the poor, was God's way of breaking into human history, redeeming humanity from injustice and violence, and bestowing power upon little ones in their struggle for freedom.[93]

Thus, we can agree that Jesus the Christ is the quintessential symbol of liberation in Christian theology. The same can be emphasized from the perspective of Spirit Christology as well. For instance, Haight points out that the Spirit of God in Christ is the Spirit of liberation and empowerment.[94] In fact, liberation is one of the fundamental criteria for a theology of religious diversity inspired by Spirit Christology. Writing from a Christocentric Trinitarian perspective that is open to the movement of the Spirit across the history of humankind, D'Costa asserts that the normativity of Christ essentially drives us to

---

91   This notion of transgressive corporeality is taken from MacDonald, *Transgressive Corporeality*, 116–143.

92   Please note that I speak of liberation in relation to social injustice and oppression. A helpful listing of different liberation theologies with respect to Christology is given by Haight. See Haight, *Jesus*, 365–370.

93   James H. Cone, *God of the Oppressed* (Maryknoll, New York: Orbis Books, 1997), 110.

94   Haight, *Jesus*, 454–456.

ENVISIONING AN EMBODIED COMPARATIVE THEOLOGY OF LIBERATION   233

... form a life that is oriented toward liberating humankind from the powers of evil, preaching the Good News to the poor, proclaiming release to the captives, the recovery of sight to the blind, and setting at liberty those who are oppressed; all messianic *actions* heralding God's kingdom through suffering self-giving love and service rather than worldly strength, coercion, and manipulation.[95]

In that sense, we may make the basic theological affirmation that the God immanent in Christ and the Spirit is the God who stands with and works to liberate the oppressed. Therefore, it is mandatory that any theological task or praxis be centered and oriented toward liberation.[96]

Turning to the Dalit context, I believe it is possible for us to claim that in possessions too, we do encounter a God who liberates and empowers the oppressed. In Hindu possessions, we may recall that the Dalit devotees who embody the goddess were seen as emboldened and empowered with the courage to speak and act in front of the (upper) caste people, re-assert their space, and so on. In Christian possessions, we saw how possessions are cathartic and offer opportunities to speak (often in 'tongues—glossolalia) as an act of resistance. We also observed that, in both Hindu and Christian Dalit possessions, the body becomes a site of collective memories to re-member their subjectivity within the caste matrix. Finally, I suggested that possessions can be interpreted as political acts, in which the iconic statue of B. R. Ambedkar, a powerful symbol of Dalit resistance, occupies a crucial place. Given these facts, in theological terms, we may therefore say, that the Christic norm of liberation is fulfilled in possessions. Accordingly, I believe we can say that God in Christ, immanent in the Dalit bodies during possessions as dynamic transgressive creativity, is also the force of liberation and empowerment. We may recall that it is this aspect of transformation of the status-quo of oppression and injustice that makes possessions *kairotic*. If these moments are *kairoi*, given that the original use of *kairos* by Jesus, as recorded in the gospels, was in relation to the Kingdom of God, we can say that possessions are instantiations and initiations of God's

---

95   Gavin D'Costa, "Christ, the Trinity, and Religious Diversity," in *Christian Uniqueness Reconsidered: The Myth of Pluralistic Theology of Religions*, ed. Gavin D'Costa (Maryknoll, New York: Orbis Books, 1990), 21.

96   Let me acknowledge here that I am not denying or ignoring other forms of praxis such as caring for sick, consoling the broken-hearted etc. However, I believe that focusing on such 'pastoral' dimensions of theology need not contradict or diminish the imperativeness of social/political liberation. In fact, I am convinced that these seemingly different modes of praxis are mutually dependent and enriching.

kingdom. Of course, it is only appropriate that these re-birthing moments of the kingdom begin with the Dalit bodies, given their affinity (and similarity) with the crucified Christ.

However, as it was pointed out earlier, transformation and liberation can be seen and understood differently in possessions. Firstly, as I had observed using Mahmood's post-liberal critique, agential reclamation, resistance, and liberation in possessions are not (only) about changing social structures. While this is surely important, I instead proposed, what Scott calls as hidden transcripts, infrapolitics, and everyday resistances, as the actual and more realistic forms of challenge and change that happen in most oppressive contexts. In that sense, the liberation that is seen in possessions is not the struggle for radical, rebellious, or revolutionary transformation, but rather for surviving and 'existing/being.' In a context where even existence is a challenge, as seen in the introduction and in chapter two, liberation for Dalits, in the most fundamental sense, is existence itself.

Against this background, we may say that God in Christ immanently embodied in Dalits enables them 'to be' in the midst of forces and powers that threaten them. This is no simple matter, for as Tillich asserts, the "courage to *be* is the key to being itself."[97] In fact, this *courage to be* is liberating power. No one has so clearly captured the liberative potential of the 'courage to be' as Cone. Recalling that the "courage to be," for Tillich is " 'the ethical act in which man affirms his being in spite of those elements of his existence which conflict with his essential self-affirmation (*sic*)," Cone equates it with Black Power and declares,

> Black Power ..., is a humanizing force because it is the black man's attempt to affirm his being, his attempt to be recognized as 'Thou,' in spite of the 'other,' the white power which dehumanizes him. ... The courage to be, then, is the courage to affirm one's being by striking out at the dehumanizing forces which threaten being.[98]

Using the same hermeneutical key, I will insist that what is resistive or liberative in possessions is the "courage to be" of the Dalits, the manifestation of 'Dalit power.' In that sense, Dalit power is the living power of God immanent with-in Dalit bodies as transgressive creativity amidst the forces of discrimination, dehumanization, and death.

---

97   Tillich, *The Courage to Be*, 181. Emphasis mine.

98   James H. Cone, *Black Theology and Power* (Maryknoll, New York: Orbis Books, 1997), 7.

ENVISIONING AN EMBODIED COMPARATIVE THEOLOGY OF LIBERATION 235

This doesn't mean that there is no desire or initiative to change the situation or the system. Rather, stories of hidden transcripts, infrapolitics, and everyday resistances tell us the contrary. There is always movement and action for change in possessions. After all, that is why possessions are transgressive, even if in subtle and creative ways. One of the creative ways we may (further) imagine liberation is by recalling the aspect of re-symbolization of evil alluded to in the earlier chapters as well as in this chapter. In possessions, even if caste or untouchability is not usually mentioned, social and political evils are re-visioned and resisted in a metaphysical language. As noted in chapter six, the Pentecostal theologian Amos Yong suggests that this dynamic actually goes back to the New Testament and early Christianity. In fact, Jesus and his followers, including Paul, spoke of the evil structures of the Roman Empire in these cryptic terms, as Principalities and Powers. And this encoded portrayal of oppressive political leadership is certainly conspicuous in the vision of John (The Book of Revelation).[99] I cannot say whether the Dalits in my study knew about this or spoke about this re-symbolization consciously. But I do believe that it is very possible that speaking of evil in a metaphysical and encoded language is more practical, and therefore, helpful in confronting caste.[100]

However, it is important to remember here the ambiguity of the symbol of God in relation to evil in Hindu goddess traditions wherein the goddess is not considered to be the polar opposite of evil (as in the case of Christianity). As we saw in chapter four, the goddess embodies evil in herself, in multiple forms, even while challenging them. Taking this into consideration, it is possible to say that we cannot speak of divine liberation, especially from the perspective of Dalits, as *wholly* 'divine.' That is, because God is not a separate entity apart from evil, God's liberating presence and power are also not completely free of the evil of oppression. Given the vulnerable nature of God as suggested by process theologians, we could say that God struggles with evil both within and without. In that sense, God is not super-human or super-natural, but rather wrestles with evil along with her equally vulnerable and fallible creation. The God revealed in Christ and in the divine possessions among Dalits is a weak and vulnerable God.[101] I believe that such a view of God and liberation implies

---

99   Yong, *In the Days of Caesar*, 145–151.

100   I can say from my own experience as a pastor, that speaking of caste and untouchability was extremely unsettling in the church. One can only imagine the plight of poor village Dalits in a caste-ridden society and church.

101   I want to note that my argument is inspired by John Caputo who convincingly makes the case for the weakness of God: "The perverse core of Christianity lies in being a weak force. The weak force of God is embodied in the broken body on the cross, which has thereby

236   CHAPTER 8

the necessity for theological enterprises that challenge oppression and fore-ground liberation (such as Dalit theology) to engage in a careful, continuous, and critical re-evaluation lest they slip into the pit of God-defending funda-mentalism and self-righteous triumphalism.

Finally, in possessions one is also able to witness the liberative motif of be-ing an alternative community. In Hindu as well as Christian possessions, the gathering of everyone in the village from all castes is imperative. We may recall Appavoo's perceptive observation: "Without community there is no posses-sion."[102] In that sense, in spite of its temporariness, possessions make possible the coming together of people of different castes. And from what we learnt from Hindu possessions, there is even a reversal of hierarchies in these com-munity gatherings. A Dalit speaks to, abuses, and in some cases even spits on the caste people, and this is not contested at all, since all these humiliating acts are hidden underneath the sacredness of the possessions. In Christian pos-sessions, this may not be the case, though, generally speaking, the church has been an avenue (mostly though not exclusively) for Christian Dalits to attain dignity and gain access to leadership positions.[103] And, as I pointed out earli-er, Dalit women take the lead in the worship, particularly during Holy Spirit possessions.

The aspect of community, along with the disruption and reversal of pow-er roles, encourage me to think of possessions in ecclesial terms. For what is the church but an intentional and inclusive community of/for all people? It is an alternative community where all bodies are knit together, transcending socially and politically constructed boundaries, by the universal divine Spirit of Christ, as his body. It is a community of healing and justice where diversity is celebrated and hierarchy is annihilated. It is a body of bodies where those who are crucified by unjust structures are centered and their well-being prioritized. Of course, the real church may not live up to these ideals, but isn't that what we (are called to) work for? Isn't the church after all the foretaste of the kingdom

---

been broken loose from being and broken out upon the open plane of the powerlessness of God. The power of God is not pagan violence, brute power, or vulgar magic; it is the power of powerlessness, the power of the call, the power of protest that rises up from innocent suffering and calls out against it, the power that says no to unjust suffering, and finally, the power to suffer-with (sym-pathos) innocent suffering, which is perhaps the central Christian symbol."

John D. Caputo, *The Weakness of God: A Theology of the Event* (Bloomington & India-napolis: Indiana University Press, 2006), 43.

102   See the section on preparation for possessions in chapter four.

103   Webster, *The Dalit Christians*, 199–228.

ENVISIONING AN EMBODIED COMPARATIVE THEOLOGY OF LIBERATION 237

of God? Jules A. Martinez-Olivieri insightfully captures the true meaning and purpose of the church.

> The ecclesia, ... is a theater of liberation. It is a mobilization of "spec-actors" who participate in the liberation of God by reproducing the logic of the gospel in specific situations. Love for God and love for others is the sacrificial performance in the crucible of life.[104]
>
> Matt. 10:18, 24–25

In that sense, what we see in possessions, I would say, is an ecclesial community in embodied action. Yes, they are fragile and fragmentary moments. Yet they happen in divine and human subjectivity embodying God as dynamic creativity, engendering, inaugurating, and building, even if only episodically, moment by moment, an alternative community. Possessions are, in that sense, truly ecclesial moments that envision and usher in the paradise envisioned by the prophet Isaiah.

> The wolf will live with the lamb,
>   the leopard will lie down with the goat,
> the calf and the lion and the yearling
>   together;
>   and a little child will lead them.
> The cow will feed with the bear,
>   their young will lie down together,
>   and the lion will eat straw like
>   the ox.
> The infant will play near the cobra's
>   den,
>   And the young child will put its hand
>   into the viper's nest.
> They will neither harm nor destroy
>   on all my holy mountain,
> for the earth will be filled with the
>   knowledge of the Lord
>   as the waters cover the sea.
>
> Isaiah 11: 6–9

---

104   Jules A. Martinez-Olivieri, *A Visible Witness: Christology, Liberation, and Participation* (Minneapolis: Fortress Press, 2016), 197.

Epilogue: Marginalized Bodies and Comparative Theology

This book was an experiment in constructing a liberative comparative theology by focusing on Dalit bodies and Dalit religious experiences. By dialogically integrating the basic frameworks of comparative theology and Dalit theology, in the first chapter, I offered a framework for a comparative theology of liberation. In the second chapter, I identified the significance of the Dalit body with respect to caste performativity, and argued that divine possessions in Dalit bodies can serve as an appropriate category for a non-textual, people/body-centered comparative theology of liberation. Building on this foundation, the second part of the book was dedicated to the study of divine possessions among Hindu and Christian Dalits. In the final part, in chapter seven, I compared them and proposed that possessions are filled with resistive and liberative potential, though in creative and unconventional ways. Based on this observation, in the last chapter, I argued that divine possessions among Dalits can be seen as *kairos* moments, when God's liberative presence creatively and consistently interrupts and transforms the society, helping us to deepen and enhance our understanding of the divine.

To conclude this book, in this epilogue, I want to make a few, but nonetheless important, observations. First, I want to recall the significance of doing a comparative theology that is located at the margins and focused on the experiences of oppressed bodies. Next, I want to acknowledge some limitations in the project that, as I will argue are, nonetheless, justifiable. Finally, I will conclude by naming the goals and objectives of the book that justify its wider relevance for the field of theology.

1 Re-Visioning Comparative Theology from and at the Margins

In this section, based on the observations and arguments made in the previous chapters, let me briefly summarize the significance and relevance of doing a non-textual comparative theology centered on marginalized bodies.

1.1 *Beyond Texts to Bodies*

One of the main arguments that I present in this book is the problem of text-centrism. In the first chapter, I pointed out the preference of text-based study of religious traditions in most comparative theological projects. Even while

EPILOGUE: MARGINALIZED BODIES AND COMPARATIVE THEOLOGY 239

I appreciate the efforts of the comparative theologians who authored these works, given the history of the relationship between the prioritization of texts and colonialism, orientalism, and Christian-supremacy, I argued for the need to move beyond texts (without actually ignoring them since, as seen in this work, we cannot do without texts completely) toward a people-centered comparative theology. And given both the theological and political significance of bodies in history, I emphasized the need for centering the body in interreligious projects.

It is my contention that a contextually sensitive and relevant comparative study of religious traditions certainly entails the need to re-turn to the body. Firstly, body enables us to concretely understand and interpret religious experiences better than texts. While texts capture the essential beliefs of religious communities, they do not necessarily present the existential religiosity of those communities (fully). This is especially true in the case of people like the Dalits whose voices are often absent in sacred texts, or if present, are given a marginal place. Focusing on bodies, particularly those of the marginalized offers an opportunity to understand how religious beliefs find expression in and empower those communities.

Secondly, a body centered comparative theology also keeps us contextually grounded. Sacred texts in all religious traditions (including Hinduism and Christianity), as invaluable as they are, often, though not always, speak from/of the past. While this is certainly important, given the significance of these texts in religious communities, studying the embodied experiences of the devotees shows us how they use those texts—oral or written—to live in the present. Bodies teach us how texts or stories from the past, such as myths and collective memories, can help communities like the Dalits to navigate their way through the complex labyrinth of caste and other such social structures.

Finally, an embodied comparative theology helps us to break out of perpetuating stereotypes and hierarchies. I noted in the first chapter how the focus on texts enables the strengthening of (the power of) caste. But there is also more. Focusing on texts often paints an unrealistic picture of society. At times, religious texts speak of an egalitarian and harmonious society that actually never exists. Or, they talk about a completely oppressive society where there is no hope for that religious tradition. Thus, often, there are two extreme views in religious texts that can be misunderstood (and misused) both by proponents and opponents of a tradition. This is especially true in the case of Hinduism in regards with caste and untouchability. But focusing on bodies turns the attention to actual religious experiences rather than reflective, and often speculative, narrations. It places the finger on the issues that affect the lives of people (such as caste), not merely basking in what the texts may unrealistically claim.

At the same time, body-centered comparative theology reveals the complex ways in which the agency of oppressed people comes to the fore. Even if there are oppressive elements that are interwoven with the religious beliefs and practices of a tradition, marginalized people (like Dalits) can still find meaning and purpose within them. Embodied experiences show us the grey areas of religion which texts are incapable of.

1.2   *Beyond Borders to Living at the Boundaries*

Comparative theology, in the simplest sense, is learning across religious borders.[1] While I agree that this "crossing borders" exercise is certainly very appealing, and indeed important, I am concerned about the assumption of the existence of concrete borders in the first place, that necessitate "passing over" and "passing back" between religious traditions.[2] Perhaps this arises from a western Christian premise of religions as separate entities that are separated by boundaries. Moreover, it may also be based on the fear of crossing and overstepping religious boundaries, and therefore, disrespecting other religious communities. The concerns are certainly justifiable. However, as we noted in this book, for those in the global south, and perhaps in the global North too, boundaries between religions are often blurred. In contrast to the tendency of western scholars to easily spot religious borders, in a context like South Asia, it is often difficult to pinpoint the borders of a religion.

This project has shown that, rather than worrying about where religious boundaries lie, a comparative theologian could/should herself stand at and with those at the boundaries. Standing with the 'boundary people,' like the Dalits, shows that they are not only at the periphery of the society (socially, economically, and politically) but also at the boundaries of religious traditions. We learnt about the hybrid nature of Dalit traditions. Dalits creatively and strategically draw from different traditions including caste Hinduism and Christianity. In that sense, Dalit religious space can be viewed as a "third space."[3] To

---

1 The title of Clooney's introductory book is a good case in point. Clooney, *Comparative Theology: Deep Learning Across Religious Borders.*

2 Paul Knitter uses these phrases throughout his book to do comparative theology. See Paul F. Knitter, *Without Buddha I could not be a Christian,* (Oxford: Oneworld, 2009), 8, 14, 31, 40 etc.

3 Inspired by the work of Arun Jones who identifies North Indian Bhakti traditions and Evangelical Christianity as "Thirdspace," and using the framework of Homi Bhaba, I have argued elsewhere that Dalit religion and Dalit bodies can be viewed as "Third spaces." Samuel, "Untouchable Bodies, Ecstasy, and Dalit Agency." See, Arun W. Jones, *Missionary Christianity and Local Religion: American Evangelicalism in North India, 1836–1870* (Waco, Texas: Baylor University Press, 2017), 3–6 & 283; Homi K. Bhabha, *The Location of Culture* (London & New York: Routledge, 1994), 56.

EPILOGUE: MARGINALIZED BODIES AND COMPARATIVE THEOLOGY

stand in this third space means there is no 'passing/moving back and forth' across borders. We can only "be still and know" (Psalm 46:10) that the Spirit of God is moving among, encompassing, and enlivening the untouchable bodies.

This doesn't mean the experiences of the Hindu and Christian Dalits are the same. No. Like in any comparative study, we noted similarities and differences. But either way, the fact is that there is a liberative divine power at the boundaries becoming visible during occasions like divine possessions. At the boundaries, standing with the Dalits, I cannot say which one is better. Even if I am a Christian comparative theologian, I cannot tell the Christian Dalits if they can learn anything from the goddess possessions of the Hindu Dalits. That would be to question to their agency. In any case, as we saw in chapter seven, Christian Dalit religiosity is deeply connected to Hindu Dalit religion. While comparative theology in general speaks of engaging in interreligious learning with humility, comparative theology at the boundaries enforces this even further. We don't need to jump across religious borders. Rather, we simply learn to humbly acknowledge and accept how marginalized people experience liberative divine power *as they themselves move across the boundaries* and draw from multiple religious sources. The people are already doing comparative stuff. A comparative theologian, at least often, simply needs the patience and the humility to watch and learn from the people.

2   Some Confessions and Justifications

While noting the significance of a body-centered comparative theology of the margins, I have to acknowledge that this comparative theology also has its limitations. Let me mention them here, along with the rationale for their inclusion. Firstly, there is the complex relationship between Hinduism and Dalits. Because of the evident rootedness of caste and untouchability in Hinduism— although as we saw earlier caste and untouchability are actually more complex than how they are perceived—there are Dalit scholars who oppose the idea of considering Dalit religions a part of Hinduism. On the other hand, there are Hindutva protagonists who seek to forcefully assimilate Dalits into Hinduism under the pretext of it being the 'home' religion of Dalits. However, I consider these two positions extreme and problematic. On the one hand, even though Dalits were/are outcastes and are treated as outsiders by caste Hindus, as we saw in chapter three, they cannot be severed from the larger Hindu theological framework. On the other hand, Dalit religions have also resisted the (conquering and) subjugating tendencies of caste Hinduism by maintaining their own distinctiveness. Therefore, I believe that we need to be aware that there is continuity between (upper-)caste Hinduism and Dalit religions even as the latter do not entirely conform to the oppressive schemes of the former. It is based on this premise that I consider Dalit religions to be a part of Hinduism. Nonetheless, I do confess that this recognition of Dalit religions as Hindu might be considered problematic in the context of casteist Hindu(tva) fundamentalism. Therefore, I believe it is my responsibility to categorically state and clarify here that I do not suggest or endorse any form of Hindutva-based ethnocentric nationalism when I say that Dalit religion can be regarded as one among the many traditions of Hinduism.

Secondly, I also want to acknowledge the common problem that appears in comparative and cross-cultural studies, viz. the historical and cultural gulf between the traditions/cultures under comparison. In this book, though the compared religious groups are both Dalits, it is important to note that they do have different religious identities. Further, one may also have difficulty in accepting the use of western concepts and frameworks to interpret a Dalit religious experience. I am aware of the vast gulf that separates the context and the language of the Dalits and theorists like Michel Foucault, Judith Butler, and anthropologists like James C. Scott and Sabah Mahmood who are my main theoretical interlocutors. Further, using Paul Tillich's concept of *kairos* to theologize Dalit possessions might sound implausible to some readers. However, we should remember that academic works today are essentially cross-cultural. And this is particularly true for Christian theology, since the fundamental method of doing theology—the method of correlation—demands a hermeneutical dialogue between the Christian tradition, including its historical interpretations that span across two millennia, and the present contextual realities in which theology is done. In other words, there is no theology that does not involve some element of cutting across time and space. Therefore, I believe that my use of western scholarship is indeed justified in spite of its broad historical and geographical distance.

Finally, in this study, my own subjective position has no doubt played a very significant role. This research is deeply influenced by my Christian liberation theological commitments. Although I tried to be openly receptive and non-judgmental in my ethnographic research and comparison of possessions, I don't believe that I ever ceased to be a liberation theologian at any point. In fact, as a Dalit liberation theologian, my interest in possessions arose from my eagerness to identify new and creative liberative aspects in the Paraiyar Dalit religion which could then be theologized. Moreover, let me recall here that this project was strongly influenced by my own identity as a Paraiyar. I wrote

EPILOGUE: MARGINALIZED BODIES AND COMPARATIVE THEOLOGY 243

this book with the awareness that the (his/her)stories (and theologies) of my subjects of study were, in a sense, my own. However, given that no academic project is ever objective or non-subjective, I believe that I can assert that these specificities and subjectivities do not, in any way, diminish the worth or integrity of this project, but rather openly affirm its investment in the cause of justice and liberation for the Dalits.

3   Looking Ahead

Like any academic work, this project was also undertaken with certain specific goals in mind. Though these aims must have been obvious throughout the book at various stages, let me list them here for the sake of clarity. Firstly, being a Dalit theological enterprise, the book has sought to identify, interpret, and celebrate Dalit agency in the midst of caste-based oppression with the intent of helping to further the cause of Dalit liberation. It is hoped that the methodological proposals and theological reflections made here will suggest possibilities of re-imagining and doing liberation theology differently, and perhaps more meaningfully, not only from the Dalit but also other marginalized perspectives. I particularly desire that the focus on the Dalit body to do constructive comparative theology will demonstrate the significance and the liberative potential of the bodies of the oppressed.

Secondly, through the prioritization of Dalit voices and experiences, I hope that this project would counter the unchecked privileging of dominant(-caste) voices in comparative theology. Moreover, the non-textual and people-centered nature of this enterprise can be seen as a challenge to text-centric modes of interreligious engagement. I also intend that the book will inspire comparative theologians to be both critical of the life-denying aspects of the traditions that they study and cognizant of their socially and politically life-affirming elements. In other words, through this work, I hope to encourage comparative theologians to be responsible and responsive to structural injustice rather than being indifferent and neutral readers.

Finally, I am keen on recognizing and upholding the need and significance of trans-global solidarities among the oppressed communities in the world. It is with this objective that I included, engaged, and dialogued with communities whose experiences are similar to that of the Dalits across the globe. By including the study of literary, theoretical, and theological resources from across the world on oppressed bodies and body politics—especially those from feminist and black perspectives—I hope that this book will have a reach and relevance beyond those familiar with the Indian society. I sincerely desire that though this project was attempted from a Dalit perspective, it would inspire more such people-centered comparative liberation theologies from other marginalized perspectives, and encourage networking and bridge-building among communities that struggle for justice across the world.

Bibliography

Aathi, Yazhan. "Missing (*En Sorkalil Thedatheer*)." Translated by Vasantha Surya. In *The Oxford Anthology of Tamil Dalit Writing*, edited by Ravikumar and R. Azhagarasan, 38–39. New Delhi: Oxford University Press, 2012.

Abraham, Shaibu. *Pentecostal Theology of Liberation: Holy Spirit & Holiness in the Society*. New Delhi: Christian World Imprints, 2014.

Alexander, Michelle. *The New Jim Crow: Mass Incarceration in the Age of Color Blindness*. New York: New York Press, 2011.

Ambedkar, B. R. *Annihilation of Caste,* The Annotated Critical Edition. London & New York: Verso, 2014.

Anandhi, S. *Contending Identities: Dalits and Secular Politics in Madras Slums*. New Delhi: Indian Social Institute, 1995.

Anderson, Allan Heaton. *To the Ends of the Earth: Pentecostalism and the Transformation of World Christianity*. Oxford & New York: Oxford University Press, 2013.

Anderson-Rajkumar, Evangeline. "Turning Bodies Inside Out: Contours of Womanist Theology." In *Dalit Theology in the Twenty-First Century: Discordant Voices, Discerning Pathways*, edited by Sathianathan Clarke, Deenabandhu Manchala and Philip Vinod Peacock, 199–214. New Delhi: Oxford University Press, 2011.

Appavoo, Theophilus. "Dalit Religion." In *Indigenous People: Dalits—Dalit Issues in Today's Theological Debate*, edited by James Massey, 111–121. Delhi: ISPCK, 1994.

Appavoo, Theophilus J. "Dalit Way of Theological Expression." In *Frontiers of Dalit Theology*, edited by V. Devasahayam, 283–289. Madras: Gurukul, 1997.

Ariarajah, S. Wesley. *Your God, My God, Our God: Rethinking Christian Theology for Religious Plurality*. Geneva: WCC Publications, 2012.

Asad, Talal. *Genealogies of Religion: Discipline and Reasons of Power in Christianity and Islam*. Baltimore and London: The John Hopkins University Press, 1993.

———. "Reading a Modern Classic: W. C. Smith's "Meaning and End of Religion."" *History of Religions,* 40/3 (Feb. 2001): 205–222.

Assmann, Jan. *Religion and Cultural Memory*. Translated by Rodney Livingstone. Stanford: Stanford University Press, 2006.

Ayrookuzhiel, Abraham. *Essays on Dalits, Religion and Liberation*. Bangalore: CISRS, 2006.

Babb, Lawrence. *The Divine Hierarchy: Popular Hinduism in Central India*. New York: Columbia University Press, 1975.

Bama. *Karukku*, 2nd edition. Translated by Lakshmi Holmstrom. New Delhi: Oxford University Press, 2012.

Barnes, Adam. "A Comparative Spirituality of Liberation: The Anti-Poverty Struggles of the Poverty Initiative and the Tijaniyya Sufi of Kiota." PhD diss., Union Theological Seminary, 2016.

Barnes, Michael. *Interreligious Learning: Dialogue, Spirituality and Christian Imagination*. Cambridge: Cambridge University Press, 2012.

Barua, Ankur. *Debating 'Conversion' in Hinduism and Christianity*. London & New York: Routledge, 2015.

Bauman, Chad. *Pentecostals, Proselytization, and Anti-Christian Violence in Contemporary India*. Oxford & New York: Oxford University Press, 2015.

Bhabha, Homi K. *The Location of Culture*. London & New York: Routledge, 1994.

Boopalan, Sunder John. *Memory, Grief, and Agency: A Political-Theological Account of Wrongs and Rites*. Palgrave Macmillan, 2017.

Bottomley, Frank. *Attitudes to the Body in Western Christendom*. London: Lepus Books, 1979.

Brown, Robert MacAfee, ed. *Kairos: Three Prophetic Challenges to the Church*. Grand Rapids, Michigan: William B. Eerdmans, 1990.

Brubaker, Richard L. "The Ambivalent Mistress: A Study of South Indian village Goddesses and their Religious Meaning." PhD diss., University of Chicago, 1978.

Butalia, Urvashi. *The Other Side of Silence: Voices from the Partition of India*. Durham: Duke University Press, 2000.

Butler, Judith & Athena Athanasiou. *Dispossession: The Performative in the Political*. Cambridge & Malden: Polity Press, 2015.

Butler, Judith. *Bodies that Matter: On the Discursive Limits of Sex*. London and New York: Routledge, 2011.

———. *Gender Trouble: Feminism and the Subversion of Identity*. New York and London: Routledge, 2007.

Caplan, Leonard. *Religion and Power: Essays on the Christian Community in Madras*. Madras: CLS, 1989.

Caputo, John D. *The Weakness of God: A Theology of the Event*. Bloomington & Indianapolis: Indiana University Press, 2006.

Chellaperumal, A. "Thamizhaga Naattar Theivangalin Panbukkoorugalum Panmuga Thanmaigalum." In *Sanangalin Saamigal*, edited by D. Dharumarajan, 45–60. Palayamkottai: Folklore Research Center, 2006.

Cheng, Patrick S. *Radical Love: An Introduction to Queer Theology*. New York: Seabury, 2011.

Clarke, Sathianathan. *Dalits and Christianity: Subaltern Religion and Liberation Theology in India*. Madras: Oxford University Press, 1998.

———. "Dalit Theology: An Introductory and Interpretative Theological Exposition." In *Dalit Theology in the Twenty-First Century: Discordant Voices, Discerning Pathways*, edited by Sathianathan Clarke, Deenabandhu Manchala and Philip Vinod Peacock, 19–37. New Delhi: Oxford University Press, 2011.

BIBLIOGRAPHY

———. "Transforming Identities, De-textualizing Interpretation, and Re-modalizing Representation: Scriptures and Subaltern Subjectivity in India." In *Theorizing Scriptures: New Critical Orientations to a Cultural Phenomenon*, edited by Vincent L. Wimbush, 95–104. New Brunswick, New Jersey and London: Rutgers University Press, 2008.

Clifford, James & George E. Marcus, ed. *Writing Culture: The Poetics and Politics of Ethnography*. Berkeley, Los Angeles and London: University of California Press, 1986.

Clooney, Francis X. *Comparative Theology: Deep Learning Across Religious Borders*. Chichester: Wiley-Blackwell, 2010.

Coburn, Thomas. *Encountering the Goddess: A Translation from the Devi-Mahātmya and a Study of Its Interpretation*. Albany: State University of New York Press, 1991.

Cone, James H. *A Black Theology of Liberation*, Fortieth Anniversary Edition. Maryknoll, New York: Orbis Books, 2016.

———. *Black Theology and Power*. Maryknoll, New York: Orbis Books, 1997.

———. *The Cross and the Lynching Tree*. Maryknoll, New York: Orbis Books, 2012.

———. *God of the Oppressed*. Maryknoll, New York: Orbis Books, 1997.

Copeland, M. Shawn. *Enfleshing Freedom: Body, Race, and Being*. Minneapolis: Fortress Press, 2010.

Cruz, Samuel. *Masked Africanisms: Puerto Rican Pentecostalism*. Dubuque: Kendall/Hunt, 2005.

D'Costa, Gavin. "Christ, the Trinity, and Religious Diversity." In *Christian Uniqueness Reconsidered: The Myth of Pluralistic Theology of Religions*, edited by Gavin D'Costa, 16–29. Maryknoll, New York: Orbis Books, 1990.

———. *Theology and Religious Pluralism: The Challenge of Other Religions*. Oxford and New York: Basil Blackwell, 1986.

Davis, Richard. *The Bhagvad Gita: A Biography*. Princeton & Oxford: Princeton University Press, 2015.

Dayam, Joseph Prabhakar. "*Gonthemma Korika*: Reimagining the Divine Feminine in Dalit Christian Theo/alogy." In *Dalit Theology in the Twenty-First Century: Discordant Voices, Discerning Pathways*, edited by Sathianathan Clarke, Deenabandhu Manchala and Philip Vinod Peacock, 137–149. New Delhi: Oxford University Press, 2011.

Dayanandan, P. "Dalit Christians of the Chengalpet Area and the Church of Scotland." In *Local Dalit Christian History*, edited by George Oommen & John C. B. Webster, 18–64. Delhi: ISPCK, 2002.

Del Colle, Ralph. *Christ and the Spirit: Spirit-Christology in Trinitarian Perspective*. New York and Oxford: Oxford University Press, 1994.

Deliège Robert. "Introduction: Is There Still Untouchability in India?" In *From Stigma to Assertion: Untouchability, Identity and Politics in Early and Modern India*, edited by Mikael Aktor & Robert Deliège, 13–30. Copenhagen: Museum Tusculanum Press, 2010.

———. *The Untouchables of India*. Translated by Nora Scott. Oxford and New York: Berg Publishers, 1999.

———. *The World of the 'Untouchables': Paraiyars of Tamilnadu*. Delhi: Oxford University Press, 1997.

Dharampal-Frick, Gita. *Interrogating the Historical Discourse of Caste and Race in India*. New Delhi: Nehru Memorial Museum and Library, 2013.

Dirks, Nicholas. *Castes of Mind: Colonialism and the Making of Modern India*. Princeton and Oxford: Princeton University Press, 2001.

Douglas, Kelly Brown. *Stand Your Ground: Black Bodies and the Justice of God*. Maryknoll, New York: Orbis Books, 2015.

Dumont, Louis. *Homo Hierarchicus: The Caste System and Its Implications*. Translated by Mark Sainbury, Louis Dumont, and Basia Gulati. Chicago and London: The University of Chicago Press, 1980.

Dupuis, Jacques. *Toward a Christian Theology of Religious Pluralism*. Maryknoll, New York: Orbis Books, 1997.

Fernández, Margarite & Lizabeth Paravisini-Gebert. *Creole Religions of the Caribbean: An Introduction from Vodou and Santeria to Obeah and Espiritsmo*. New York and London: New York University Press, 2011.

Flood, Gavin. *An Introduction to Hinduism*. New York: Cambridge University Press, 1996.

Foucault, Michel. *Discipline and Punish: The Birth of the Prison*. Translated by Alan Sheridan. New York: Vintage Books, 1995.

———. *Power*. Edited by James D. Faubion, Translated by Robert Hurley et al. New York: The New York Press, 2000.

Fulkerson, Mary McClintock. "Contesting the Gendered Subject: A Feminist Account of the *Imago Dei*." In *Horizons in Feminist Theology: Identity Tradition, and Norms*, edited by Rebecca S. Chopp and Sheila Greeve Davaney, 99–115. Minneapolis: Fortress Press, 1997.

Ganguly, Debjani. *Caste, Colonialism and Counter-Modernity: Notes on a Postcolonial Hermeneutics of Caste*. London and New York: Routledge, 2005.

Geevarghese Mor Coorilos, "Dalit Theology and its Future Course." In *Dalit Theology in the Twenty-First Century: Discordant Voices, Discerning Pathways*, edited by Sathianathan Clarke, Deenabandhu Manchala and Philip Vinod Peacock, 168–177. New Delhi: Oxford University Press, 2011.

Gorringe, Hugo. *Untouchable Citizens: Dalit Movements and Democratization in Tamilnadu*. New Delhi, Thousand Oaks and London: Sage Publications, 2005.

Guha, Sumit. *Beyond Caste: Identity and Power in South Asia, Past and Present*. Leiden: Brill Publications, 2013.

Haight, Roger. *Dynamics of Theology*. Maryknoll, New York: Orbis Books, 2001.

———. *Future of Christology*. London and New York: Continuum, 2008.

———. *Jesus: Symbol of God*. Maryknoll, New York: Orbis Books, 1999.

BIBLIOGRAPHY

Hawley John S. and Mark Juergensmeyer. *Songs of the Saints of India*. New Delhi: Oxford University Press, 2004.

Hawley, John Stratton. "Naming Hinduism." *The Wilson Quarterly* (Summer 1991): 22–41.

Humes, Cynthia Ann. "Power in Creation." In *Breaking Boundaries with the Goddess: New Direction in the Study of Saktism*, edited by Rachel McDermott & Cynthia Ann Humes, 297–333. New Delhi: Manohar Publications, 2009.

Hunsinger, George. "Karl Barth and Liberation Theology." *The Journal of Religion*, 63/3 (7/1983): 247–263.

Ilaiah, Kancha. *Why I am not a Hindu: A Sudra Critique of Hindutva Philosophy, Culture and Political Economy*. Calcutta: Samya, 2002.

Inglis, Stephen. "Possession and Pottery: Serving the Divine in a South Indian Community." In *Gods of Flesh Gods of Stone: The Embodiment of Divinity in India*, edited by Joanne Punzo Waghorne and Norman Cutler, 89–101. Chambersburg: Anima Publications, 1985.

Isherwood, Lisa and Elizabeth Stuart. *Introducing Body Theology*. Sheffield: Sheffield Academic Press, 1998.

Jaffrelot, Christophe, ed. *Hindu Nationalism: A Reader*. Princeton and Oxford: Princeton University Press, 2007.

Jeremiah, Anderson H. M. *Community and Worldview among Paraiyars of South India*. London: Bloomsbury, 2013.

Jeyaraj, Daniel. "Indian Participation in Enabling, Sustaining, and Promoting Christian Mission in India." In *India and the Indianness of Christianity: Essays on Understanding—Historical, Theological, and Bibliographical—in Honor of Robert Eric Frykenberg*, edited by Richard Fox Young, 26–40. Grand Rapids and Cambridge: William B. Eerdmans, 2009.

Jones, Arun W. *Missionary Christianity and Local Religion: American Evangelicalism in North India, 1836–1870*. Waco, Texas: Baylor University Press, 2017.

Jordan, Mark D. *Convulsing Bodies: Religion and Resistance in Foucault*. Stanford: Stanford University Press, 2015.

Kahl, Brigitte. *Galatians Re-Imagined: Reading with the Eyes of the Vanquished*. Minneapolis: Fortress Press, 2010.

Kale, Madhavi. *Fragments of Empire: Capital, Slavery, and Indentured Labor in the British Caribbean*. Philadelphia: University of Pennsylvania, 1998.

Kakar, Sudhir. *Shamans, Mystics, and Doctors: A Psychological Inquiry into India and its Healing Traditions*. Chicago: The University of Chicago Press, 1982.

Kapadia, Karin. *Siva and Her Sisters: Gender, Caste, and Class in Rural South India*. Boulder, San Francisco & Oxford: Westview Press, 1995.

Kärkkäinen, Veli-Matti. *Christology: A Global Introduction*, 2nd ed. Grand Rapids, Michigan: Baker Academic, 2016.

Keller, Catherine. *On the Mystery: Discerning Divinity in Process*. Minneapolis: Fortress Press, 2008.

King, Richard. *Orientalism and Religion: Postcolonial Theory, India and the 'Mystic East.'* London and New York: Routledge, 2002.

Kinsley, David. *Hindu Goddesses: Visions of the Divine Feminine in the Hindu Tradition*. Berkeley, Los Angeles: University of California Press, 1988.

———. *Hinduism from a Cultural Perspective*. Englewood Cliffs: Prentice Hall, 1982.

Kittel, Gerhard, ed. *Theological Dictionary of the New Testament*. Vol. III. Translated and edited by Geoffrey W. Bromiley. Grand Rapids: Wm. B. Eerdman, 1965.

Knitter, Paul F. *Introducing Theology of Religions*. Maryknoll, New York: Orbis Books, 2011.

———. *No Other Name? A Critical Survey of Christian Attitudes Toward the World Religions*. Maryknoll: Orbis Books, 1985.

———. *Without the Buddha I Could Not be a Christian*. Oxford: Oneworld, 2009.

———. "Toward a Liberationist Theology of Religions." In *The Myth of Christian Uniqueness: Toward a Pluralistic Theology of Religions*, edited by John Hick and Paul F. Knitter, 178–200. Maryknoll, New York: Orbis Books, 1987.

Laksana, A. Bagus. "Comparative Theology: Between Identity and Alterity." in *The New Comparative Theology: Interreligious Insights from the Next Generation*, edited by Francis X. Clooney, 1–20. London and New York: T & T Clark, 2010.

Lampe, G. W. H. *God as Spirit: The Bampton Lectures, 1976*. Oxford: Clarendon Press, 1977.

Lott, Eric J. "A Missionary's Dilemma: The Emerging Dalit Identity" *Gurukul Journal of Theological Studies*, 24/ 2 (June 2013): 6–17.

Maanen, John Van. *Tales of the Field: On Writing Ethnography*. Chicago and London: The University of Chicago Press, 1988.

MacDonald, Diane L. Prosser. *Transgressive Corporeality: The Body, Poststructuralism, and the Theological Imagination*. Albany: State University of New York Press, 1995.

MacPhail, Richard D. "Finding a Path in Others' World: The Challenge of Exorcism." In *Popular Christianity in India: Riting Between the Lines*. Edited by Selva J. Raj & Corinne G. Dempsey, 141–162. Albany: State University of New York Press, 2002.

Mahmood, Sabah. *Politics of Piety: The Islamic Revival and the Feminist Subject*. Princeton & Oxford: Princeton University Press, 2005.

Manchala, Deenabandhu. "Expanding the Ambit: Dalit Theological Contribution to Ecumenical Social Thought." In *Dalit Theology in the Twenty-First Century: Discordant Voices, Discerning Pathways*, edited by Sathianathan Clarke, Deenabandhu Manchala and Philip Vinod Peacock, 38–54. New Delhi: Oxford University Press, 2011.

Martinez-Olivieri, Jules A. *A Visible Witness: Christology, Liberation, and Participation*. Minneapolis: Fortress Press, 2016.

BIBLIOGRAPHY

Masilamani-Meyer, Eveline. "The Changing face of Kattavarayan." In *Criminal Gods and Demon Devotees,* edited by Alf Hiltebeitel, 69–104. New York: State University of New York Press, 1989.

Massey, James. "An Analysis of Dalit Christian Issue with Special reference to 1950 Presidential order," In *Dalit Christians in India,* edited by R. R. Patil & James Dabhi, 73–97. New Delhi: Manak Publications, 2010.

———. *Dalits in India: Religion as a Source of Bondage or Liberation with Special Reference to Christians.* New Delhi: Manohar Publications, 1995.

———. "History and Dalit Theology." In *Frontiers of Dalit Theology,* edited by V. Devasahayam, 161–182. Madras: Gurukul, 1996.

———. "Revisiting and Resignifying the Methodology for Dalit Theology." In *Revisiting and Resignifying Methodology for Dalit Theology,* edited by James Massey and Indukuri John Mohan Razu, 51–69. New Delhi: CDS, 2008.

Masuzawa, Tomoko. *The Invention of World Religions: Or, How European Universalism Was Preserved in the Language of Pluralism.* Chicago and London: The University of Chicago Press, 2005.

McDonald, Diane L. Prosser. *Transgressive Corporeality: The Body, Poststructuralism, and the Theological Imagination.* Albany: State University of New York Press, 1995.

Mesle, C. Robert. *Process-Relational Philosophy: An Introduction to Alfred North Whitehead.* West Conshohocken, Pennsylvania: Templeton Press 2008.

Meyer, Eveline. *Aṅkaḷaparamēcuvari: A Goddess of Tamilnadu Her Myths and Cult.* Stuttgart, Germany: Steiner Verlag Wiesbaden GMBH, 1986.

Moffatt, Michael. *An Untouchable Community in South India: Structure and Consensus* (Princeton: Princeton University Press, 1979).

Michael, S. M. "Introduction." In *Dalits in Modern India: Visions and Values,* 2nd edition, edited by S. M. Michael, 13–41. New Delhi: Sage Publications, 2007.

Miles, Margaret R. *Bodies in Society: Essays on Christianity in Contemporary Culture.* Eugene, Oregon: Cascade Books, 2008.

———. *The Word Made Flesh: A History of Christian Thought.* Oxford: Blackwell Publishing, 2005.

Mines, Diane P. *Caste in India.* Ann Arbor, MI: Association for Asian Studies, 2009.

———. *Fierce Gods: Inequality, Ritual, and The Politics of Dignity in a South Indian Village.* Bloomington and Indianapolis: Indiana University Press, 2005.

Moltmann, Jürgen. *The Way of Jesus Christ: Christology in Messianic Dimensions.* Translated by Margaret Kohl. New York: HarperSanFrancisco, 1990.

Monikaraj, D. "Biographical Musings I—Vethamanickam," In *Frontiers of Dalit Theology,* edited by V. Devasahayam, 206–230. Madras: Gurukul, 1996.

Moon, Vasanth, comp. *Dr. Babasaheb Ambedkar: Writings and Speeches: Volume. 3.* Bombay: Government of Maharashtra, 1987.

252   BIBLIOGRAPHY

———, comp. *Dr. Babasaheb Ambedkar: Writings and Speeches: Volume 5*. Bombay: Government of Maharashtra, 1987.

Moyaert, Marianne. "Unpublished Inaugural Lecture." Vrije Universiteit Amsterdam. November 1, 2014.

———. "Christianity as the Measure of Religion? Materializing the Theology of Religions." In *Twenty-First Century Theologies of Religions*, edited by Elizabeth J. Harris, Paul Hedges & Shanthikumar Hettiarachchi, 239–266. Leiden & Boston: Brill Rodopi, 2016.

Nicholson, Andrew J. *Unifying Hinduism: Philosophy and Identity in Indian Intellectual History*. New York: Columbia University Press, 2010.

Nirmal, A. P. "Doing Theology from a Dalit Perspective," in *A Reader in Dalit Theology*, edited by Arvind P. Nirmal, 139–144. Madras: Gurukul, 1990.

Nirmal, Arvind P. "Towards a Christian Dalit Theology." In *A Reader in Dalit Theology*, edited by Arvind P. Nirmal, 53–70. Madras: Gurukul, 1990.

Nongbri, Brent. *Before Religion: A History of a Modern Concept*. New Haven: Yale University Press, 2013.

Northrup, David. *Indentured Labor in the age of Imperialism 1838–1914*. Cambridge: Cambridge University Press, 1995.

Oddie, Geoffrey. *Imagined Hinduism: British Protestant Missionary Constructions of Hinduism, 1793–1900*. New Delhi, Thousand Oaks, California & London: Sage Publications, 2006.

Olivelle, Patrick, trans. *The Law Code of Manu*. New York: Oxford University Press, 2004.

Olson, Carl, trans. *Hindu Primary Sources: A Sectarian Reader*. New Brunswick and London: Rutgers University Press, 2007.

———, trans. *The Many Colours of Hinduism: A Thematic-Historical Introduction*. New Brunswick, New Jersey: Rutgers University Press, 2007.

Paden, William E. *Interpreting the Sacred: Ways of Viewing Religion*. Boston: Beacon Press, 1992.

Panikkar, Raimon. *The Cosmotheandric Experience: Emerging Religious Consciousness*. Maryknoll: Orbis Books, 1993.

Parattai. *Dalit Samayam*. Madurai: Parattai Kalvi mattrum samuga Arakattalai, 2010.

Patil, R. R. & James Dabhi. "Introduction." In *Dalit Christians in India*, edited by R. R. Patil & James Dabhi, 1–14. New Delhi: Manak Publications, 2010.

Peacock, Philip Vinod, "In the Beginning is also an End: Expounding and Exploring Theological Resourcefulness of Myths of Dalit Origins." In *Dalit Theology in the Twenty-First Century: Discordant Voices, Discerning Pathways*, edited by Sathianathan Clarke, Deenabandhu Manchala and Philip Vinod Peacock, 74–92. New Delhi: Oxford University Press, 2011.

Pelikan, Jaroslav. *Jesus Through the Centuries: His Place in the History of Culture*. New Haven and London: Yale University Press, 1985.

BIBLIOGRAPHY

Pierris, Aloysius, *Fire and Water: Basic Issues in Asian Buddhism and Christianity*. Maryknoll, NY: Orbis Books, 1996.

Pilavendran, K. "Nattar Theivangalin Thiriburuvakkangal." In *Sanangalin Saamigal*, edited by D. Dharumarajan, 91–104. Palayamkottai: Folklore Research Center, 2006.

Pinn, Anthony B. *Embodiment and the New Shape of Black Theological Thought*. New York and London: New York University Press, 2010.

Pinnock, Clark H. "An Inclusivist View," in *Four Views on Salvation in a Pluralistic World*, edited by Dennis L. Okholm and Timothy R. Phillips, 95–123. Grand Rapids: Zondervan, 1996.

Pintchman, Tracy. *The Rise of the Goddess in The Hindu Tradition*. Albany: State University of New York Press, 1994.

Ponnaiah, James. "Rituals and Ritual Power of the Broken People: A Debate Over Strategies." *South Indian Folklorist* 9 (2010): 17–40.

Prabhakar, M. E. "Christology in Dalit Perspective," In *Frontiers of Dalit Theology*, edited by V. Devasahayam, 402–432. Madras: Gurukul, 1996.

Rahner, Karl. *Theological Investigations*, vol. XII, *Confrontations 2*. Translated by David Bourke. New York: Seabury Press, 1974.

———. *Theological Investigations*, vol. XVII, *Jesus, Man, and the Church*. Translated by Margaret Kohl. New York: Crossroad, 1981.

Raj, M. C. *Dalitology: The Book of the Dalit People*. Tumkur: Ambedkar Resource Center, 2001.

Raj, Y. T. Vinaya. "Envisioning a Postmodern Method of Doing Dalit Theology." In *Dalit Theology in the Twenty-First Century: Discordant Voices, Discerning Pathways*, edited by Sathianathan Clarke, Deenabandhu Manchala and Philip Vinod Peacock, 93–103. New Delhi: Oxford University Press, 2011.

Rajkumar, Peniel Jesudason Rufus. "Hunting Using Hoax: Dalits, Caste and the Conversion Debate in India." In *Mission At and From the Margins: Patterns, Protagonists and Perspectives*, edited by Peniel Jesudason Rufus Rajkumar, Joseph Prabhakar Dayam and I. P. Asheervadham, 248–260. Eugene, Oregon: Wipf & Stock Publishers, 2014.

———. "Re-Cast(e)ing Conversion, Re-visiting Dialogue: Indian Attempts at an Interfaith Theology of Wholeness." *Journal for the Academic Study of Religion* 26/2 (2013): 157–171.

Rajkumar, Peniel. *Dalit Theology and Dalit Liberation: Problems, Paradigms and Possibilities*. Farnham, Surrey: Ashgate, 2010.

Ramapandi, K. "Naatarvayamaakath Theivangal." In *Sanangalin Saamigal*, edited by D. Dharumarajan, 147–156. Palayamkottai: Folklore Research Center, 2006.

Ramaswamy, Sumathi. *Passions of the Tongue: Language Devotion in Tamil India, 1891–1970*. Berkeley: University of California Press, 1997.

Rao, Anupama. *The Caste Question: Dalits and the Politics of Modern India*. Berkeley, Los Angeles and London: University of California Press, 2009.

Rapaka, Yabbeju "The Indian Pentecostal Church of God in Andhra Pradesh, 1932 to 2010: A study of Dalit Pentecostalism." PhD diss., Regent University, 2011.

Roberts, Nathaniel. *To Be Cared For: The Power of Conversion and Foreignness of Belonging in an Indian Slum*. Oakland: University of California Press, 2016.

Rodrigues, Valerian, ed. *Essential Writings of B. R. Ambedkar*. New Delhi: Oxford University Press, 2002.

Roy, Arundhati. "The Doctor and the Saint." In B. R. Ambedkar, *The Annihilation of Caste*, The Annotated Critical Edition. London and New York: Verso Books, 2014.

Samuel, Joshua. Book Review of *Tastes of the Divine: Hindu and Christian Theologies of Emotion* by Michelle Voss Roberts, *The Ecumenical Review* 68.1 (March 2016): 157–159.

Samuel, Joshua. "Comparative Theology as People's Theology: A Proposal from a Dalit Perspective." Paper presented at the International PhD Seminar, Pietermaritzburg, October 4–6, 2014.

Samuel, Joshua. "Towards a Comparative Theology of Liberation: Exploring Comparative Theology's Relevance for Doing Indian Liberation Theology." *Interreligious Studies and Intercultural Theology* 1/1 (2017): 47–67.

Samuel, Joshua. "Dalits and Conversions." Paper presented at the 'Interfacing for Emancipation' conference, Bangalore, August, 2010.

Samuel, Joshua. "Practicing Multiple Religious Belonging for Liberation: A Dalit Perspective." *Current Dialogue* 57 (December 2015): 78–87.

Samuel, Joshua. "Untouchable Bodies, Ecstasy, and Dalit Agency: Charismatic Christianity in a South Indian Village." Paper Presented at the 'World Christianity Conference,' Princeton Theological Seminary, March 15–18, 2019.

Savarkar, Vinayak Damodar. *Hindutva: Who is a Hindu?* New Delhi: Hindi Sahitya Sadan, 2005.

———. "Hindutva: Who is a Hindu?" In *Hindu Nationalism: A Reader*, edited by Christophe Jaffrelot, 87–96. Princeton & Oxford: Princeton University Press, 2007.

Schillebeeckx, Edward. *Christ the Sacrament of the Encounter with God*. London: Sheed and Ward, 1977.

Schüßler, Werner. "Tillich's life and works." In *The Cambridge Companion to Paul Tillich*, edited by Russel Re Manning, 3–17. Cambridge & New York: Cambridge University Press, 2009.

Scott, James C. *Domination and the Arts of Resistance: Hidden Transcripts*. New Haven: Yale University Press, 1990.

———. *Weapons of the Weak: Everyday Forms of Resistance*. New Haven: Yale University Press, 1985.

Sherinan, Zoe C. "Dalit Theology in Tamil Christian Folk Music: A Transformative Liturgy by James Theophilus Appavoo." In *Popular Christianity in India: Riting Between the Lines*. Edited by Selva J. Raj & Corinne G. Dempsey, 233–253. Albany: State University of New York Press, 2002.

BIBLIOGRAPHY

255

———. *Tamil Folk Music as Dalit Liberation Theology*. Bloomington and Indianapolis: Indiana University Press, 2014.

Shrirama. "Untouchability and Stratification in Indian Civilisation." In *Dalits in Modern India: Visions and Values,* 2nd edition, edited by S. M. Michael, 45–75. New Delhi: Sage Publications, 2007.

Sigurdson, Ola. *Heavenly Bodies: Incarnation, the Gaze, and Embodiment in Christian Theology*, Translated by Carl Olsen. Grand Rapids, Michigan: William B. Eerdmans Publishing, 2016.

Singaram, Charles. *The Question of Method in Dalit Theology: In Search of a Systematic Approach to the Practice of an Indian Liberation Theology*. Delhi: ISPCK, 2008.

Sivakami, P. *The Grip of Change*. Chennai: Orient Blackswan, 2009.

Sobrino, Jon. *Jesus the liberator:* A Historical-Theological Reading of Jesus of Nazareth. Translated by Paul Burns and Francis McDonagh. Maryknoll, New York: Orbis Books, 1993.

———. *No Salvation Outside the Poor: Prophetic-Utopian Essays*. Maryknoll, New York: Orbis Books, 2008.

Swamy, Muthuraj. *The Problem with Interreligious Dialogue*. London and New York: Bloomsbury, 2016.

Sweetman, Will. "Unity and Plurality: Hinduism and the Religions of India in Early European Scholarship" in *Defining Hinduism: A Reader*, ed. J. F. Llewellyn (New York: Routledge, 2005).

Taylor, Mark Kline. *Paul Tillich: Theologian of the Boundaries*. London and San Francisco: Collins, 1987.

Thass, Iyothee. "A Unique Petition" In *The Oxford Anthology of Tamil Dalit Writing*, edited by Ravikumar and R. Azhagarasan, 218–221. New Delhi: Oxford University Press, 2012.

Thatamanil, John J. "Comparative Theology after "Religion."" In *Planetary Loves: Spivak, Postcoloniality, and Theology*, edited by Stephen D. Moore and Mayra Rivera, 238–257. New York: Fordham University Press, 2011.

———. *The Immanent Divine: God Creation, and the Human Predicament: An East West Conversation*. Minneapolis: Fortress Press, 2006.

Thomas, V. V. *Dalit Pentecostalism: Spirituality of the Empowered Poor*. Bangalore: Asian Trading Corporation, 2008.

Thumma, Anthoniaraj. *Dalit Liberation Theology: Ambedkarian Perspective*. Delhi: ISPCK, 2000.

Tiemier, Tracy. "Comparative Theology as a Theology of Liberation." in *The New Comparative Theology: Interreligious Insights from the Next Generation*, edited by Francis X. Clooney, 129–149. London & New York: T & T Clark, 2010.

Tillich, Paul. *The Courage to Be*. New Haven: Yale University Press, 1956.

———. *The Protestant Era*. Translated by James Luther Adams. Chicago: The University of Chicago Press, 1953.

———. *Systematic Theology*. Vol. I. Chicago: University of Chicago Press, 1973.

———. *Systematic Theology*. Vol. II. Chicago & London: The University of Chicago Press, 1975.

———. *Systematic Theology*. Vol. III. Chicago: The University of Chicago Press, 1963.

Turman, Eboni Marshall. *Toward a Womanist Ethic of Incarnation: Black Bodies, the Black Church and the Council of Chalcedon*. New York: Palgrave Macmillan, 2013.

Valerian, Rodrigues, ed. *The Essential Writings of B. R. Ambedkar*. New Delhi: Oxford University Press, 2004.

Viswanath, Rupa. *The Pariah Problem: Caste, Religion, and the Social in Modern India*. New York: Columbia University Press, 2014.

Viswanathan, Susan. "The Homogeneity of Fundamentalism: Christianity, British Colonialism and India in the Nineteenth Century." *Studies in History*, 16/2 (2000): 221–240.

Voss Roberts, Michelle. *Dualities: A Theology of Difference*. Louisville: Westminster John Knox Press, 2010.

Voss Roberts, Michelle. "Gendering Comparative Theology," in *The New Comparative Theology: Interreligious Insights from the Next Generation*, edited by Francis X. Clooney, 109–128. London and New York: T & T Clark, 2010.

Voss Roberts, Michelle. *Tastes of the Divine: Hindu and Christian Theologies of Emotion*. New York: Fordham University Press, 2014.

Webster, John C. B. *Dalit Christians: A History,* 2nd edition. Delhi: ISPCK, 1994.

Webster, John C. B. *Religion and Dalit Liberation: An Examination of Perspectives*. New Delhi: Manohar Publications, 1999.

Webster, John C. B. "Who is a Dalit?" In *Dalits in Modern India: Visions and Values,* 2nd edition, edited by S. M. Michael, 76–88. New Delhi: Sage Publications, 2007.

Whitehead, Alfred North. *Process and Reality; An Essay in Cosmology*. New York: The Free Press, 1985.

Whitehead, Henry. *Village Gods of South India*. Calcutta: Association Press, 1921.

Widlund, Ingrid. *Paths to Power and Patterns of Influence: The Dravidian Parities in South Indian Politics*. Uppsala, Sweden: Uppsala Universitet, 2000.

Wigg-Stevenson, Natalie. *Ethnographic Theology: An Inquiry into the Production of Theological Knowledge*. New York: Palgrave-Macmillan, 2014.

Wilfred, Felix. *The Sling of Utopia*. Delhi: ISPCK, 2005.

Wilson, K. "An Approach to Christian Dalit Theology." In *Towards a Dalit Theology*, edited by M. E. Prabhakar. Delhi: ISPCK, 1989.

Yong, Amos. *In the Days of Caesar: Pentecostalism and Political Theology*. Grand Rapids, Michigan: William B. Eerdmans, 2010.

Younger, Paul. *Playing Host to the Deity: Festival Religion in the South Indian Tradition*. New York: Oxford University Press, 2002.

Zelliot, Eleanor. *From Untouchable to Dalit: Essays on the Ambedkar Movement*. New Delhi: Manohar Publications, 1998.

BIBLIOGRAPHY   257

Online Sources

"11 major incidents of violence against Dalits which show how badly we treat them." *News*. Accessed on September 27, 2018. http://www.indiatimes.com/news/india/11-major-incidents-of-violence-against-dalits-which-show-how-badly-we-treat-them-258944.html.

"4 Dalits Stripped Beaten up for skinning dead cow." *The Times of India*. Accessed on September 12, 2016. http://timesofindia.indiatimes.com/city/rajkot/4-Dalits-stripped-beaten-up-for-skinning-dead-cow/articleshow/53184266.cms.

"A Voice for Dalit Women in India: Ruth Manorama Speaks Out Against Caste-Based Discrimination." Accessed on September 26, 2016. http://www.democracynow.org/2015/9/29/a_voice_for_dalit_women_in.

"After Una atrocity Dalits protest and refuse to dispose of carcasses in Gujarat." *The Hindu*. Accessed on September 24, 2018. http://www.thehindu.com/news/national/other-states/dalits-protest-refuse-to-dispose-of-carcasses-in-gujarat/article8918558.ece.

"Bahujan Samaj Party." Accessed on May 20, 2018. http://www.bspindia.org.

"Boston #chalouna protests." *Dalit Camera*. Accessed on September 24, 2018. http://www.dalitcamera.com/boston-chalouna-protests/.

"Crime against Scheduled Castes." *The Economic Times*. Accessed on September 27, 2018. http://economictimes.indiatimes.com/news/politics-and-nation/crime-against-scheduled-castes-steep-spike-in-gujarat-most-number-of-cases-in-up/articleshow/53329482.cms.

"Dalit student from JNU commits suicide." *First Post*. Accessed on September 27, 2018. http://www.firstpost.com/india/jnu-dalit-student-suicide-when-equality-is-denied-everything-is-denied-wrote-27-year-old-j-muthukrishnan-3333050.html.

"Ghar Wapsi." *The Indian Express*. Accessed on September 21, 2018.

"Missing girl's body found in well in Ariyalur." *The Times of India*. Accessed on September 27, 2018. http://timesofindia.indiatimes.com/city/trichy/missing-girls-body-found-in-well-in-ariyalur/articleshow/56590309.cms.

"Periyapalayam." https://villageinfo.in/tamil-nadu/thiruvallur/uthukkottai/periyapalayam.html. Accessed on April 3, 2017.

"To deny Dalits entry 'upper castes' cancel temple fest in Hassan." *The Hindu*. Accessed on March 12, 2018. http://www.thehindu.com/news/national/karnataka/to-deny-dalits-entry-upper-castes-cancel-temple-fest-in-hassan/article8379078.ece.

"Vichur." https://villageinfo.in/tamil-nadu/thiruvallur/ponneri/vichoor.html. Accessed on March 20, 2017.

Beltz, Johannes. "The Making of a New Icon: B. R. Ambedkar's Visual Hagiography." *Journal of South Asian Studies* 31/2 (2015): 254–265. Accessed on September 25, 2018. http://www.tandfonline.com/doi/full/10.1080/02666030.2015.1094210?src=recsys.

Clarke, Sathianathan. "Viewing the Bible Through the Eyes and Ears of the Subalterns in India." Accessed on January 16, 2018. http://www.religion-online.org/showarticle. asp?title=2444.

Melanchthon, Monica Jyotsna. "Dalit, Bible and Method." *Society of Biblical Literature.* Accessed on January 16, 2018. https://www.sbl-site.org/publications/article.aspx-?ArticleId=459.

Namala, Annie. "Violence against Dalits: There is a discernible pattern to this madness." Accessed on September 27, 2018. http://indianexpress.com/article/blogs/dalit-violence-gujarat-gau-rakshaks-2930876/.

Interviews

Ambrose, Elisa. Interview by author. Audio Recording. Thannirkulam, India July 2, 2016.

Jayaharan, John. Interview by author. Audio Recording. Madurai, India, July 21, 2016.

Jayaharan, John. Interview by author. Audio Recording. Madurai, India, July 18, 2016.

Jayaharan, John. Interview by author. Audio Recording. New York, United States of America, April 12, 2016.

Jeyapal, Balasubramanium. Interview by author. Audio Recording. Chekkanur, India, July 22, 2016.

Jyothi. Interview by author. Audio Recording. Vichur, India, June 15, 2016.

Kodangi. Interview by author. Audio Recording. Chekkanur, India, July 23, 2016.

Kondaivilai. Interview by author. Audio Recording. Madurai, India, June 22, 2016.

Pastor's wife. Interview by author. Audio Recording. Thannirkulam, India, July 2, 2016.

Patrick, Gnanapragasam. Interview by author. Audio Recording. Madurai, India, July 20, 2016.

Rani. Interview by author. Audio Recording. Vichur, India, July 25, 2016.

Sahayam. Interview by author. Audio Recording. Madurai, India, June 24, 2016.

Sankar. Interview by author. Audio Recording. Vichur, India, July 10, 2016.

Soorya. Interview by author. Audio Recording. Periyapalayam, India, July 16, 2016.

Sudha, Agnes. Interview by author. Audio Recording. Vichur, India, June 15, 2016.

Sumathi, Mercy. Interview by author. Audio Recording. Vichur, India, June 15, 2016.

Temple Priest. Interview by author. Chekkanur, India, June 23, 2016.

Index

Aathi, Yazhan 3

Ambedkar B. R. 7–8, 16, 19–22, 180, 198–200, 233–234

Anderson-Rajkumar, Evangeline 51, 147–148

Appavoo, James Theophilus 22–23, 48, 115, 144, 164–165, 181, 236

Aryan 25–26, 93, 97–98, 145

Avi kattu 159

Bama 59

Bhagavad Gita 81–82

Bhakti traditions 17–20, 113, 240–241
  Ravidas 17–19
  Chokamela 18–19
  Assertion 14, 16–17, 20, 43, 46, 62–63, 71–72, 93–94, 101–102, 104, 130–131, 135, 168, 191–194, 196–201, 204, 217–218, 226–227, 231

Bible 39–40, 81–84, 128, 157, 164–166, 182

Binarism 42–43, 46–47, 145

Black Lives Matter 189

Boopalan, Sunder John 60

Brahmins 8–9, 12, 18, 21–22, 81–82, 84–85, 87–88

Brahmanic/al 6–7, 12–13, 16, 20, 39–41, 60–62, 65, 82–88, 93, 97–98, 106, 109, 112–113, 122–123, 126

Butler, Judith 28, 57–59, 61, 188, 190, 242

Body/Bodies
  Dalit body 6–7, 28, 29, 51, 56, 70, 73–76, 147, 186–188, 196–199, 215–216, 218, 226–227, 238, 243
  In Christianity 66
  Also   see Butler, sacrament, possessions

Brubaker, Richard 97–98, 102, 105, 109, 179

Buddhism 20–22, 79–82, 135–137, 200

Caste 7
  System
  Discrimination 38–39, 54

Chamar 17–18, 89, 131

Chandala 52–53

Panchama 52–53

Ceri 89–90, 96, 99, 194–195

Christ (also see Jesus) 30–31, 69–70, 132, 136, 141, 143–144, 146–147, 161–162, 210, 212–213, 218–221, 224

Christian centrism 46

Clarke, Sathianathan 22–23, 25–26, 43–45, 48–49, 89–91, 96, 98–100, 103–104, 106–108, 111–112, 145–147, 157–159, 224–225

Comparative Theology
  and pilgrimage 33–34
  Text-centrism 35, 73–74, 238–239
  Liberation 34, 53
  Introduction 32–34

Colonialism 9–10, 27–29, 35–36, 47–48, 80–81, 87–88, 112–113, 145, 179, 195, 238–239

Collective memories 122, 197, 233–234, 239

Comparative category 56, 72–73, 91, 150, 160–161, 226–227
  vague comparative category 73
  Divine possessions 73

Cone, James 70–71, 142–143, 227–228, 232, 234

Construction of Hinduism 36, 39, 80, 170–171

Conversion 26–27, 82–83, 118, 127, 166, 170–171, 179–180, 208

Copeland, Shawn 70

Crucified people 71

Dalit
  Christology 142–144
  Meaning 16–17
  Christianity 127, 166, 168, 170–171, 181–182
  Reservations 137
  Panthers 16, 26–27
  Identity 42, 44–46, 51–53

Dalit religion 22–25, 28–29, 48–49, 79, 81, 88, 104, 164, 175, 187–188, 200, 217, 240–243

Dalit theology
  Introduction 41
  New Directions 42
  God-Talk 141, 145, 147

Dayam, Joseph Prabhakar   22–23, 48,
    100–102, 104
Deliège, Robert   11–15
Disciplining   6–7, 61, 73–74, 163
Divine possessions What Are   106
    Christian   74–75
    Hindu   74, 181–184, 186–187, 200–201,
        212–213, 217, 219–220, 225, 233–234, 236
    Goddess   109, 156, 170–171, 241
    Temporary & Enduring   107, 109
Drum
    Dalit drum   25–26, 111–112, 164, 181–182
    Parai   25–26, 111–112, 164–165, 181–182,
        198–199
Dumont, Louis   12–14, 58

Ecstasy   150–151, 156, 164–166, 168, 183
Empowering Becoming   232
Ellaiamman   89–90, 94, 99–100, 102–104
Essentialism   45
Ethnography   23, 50–51
Evil
    Reimagining   169, 196

Flood, Gavin   85–88, 91–93
Foucault, Michel   28, 58, 61–65, 188–189,
    242

Gandhi   135–136, 140, 179–180
Goddess
    See Ellaiamman, Mariamman
    Dalit goddesses   28–29, 79, 91, 93–99,
        185–186, 198–199
    Devi-Mahatmaya   92–93, 103
    Great Goddess   91–94, 125–126, 184–185
    Periyapalayathamman   97–98, 111–113, 184
    Gonthemma/Gonthelamma   100–102
    Ambivalent   102–104
Grace   30–31, 69, 72, 101–102, 144, 166–167,
    206–207, 222, 224–225, 227–228
    Possessions as grace   119, 165–166, 175,
        186, 212–214, 225, 230
Grammar of the bodies   60–63, 65, 188

Hidden Transcripts   30, 191, 217, 234–235
Hindu Nationalism   62, 84–85
Hindutva   62, 137–140, 241–242
Holy Spirit possessions   150, 164–169, 175,
    181–183, 195–196, 199, 225, 236

Identitarianism   44
Ilaiah, Kancha   79–80
Immanent/Immanence   30–31, 224
Inclusivist   30–31, 223
Infrapolitics   30, 193–194, 217, 234–235
Isaiah   142, 237

Jati   9, 87–88
Jeremiah, Anderson   176–180, 200
Jesus (also   see Christ)
    As Dalit   142–143
    And lynching   71
    Embodiment   68–69
    And Dalit liberation   141–144
    As Great *Kairos*   210–213, 215–216, 218–220

Kairos   30–31, 205
    In the Bible   206
    In South Africa   206–207
    In Central America   207
    In The Road to Damascus   207–208
    In the U.S. context   208
    Paul Tillich   208
    Possessions as *kairos*   213
    Re-visioning *kairos* as possessions   215
Kapadia, Karin   106–110, 113–116, 119, 122,
    124–126, 182–183, 186, 194–195, 200–201
Karma   87
King, Richard   36, 39–40, 83–85
Kinsley, David   7–8, 87–88, 91–92, 95, 117,
    124–125
Kodangi   107–108, 122–124

Mahmood, Sabah   54–55, 190–191, 203–204,
    234, 242
Marian possessions   159–162, 181–182
Mass Movements   26–27, 127, 131, 141, 161,
    170–171, 199
Masuzawa, Tomoko   35
Malas   100–101, 131, 135, 178–179
Madhigas   117, 178–179
Manu Dharmasastra   8, 25–26, 52–53, 231–232
Mariamman
    Goddess   5, 94–100, 102–104, 117–118, 120,
        184–186
    Myth   94, 99–100, 103–104
    Guyana   112–113
Methodological exclusivism   42
Mines, Diane   8–9, 109, 117–118, 125, 198–199

INDEX

261

Moksha 87
Myths 86–87, 90, 92–94, 98–100, 103–105, 123–124, 239
    Emancipatory mythography 90, 99–100, 103–104

Nirmal, Arvind 41–42, 46–47, 50, 141–143
Non-othering theology 51

Occupy Movement 189
Oddie, Geoffrey 36, 82–85
Orientalism 9–10, 28–29, 36, 83–84, 179, 238–239
Outcaste 6–7, 9, 20, 25–26, 52–53, 58, 65, 89–90, 125, 241–242

Paraiyar
    History 25–27
    Paraiyar religion 94, 175 (also see Dalit religion)
Panikkar, Raimon 216
Pathos 42, 48, 142–146, 236
People-centered theology 50
Performativity 59–60
Pey 106–107, 114–115, 119, 156, 169, 185–186
Possessions
    Arul varuthal/Arulooruthal 117–118, 125
Prabhakar, M. E. 142–144
Purity and pollution/impurity 10, 12–14, 18–19, 52–53, 66–67, 101–102, 108, 113–114

Queer 122

Rajanaiken 128, 130–131
Rajkumar, Peniel 40–41, 43–44, 140, 143–146
Religion
    Construction of 80–81
    See Construction of Hinduism, Dalit Christianity, Paraiyar and Dalit religion
    Resistance
    Dalit resistance 7, 22, 51, 99–101, 106, 193–194, 198–199, 233–234
    Alternative modes of resistance and liberation 30–31, 46, 54–55, 175, 190–191, 201, 217, 224, 230
Rice Christians 135–136, 166

Roberts, Nathaniel 151–152, 154, 166–169, 177–180, 199–200

Saamiyadi 96, 98, 107–108, 111, 118, 120–121, 123, 125, 156, 181, 183–184, 201–202
Sakti/Sakthi 92–93, 98, 119–120, 156
Sanskrit/Sanskritic 16, 28–29, 39–41, 81–84, 88, 91, 93, 97–98
Sacraments
    Body as sacrament 69–70
    Dalit body as sacrament 70, 215–216, 226–227
    Baptism 29, 75, 130, 160, 162, 164–166
    Eucharist 160–162
Samsara 87
Slums 94, 151–152, 166–168, 177–178, 184, 199–200
Spirit Christology 30–31, 75, 205, 213, 218–220, 224–225, 228, 230, 232–233
    and religious diversity 221
Sudra 8–9, 21–22, 130, 157–159, 231–232
Suffering
    God 71–72, 142–143, 146, 159–160, 226, 226n72, 233, 235–236
    Goddess 104
    Dalit/oppressed 43, 46, 72, 143–144, 146, 170, 197, 215–216, 226–227
Symbol
    Christ 30–31, 218–220, 224–225, 227–228, 232–233, 235–236
    Cross 71, 142, 226–227
    Dalit body 196–197
    Goddess 93, 99, 101–104, 184–188, 198–200
    Bible 158–159

Tillich, Paul 30–31, 75, 185, 205, 208, 213–214, 216, 218–221, 226–227, 230, 234, 242
Thatamanil, John 33–34, 73, 225–226, 229
Transgressive Creativity 30–31, 224, 228, 232–234

Untouchables 5–9, 11–17, 19–22, 143–144
Untouchability 7, 11, 14–16, 51, 54, 56–57, 101–102, 169–170, 235, 239–242

Varna 9, 65, 87–88
Vedas 129, 157–158

Vedamanickam, Maharasan 129
Vellalakantan 117–118, 125
Victorization 145
Victimization 145–146
Vinayaraj Y. T. 148–149
Viswanath, Rupa 132, 134–137
Voss Roberts, Michelle 34, 40–41, 49, 53–54

Violence
  against Dalits 6–7, 52–53, 62, 99, 114, 121, 123–124, 138–139, 147–148, 186–189
  in the U.S. 62–63, 189, 208

Webster, John 16, 131–132, 135–137
Whitehead, Alfred North 225, 228–229
Wilfred, Felix 49, 90–91,

Printed in the United States
By Bookmasters